Rave Reviews for
Edward Humes'
MISSISSIPPI MUD

Books by Edward Humes

Buried Secrets
Murder with a Badge
Mississippi Mud: A True Story from a Corner of
  the Deep South*

*Published by POCKET BOOKS

Mississippi MUD

A TRUE STORY FROM A CORNER OF THE DEEP SOUTH

EDWARD HUMES

POCKET BOOKS

New York   London   Toronto   Sydney   Tokyo   Singapore

POCKET BOOKS, a division of Simon & Schuster Inc.
1230 Avenue of the Americas, New York, NY 10020

ISBN: 0-671-53505-6

First Pocket Books printing December 1995

10 9 8 7 6 5

POCKET BOOKS and colophon are registered trademarks of Simon & Schuster Inc.

Cover photo © David Muench/Tony Stone Images

Printed in the U.S.A.

To Gabrielle, for reminding me that each day is a delight

ACKNOWLEDGMENTS

My heartfelt thanks to everyone who helped me slog through the mud. Captain Randy Cook of the Harrison County Sheriff's Department was particularly generous in allowing me to tax his time, patience, and hospitality. I also wish to express my gratitude to U.S. Attorney George Phillips, First Assistant Kent McDaniel, Detectives Gerald Forbes and Richard O'Bannon of the Biloxi Police Department, Captain D. K. Basco and Lieutenant Lee Freeman of the Louisiana State Penitentiary at Angola, Harrison County Sheriff Joe Price, Biloxi City Councilwoman Dianne Harenski, Greg Broussard, Gurvir Dhindsa, and attorneys Rex Jones, Kelly Rayburn, and Mike Adelman.

Becky and John Field and their family offered the greatest of gifts—they always made me feel welcome, in good times and bad. I wish them luck and health.

Donna Wares, my wife and partner, made this book—and everything else—possible.

And, finally, I wish to thank the Sherry and Sposito families, and Lynne Sposito, whose courage and determination continue to amaze.

Mississippi Mud is that purest form of poker, a game in which the cards become irrelevant and the ability to bluff and betray fellow players reaps the greatest reward. The name is synonymous with a certain brand of corruption in the Magnolia State, undisguised and unashamed. By either definition, lying is an art form in Mississippi Mud, morality a fool's distraction.

Mississippi MUD

PROLOGUE

Monday, September 14, 1987
Biloxi, Mississippi

The city's worst day began quietly enough, when a used
car salesman discovered one of his cars missing, an
anonymous-looking yellow Ford. The theft was strange,
because the boxy Fairmont was about the least valuable car
on the lot, so ordinary, it seemed invisible—like an undercover police car. Or a getaway car.

The day ended quietly, too, with a muted popping noise,
much like the sound of a newspaper rolled loosely into a fly
swatter and slapped on a tabletop. Few people heard those
nine innocuous pops, and those who did would never speak
of them. Yet those sounds would destroy a family, alter
countless lives, transform a city. Little would remain the
same in Biloxi in their wake.

Between those two events, Vincent and Margaret Sherry
lived as they always had, taking no special precautions,
exhibiting few outward fears. He went to the county courthouse that morning as always, where he had served as judge
of the Circuit Court for the past eleven months. She, as
always, worked much of the day on her one great
obsession—exposing Biloxi's legendary corruption, in
preparation for a mayoral campaign many Biloxians believed would earn her reign of city hall.

During that last day, Vince Sherry also found time to jog,
to kibitz with his law partner, to get his thick shock of
brown hair cut at the local Air Force base barbershop
(where he enjoyed the privileges of a retired colonel), and to
gas up his battered station wagon in preparation for a trip
Tuesday to Baton Rouge. The Sherrys planned to take the
day off to visit their youngest daughter at her college

campus and to have cataracts removed from one of their beloved dachshunds, Meaux.

Margaret Sherry spent part of Monday shopping for clothes for her increasingly round five-foot frame, buying two electronic calculators, planning a United Daughters of the Confederacy convention she was chairing the next month, and speaking to three friends on the telephone about her plans to allege scandals in city government. At one time or another during the day, she told people she had been working with the FBI, that she now had enough evidence to expose a major corruption case in the city, and that she would try to put the man she hated most—the mayor of Biloxi—in jail.

"You can't talk like that without evidence," one of her friends warned upon hearing this final pronouncement.

"Don't you understand? I have the goods," Margaret said in her quiet, commanding way. "I have the documentation."

She told another friend that she planned to make her claims public the next day, at Tuesday's city council meeting, when the city's budget was to be adopted.

Oddly, her last conversation of the evening was cut short, in midsentence, just as Margaret was about to say good night to her friend, Dianne Harenski, an occasional ally on the city council. This was after 7 P.M., and Vince had been clamoring in the background. He was hungry, he was saying, it was time for dinner. Margaret's friend could hear him clearly. A minute or two later, when the phone clicked dead in her hand, Harenski simply assumed Margaret had rushed off the line to appease her hungry husband.

Later—minutes or hours, no one can say for sure—that anonymous yellow Ford cruised by the Sherrys' ranch-style four-bedroom home on Hickory Hill Circle, then stopped down the block. The lonely street was empty, its houses locked tight against the thick, wet air of the Gulf. The only sounds piercing the humidity were the whir of crickets hidden in dense lawns, the dry flap of bats overhead.

Vince was still wearing his blue seersucker pants and white shirt from court that day, his trim frame stretched out on the couch in the den as he watched the Atlanta Braves on television. The knock on the door brought him to his feet.

He shunted the barking dachshunds, Meaux and Fritz, into the master bedroom, where Margaret was midway between dressed and undressed, then he pulled the door shut. He muted the television and tossed the remote control onto the coffee table, which, like many areas of the house, sat obscured beneath a burial mound of papers, magazines, newspaper clippings, and legal files, some of it his, some of it Margaret's. They were voracious readers, and they threw out nothing. Then he opened the front door and waved in whoever had knocked.

They walked back to the den, where Vince and his company that night may have chatted awhile. Vince could have even offered a visitor a cup of tea—police would later find a lone, used bag of Lipton's sitting on the kitchen counter, a cup rinsed and on the drainboard. Then again, business may have overtaken politeness immediately, and Vincent Sherry may have turned around, still smiling in greeting, to face a .22-caliber Ruger automatic, the black tube of a silencer sitting fat and obscene on the lip of its barrel.

Inside the bedroom, Margaret had stripped to her bra and panties, her glasses on the bureau, her gray-streaked brown hair tousled. As she reached up to take off an earring, she heard, faintly, that popping noise, followed by a vague sound of movement in the living room. Perhaps, her family would later speculate, she shook her head and smiled, thinking: There goes Vince, swatting flies again. She loved him dearly, but Vince had been a cleanliness bug throughout all his fifty-eight years, the type who washed his hands *before* using the bathroom, who flushed with his foot, who would never have something as unsanitary as a flyswatter around the house. Vince would use a newspaper, flailing about the room, knocking over books and papers. Then he'd throw the offending page with its flattened insect into the trash, as if disposing of toxic waste. It always made Margaret laugh.

After a moment, the bedroom door glided open, a slight creaking. The dogs rushed out, yapping. Margaret did not grab for her housecoat draped over the television—what would be the point? After nearly forty years of marriage, why bother trying to cover up the ravages of time when your

husband walked in the room? Margaret would hardly have
looked up at the blurry form in the doorway. She was so
nearsighted without her glasses.

Then there was that swatting sound again, two pops,
louder now, followed by the sound of something hitting the
wall behind her. This wasn't fly swatting, after all. The
sound was coming from the doorway, from a man who was
approaching her now, flying at her, coat flapping, a man she
must have finally realized wasn't Vince, even as the sharp
odor of cordite filled the room. This smell she knew well
because she was a crack shot herself, could shatter a bottle
at one hundred yards with a .22 rifle by the time she was
twelve, that pungent aroma stinging her nostrils with every
shot. She slid to the floor, a gold-ball earring clutched in her
right hand, the other still dangling in place, as the man who
wasn't Vince loomed over her.

She never heard those last four quiet pops. Consciousness, identity, dreams, fear—all were obliterated before the
sound of that first silenced shot stopped echoing. And the
day ended as quietly as it had begun, with a nondescript
Ford disappearing down a deserted street, the sound of dogs
barking muffled behind a closed front door.

PART 1

Lynne

There is no fate that cannot be surmounted by scorn.

—Albert Camus, The Myth of Sisyphus

CHAPTER 1

Without warning or symptom, the twentieth century's version of Plague came calling on Lynne Sposito at exactly ten minutes past two on the afternoon of September 16, 1987. She'll always remember the kitchen clock's position then, because the moment marked her permanent passage from normalcy. This was the day her life changed, irrevocably, in ways as incomprehensible then as they remain now, for such is the power of death, grief, and obsession to mold us, whether we will it or not. Such is the power of that disease called homicide to change everything.

Lynne's oldest brother, Eric Sherry, was on the line, telephoning from his home in Florida, searching for a way to explain to his big sister what had happened to their parents.

"There's no easy way to say this," he finally said, voice crackling with strain, as if he was lifting something heavy. "So I'll just say it: Mom and Dad are both dead."

The things that go through your mind at a time like that, Lynne would later marvel. She and a neighbor had returned home from shopping for furniture a short while ago—the Spositos had just moved to Raleigh, North Carolina, and much of their new brick Colonial sat barren of decor. Now she stood in the kitchen, face gone white, waving off her friend, who kept asking "What's wrong?" She couldn't make the transition from end tables to the fact that she would never hug her parents again. She'd never argue with her father. Never smell her mother's perfume. Never.

"What? What do you mean?" she asked, bafflement making her whisper. She still cradled the phone casually between chin and shoulder, the way you would hold it while answering a survey or ordering from a catalog. She transferred the receiver to a sweaty, cold fist. "Was it an accident?"

"No, it wasn't an accident," Eric said. "They were killed."

Again, Lynne groped for comprehension: What her younger brother was saying made no sense to her. She had unpacking to do, a job interview at a medical center set for that afternoon, dinner to get ready. How could her parents be dead? She had just talked to her mother a few nights before. Then she remembered a family friend in Biloxi who had lost his parents in a gas explosion. "Was there an explosion, Eric? Did the gas main blow up?"

"No, Lynne. They were killed by some*one*. They were found today. That's all I know."

They were killed. They were found. Her parents, it seemed, had become inanimate objects, things to be discovered, like lost car keys. The words filled her head, threatening to drown out everything else Eric was saying.

She heard him dimly after that, though later she would remember every word, replaying the conversation over and over. Eric told her their father's law partner in Biloxi, Pete Halat, had found the bodies. A friend of Eric's in Florida had called within the hour to offer her condolences after hearing about the murders on the radio—assuming, incorrectly, that Eric already knew. When Eric placed a frantic call to Halat to ask what happened, he found out their youngest sister, Leslie—still "the baby" to Lynne, though she would turn twenty in a month—also had learned of the murders, and just as abruptly as Eric. She had called the law office to complain about her parents standing her up the day before, only to have a lawyer clumsily tell her to find her roommate and sit down, he had some bad news to give her. Now she was on her way to Biloxi, Eric said. Lynne pictured Leslie's five-foot form hunched at the wheel, grimacing, with knuckles white and gas pedal floored.

"Vin doesn't know yet, though," Eric said, anticipating Lynne's next question. At twenty-seven, one year younger than Eric, Vincent Sherry III—Vin to his family—was the most mercurial of the four Sherry children, the one most likely to do something rash or vengeful once he heard the news.

"I'll tell Vin," Lynne found herself saying, vaguely surprised she could speak at all. Then she realized she had no idea what to say to Vin. "What can I tell him, Eric?"

"I don't know anything, Lynne," Eric sighed. Halat had refused to give him any details by telephone, he said. Pete wanted to talk to them in person first. "Get down here quick," that was all he said.

"You've got to get to Biloxi as soon as you can, Lynne," Eric said. "I'm heading out the door now."

Later, Lynne couldn't remember saying good-bye, only staring at the telephone on her kitchen wall, the receiver mysteriously back in place on its cradle, her friend still asking what was wrong, barely audible, like a television set with the volume way down, drowned out by a roaring in Lynne's ears that threatened to drive all thoughts from her mind, all warmth from her soul.

"My mom and dad are dead," she heard herself say. The enormity of it had just begun to dawn on Lynne as she uttered the words, then watched her friend instinctively recoil, as if murder could be somehow contagious.

What would she tell her seven-year-old daughter, Beth, she wondered? The little girl had just announced how happy she was that Grandma planned to visit in a month. Or Tommy, her moody thirteen-year-old—what would she say to him? He had always blossomed in the small-town security of his grandparents' Biloxi home. No more. How could she tell Cathy, the oldest sixteen-year-old Lynne had ever known, a girl who just a week earlier spent an hour on the phone with her grandmother, laying plans for Margaret's next mayoral campaign. Worst of all, whatever she managed to tell them, she would have to do it alone—her husband, Dick, was out of the country on business. Again. Lynne found herself cursing his new job, his success, his long trips away. She needed him here, now, their seventeen years of shared history to blunt the agony. She felt an insane urge to run from the house, to tell no one, not even Vin or the kids. Impossible, of course. But she allowed herself that brief moment of fantasy, that maybe, just maybe, it would all go away if she simply ignored it.

And then Lynne remembered a conversation she had
with her mother four months earlier, so innocuous at the
time, so ominous now. Mom had known, Lynne realized.
She knew this was coming. And terror began to compete
with bewilderment, a row of bass drums thumping in Lynne
Sposito's chest.[1]

"Things are getting hot down here," Margaret Sherry had
told her daughter. "Maybe too hot to handle."

On the other end of the telephone, fifteen hundred miles
away and living in Virginia at the time, Lynne had steeled
herself. Her mother had spoken for years of exposing
Biloxi's corruption—so often, it had begun to sound com-
monplace to Lynne, like family gossip. Truth be told, Lynne
wasn't much interested in the political machinations of
Biloxi, Mississippi, that so consumed her mother. So she
would just say, sure, Mom, uh-huh, Lynne's mind on her
three kids, or the dinner bubbling on the stove, or her plans
to return to nursing now that her children were old enough.
If her mother noticed the lack of interest, she never let on.

"I've nearly got enough," Margaret was saying. "I'm
going to blow the lid off this town." And then she added that
last, strange remark: "I just hope to God they don't come
after my children."

Odd as this sounded to Lynne—odd enough, certainly, to
stick in her memory—she still didn't say anything. It was
just Mom going off again, overdosing on politics. Nothing
her mother might have discovered could be that serious, she
figured.

So the forbidding words had melted into the hiss of the
telephone lines. Then Lynne said something like, oh, Mom,
come on, and the subject changed, to grandkids' report
cards and plans for Margaret to visit in the fall. Lynne never
did ask her mother what she had meant about them coming
after her children, nor did she raise the implied
alternative—that "they" might skip the kids and go directly
after the parents.

Later, when the internal chant of *How did I miss it?* would
grow especially fierce, Lynne would lie awake nights and
relive that conversation, her mother's soft drawl in her ear,
memories weighted with regret and the leaden anguish of
having heard without listening. Even Lynne has to admit

she couldn't have changed what happened, but this truth offers little comfort. On those sleepless nights, when the longing left by lost chances lays another layer of brick and mortar around her heart, Lynne Sposito can't help but wish she had asked her mother one thing: to tell her exactly who *they* were.

So Lynne could make them pay.[2]

"I've got to take care of my kids," Lynne said as she slumped into a chair in the dining room.

Her friend, Kathy Pierson, poured a tumbler full of water for each of them. Lynne drained the glass, barely tasting its contents, growing keenly aware of Kathy watching her intently. She ran a hand through her short blond curls, a tall woman with a pale, round face and a small mouth that tended toward a curt, even disapproving expression whether she intended it or not (a tendency that served her well, however, during her years as a head nurse). Now, she imagined, she must be the color of some of the emergency room patients she used to treat for shock, a chalky hue that always told her to watch closely, something bad was about to happen. That's how her friend seemed to be looking at her now, waiting and watchful. Lynne looked up and repeated, "I have to take care of my kids."

Kathy offered to pick up Lynne's seven-year-old, Beth, at the school bus stop that afternoon and keep her next-door for a few hours while Lynne did what she had to do. Lynne nodded at her neighbor with relief. She had some difficult telephone calls of her own to make.

The people at Tommy's junior high and Cathy's high school were understanding, if shocked, at Lynne's request that they be granted an extended leave because their grandparents had been murdered. In her shock, Lynne had phrased her request in the blandest of terms, without preamble, exactly as she would have called to say one of her children was home sick with a sore throat. The school officials said the kids could take off as long as needed, and Lynne said she would pick them up shortly.

They also asked a question that, in the next few days, would become a familiar refrain: Is there anything we can do? *Just let us know if there's anything we can do.* This would spill off many lips, and little time would pass before these offers from virtual strangers started grating on Lynne. What could you say? Thanks, sure, I appreciate that, knowing it was a *pro forma* remark, like the excuse me you get when someone bumps you in the elevator. It was more to relieve the speaker than the person receiving the offer, a way of maintaining the illusion that the unfixable can somehow be fixed, a bumbling ritual to dismiss and deny death. Soon Lynne had little patience for it. What did these strangers know of her parents, the people who taught her to love Broadway musicals and Inspector Clouseau and Russian folk tales, who had supported the segregationist George Wallace, even while writing checks to the United Negro College Fund?

In the first hours of that endless afternoon, what Lynne wanted most was to talk to her husband, Dick. Perversely, frustration at her inability to do so kept her emotions in check, kept her functioning with something bordering on efficiency. She had decided she would not break down until she could talk to her husband, and that emotional dam held all day.

Dick Sposito traveled abroad at least once a month in his position with a Paris-based telecommunications conglomerate. He had left for France the day before. Thirty minutes of calling failed to get Lynne through to him. It was maddening: She didn't even have the right number for his new office in the company's Raleigh headquarters. The number she knew—his direct line—rang endlessly, unanswered. Finally she got through to his division's secretary in Raleigh, who promised to find Dick in Paris.

With Dick out of touch and Eric and Leslie driving to Biloxi, Lynne had no one to talk to. She could not bear the thought of immediately calling Vin and making him feel as she did. Better he have a few more moments of happy ignorance, she thought. Better she try to learn more before calling. The question of what could have happened—and why—ate at her. Lynne realized she couldn't possibly wait until she got to Mississippi for answers. So she called her father's law office in Biloxi and asked for Pete Halat.

She did not know what to expect from her father's law partner. Lynne had never considered Biloxi home—she lived there only a few years in the sixties, long before the Halat and Sherry law firm came into existence in 1981.

Vincent Sherry had been a judge advocate in the Air Force, a full colonel, and the family had moved around constantly during Lynne's childhood—the South, Big Sky country, Bermuda, Washington. Her brief time in Biloxi began in 1965 when she was in eighth grade, and ended two years later in favor of an outpost in Okinawa, Japan. By the time Vince retired from the military in 1970, choosing Biloxi as his new, permanent home and, later, Pete Halat as his new law partner, Lynne had married an airman she met in Japan and was living in her husband's hometown in Ohio. So she knew Pete only from visits to her parents' home and phone calls to her dad's office.

Still, who else could she call now? Pete Halat had been Vince's law partner for six years, his best friend even longer—which was saying a lot for her father, a man who seemed garrulous and friendly to the casual observer, but who allowed few people truly close. Many times over the years, Lynne had known the pain of feeling like one of those people Vince kept at jovial arm's length.

"I have to know what happened, Pete," Lynne said when she finally got Halat on the line.

"I don't want to tell you anything over the phone, honey. I don't want you upset traveling." Pete's voice was deep, honeyed with a Mississippi drawl that made him sound older than his forty-five years, reassuring—a good voice for a lawyer, Lynne thought. Her father had always said he was a master in the courtroom. "Y'all just get down here, and we'll talk then."

"Pete, nothing could be worse than my own imagination," she said, struggling to sound dispassionate, to draw on her nurse's studied professionalism in dealing with grief—training that, until this day, had always been reserved for other people's heartache. To her mild surprise, Lynne found she could do it: Her voice was a stranger's. "Please. Tell me what happened."

Silence. Then, finally, "What do you want to hear?" Pete sounded tired, almost wary, Lynne thought. He'd been through a lot, too, she guessed.

"Were they shot or were they stabbed?" Lynne asked.

"Shot."

"Once, or more than once?"

"More than once."

Then the hardest question. "Did they die right away, or did they suffer?" Lynne closed her eyes as Pete hesitated.

"I don't know, Lynne. I think they died right away. I don't know."

Halat explained then how the courthouse staff had called him that morning to ask what had happened to Judge Sherry. He had a full docket awaiting him, but he hadn't shown up for court. Vince was renowned for his tardiness—both he and Margaret lived on Hong Kong time, Pete liked to say—but this had seemed odd even for Vince. Pete told Lynne he had driven out to the Sherry house on Hickory Hill Circle and saw that both Margaret's and Vince's cars were in the driveway. When he knocked on the door, though, no one answered. He just heard the dogs barking inside. Then Pete leaned against the door to peer through a window. As his weight shifted, his elbow pushed the door open, Lynne would later recall him saying. Apparently, the front door had been slightly ajar, just enough to keep it from latching.[3]

"I walked a little into the house, and I saw your dad's feet. I didn't want to see any more. I didn't want to go in any further. I didn't want to find your mom."[4]

The police had done the rest. They went in and found the bodies, right after Pete called them, about eleven o'clock that morning Mississippi time. Noon in North Carolina. Lynne closed her eyes again, saw herself picking out end tables and going to lunch with her neighbor. A few hours ago she had been buying furniture, and all the while her parents were lying there dead, someone's bullets in them. Someone who hated them enough or feared them enough to kill them.

"I'm so sorry," Pete told her. "I'll do anything I can for you and your family." Lynne heard the sincerity in his voice and thanked him. She'd see him soon, she said before hanging up.[5]

She tried Dick's office again. Still no word from Paris. It was dinnertime there, midevening, and he wasn't at his hotel. Barely an hour had passed since she received the news from Eric. It seemed so much longer.

Reluctantly, Lynne began calling the endless web of relatives and close friends who had to be told. First came Vin in Northern California's wine country. He dropped the phone and wailed when Lynne finally forced herself to call, finding no better way to break the news than Eric's abrupt, shattering pronouncement. She told him what little she had learned from Pete Halat, then, as he agonized over when to come, assured him it would be fine if he came a day or two later so his wife could accompany him. She would take care of things. Vin was already talking about getting a gun, and Lynne was happy to encourage him to wait—she did not want him traveling alone.

After Vin, the other calls seemed easier. Or maybe she was just numb, Lynne thought, the coldness in her hands spreading throughout her body and mind.

She had made calls about deaths in the family before— somehow, the oldest child was always expected to handle such chores—but always the message had been cushioned by old age or sickness, the expectation of mortality. Never like this. She had talked to her mother just that past Sunday. Innocuous, normal, we-just-got-back-from-the-grocery-store talk. Now these calls Lynne was forced to make turned into bitter replays of when she had received the news. "Mom and Dad are dead," she said over and over. "No, it wasn't an accident. It was on purpose."

When, on the fifth or sixth call, her mother's aunt dropped the phone and started screaming, the receiver banging against the floor as it swung on its coil, Lynne knew she couldn't make one more call. Instead, she left the house to get her daughter Cathy at school, memories briefly crowding out fears and suspicion as she went through the mechanics of driving her car without hitting anything.

This is how Lynne Sposito remembers her father:

He was a man of penetrating intelligence, with encyclopedic knowledge of the law, history, and world affairs. He was fluent in five languages—he used to read the story of *Peter and the Wolf* to Lynne in Russian. Better that way, he insisted. You lose too much in the translation. His doctoral thesis on the judicial system of South Vietnam, a country and people he had come to love during military tours in the Orient, made him one of the few non-Vietnamese experts on the subject. This specialty proved an eclectic choice at best, since he earned his Ph.D. two short years before Saigon fell and its judicial system ceased to exist.

He was given to great—some said excessive—acts of charity, once handing a down-and-out hitchhiker his coat on a cold winter night, then letting him steal a carload of Christmas gifts intended for the Sherry family. He refused to notify the police. "That fellow needs those things more than we'll ever need them," he told an apoplectic Margaret upon returning home.

He was not a handsome man in any classical sense, but there was an unmistakable magnetism about him, and women often sought him out, much to Margaret's annoyance. He had high blood pressure, bouts of severe headaches, an ability to coin funny or cruelly accurate nicknames for virtually anyone (Biloxi's edgy mayor was "Norman Bates"), and a mercurial temper that led him into epic battles with his wife. At the same time, he was possessed of Old World courtly manners and a professorial vocabulary—he loved to use words so obscure they would send his family scrambling to the dictionary to see if they'd been praised or insulted. Knowledge was its own reward, he always said. More than anything, Vincent Sherry fervently believed ignorance, not evil, to be humanity's worst sin.

Yet this man who could be so kind to strangers, who was so humane a judge that men he sentenced to prison sent him thank-you notes and Christmas cards—this same Vince Sherry found it impossible to express his love to his children. "Don't let people get too close," Vince often told Lynne. "If they get too close, they'll know how to hurt you."

This was the life lesson of a man whose absentee father had appeared one night and attempted to smother him with a pillow. Vince was only thirteen at the time. His mother had heard the commotion and dispatched Vince Senior with a cast-iron fry pan to the head. Vince Junior had the privilege of helping drag his father's semiconscious body out the back door. They didn't see him again for years.

Lynne Sposito grew up struggling to please her father, vying for that closeness Vince so rarely granted. But it always seemed her grades were never quite high enough, the boyfriends she brought home never quite good enough, her appearance never quite perfect enough. Vince believed that providing a roof, schooling, clothes, and food clearly showed his love, that his children would automatically know how proud he was without him having to say it aloud—the miscalculation of a child whose father provided nothing but beatings and abandonment. For years, Lynne secretly took her father's silence to mean one thing: The smartest man she knew thought she didn't measure up.

And then, just a few years ago, when Vince's mother was sick and dying, she had confided in Lynne how much she wished her son would say he loved her. He had been a small child the last time she heard him say so. A few days later, Lynne telephoned Biloxi and confronted her father with her dying grandmother's request. "Tell Grandma you love her, Dad. Do me a favor and just tell her. It would mean a lot to her."

Vince was outraged by this, surprise and—could it be fear?—in his voice. "What in the hell are you talking about?" he huffed. "Jesus Christ, Lynne, I pay her utility bills, I send her flowers, I call her every couple of days. She knows I love her!"

Things, Lynne thought, all the things he's done. He doesn't get it, she realized. She pushed him, repeating the request, and finally he agreed. Yes, sure, I will do it. End of subject.

Then they chatted for a while. Vince gradually calmed down. But just as they closed the conversation, ready to say good night, Lynne said, "Daddy?"

"What?"

"I love you."

The pause was so long, longer than Lynne could hold her breath. Finally, Vince said, "I do you, too."

The memory can always make Lynne laugh. Even on September 16, 1987, on the worst day of Lynne's life, her brilliant, eloquent father's inability to utter one simple word could make her chuckle. *I do you, too.* Because to Lynne, there was total freedom, a complete release, in hearing her father stammer that lame reply, so heartfelt, so difficult, coughed up from his soul. Any hang-ups I ever had, she would later say, about not being loved, about not being smart enough, all of it just melted away. It was Dad's problem, not mine. Dad couldn't say it, because of the way *he* was, not me.

You take your comfort where you can find it: At least,

Lynne told herself as she drove to her own daughter, she had forgiven her father for the coldness. And in his own way, he had finally told her he loved her. It had even become a running joke between them. The last time they had spoken, she had teased him, as she had done so many times before. She had said, "Dad, I do you, too."

Vince Sherry had a wonderful laugh.

Lynne walked toward the school gym where Cathy had just finished basketball practice and spotted her daughter walking out the door. She waved Cathy over. She was a younger version of Lynne—tall, blond, willowy thin, the way Lynne had been twenty years before when she was Cathy's age.

"Get your books, whatever you need," Lynne said. "You won't be back in school for a while."

Cathy's uncertain smile faded, her sixteen-year-old face finding lines no one her age should have. "Did something happen to Daddy?" Visions of terrorists aboard the Concorde swept through her head.

Lynne shook her head. "No, I'm trying to get hold of him. He's fine." Cathy picked up her books and they were heading out of the building when Lynne cleared her throat. "It's Grandma and Grandpa. They've been shot."

Cathy Sposito was the one member of the family who had hung on every one of her grandmother's words when it came to politics. They religiously discussed the latest Biloxi scandals on the phone. Bright and sophisticated for her age, she had helped with Margaret Sherry's 1985 mayoral campaign, and she had planned to work even harder in 1989. Cathy stopped walking and grabbed her mother's arm.

"Where the hell was Gerald Blessey?" she asked.

Gerald Blessey. He was mayor of Biloxi that year, a liberal Democrat, a self-described reformer, a lawyer and decorated Vietnam veteran, popular in the city's substantial, if poorly franchised, black community. And he was Margaret Sherry's nemesis. There was no other way to put it: Margaret Sherry hated Gerald Blessey, bitterly, thoroughly, publicly, and the mayor gave every indication of feeling the same way about her.

The enmity went back six years, to the start of Margaret's political career. An old-style Goldwater Republican, Margaret had been elected to the Biloxi City Council in 1981. She quickly became a voting bloc of one within the Democrat-dominated body, invariably on the short end of six-to-one roll calls. The new mayor elected that same year—widely acknowledged at the time as one of the most liberal elected officials in Mississippi—quickly became Margaret's most despised target. He pursued a vision of progressive reform and government activism that was anathema to a bedrock conservative like Margaret. The sideshow of Mayor Blessey's and Councilwoman Sherry's vitriolic arguments in the colonnaded council chambers soon overshadowed all else that went on in the room, dominating news reports and the council's time. Margaret accused Blessey of everything from misspending government funds, to forcing council members to adhere to scripted meetings, to having his police department investigate her, to complicity with underworld crime figures and the city's most notorious vice merchants. None of her allegations was ever proved. Blessey, in turn, called his most rabid opponent a voice from the past, insensitive and racist. Among other things, he attacked her for opposing a city holiday honoring the birth of Dr. Martin Luther King, a volatile issue in the polar racial politics of the Deep South. And he pointed out that it was Vince Sherry, then a criminal defense lawyer, who profited from crime and vice, not he.

In 1985, Margaret gave up her council seat to run against the incumbent mayor. To no one's surprise, the contest distinguished itself primarily for its bitterness. Mayor Blessey's patrician, aloof manner combined with rough economic times to alienate many voters, broadening Margaret Sherry's appeal. In the end, though, he still managed a bare five-hundred vote margin of victory over Margaret in a city divided.

But to Blessey's chagrin, Margaret did not go away. She took on the role of Biloxi's most prominent gadfly, appearing at council meetings to voice opposition to the mayor's policies, using the voter referendum process to block his proposals and bond issues. Off the council, Margaret began to enjoy more power to foil Blessey than she had when she was on it, and she made no secret about her plans to run again for mayor in 1989. Many political observers believed she would win, her prominence boosted by Vince's rise to the bench, an appointment bitterly opposed by Mayor Blessey.

If Margaret seemed confident, perhaps it was because she had an insurance policy: She had been working with the FBI, trying to document corruption in city hall. Unable to contain her glee, Margaret had told as many as a dozen people in Biloxi of her "undercover" work.

Now Lynne had to wonder: Did Margaret find something so damning that she and Vince had to be eliminated? Was that why she had made that cryptic remark about them coming after her kids? Lynne had no evidence to support this, just suspicion. Still, she couldn't help but ask herself the very same question her daughter had posed in the school gym: Where in the hell *was* Gerald Blessey?[6]

It was seven o'clock that night in Raleigh before Dick Sposito finally found the stack of urgent messages to call home. At first, Lynne sounded normal to him—painfully, impossibly normal. "Hello, Dick. I'm so glad you called." Then the iron control she had maintained all day finally began to slip.

"Dick, Mom and Dad have been killed. Someone shot them." The words were coming in a rush now, barely any space between them. "You've got to come home. I've got to go to Biloxi."

Dick Sposito, unflappable, soft-spoken, tried to absorb what his wife was telling him, then attempted to coax some details from her. She could hardly talk anymore. This was the conversation she had longed for all day, but when it finally came, she found no more words, barely able to explain to him what had happened. He told his wife she should go to Biloxi without him. There wouldn't be a flight until morning. It would be twenty hours or more before he could get there from Paris. "Don't wait for me. Just get on down there. I'll meet you there as soon as I can."

Lynne said okay, then started to cry. She found she couldn't stop, fierce, gulping sobs. She handed the phone to a friend, a secretary at Dick's company who had come over to help, and who began making plans for Dick's trip home. Lynne fled the kitchen, pounding up the stairs and locking herself in her bedroom. She buried her face in her pillow, framed photos of her parents beside her.

CHAPTER 2

Biloxi, Mississippi, 1987

The cancerous heart of Biloxi, known simply as The Strip, squats low and ugly along U.S. Highway 90, a road whose asphalt lies atop the ancient ruts of the Old Spanish Trail, the preferred route of smugglers, cutthroats, and thieves for the better part of three centuries.

The Strip is everything Biloxi pretends not to be. It lies past the retirement-home-turned-tour-bus-stop of that ultimate Southern gentleman, Jefferson Davis, past the mothballed Air Force jet skewered atop a giant pylon and plopped onto the median like some child's dusty model, past the beachfront antebellum mansions with their white columns and oak trees bearded with Spanish moss.

Such symbols of the genteel South on Highway 90, of small-town boosterism for the military, of wealth and grace and a glorious past, all of it gives way to The Strip's squalid hodgepodge of striptease joints and miniature golf, cheap motels, fast-food restaurants, and bars. Here the out-of-town rubes are cleaned out in floating dice and card games. Scams, break-ins, and violent ends are plotted on The Strip, and a stream of hopeless men and women meet beneath the neon, playing venereal roulette for fifty dollars or less in a tangle of sweaty bodies and dirty sheets.

A narrow beach of bright white sand separates the four lanes of blacktop from the steel blue arc of the Gulf of Mexico, but even that apparently virginal escape from the relentless 99s of Biloxi summer (99 degrees, 99 percent humidity) is a mirage. The beach is artificial, its sand dredged up from the sea bottom and sprayed on the rocky shore like so much stucco, paid for by a local tax that, after thirty-some years, is still soaking residents with its questionable benefits. The summery seascape of daylight gives way to a far more ominous terrain at night, where furtive drug deals are struck and teen-aged girls sell themselves for a few lines of coke. The Biloxi police trawl the beach at night whenever arrest statistics need a boost.

This stark contrast in geography illustrates a broader urban schizophrenia that lies at the center of Biloxi's dual persona. Its people pride themselves on maintaining a bastion of Old South virtue, even as they permit their city of fifty thousand to continue in its centuries-old role as center for wide-open corruption.

In decades past, a succession of corrupt mayors, police chiefs, and sheriffs resisted all attempts at reform, allowing illegal gambling, prostitution, and countless other criminal enterprises to flourish openly. They stuffed their own pockets and the city's coffers by exacting a tithe on vice, skimming a percentage of the take in exchange for protection. Even squad cars and deputies' uniforms were underwritten by vice.[1]

In the sixties, *Look* magazine compared the region's physical beauty to the French Riviera, but it was the Eastern Mafiosi, not the jet set, who vacationed here. At the same time, a separate group of thugs, killers, safe-crackers, and con men who came to be known as the Dixie Mafia made The Strip their headquarters, taking over the gambling, the prostitution, and the drug dealing, then fanning out across the other states of the Old Confederacy to plunder banks, steal cars, and, when times got tough, to rob and kill one another.

In the seventies and eighties, little seemed to change. A laundry list of indictments lodged against officials of government and law enforcement reinforced the cynicism of Biloxi's residents and its legion of critics (the residents of the rest of the state of Mississippi), but accomplished little else.[2] It got so bad that some citizens of the adjacent town of Gulfport, Mississippi, always quick to point out that they most certainly were *not* from Biloxi, began routinely referring to the road that marks the border between the two towns as the Gaza Strip.

Lynne Sposito and her family passed down The Strip as they drove in from the airport on Thursday morning, the day after Vincent and Margaret Sherry were found dead in their home. Sunlight flashed off the garish, sequined sign atop the most notorious strip joint in Biloxi, the cavernous Golden Nugget, which continued as a front for prostitution, drugs, and gambling even while the city closed down its competitors. The owner's daughter had been Mayor Blessey's personal assistant, another point of contention for Margaret. She had promised to shut down the clubs if elected, despite Vince's odd friendship with the Golden Nugget's owner, an old-timer in the Dixie Mafia named Mike Gillich. Now that would never happen.

The harsh morning glare and Lynne's tired, gritty eyes made the souvenir shops with their displays of garish T-shirts and genuine driftwood sculptures appear far more wretched than her earlier memories of Biloxi. And yet, the graceful mansions and gentle, empty beachscape that abutted The Strip seemed incongruously peaceful in the wake of double assassination. Against that serene backdrop, the street corner newspaper boxes seemed all the more jarring, with their banner headlines, large enough to read from the car: SHERRYS SHOT, KILLED.

Vince and Margaret were one of Biloxi's most prominent couples, and the newspapers in Mississippi, and as far away as New Orleans, had covered the story to the saturation point. Seeing the family's tragedy reduced to such black-and-white simplicity was a punch in the stomach to Lynne. But later, she and her family would pore over the newspapers, greedy for information, reading and re-reading each story until the words no longer made sense.

Eric and Leslie sat with Lynne and her three children in the car, as shocked by it all as she was. Her brother and sister had greeted Lynne at the airport; Lynne's other brother, Vin, would be coming later. The police wanted to question them right away, but before going there, Eric said, Vince's law partner wanted to see them. That was fine with Lynne. The whole family felt disconcerted that the city police department had assumed control of the murder

investigation—a department commanded by the man they
so disliked and whom they considered a logical murder
suspect, Mayor Blessey.

"Pete says before we go anywhere, we should go talk to
him," Eric told Lynne. "We need to go there first." They
dropped off Tommy and Beth at a friend's house—but not
Cathy, who insisted on staying with Lynne—then drove to
see Pete Halat.

The night before, Halat had promised Eric he would use
his contacts to try and find out what happened to Vince and
Margaret—and why.[3] Anticipating more information had
been Lynne's only comfort through the long, sleepless night
of packing and waiting, staring at the clock until she and her
children could finally drive to the airport for the first flight
out. As she had watched her seven-year-old daughter rise
from bed to stare out the window, then ask if someone was
going to come kill her, too, Lynne had been glad that Pete
Halat, at least, could be counted on to help them.

The Halat and Sherry law office was housed in a restored
early-twentieth-century brick building on the Vieux
Marche, an otherwise dispirited pedestrian mall in Biloxi's
less-than-thriving downtown. The Vieux Marche was the
weedy, half-vacant ghost of a failed urban renewal project
touted by successive city administrations—another white
elephant, according to Margaret Sherry. The thriving center
of business and commerce envisioned when the restoration
project was conceived had quickly given way to empty
storefronts, a welfare office, a plasma donation center, the
shuffle of pedestrians with nothing to spend and nowhere to
go. Crabgrass sprouted between the cobbles. Even the
household loan company—the type that advertises "Problem credit? No problem!" and charges interest rates that
could finance a space shuttle launch—had gone out of
business. But Halat and Sherry had seemed to prosper, and
though Vince drove former rental cars he bought second
hand, Pete had a Mercedes and an expansive house with
purplish paint, a favorite color of his artist wife.

Pete Halat greeted Lynne, Eric, Leslie, and Cathy solemnly, almost paternally, asking about their trip, about how
they were holding up, telling them how devastated he was to
lose his best friends in the world. He hugged Lynne.

She thought he wasn't a bad-looking guy, dressed in an

immaculate white shirt and tie, a little sharp featured
maybe, eyes a bit too small, brown hair a trifle shaggier than
fashionable—but overall, charming.

"I'll help you in any way I can," Halat assured them.
Then, as Lynne rubbed her eyes, he added, "Sweetheart,
don't pick at your face."

At forty-five, Halat was only ten years older than Lynne.
But she was distracted and, anticipating his help, in a
forgiving mood. She chalked up his patronizing to grief and
discomfort at having to discuss his best friends' murder
with their children.

At Pete's request, Lynne and Eric followed him into the
law library for a private talk. They sat at the library table,
amid the shelves of law books and the smell of leather and
cloth bindings, knowing that Vince Sherry had spent countless hours in that room, flipping through the heavy volumes.
Lynne found herself inhaling deeply, hoping to find some
trace of her dad, but there was only the musty odor of pages
slowly aging.

Eric started to ask what Pete had found out, but Halat cut
him off. "Listen, there's something you need to understand," he said slowly. "There is nothing you can do to
bring your parents back to life. Nothing. The best thing you
can do is drop it."[4]

Lynne and Eric looked at one another, confused. How
could he be saying this? He was Vince's best friend. Then
Lynne thought she understood: Pete must have found
something out from his contacts in law enforcement or his
criminal clientele—something bad. Now he wanted to
protect them instead of passing on the information. Lynne
and Eric demanded he explain himself. "Was it Blessey?"
Lynne asked. "Is that why you want us to drop it?" They
begged him to tell them more.

Halat refused to elaborate. He had no information for
them, he said. He just wanted them to drop it, to mourn
their parents, then go home and get on with living—for
their own good.

Later, after Lynne described her meeting with Halat,
Cathy told her mother, "I don't trust him, Mom."

Cathy had never liked Pete. At age three, during a family
visit to Biloxi, she had objected to his clowning around and
putting his head on Lynne's lap while posing for a holiday

photo, telling him, "Get off my mom!" Then she announced—right in front of the man—that he had "evil eyes." Her opinion had remained unchanged over the next thirteen years.

Lynne, however, thought her daughter was being a little hard on Pete. Her father did not have many close friends. If he trusted Halat, that was good enough for Lynne. "He's just trying to help," she said.

Cathy didn't answer. She crossed her arms and stared silently out the window as they drove to their interviews with the Biloxi police.

CHAPTER 3

The Biloxi Department of Public Safety is housed in a condemned elementary school west of downtown, just a couple of blocks inland from The Strip. Its rank-and-file work areas were nominally refurbished with chipped and lumpy metal desks, cheap wood paneling, and stained industrial carpeting of uncertain coloration. The old and yellowed porcelain water fountains still dispense tepid, tinny water in the hallways, and the bathrooms still have rows of enormous floor-length urinals designed for all heights and aims. The chief occupies what had been the principal's office.

The Special Investigations Office, which served as head-quarters for the Sherry murder investigation, had been a fourth-grade classroom, divided now by cheap plywood partitions and piled high with papers and old case files. Several investigators working there had sat in that same classroom decades earlier, pursuing Dick, Jane, and the times tables long before they were assigned to one of the most sensational murder cases in Mississippi since the Civil War.

The Sherry killings drew statewide, then national headlines. *Newsweek, The New York Times,* the *Los Angeles Times,* ABC News, all joined the hunt, bringing enormous pressure to bear on the small city police department, which possessed a mere seventy sworn officers, including the lieutenant dog catcher. In Biloxi, the murders managed to penetrate the numb tolerance of violence fostered by an age of brutal ends and weekly true-crime miniseries. Gun sales soared after news of the murders broke. Strangers in the neighborhood were no longer universally greeted with Southern courtesy, but sometimes with suspicion and nervous calls to 911. You just don't walk into a house in an affluent, country-club subdivision in Biloxi, mere footsteps from the Sunkist golf course, blow away a sitting judge and his mayoral candidate wife, then vanish into the night. The Dixie Mafia crooks had been killing each other on The Strip for years—that was almost tolerable, a bludgeoning here, a stabbing there. But the Sherry killings were different—a judge, a politician. Everybody knew them, or at least knew of them. As corrupt and venal as the city of Biloxi could be, things like this just didn't happen. Until now.

The mayor and his public safety director wanted a swift solution to the case, they declared, trumpeting their massive task force committed to solving the heinous crime, the rhetoric predictable. But their initially hopeful pronouncements to the media quickly gave way to quiet despair inside the old elementary school. Thirty hours after the bodies were found at 203 Hickory Hill Circle, the task force of investigators from Biloxi P.D., with help from the Harrison County Sheriff, the Mississippi Highway Patrol, the district attorney, the state Attorney General, and the FBI, knew little more than the Sherry children had learned from a few harried phone calls and a visit to Pete Halat. Which is to say, they had a passel of suspicions, but no real idea who killed the judge and the candidate, or why. Some client of Vince's? A defendant who came before him during his fourteen months on the bench? An enemy of Margaret's? The possibilities seemed endless. They weren't even sure *when* it happened—that's how clean a job this had been.

All the police knew for sure was that the murder had been well planned and professional. There were no telltale fingerprints in the house, no murder weapon left behind. By the time Lynne Sposito had arrived in town, police scuba divers were in the process of searching for the gun in Biloxi's back bay, not far from the Sherrys' home, as well as in every alligator-and-snake-ridden water hazard at the neighboring golf course. Everyone knew this to be a hopeless exercise. The gun could be anywhere.

Inside the house, detectives concluded, nothing much had been disturbed by the killer—there were no obvious signs of anything missing. Vince's wallet still sat in his back pocket. Margaret's black purse lay atop a copy of the city's proposed budget for 1988, the credit cards and forty-two dollars and change untouched inside. The small safe appeared unmolested. Robbery had not been a motive.

A .22 automatic, most likely a Ruger, judging from the markings on the shells and bullets, had killed the Sherrys. The small caliber required an expert's aim to ensure fatality, while the low mass and velocity of the bullets guaranteed little noise and few, if any, exit wounds. The lead projectiles would have ricocheted inside the victims, maximizing damage to organs and blood vessels. The .22 is the weapon of choice for marksmen and assassins, and the killer had been both. All but one of the shots were fired in pairs, spaced tightly—"double taps," the pros call them, for the quick, twin flicks to the trigger that fire off two rounds in rapid succession. Even the two bullets that missed Margaret were found embedded in the bedroom wall less than one inch above Margaret's height, right next to one another, a barely errant double tap.

It appeared Vince had been shot first, bullets fired from less than two feet away into his face as he stood looking at the gunman, sending him pinwheeling backward, arms flailing, blood spraying on walls, ceiling, his clothes, and his yellow vinyl reading chair. The first shot, it appeared from the burns and black gunpowder stippling his skin, had come with the barrel inserted into his mouth. His hands may have gripped the barrel. The bullet sheared off a row of his teeth, sending white fragments of enamel and silver fillings sailing through the room. Vince always boasted about his perfect teeth, brushed and flossed with care—how that shot must have hurt, Lynne would later say, her own teeth gritted.

Next, the killer had pumped four shots straight down into Margaret's head, killing her instantly. There was no spray of blood, just a rivulet of crimson down one cheek and the side of her neck, soaking her bra. She had somehow slumped down into a sitting position, her legs straight out in front of her, feet under her dresser, her back against the bed, hands cupped at her sides, still holding one earring. Had she fainted in this unlikely position? Was she cowering? Had the gunman ordered her to sit down? Investigators could not tell.

When Margaret was dead, investigators theorized, the killer returned to deliver a final shot to the judge, striking him just below his right eye, perhaps a *coup de grace* to silence his struggles. From the spray of blood around him, they could tell he had lived for a while after first being shot, which led them to believe Vince listened to his wife die before the final shot came to end his agony.

The only traces, aside from the nine Remington-brand brass shells ejected from the automatic pistol, were bits of plastic foam scattered around the bodies, some on Vince's chest as he lay in the den, some caught in Margaret's hair as she sat slumped wearing only her bra and panties. The police theorized that the shooter had muffled his shots with a pillow or seat cushion, which would explain why no neighbor heard the gunshots. It could also explain why Margaret appeared to have been surprised by the killer after Vince had been shot—she simply didn't hear it. The only problem with this theory was that no pillows or cushions seemed to be missing from the home. The police divers added pillows to the list of items to be searched for, but none turned up. It seemed odd that a stone-cold killer would walk out carrying a pillow with nine smoking bullet holes in it, but no other explanation for the foam leapt to mind.[1]

Establishing the time of death also posed a major problem. A city councilwoman, Dianne Harenski, told police she talked to her friend Margaret by telephone between 7 and 7:30 P.M. Monday. She was sure of the time because *Wheel of Fortune* was on TV when she placed the call. Vince had been grousing in the background about wanting to go to dinner when the call was abruptly cut short, before the two women had completed their good-byes. Vince and Margaret could have died then and there, the police thought at first, but the contents of their stomachs suggested they probably went on to eat dinner later that night. This was far from certain, though, because the bodies had begun to decompose in the hot, closed house, making precise calculations difficult. The remains of large salads in their stomachs could have been a late lunch, though dinner seemed more likely to the coroner, based on calculations of the rate of human digestion.

There was one other witness, a parole officer who recalled receiving a telephone call from the judge on Tuesday morning, the day before the bodies were found. Vince had a question about a parolee who flunked his drug test—he wanted to cut the kid a break rather than revoke his parole. The parole officer was certain the call had been Tuesday morning. The contradictory information seemed irreconcilable, and a canvass of the neighbors failed to produce any leads. Nobody knew anything.

The killer had chosen an ideal time to strike: just before the Sherrys were to leave town to visit a veterinary hospital and their daughter Leslie in Baton Rouge. This meant they would not be missed in Biloxi for many hours, perhaps days, leaving ample opportunity for a clean getaway, for memories of passing cars and faces to fade in the neighborhood, for alibis to be constructed, if necessary. The implication: the killer had observed the Sherrys for a time, learned their habits and plans, and timed the hit so that it just preceded their trip.

Or, there was another possibility, the one the Sherry children had locked on: The killer knew Vince and Margaret well enough to know exactly what they were doing that night, and when best to strike.

The behavior of the Sherrys' beloved dogs, Meaux and Fritz, supported this theory to an extent. The two dachshunds would not have attacked a friend. They hadn't bothered Pete Halat, for instance, when he had come in to discover the bodies. But when two strange policemen showed up a short time later, Meaux had stood sentry in front of Vince, then rushed into the bedroom to keep the police away from Margaret, barking and baring his fangs. The first two patrolmen who arrived at the house couldn't touch the bodies, so ferocious was the little dog's efforts to save his two motionless masters, who had doted on those animals, called them The Boys, their two newest sons. Even Vince, who had made Lynne wash her hands with bleach when she touched a dog as a child, let The Boys kiss him on the lips and sleep next to him in bed. Leslie Sherry was convinced only a friend could have done it. Only a friend could have gotten past The Boys without being bitten or hurting the dogs. And whoever it was might be feigning incredulity and grief along with the rest of the city right now.

Halat had told the police he went to the Sherrys' home Wednesday after Vince's court clerk called wondering why he failed to show up for work. Halat got no answer when he tried calling the Sherry home, then sent his wife, Sandra, over to check on things. She called back to say both Vince's and Margaret's cars were parked in the driveway, but no one answered the door. So Pete and a lawyer in his employ, Charles Leger, drove over in Pete's Mercedes.

Halat's description of what followed had been vivid. "I looked into the, I looked in the, ah, room there, through the glass in the door, and I could see the puppies, the dogs . . . I saw some dog excrement on the rug. This kinda alarmed me a little bit . . . In an attempt to check to see if the door was locked, I put my hand on the door latch; I pressed down and it was open. As the door opened an odor came from the room and I immediately perceived in my mind something was wrong. . . .

"I very slowly walked through the hallway, through the entranceway, through the living room, and as I approached the door to the kitchen, I, I saw Mr. Sherry laying on the floor on his back, his feet toward the front door and his head toward the sliding glass door. It was my initial impression at that time that Mr. Sherry was dead. I turned around and went out and told [a neighbor] to please call the police as quickly as he could.

"I had no idea that Mrs. Sherry was in the house, but I did not re-enter the house, for reasons that I can't explain right now."

Halat told the police that he had no clue who might have

killed the Sherrys or why. Although rumors had begun to
float around the city to the contrary, Halat was certain that
neither of them had received any threats and was equally
certain that if they had, the Sherrys would have confided in
him before anyone else. He was their best and most trusted
friend and confidant, he said.

"I'm not in favor of the death penalty," Halat concluded,
"but if y'all catch this guy and he's convicted, I'll volunteer
to pull the switch."[2]

Halat's statement seemed so complete that the Biloxi
detectives saw no need for more than a cursory talk with the
law firm associate Halat had brought to the house that
morning, Chuck Leger. Two years would pass before investigators would correct that mistake and ask for Leger's
distinctly different version of events that morning.

Without any hard evidence, the task force investigators
were forced to cast about for potential suspects, hoping that
luck would take them where facts could not. So far, they had
little to show for their efforts. Dozens of useless tips about
suspicious men in the vicinity were doggedly checked.
Composite drawings of two men—whose crime consisted of
asking for directions to the Sunkist Country Club on the
day of the murders—were circulated. No evidence against
them existed other than the fact that they had expressed a
desire to visit a golf course near the Sherry home on the day
before the murders. But such was the desperation of the
police department to show progress, to have something to
hand out at the press conferences. Newspapers statewide
dutifully published the composites, generating dozens of
spurious tips. The men depicted in those artist's renderings
were never identified, however—fortunately for them.

The task force briefly considered Pete Halat as a potential
suspect. The politically wired and ambitious partner would
be a good place to turn in any homicide. He was the last
person to see Vince Sherry alive, and he was the first to find
the bodies. But the detectives saw no motive. Vince, with
his perilously high blood pressure, had been turned down
for an insurance policy on behalf of the firm and Pete. Halat
didn't get a penny from Vince's death. If anything, his
practice stood to suffer. And even the kids said he was
Vince's best friend.

Next, one by one, the task force looked at Vince's former clients. They considered a cocaine-smuggling preacher from Gulfport who had accused Vince of taking a big fee, then selling him out. There was a Chicago mobster and Colombian cocaine smugglers to consider, as well as the king of Biloxi's Strip, Mike Gillich. Vince's files were a veritable *Who's Who* of Gulf Coast crime.

Most promising of Vince's former clients was Betty "Diamond Betsy" Inman, a Tennessee-based cocaine smuggler who earned her nickname from an Imelda Marcos–style hoard of drug-financed jewels, furs, clothes, and shoes stashed in her Nashville condo. Years earlier, she had paid for Vince's legal representation in Mississippi and Puerto Rico by signing over her two Lincolns, a Dino Ferrari, a motor home, and a pile of cash. (The corpulent, occasionally incoherent trafficker also suggested he dump Margaret and run off with her as part of the retainer, a package deal Vince politely declined.) When she drew a prison term despite Vince's best efforts, Inman decided Sherry had betrayed her. Her love letters turned to threats. The task force heard that Betsy had told associates Vince had looted her possessions, swearing she'd kill Sherry if given the chance.

But Diamond Betsy had been in jail when Vince and Margaret died, the task force soon found. Her threats, apparently, had been idle ones.

The task force would spend weeks pursuing clients of Vince's, without success. It was all speculation. Without evidence from the crime scene or witnesses to implicate a particular person, there was nothing to really investigate. The police ended up telephoning or visiting these clients of Vince's and, in essence, bluntly asking them to confess. No one did.

Faced with so many dead ends, the much-publicized task force began to dwindle in size after a handful of days as its members found less and less to do. They knew a truism of the field of homicide investigation: Except for a tiny majority of cases, murders are solved within forty-eight hours of their commission. Or they are never solved at all.

If the police had trouble finding a suspect, the rumor mill in Biloxi did not. Within hours of the discovery of the bodies, rumors that Biloxi's favorite son, Mayor Blessey, might be a viable suspect were being discussed avidly in grocery store lines and over morning coffee across the Mississippi Gulf Coast. Certainly Lynne's suspicions, her whole family's, focused on the mayor. She was certain her mother's worst political enemy had to be involved, and many townspeople reinforced that suspicion, relishing the gossipy intrigue. One woman approached Lynne later, at her parents' wake, and said, "Seventy-five percent of Biloxi thinks Mayor Blessey did it, darlin'. The other twenty-five percent are related to him."

This suspicion was studiously ignored by the Biloxi police officials in charge of the case in all their public pronouncements and investigative actions. In one press conference, Director of Public Safety George Saxon admitted that, three days after the bodies were found, investigators still could not determine the motive for the murders. Yet in almost the same breath, he declared, "Politics had nothing to do with the killings." Gerald Blessey sat next to him at the conference.

Lynne saw in this a huge conflict of interest, but the truth was, even outside investigators brought in to help the city police department agreed that there was absolutely no evidence to link the mayor to the murders.

Still, Lynne had a point: The city's director of public safety and his police chief served at the mayor's pleasure, and Gerald Blessey had made it abundantly clear that he would not be considered a suspect simply because he and the victims were enemies. The fact that Blessey was out of town during the time of the murder and had uncharacteristically missed a crucial city council meeting Tuesday, just as Margaret had, was duly noted, though it was never couched in terms of an alibi.

A sheriff's detective on the task force who asked to question Blessey, if only as a matter of routine, was told by the sheriff at the time not to pursue it.[3] This got back to Lynne eventually, infuriating her and compounding suspicions of coverup and complicity.

Long before that, from her first day in Biloxi—even while Leslie Sherry spoke of how only a friend could get past her parents' dogs—Lynne Sposito had focused on her mother and father's worst enemy: Mayor Gerald Blessey. On that first day in Biloxi, she walked into the city police department expecting the worst from the police department the mayor commanded.

And even then, Lynne had no idea just how bad it would get.

CHAPTER 4

If the Sherry children arrived at the converted school- . house fearful and distrustful of the mayor's police department, the two detectives assigned to question them only exacerbated those feelings. They separated Lynne, Eric, and Leslie for individual interrogation, a police tradition more often used with criminal suspects than with grieving families. Leslie went first, while Eric and Lynne paced and fretted in a cluttered hallway.

The youngest Sherry and the only one who had still lived with Vince and Margaret when home from college, Leslie seemed a logical starting point to the police—the family member most likely to have recent, relevant information. She immediately brought up a key detail the detectives had not heard about before. Wherever Vince Sherry went, Leslie said, he carried a black appointment book. Upcoming appointments, court hearings, dinner dates—everything he did or planned to do—would be there. If anything could help police learn whom he was planning to see at the time of the murders, that book could do it, Leslie said.

"His black book went with him wherever he went 'cause, as intelligent as he was, he was scatterbrained and he needed his book to know where he was supposed to be," Leslie told Detective Otto "Buddy" Wills and his newly assigned partner in the case, Harrison County Sheriff's Investigator Greg Broussard, sent by the sheriff to assist the city-run task force. Leslie was surprised when the two investigators told her they knew nothing of this appointment book. They, in turn, were surprised that Vince's best friend, Pete Halat, had somehow forgotten to mention this potentially crucial piece of evidence.

"If he forgot it," Leslie said of her father, "I could expect him back within fifteen minutes. . . . They both had one, but he was fanatic about bringing his with him everywhere."[1]

With that simple revelation, the detectives learned the killers had taken something from the home after all. Though it could still be buried in the mounds of files and papers at the house, the book should have been readily apparent, near the judge's jacket or car keys, or in his coat pocket. Yet their initial search of the house had not uncovered it. They would search again, now that they knew what to look for. But that book was gone. They were sure of it.

And that could mean only one thing, Broussard and Wills decided. The Sherrys had known their killer, probably had dinner with him. Why take the appointment book, unless it named the last person to have seen Vince and Margaret alive? And that last person was their murderer.

Eric Sherry spoke to the police after Leslie, alone with the two investigators in a small office. Unlike the detailed questions they had asked of Leslie about Vince's and Margaret's habits, likes and dislikes, the round and balding Wills and his thin, dark partner, Broussard, seemed most interested in asking Eric two things: to describe what he knew about the murders, and to detail his trip to Biloxi the night before.

With their poker faces and seeming solicitousness, the two investigators neglected to mention the reason for these questions—that they had already heard from three witnesses whose accounts left them wondering about Eric and the sincerity of his grief. One person saw Eric in town Wednesday afternoon—within a few hours of the discovery of the bodies—when he should have been at home in Florida. A friend of the family, meanwhile, had told police that Vince and Margaret had confided that they were having "major problems" with one of their sons, which the friend understood to be Eric. And yet another witness—no less than the head of the police department, Director of Public Safety George Saxon—had seen Eric Wednesday evening, and concluded that his behavior seemed far too cold and calculating for someone who had just learned his parents had been murdered. "He walked up to me like any passerby and said, 'What's going on here?'" Saxon recalled. "All he asked was, 'Where are the dogs?' No crying, no upset. Just cold." Finally, Wills and Broussard had been tipped off about something else concerning Eric, something secret in his past. They were keeping this to themselves for the moment, but it was explosive enough to raise serious questions about who Eric Sherry was, and what he thought of his parents—placing him on the list of potential suspects.

Point by point, however, and seemingly without realizing he was doing it, Eric exploded the theory that the Sherry murders were a case of parricide. First he explained how he had received a telephone call at his home in Fort Walton Beach, Florida, Wednesday afternoon from a friend who had heard about the murders on the radio within an hour of their discovery. He had immediately called Pete Halat and his sister Lynne, then jumped in his car and made the two-and-a-half hour drive to Biloxi as fast as he could. That's why he was in town by late afternoon, early evening. There was nothing strange about it.

Once in Biloxi, Eric recalled, he was not allowed inside or even near the house, which had been cordoned off with yellow plastic tape while dozens of cops and other officials milled about outside. It was then that George Saxon briefly spoke with Eric and concluded he seemed oddly calm. He didn't know Eric had always been a stoic, refusing as a child to cry even when Vince spanked him. At age twenty-eight, Eric remained much the same. He had sounded just as cold and distant when he phoned Lynne—but she, of course, knew him, knew it was his defense against anguish. Believing as he did that Biloxi officials had something to do with the murders, he was not about to show how upset he was in front of the mayor's hand-picked public safety chief, Eric would later say. "I wouldn't give them the satisfaction."

After stopping at the house, Eric told his interrogators, he next had driven to Pete Halat's house, where the Sherrys' friends had gathered to mourn. Pete pulled Eric aside and explained how he had found the bodies, a story Eric repeated for the policemen interviewing him. Eric displayed no inside knowledge of the murder scene—the sort of slip the murderer might make—just an abbreviated version of Halat's tale. Each of the Sherry children repeated a similar story, though for some reason, they remembered Halat telling them he had only seen the bottom half of Vince's body, not his face, before he fled the house. Yet Pete had told the police he had seen the whole body, and even described accurately Vince's position, with his head near the sliding glass doors in the den. The children also remembered Halat saying his elbow accidentally pushed open the Sherrys' front door as he peered in, while he told police he opened it purposely. Even so, Eric's account raised no red flags for the detectives.

As for the issue of trouble the Sherrys were having with a son, Eric and, later, Lynne explained it was their younger brother, Vin, not him. Nine years earlier, an eighteen-year-old Vin had left the Sherry home in Biloxi to live with Lynne after a terrible argument with his mother because she had searched his room. Margaret and her youngest son eventually made up, but only after years of tension. Eric was reluctant to speak ill of his brother, but the investigators soon realized that if the Sherrys were having problems with a son, it had to be Vin. And he had been three thousand miles away at the time of the murders.[2]

The detectives had little else to ask Eric. He had no idea they had him down as a possible suspect, nor did he realize that he had mostly—though not completely—allayed those suspicions.

Lynne, however, saw a few minutes later exactly where they were headed, even though her interview began innocuously enough: The investigators' first question was how many children did Vince and Margaret have. When Lynne answered four, thinking the question odd, as she knew the police already had that information, Detective Wills refined the question. How many of those four are *natural* children?

"What?" Lynne asked, stunned, a bit frightened.

"How many are the natural children of Vincent and Margaret Sherry?" When Lynne could do nothing but stare, the detective added, "We just heard a rumor that one of you is adopted, and we'd just like to know if that's true."

The police, somehow, had found out one of the Sherry family's deepest secrets, Lynne realized: that Eric Sherry was adopted. Not even he knew it, Lynne believed. Eric had been born to Margaret's black-sheep brother and his Japanese wife, who separated shortly after his birth. Margaret and Vince had adopted Eric at age seven months when his mother returned to Japan and his father confessed he was not up to the task of single fatherhood. Few people knew the truth of Eric's origins—the Sherrys hadn't wanted him to feel unloved as a child, and as he grew older, they lacked the courage to tell him who his parents were, for fear he would resent the deception or, worse, express a desire to live with Margaret's irresponsible brother.

"I don't see what that has to do with anything," Lynne snapped.

"Well, we have to operate under the possibility that this person just found out he was adopted, and was so upset with your parents that he killed them."

Lynne thought for a moment she was going to throw up. It all seemed so hopeless. They'd never catch the killer. The police—detectives who worked for the mayor, the man she considered the real prime suspect—were trying to pin the murder on her brother. It only seemed to confirm her worst fears—that the police were part of some terrible conspiracy. Eric would be crushed if he found out he was a target. It never occurred to her that he really might have something to hide.

Somehow, though, instead of raging at the two investigators, she managed to respond with a cold precision, once again finding that detached feeling, as if she was talking about somebody else's murdered parents. She kept telling herself that if she cried and yelled, they would never take her seriously again. She had to be like a surgeon entering the operating theater, cool, objective, analytical.

"Well, that's a really neat theory," she said, "except for one thing. This person doesn't know about the adoption."

"You can't know that," one of the policemen responded.

"Look," Lynne said, "do you understand? I'm seven years older than the next kid. I would have to have been a complete idiot not to know that the child was adopted. I was the only one who knew, besides my parents. But if that person was so upset that he killed Mom and Dad over it, don't you think he would have been a little bit pissed at me, too, for keeping the secret? We've not even had a point in our relationship where it's been strained, much less angry with each other. Not to mention the fact that to come home and play the grieving son, he'd have to be a sociopath. Which he is not."

The two investigators did not look convinced. But they eased up a bit, explaining they just had to check out every angle. It didn't mean they really believed Eric did it.

Lynne was not mollified. She said, "You've got to promise me something: Please don't tell Eric. I swear to you, he doesn't know. If you tell him, he'll feel like he's lost everything. Please. If it comes down to it, I'll tell him. But for now, just don't do that to us."

The two detectives looked at one another, then nodded. The subject of the adoption would remain closed for the time being. It was a lousy angle anyway. There was no evidence against Eric. They had been honest with Lynne: At that point, they did not really believe Eric Sherry had killed his parents, no matter what their boss said. That would change in time, however. Eric did, indeed, have things to hide, they would soon decide.[3]

At the end of the day, the Sherry murder task force gathered in a conference room to review two days of investigation. What they knew could be summed up easily: They had no meaningful witnesses, no evidence, and no idea who killed the Sherrys.

Even public pleas for information about where the Sherrys dined Monday evening led nowhere. The last time they were seen outside their house was around 5:30 P.M. on Monday, September 14. Vince had picked up three dozen sandwiches at the air base to bring to the home of a fellow judge whose father had died. He delivered them, then returned to the base for a haircut. Finally, he had stopped by the law office for a chat with Pete Halat, gassed up his car, and, as far as the police could find, he had gone home. The trail ended there.

Margaret was seen about the same time, maybe a half hour later, at the base exchange, where she browsed through the clothes racks, then bought two calculators. These were found still in the plastic shopping bag from the exchange, hanging on a doorknob off the den, the receipt inside dated September 14, 6:30 P.M. After making that purchase, she had gone home and had several telephone conversations, one of which was cut short, either by accident or by the arrival of a killer. After that, the task force had drawn a blank on both Sherrys, except for one witness, the parole officer, who recalled the Tuesday morning conversation with Judge Sherry.

Motive also remained a mystery. Detectives had heard rumors of threats against the Sherrys—several friends mentioned it when questioned, one even recalling Margaret speaking of a "contract" on her life. But, again, Pete Halat's firm statement that there could not have been any serious threats without his knowing closed off that avenue of inquiry.

Then there was Margaret's supposed work with the FBI. Lynne Sposito, along with several friends of Margaret's, had investigators half convinced that subject might be worth exploring, whether the mayor liked it or not. Lynne had been adamant with detectives: Margaret had been helping the FBI investigate alleged city corruption, particularly in Biloxi's waterfront redevelopment project, the centerpiece of Mayor Blessey's attempt to stimulate the city's moribund economy. Because of what Margaret claimed to have uncovered, she had expressed fears about her and her family's safety shortly before the murders, Lynne told the police. That remark of Margaret's about them coming after her kids kept gnawing at Lynne.

Once again, though, Pete Halat discounted this notion, assuring police the Sherrys had received no threats. Then FBI Agent Royce Hignight—the Sherrys' friend and neighbor, and a senior agent on the Coast—flatly denied any such investigation existed. Sure, Margaret had talked to him, the agent confirmed, but she had nothing of value. There was no investigation. Period. And that closed off Margaret's search for corruption as a possible motive, so far as the task force was concerned. Neither Mayor Blessey nor any other city official would be added to the list of suspects.

The list would not remain empty, however. Late on September 17, a few hours after the Sherry children left the police department feeling uninformed and fearful, two things happened that gave investigators one firm suspect, as well as a puzzling contradiction.

First, a friend of Eric Sherry called to tell police that she had run into him in Florida a week earlier, during the Labor Day weekend. Eric had told her he planned to be in Biloxi the following week, on Sunday and Monday, September 13 and 14—the last days of Vincent and Margaret Sherry.

Hours before the police learned this, Eric had sat with Broussard and Wills and somehow failed to mention these travel plans. That glaring omission was as bad as an outright lie as far as the police were concerned. It didn't matter whether he actually made the trip—it sounded bad, like he was hiding something. It put Eric Sherry right back on the suspect list. At the top. The task force began investigating him in depth.

The second occurrence came at the end of the day, after the task force folded for the evening. The sheriff's dispatcher forwarded a call to Greg Broussard's home. Ruthie Smith, Judge Sherry's court reporter, wanted to talk. She reopened another avenue that investigators had all but discounted earlier in the day.

"I've got a tape you ought to hear," she told Broussard. "It's of Judge Sherry, on the bench. Talking about receiving threats on his life."

CHAPTER 5

The woman had stood before Circuit Judge Vincent Sherry near tears. She feared the man charged with nearly killing her—her own husband—would try again.

"I can't do anything without watching for him," the woman had pleaded to the judge that May, five months before Vince Sherry would die. ". . . Somebody is out there who can get a gun any time he wants it."

High on his bench, the judge promised the abject woman that her husband would be tried and justice done—have no doubt of that, he vowed. Then, as his stare turned inward, he begged the woman not to let threats and fears govern her life—even as he seemed to forget for a moment that she was standing there. Speaking of his own recent experiences with intimidation and jeopardy, Judge Sherry silenced the courtroom by choosing that moment to break a lifelong habit of poker-faced privacy with an extraordinary statement.

"Would you believe, dear lady, that in the past two weeks, I've had an out-of-state threat on my life, and an in-city threat on my life?" Vince Sherry announced, the stenographer's tape recorder picking up each word. "And I know where it's coming from. But I'll see myself in the pits of hell before I'll be afraid of these people."

An assistant district attorney—an officer of the court charged with enforcing the laws of Mississippi—sat at her oak prosecutor's table, saying nothing. True, she worked for a district attorney who boasted heartily of his delight in making Judge Sherry white around the mouth—either from tight-lipped anger or from a milk of magnesia mustache, whichever came first. Still, this was an unusual comment, even from her boss's political enemy. Maybe the prosecutor didn't take the judge's words seriously. Maybe she simply wasn't listening. For whatever reason, the district attorney of Harrison County, Mississippi, did nothing after a sitting judge spoke openly of threats on his life.

Instead, Judge Sherry continued to console the woman quivering before him as her husband stared from the defense table.

"Believe me, I identify with you on this business of cheap threats against your life," Judge Sherry declared. "But as you pointed out to me, he's done it to you once. These clowns that are after me haven't gotten me yet."

No one thought to ask the source of the threats, a reference eerily similar to words spoken by Margaret Sherry to her daughter that same month. The hearing simply ended. The defendant was hauled off, the woman drifted away, and the judge and his clerk began moving through the court's daily calendar of murder, divorce, theft, and contract dispute. The endless bits of suffering and outrage that fill courthouses daily throughout the nation, a thousand dramas a day both momentous and petty, drowned out Vince Sherry's personal demons as the clerk called the next case.[1]

Detectives played the court reporter's tape of that May 12, 1987, hearing over and over, but no matter how many times they replayed it, no keys to the fatal events of the following autumn appeared. No name was whispered on that tape, no accusation explained. Vincent Sherry may have known his killer. But all he left behind was an unheeded warning, a man's strong voice with clear diction and perfect grammar, a moment out of time preserved forever on a thin brown piece of magnetic tape, both prescient and meaningless. And you can't help but listen to it and long for more.

There had indeed been threats against at least one of the Sherrys, despite Pete Halat's avowals, which now seemed a bit odd. One threat was from out of state, one from within the city—that's what Judge Sherry had said. It was a frustrating puzzle for the police, hearing a victim of a contract killer express fear of his impending demise, yet fail to name the source. Again, they wondered if his work as a lawyer, his duties as a judge, or the politics of his wife had led to the threats. The tape provided no illumination. Investigators renewed efforts to call friends of the Sherrys who might have heard them speak of threats, and although several people did recall Margaret mentioning these fears, she was never specific. No useful details cropped up.

The mystery of the missing appointment book still plagued task force members as well, as they frantically sought to retrace the Sherrys' final day. Once Leslie Sherry had informed the police of its existence, they searched the house, the judge's chambers, and his law office, without success.

Finally, in desperation to trace the Sherrys' last appointment, the task force dispatched an officer on a peculiar quest: rooting through every salad bar on the Mississippi Gulf Coast, looking for precisely the right mixture of shredded carrots, almonds, green peas, raisins, and kiwi to match the plastic bags of stuff the medical examiner had pulled from the stomachs of Vincent and Margaret Sherry. If only they could figure out where the Sherrys ate that night—and who sat across the table from them—investigators felt certain they'd find their killer.

But when detectives finally found the one restaurant that could have served the Sherrys that night, right down to the last garbanzo bean, they came up empty. No one at the Golden Corral remembered seeing either Vince or Margaret on the night of September 14, 1987. This seemed unlikely—the Sherrys could not have eaten there without leaving their distinctive imprint. They didn't just enter a restaurant and sit down. They worked the crowd, finding a dozen acquaintances to greet and shake and clap on the back, Vince flirting with the women, Margaret sharing her latest take on Biloxi intrigue and corruption. They were born politicians, never a birthday forgotten or a funeral unattended. They drove restaurant hostesses crazy because it always took them ten minutes to walk from the door to a table.

Except for the one night that counted, no one remembered a thing.

While the police searched salad bars for slices of kiwi and listened to Judge Sherry foretell his own death, Lynne Sposito started looking for her own answers. On the morning of Friday, September 18, in the hours before her parents' wake, she and her brother Vin, who had arrived in town the day before, left their beachside motel and drove to their parents' house. It was still cordoned off and under guard, so they decided on impulse to go next-door. They only knew their parents' neighbor by sight, an occasional wave and hello, but it seemed worth a try. As the policemen guarding her parents' house gazed at them with apparent disinterest, Lynne knocked on the door.

It cracked open. A young man, eyes wide, thinning hair disheveled, peeked out, then waved them in the door, opened just enough for them to squeeze through. "Quick, quick, come in," he hissed. Brett Robertson slammed the door shut behind them so fast it almost caught Lynne's foot.

Lynne and Vin started to ask Robertson if he had seen

anything suspicious Monday night or Tuesday morning—
the newspapers, not the police, having provided this possible time frame for the murders. But the man silenced them.

"Don't you know what's going on?" he asked.

Lynne began to think something was wrong with this
person. This attempt at amateur detecting was turning into
a colossal waste of time. "Of course we know," she said
patiently, as if speaking to someone impaired. "Our parents
were shot and killed."

"No, no, you don't understand," Robertson said. They
were still standing in the entryway, and he gave no indication that he was going to invite them any further into the
house. He merely said quietly, "I saw the guy."

"What?" Vin and Lynne barked the same question simul-
taneously. "What guy?"

Now Robertson looked at them like they were the idiots.

"I saw the car. Or I saw a car, outside the house that night,
Monday night, about ten o'clock. As soon as I saw it, I
thought, That looks like a narc car. A yellow Ford Fairmont."

To Lynne and Vin, who had spoken to the police, who
had read every word in every newspaper written about the
case, this was stunning. As far as the police knew, no one in
the neighborhood had seen anything.

Yet here was Robertson gauging their reactions, pausing
for effect. As nervous as he was, he wanted to impress his
visitors with this bombshell.

"I saw who was driving it—this Biloxi cop," Robertson
said. "He was plainclothes, but I recognized him . . .
because he stopped me a few years ago. So, okay, I see him
that night, and at first, I thought he was just sitting outside
to watch me. But now I think he was driving the car for the
people that killed your parents."

"Are you sure?" Lynne had to ask. It was just too
incredible: a cop outside the house at the time of the
murders. Her head felt like it was about to explode. If it was
just a coincidence, she thought, then the police would have
mentioned it. It would have been all over the news. A cop
patrolling the neighborhood in an unmarked car would have
been an invaluable witness. But there had been nothing. If
Robertson was telling the truth, it meant the cop had kept
silent about his presence that night on Hickory Hill Circle,

saying nothing about the yellow Ford at the scene of the crime. Which could mean only one thing. Lynne asked again, "Are you certain?"

"Yeah, I'm sure," Robertson said. "I know this guy."

"Did you tell anyone?" Lynne demanded. "Did they come around and talk to you? There were supposed to be cops all over this neighborhood after they found Mom and Dad."

"Yeah, they came around. I told them I saw a car, but I didn't, you know, tell them anything much about it."

"Why not?" This was just too much for Lynne. How could someone sit on something like this?

Robertson just shook his head, looking small and scared. "Because the cop who came around knocking on my door is the same one that was driving the car."

"Jesus," Vin whispered.

Robertson was not about to say to the policeman, gee, yeah, I saw someone on the night of the murder: you. So he had just mentioned seeing a strange car in the neighborhood, and left it at that. Now he wouldn't talk to anyone at the Biloxi Police Department, he said. How could he know whom to trust? Lynne sympathized: She felt the same way.

The reluctant witness said he didn't know the name of the policeman he had seen, so Lynne asked for a complete description. She took careful notes, a precaution that would soon become a habit. Robertson said he had not seen the man step outside the yellow Ford that night. He just saw him driving. Nor had he seen anyone go in or out of the house. But it was the cop who had once questioned him before, or his twin. He was over six feet tall, two hundred seventy-five pounds, maybe three hundred, a big, heavy man. He had brownish black hair, parted in the middle, a thin beard, glasses.

"He doesn't usually drive that Ford," Robertson said. "He normally has a white Chevy Caprice or Impala."[2]

There wasn't much else to say. Lynne said she knew someone at the sheriff's department she could trust. Would Robertson talk to him? Or the FBI? He said he would.

Vin and Lynne left dazed, knowing they had to get ready for the wake but too stunned to do more than sit in their car and stare at their parents' house, at the policemen standing outside. It could all be a mistake, or a fabrication, or some bizarre coincidence—yet it was so tempting to believe the worst. Robertson was so genuinely terrified. His story confirmed all their fears. The mayor wasn't just behind the murder, Lynne thought—he had his cops do the job. And now they had taken charge of the case, tidying up any loose ends.

At the wake, Lynne pulled Sheriff's Investigator Greg Broussard aside and told him about Robertson and the yellow Ford. She decided she had to trust someone—at least, as a sheriff's employee, he could not be influenced by city hall. He was independent of the Biloxi police. And Lynne did not yet know of the intensifying interest in her brother Eric.

Until that moment, the police had not been looking for any particular getaway car, Broussard confirmed, sounding disgusted by the investigative lapse. No connection had been made between the murder and the theft from the used car dealer where the Ford had been reported missing. As far as the task force knew, there was no reason to associate a routine car theft with an extraordinary murder case. Now, thanks to Lynne, that connection had been made. Broussard and his partner, Buddy Wills, finally had a tangible lead: The task force would launch a search for the yellow Ford. A press release and description would be released immediately, he promised.

After hearing Lynne repeat Robertson's description of the Ford's driver, Broussard mused, "Sounds like Ric Kirk."

Kirk was a heavyset Biloxi detective who had been assigned to narcotics and who, records would later show, had questioned Brett Robertson during a neighborhood canvass the day the bodies were discovered.[3]

"Do you know," she asked the sheriff's investigator, "if this Ric Kirk drives a white Chevy Impala or Caprice?"

Broussard looked surprised. "Well, yeah," he said. "I believe he does. Why do you ask?"[4]

But Lynne had stopped listening. In her mind, Brett Robertson's story had been confirmed. And the Biloxi police officers stationed around the funeral home to provide security for the family of Biloxi's most prominent murder victims suddenly seemed less a comfort, and more a menace.

CHAPTER 6

Twelve hundred people attended the wake for Vincent and Margaret Sherry. The people at the funeral home could remember few turnouts to rival it. The only one absent who had been expected to attend was Vincent Sherry Jr. himself. His closed coffin sat empty as the mourners passed by, his gold-framed picture atop the casket lid, but his body missing, unbeknownst to all but a handful of the guests.

Vince's body had been removed to the medical examiner's office that morning for a second autopsy in order to resolve a forensic puzzle: an unaccounted-for bullet.

Nine brass shells had been found in the house Wednesday, ejected from the murder weapon and sent skittering across the living room and bedroom floors, rolling under chairs, tables, and bed. Semiautomatic handguns use the expanding gases of burning gunpowder not only to power bullets down the barrel and into human flesh, but also to eject each expended shell—the hollow metal package that contains gunpowder, primer, and bullet. Since there is always one shell for every bullet, nine shells meant nine bullets had been fired, a full magazine for the Ruger auto. But there was a discrepancy.

Two bullets had plowed into the bedroom wall above Margaret's dresser, where she had been standing when the killer entered the room. Four more lead projectiles had passed into Margaret's head. Two bullet wounds—one in the mouth, one below his right eye—had been noted during Vince's first autopsy. That made for a total of eight slugs. Where was the ninth bullet?

This was of vital importance. Murder weapons can be matched to the bullets they fire. The problem was, the eight in hand were badly deformed. The police needed to see if the ninth was in better shape, which is why a second autopsy had been ordered, once an inch-by-inch search of the house failed to turn up the missing slug.

While the wake went on, the medical examiner found the ninth bullet had been inside Vince Sherry all along, disappointingly smashed beyond usefulness as it crashed through Vince's teeth and the thick bone of the human skull. Another double tap had been mistaken for a single wound.

Still, Vince's absence at the wake provided a strange source of comfort for the family, even a measure of amusement. "Well, Dad, you did it," Lynne whispered out of the corner of her mouth to her sister and two brothers. "We always said you'd be late for anything, even your own funeral. And you actually pulled it off." Then all four of them covered their faces, as the other mourners turned away in embarrassment, mistaking laughter for sobs.

Lynne roamed through the gathering at the funeral home, Dick Sposito at her side, exhausted from his long flight from France, still trying to absorb everything Lynne told him about her visit with the police—and with Vince and Margaret's neighbor. After his arrival, he had immediately sat down and drawn a flowchart of possible suspects and motives, a methodical accountant's approach that formed a perfect counterpoint to Lynne's tendency toward instinctive reactions and gut solutions.

Dick's quiet, calm presence fortified Lynne and their children, who had been having trouble eating and sleeping. Whenever they were in their motel room, Tommy restlessly paced. Cathy obsessively read the newspapers and watched the television news, deep circles forming beneath her eyes. Beth kept asking if Grandma and Grandpa could maybe wake up. All were frightened. Lynne was at a loss, but Dick solved part of the problem—the nighttime fears—by proposing they all sleep together in the same motel room along the beachfront, crowded but safe, the Sherry house still off limits and occupied by police technicians. Not that any of them would want to sleep in that house ever again.

At the wake, Lynne clutched Dick's hand hard each time she caught sight of Gerald Blessey. Lynne studiously avoided the area of the funeral home where the mayor stood. She had wanted to bar Blessey from attending, but Pete Halat had insisted he be allowed to come. Blessey was a public figure, he told Lynne, as were Vince and Margaret. He had to come. Lynne had reluctantly acquiesced, then gratefully accepted Pete's offer to handle the media as well. Halat also promised to keep Vin and Blessey as far apart as possible, anticipating an outburst if the two came together.

During one pass through the crowd, accepting condolences, hugs, and handshakes from people she hardly knew, Lynne became aware of Pete Halat behind her, talking to the medical examiner in a hushed voice, unaware that Lynne was within earshot. They were discussing a witness the police had found who remembered talking to Vince Sherry on Tuesday morning. The medical examiner lacked the details, but this turned out to be a garbled reference to the parole officer who claimed to have had a phone conversation with Vince. The time of death had not been firmly established—various tests were still underway—but the medical examiner told Halat that, because of this witness, it appeared the judge had been alive on Tuesday.

"That's impossible," Lynne thought she heard Halat proclaim. "They were long dead by then."[1]

The pair moved out of Lynne's hearing after that, but she wondered what Pete had meant by that remark, what made him so sure. No newspaper had reported this. No one she talked to at the police department would commit to a firm time of death. Even the medical examiner was unsure—she had just heard him say so—and he was the person responsible for determining the time of death. It was strange.

Lynne might have forgotten about it, but a few days later, Halat was proved right. The medical examiner's tests pinpointed the time of death at Monday night. The parole officer had been mistaken. Just as Halat suggested, Vince was long dead by Tuesday morning. Lynne had to wonder how Pete Halat possibly could have known that.

Later that evening of the wake, during the rosary, two women sat talking, speculating about who had come to the wake and who had not, a kind of *Who's Who* in Biloxi. It was little more than gossip. But then one of them said, "Do you realize that the person who killed them could be right here in this room, pretending to be a friend of the family, just like they did to get in the house?"

The women didn't notice the blond sixteen-year-old sitting nearby, who stiffened, then blanched at their words. They had never met Cathy Sposito, and they had no way of knowing their idle rumination would so profoundly affect her. It had never occurred to Cathy that the killers of her grandparents could be so bold as to show up at the wake. Now she turned to look at the people around her, wondering which solemn expression masked a murderer certain he'd never be caught. Who was the chameleon? She began to shake.

Lynne was chatting with someone when Dick grabbed her elbow and whispered, "You've got to come quick, something's wrong with Cathy." He guided Lynne to the back of the funeral home, where two rooms with chairs and beds had been set aside to help get the family through the long day and evening. She could hear the weeping coming from behind one of the closed doors.

Inside, Lynne found her daughter curled in a fetal position on one of the beds, gripping her legs with damp, cold hands, her whole body quaking as if someone were shaking the mattress beneath her. "What is it, honey?" Lynne cried out. "What's wrong?"

"Oh, Mommy, just hold me. Hold me!" Cathy's teeth were chattering as she spoke, tears running down her cheeks.

Lynne climbed onto the bed and hugged her daughter, curling around the girl as if shielding from blows, then asked again what was the matter.

"Oh, Mommy, I heard them talking—about how the killers could be here right now. Right here! They could be here, Momma. They could think we know what Grandma did, what Grandma knew. We could be next. They could be here and we don't know it. Maybe they'll want to kill us, too." Cathy was sobbing now, the tremors wracking her body.

Lynne comforted her daughter, feeling the sobs slow as she told Cathy hush, that everything would be fine. No one will ever hurt my children, Lynne whispered, her voice gentle but her teeth clenched.

The next day, the day of the funeral, the four Sherry children walked into the cathedral arm in arm. Five hundred people packed the church, the mayor, the governor, and a platoon of judges among them. Detectives Wills and Broussard stood in the back, scanning the faces, looking for suspects, watching Eric Sherry carefully.

The Requiem Mass was held in Latin by the bishop of Biloxi, a special request in honor of Vince, who preferred the ancient ritual language of Rome and who, of course, would have understood every word. The traditional "Ave Maria" was sung in a tenor's clear, strong voice, but so was the Protestant hymn "Amazing Grace," in honor of Margaret's relatives—she had converted to Catholicism only after marrying Vince, ending up the more devout of the two.

As the bishop finished his homily, Pete Halat sprang up and took the lectern to deliver a eulogy—something that seemed to surprise Lynne and her family. They looked up and there stood Pete, the coughs and rustling in the congregation silenced, first by his quiet determination, and then by the moving, heartfelt words that followed.

"Why?" he began, anger and sorrow twisting his narrow, tanned face. "Why has God deemed to take Vince and Margaret from us, and allowed the wild animal who committed this heinous crime to remain in our midst, lurking in the dark, perhaps even befriending a prospective victim so that he might use that confidence to get close enough to strike his deadly blow!"

Lynne shivered at the thought, then glanced at her daughter, who sat stiffly in the hard wooden pew, eyes down. Exactly the same fear had shaken Cathy the night before—fear of the enemy disguised as a friend, hatred masked as love. Lynne couldn't stop herself from scanning the faces around her, as if the animal in the dark would somehow reveal himself if she gazed intently enough. She finally forced her eyes back to the lectern.

"I particularly remember an incident," Pete was saying, "when, on his jogging circuit, Vince stopped by my house, came in, and asked for a glass of milk. As was my custom with Vince, I pointed to the cabinet and said, 'The glasses are still kept there.' My wife, Sandra, admonished me that that was no way to treat a guest. My automatic response was, 'Vince is not a guest. He's kin.'"

Leslie began to weep softly. Lynne felt a thickening in her throat as Pete said, "I cannot possibly measure my personal loss against that of Vince and Margaret's children and grandchildren and family members, but indeed, my loss is great. . . . I considered them family."

Anecdotes and praise followed, tributes to Vince's generosity, his intellect, even the piano lesson he took on his last day of life—he planned, Halat said, to surprise his wife by performing her favorite song. This was the first Lynne had heard of it, so like her father. Halat spoke of Margaret's fierce integrity, her political acumen, her grace at losing the mayor's seat she had coveted. He painted a broad, touching portrait of people he clearly loved.

Yet, one other moment in that eulogy would stick in their memories, something just a little hard and calculated buried within the genuine emotion of Halat's farewell to friends, even his use of Vince's trademark words of goodbye, "And so, my friend, I'll see you anon."

Toward the end of his remarks, Halat said, "I believe Margaret would like to be remembered as a leader who was more interested in the people than in her personal gain. And I believe she would want us to continue her good fight for honest, open, and accountable government."

Lynne and Eric looked at one another at that moment, startled by these words, and sharing the same thought at their meaning: Obliquely yet unmistakably, Pete Halat had just announced his intention to run for mayor in Margaret's stead. No one else caught it, but there it was, recorded for posterity when Halat distributed copies of his speech, a transcript prepared by his office staff, memorializing his words in praise of the Sherrys.

A few weeks later, Halat would confirm Lynne's and Eric's impression by telling the local newspaper he was probably going to run for mayor—an office Margaret's nemesis, Gerald Blessey, eventually decided to abandon without seeking a third term.

"I wouldn't have considered it with Margaret in the race," Halat told the newspaper.

Only a few close friends of Margaret's knew she had kept a list in her purse in the months before her death—names of people she considered likely opponents in her next run for mayor. Periodically, she crossed one name off the list, added another. She had updated it shortly before her death. Not even Lynne knew about it at the time.

The name of the Sherrys' good friend, Pete Halat, had been jotted down on that list.[2]

At the funeral, though, Lynne gave Halat's ambitions only fleeting attention, focusing instead on his glowing tribute. The memories he evoked stayed with her as the Sherry children drove to the cemetery in a long procession, passing the flags at half-mast, the policemen in dress uniforms saluting the hearses as they passed. Lynne was vaguely surprised by all the pomp—they were just Mom and Dad to her.

Each son and daughter placed a single rose on the caskets, Lynne quietly weeping as she laid her flower, Eric kneeling before his mother's coffin and gently kissing the lid, Vin stiffly wiping away tears, Leslie's face so twisted by grief she was unrecognizable, a tableau of anguish captured for the next day's front page.

CHAPTER 7

From the moment she arrived in Biloxi, Lynne Sposito wanted to see the house. Partly, this was to reclaim already receding memories, to grasp some lasting trace of her parents—a forgotten tin of her mother's infamous rum cake, the aroma of her father's cigars (the ones he smoked only when he wanted to irritate Margaret). But more than that, she wanted, even needed, to walk through that front door, into the living room, on to the den, then finally the bedroom—to tread the same path the killer had taken, eyes wide, to see what he had seen. Maybe she would understand it then. Maybe she would see something the police had missed. Maybe something about this crime might finally make sense.

In the past week, her family had been dissected and discussed in that privacy-killing, dispassionate way only murder permits, with its evidence technicians and burning television lights. Vince's and Margaret's every word and deed had been replayed with a new, ominous coloration in place. It went beyond Eric's adoption. The police wanted to know, as casual as if asking the time: Did your father go to whores? Was he on the take? Did he fool around on your mom? Was Margaret a racist? Would she have known if your dad was corrupt? It seemed almost an accusation: What could Margaret and Vincent Sherry have done to warrant their own deaths?

That was why Lynne needed to visit the house. She needed to see for herself, without the jaundice of suspicion the police seemed to carry with them. Then, she believed, she might understand what happened, and why.

For an entire week, the task force had held her at bay. Wait until the scene is processed. Wait until the FBI team from Quantico is through. Wait until the whole place is dusted for fingerprints, until it is swept for hairs and fibers, until the direction and velocity of each bullet and spatter of blood is measured and calculated. So Lynne had waited, impatient, straining. It was why she had gone out to the neighborhood and talked to Brett Robertson—the itch to see, to do something. To help set things straight.

Now the day had finally come. The police had called and said they wanted the family to go in. That's how they put their request; It was time to go in, the way the commander of a Marine company or a SWAT team says, *We're goin' in*. And that was how it felt. Buddy Wills and Greg Broussard wanted to use the Sherry children's eyes, their familiarity with the surroundings, their knowledge of their parents' habits—even their intuitions—to better interpret the evidence left in that house. It wouldn't be pretty, Broussard had warned. But it was important. It could help catch a killer.

This is what Lynne had been waiting for, and she had

promised to be there without hesitation. So why, Lynne asked herself, as she stared at her reflection in the motel bathroom mirror, did she suddenly dread entering that house?

No answer suggested itself as she surveyed the short blond hair in the mirror, the hastily combed perm, the circles under her eyes, the extra thirty pounds she kept meaning to lose, the mouth that of late looked wrinkled and tight, as if she had forgotten how to smile. Yes, she needed to see what had been left behind. Yet, once that threshold was crossed, there would be no more indulging the fantasy that it had all been some terrible mistake. She would see it, smell it, know it in her bones. It wasn't that she feared the house or the killer—only the certainty that her parents were truly gone. Nothing the police or the newspapers said could come close to slamming home that realization like a visit to Hickory Hill Circle.

Lynne traded the motel room for the harsh, gray glare of Biloxi morning. It was Tuesday, September 22, six days since Vincent and Margaret Sherry were found dead, and Lynne Sposito was going home for the last time.

Even after a week, the stench assaulted the nostrils, a mixture of dog droppings, bodily fluids, the scent of blood. Policemen had sealed the windows that first day, a safeguard against any attempts to tamper with evidence. This was probably a precaution without purpose, since the killers had possessed up to two days to remove any damning evidence before the murders were discovered, and they undoubtedly had done so long before the bodies cooled. The walls and carpets in that closed house seemed to Lynne to radiate the scent of death. Lynne and her sister, Leslie, surveyed the yellow tape barriers draped and stuck everywhere, the black graphite fingerprint powder that dusted surfaces throughout the house, the general rummaging—as if the house had been pillaged.

None of this mattered at the moment, though. Only the blood in that room shocked—and angered—Lynne. Trails of dry, brown blood streaked the sliding glass door that led from the den to the yard. Blood had pooled on the vinyl cushions of Vince's yellow reading chair, and on the carpet below, where strips of tape outlined the spot on which

Vince's supine body was found, a ghastly silhouette. A trail
of blood led to that taped figure, stretching back from the
spot Vince had occupied when the first bullet slammed into
his face.

"I asked you people if they died right away," Lynne said,
her voice a quiet monotone. The four investigators taking
part in this walk-through watched Lynne warily, Leslie
brooding at her side. "I asked you if it had been quick for
them, and you told me, yeah, it was quick. Now, you told
me one lie. Don't tell me any more."

The detectives continued staring at her blankly. Lynne
saw that it had been a good idea to insist that she and Leslie
come to the house together—the police had wanted Leslie
alone at first, as her memories of the house were freshest.
But at Lynne's suggestion, the four Sherry children had
made a pact to face painful tasks in the next few days
together, or at least in pairs. That way, there always would
be at least one other person to talk to who had been through
the same experience, the same shock. The way Leslie had
clutched her hand after walking into that stifling house—
and the anger she now felt boiling within her—told Lynne
she had been right to resist being bullied into waiting
outside.

"I'm a nurse, for Christ's sake," she continued, the words
heated now, louder, pushed through gritted teeth. "You
don't pump arterial blood after you're dead. You don't wind
up clear across the room with your blood on the opposite
wall if you die instantly. Don't lie to me."

The one comfort Lynne had allowed herself—that her
parents had not suffered—had been stripped from her.
There was no denying it. Broussard and Wills, who were at
this time functioning as the primary field investigators on
the task force, apologized, saying they were sorry for playing
down Vince's death. But Margaret really had died quickly,
they promised, four head shots, instantaneous, no time
even for the nerve cells to fire off a pain message to her
brain. That was gospel, they swore as they stood in the
bedroom, explaining Margaret's position in death. They
had thought it would be easier on the family to say the same
of Vince, to keep to themselves how he must have been left
there, bleeding and helpless, perhaps listening to his wife
die before the assassin finished him off. They had no idea

Lynne would deduce the significance of all the blood. They assured her their intentions, though deceptive, had been honorable.

"I understand," Lynne said. "But I can handle anything if I know what I'm handling. Once you accept the reality of somebody feeling the need to do this to your parents, you can handle just about anything—as long as somebody doesn't jerk you around. So if you can't tell me something, fine. Just tell me you can't tell me. But don't lie to me."

Broussard and Wills agreed. They looked at Lynne with new respect. They would not underestimate her again.[1]

Together, they walked through the house, room by room—the four investigators, Lynne, and Leslie. At the investigators' direction, the two daughters looked for anything that might be missing, particularly pillows because of the singed foam scattered around the bodies.

The walk-through, then, became a painful tour of Sherry family memories—the framed front page from the *Sun Herald* when Margaret barely lost the mayoral race, the photo of a black-robed Vince taking the oath of a circuit court judge, the diplomas and degrees, Vince's in law and political science, Margaret's in mathematics and art, wonderful accomplishments crammed carelessly in a closet.

In each room, Wills or Broussard asked the same questions: Is anything out of place? Is anything missing? Each time, Leslie and Lynne shook their heads no. The killers, it appeared, had taken nothing, at least nothing obvious—except for Vince Sherry's appointment book.

In the kitchen, Lynne walked to the counter near the sink and picked up a plastic seven-day pill dispenser—her mother's, for blood-pressure and thyroid medication. Lynne popped it open, looked inside, and said, "They were dead Monday night by ten o'clock."

This abrupt pronouncement startled the investigators—as far as they knew, a firm time of death had not yet been determined. But to Lynne, it suddenly seemed clear. She showed them how each daily compartment in the medicine container held seven pills. Sunday's was empty. Monday's had two pills left inside. Margaret had taken her morning medication on Monday, September 14, but had never removed her evening dosage. Margaret's and Vince's

nightly movements had attained ritual status, unvaried for
years, Lynne explained: Every night, after the ten o'clock
news, which they watched religiously, Margaret had a big
glass of milk and took her last pills of the day. You could set
your clocks by the regularity of Mom and Dad's nocturnal
habits, she said. "Mom was dead by ten o'clock, ten-thirty
tops. There is no doubt. She never missed her pills."

This revelation, combined with Margaret's phone conversation with her friend Dianne around seven o'clock Monday night, gave Broussard and Wills enough information to
narrow the time of death to a three-hour window, between
seven and ten o'clock on the night of September 14. The
sighting of the yellow Ford at ten or so that Monday night
took on greater significance. It was no longer simply a
strange car that might be relevant to the investigation; now
it was a suspicious car in the neighborhood at exactly the
time of the murder.

It wasn't much, but finding evidence the police had
overlooked gave Lynne the feeling of contributing to the
case, of helping bring the killers to justice. But it also begged
the question: Why hadn't the police asked about this pill
container on their own? It had been in plain view. Lynne
would learn later this was only one of many oversights by
the often fragmented, leaderless task force.

The walk-through ended in one of the extra bedrooms
that had been used as an office, piled high with papers,
much of the clutter from Margaret's personal investigation
of how the city was using—or, as she believed, misusing—
federal grant money. The entire Sherry family would spend
the next several days working with the investigators, going
through these papers and the others spread through the
house, retracing Margaret's thinking and findings, reading
Vince's mail, burrowing through bank receipts—anything
that might suggest a motive for murder.

They looked everywhere. There was the heating vent
Margaret used to stash papers. Empty. They pulled books
off the shelf and shook them, looking for messages tucked
into the pages. Nothing. At one point, one of the investigators asked Lynne, "Where's your dad's toolbox?"

"Dad didn't have a toolbox," Lynne said. "But Mom's is
in the closet."

The task before them was monumental. The Sherrys were

packrats when it came to their documents, with utility bills and canceled checks going back to the 1970s, boxed and filed, utterly useless.

They also kept answering machine tapes, piling used cassettes in a cardboard box instead of recording new messages over the same tape. Theorizing that Vince and Margaret kept those old tapes for a reason—more threats, perhaps?—the investigators began replaying them one by one. As Leslie and Lynne rummaged through the old files in their mother's office, they suddenly heard, drifting in from the next room, their father's rich, clear voice.

"Hi, hon, pick up," Vince was saying. He had been calling his wife from work. "I'm on my way home. Do you need me to pick up anything at the store?"

The pedestrian normalcy of that recorded call left both women speechless, frozen in place, papers quivering in their hands. The tape was from a week or so before the murders, a lifetime ago, when what to get at the market seemed the most pressing of concerns. The machine had clicked, cutting off Vince's voice, Margaret picking up and no doubt telling him to bring home some milk or some ice cream or a dozen eggs. The ordinariness of the call, in that house the Sherry children could never forget and never again love, opened all their wounds, each word a razor stroke.

The tape found in the machine on the day of the murder was no less poignant: Friends had called on Tuesday and Wednesday, right up to the time the bodies were found. The machine had clicked on and off mindlessly, continuing to answer the phone and recording messages, each caller's voice echoing in the house as the Sherrys lay unmoving, unnoticed. Norma had called Margaret about the seafood festival. A councilman called to discuss the city budget with her. Fred wanted to remind Vince of a meeting the following Sunday. The local librarian called to say a book was in. Then Leslie's voice appeared, the message she left making it clear she was a little miffed, a little impatient: Where were you? Why did you stand me up? This had been left Tuesday, when the Sherrys missed their lunch date and veterinary appointment in Baton Rouge. A week later, the sound of her anger replayed was mortifying, the thought of her carping into that machine as her mother and father lay murdered almost unbearable.

From Wednesday, the tape had preserved a call from Pete Halat's secretary, then from Halat himself—attempts to find out why Vince failed to come to court that morning. Then came a flurry of messages left just after eleven o'clock, when the first report of a possible homicide at the Sherry home went out on the police radio: Two friends of the family left messages, as had a radio news reporter, a court clerk, and a police dispatcher, all calling back-to-back, wanting to know the same thing, if anyone was home. All wanted to know: Was it true? Had there been a shooting?

No one had picked up those calls, of course. Pete Halat had dashed in and out already, and the police had yet to arrive. The tape ended, with the silence that followed a last plaintive question from a friend: "Is anyone there? Is anyone there?"

On the other side of that tape, older calls had been recorded. One of them raised investigators' suspicions. John Field, a former Biloxi cop who had left the force under a cloud years earlier, had called to tell Vince, "Come on over. The ice cream's ready."

That same morning of the walk-through, the police had cracked open a safe that had been brought from the Sherrys' bedroom closet to the police department. Amid the old insurance policies and other assorted, innocuous documents, the police found a three-by-five sheet of notebook paper with a row of what appeared to be figures in kilo amounts. Suspicions immediately flared that Vince might have been involved in drug trafficking—measurements in kilograms are, among other things, the hallmark of cocaine dealers. The police already knew Vince had represented a number of heavy traffickers. Then there was his friendly associations with the Gulf Coast's criminal element—his address book had been filled with gangsters, crooks, and other assorted toughs, right next to the senators, congressmen, and judges he also counted as friends. He was friends with a corrupted judge, a corrupted sheriff, a variety of notorious gangsters. Vince, the police had concluded, liked to rub elbows with the dark side. Maybe, they theorized, he had crossed over the line himself.[2]

Now, in this context of suspicion, the telephone message reference to "ice cream" was not seen as a simple invitation to dessert, but as a possible reference to cocaine. Maybe a shipment had just arrived and this was code—coke was often called snow, flake, white lady. Why not ice cream? Drug deals had led to more than one murder, the police knew, and Vince, with his lawyer's connections and criminal friends, could easily have gotten involved. Poor Margaret could have simply been dragged down with him.

The suspicions did not pan out, however, no matter how odd the kilo figures mixed in with other ordinary family papers might seem. When task force investigators went to question John Field about the message machine tape, he went to his freezer and hauled out a bucket of strawberry ice cream his wife had made.

"Vince loved Becky's ice cream," a tight-lipped Field told his inquisitors, in that same deliberate, hoarse basso voice so recognizable on the Sherrys' answering machine, though now it was dripping with contempt. "Y'all got any other hot leads like this one?"

Nevertheless, the paper with the kilo amounts was sent to the FBI crime lab to see if there were traces of cocaine on it. The drug is persistent and pervasive, often contaminating money and papers used by people who handle the substance. The paper would later come back clean, another puzzle piece that didn't fit.

"You keep saying it was clean, a clean job, nothing left behind," Lynne said during a pause in the tape playing and rummaging. "Now we're saying nothing's missing. What else can you tell us? What does this mean?"

"Well, one thing we can tell you is, it's a contract hit," Broussard replied. "Every step of the way was professional."

"How can you tell that?" Lynne wanted to know.

"Because they used a twenty-two."

Lynne was still innocent in these matters, though that, too, would change. She asked them why the caliber of the gun meant anything.

"Well, a twenty-two will penetrate the skull once, but it usually won't come out," Broussard explained. "It does a lot of ricochet damage, and this person knew where to aim. Plus, they're easy to obtain, and they're easy to get rid of."

Lynne was surprised. She had been wondering about the killer's choice of gun. "God, if I was a contract killer, I'd figure you'd use a cannon, as big a gun as you could get," she suggested.

The investigators shook their heads. The pros don't need the cannons. They use finesse. They hit where they're aiming. They know just the right gun to use, just the right amount of firepower, no more, no less.

"So what you're saying is, either a hit man killed my parents, or a cop."

The room went silent. The Biloxi police had officially discounted the reported sighting of an officer driving the yellow Ford that night, but Lynne had not. She was curious to see what reaction she'd get. Finally, one of the policemen asked what she meant.

"Well, you guys would know how to fake a contract killing," she said, backing off from a direct accusation against one of Biloxi's finest. "Someone like me would come in and use a cannon. I wouldn't know how to make it look like a professional job. A cop would."

The subject changed after that, but Lynne had made her point. She was saying no one, from her perspective, was above suspicion. They could go after her brother. But, if necessary, she would go after them.

They did go after Eric, that same day. Later in the afternoon, Leslie and Lynne met their brother at the Halat and Sherry law office to root through papers and to box up Vince's books and personal possessions. Broussard and Wills showed up after a while, ostensibly to ask Eric and Leslie some follow-up questions.

But the subject eventually came around to Eric's travel plans: Was he or wasn't he planning a trip to the Gulf Coast around the time of the murders, as they had been told? Eric said yes, he had planned to go to New Orleans, little more than an hour's drive from Biloxi, for a disc jockey job that weekend, and to spend some time on the Coast as well. The trip fell through when he had to work his regular job in Florida, which is why he failed to bring it up to the police before. "I didn't think it was worth mentioning," he said.

The investigators stared impassively at Eric, his longish,

dark hair, his thin mustache—so unlike the other Sherry children. Did he know the truth about his origins, they wondered, had it eaten at him?

They didn't mention the little talk they had had with a policeman back in Eric's city of residence, Fort Walton Beach, Florida, who told them Eric had been off from his regular job at the time of the murder—another contradiction to fuel their suspicions. Nor did they mention how the police suspected him of small-time drug dealing out of the dance club where he deejayed. This allegation had resonated with the kilo notations in Vince's safe, and with another tip they received: that Vince had used his influence to save his son from a drug rap, pinning it on a Biloxi dealer who then sought revenge. Though this tip later proved false, as did the information about his work schedule, the list of reasons to suspect Eric kept on growing as far as the police could see. He had been seen around town since the murders, hanging out in seedy bars known for drug dealing and other questionable activities, huddling with known criminals and their children, including several offspring of Dixie Mafia killers and vice lords. He would later tell Lynne he had been trying to unearth information from these lowlifes he knew from high school. But to the police, it was almost as if Eric was begging to be considered a suspect. And he seemed not to have a clue.

Lynne, however, listened to the questioning warily, still worried the police might spring the subject of the adoption to see how Eric might react. They didn't, but their inquiries took an equally ominous turn.

"There's really not much to this," Wills said, after they had queried him about his planned trip to the Coast. "But we'd like you to think about taking a polygraph test."

Eric seemed genuinely perplexed at this request. "A lie detector test? Me? Why?"

"Well, because of the trip you were planning out here, and some other things, we'd just like to get it out of the way, to completely rule out you having anything to do with this. Then we can go on with other things, and forget about it. It's just a formality."

Lynne shifted uncomfortably in her chair. Eric was still looking puzzled, sitting there behind his father's desk,

Vince's blotter and pencils and framed photos there on the desktop, as if he might walk through the door and sit down to work any minute.

"What do you think, Lynne? Should I do it?"

Lynne thought, God, they're going to hook him up to that machine and ask him about the adoption. They'll have their answer—and Eric will feel like he's lost everything. She couldn't let that happen. "I don't think you should, Eric," she said, thinking fast. She turned to Wills and Broussard. "You're putting Eric in a no-win situation."

"What do you mean?" one of the detectives asked.

"My God, we just buried our parents. If he blows it because he's nervous or upset, you're gonna say you've got your person. You'll stop looking. And if he passes it, you can always say he's a sociopath, he could be lying and still pass it. Or he's on drugs, he could pass it. There's no way this would do anything but hurt him."

The detectives exchanged a look, as if to say, we should have button-holed Eric when he was alone, got him to agree to the test without Lynne around. Then he couldn't have backed down—it would look too bad for him.

Lynne took their silence as encouragement. She turned to Buddy Wills and asked, "If it were your parents, would you take it?" After a moment, he surprised Lynne by saying he didn't know. Then she looked at Broussard.

"Probably not," he said. She knew then that she had been right to trust him. Other investigators would have said whatever they had to say to get the result they wanted—believing that to be their job. But Broussard had been honest. He turned to Eric and said, "Just think it over."

After they left, Eric wanted to know why Lynne had been so vehement about him not taking the test. "It's not that big a deal, Lynne. I didn't go to New Orleans. I didn't see Mom and Dad. I sure as hell didn't kill them."

"I know that, Eric. But it's bullshit. And we've been through enough. You don't need to go through any more."

Eric shrugged and, to his sister's relief, didn't press further. "You're the one thinking of all the questions to ask. I'll leave it to you."

The issue would have died then and there if it had been up to Lynne. But it would not go away. Under pressure from

Biloxi's director of public safety—and later from the mayor himself—Wills and Broussard, then their predecessors, would continue to ask Eric to submit to a lie detector test. Privately, they assured Lynne they would not broach the question of his adoption if he agreed to the test, but she continued to refuse.

The idea that they were sniffing around after Eric while ignoring the mayor as a suspect had Lynne beside herself. She still believed Gerald Blessey, and therefore his entire police department, had a conflict of interest because of his enmity with the Sherrys. Few people other than the family and Mayor Blessey's most fervent opponents endorsed this position. Surrendering jurisdiction of a murder case solely on the basis of political differences with the victims would be legally unprecedented, not to mention intensely embarrassing for the city and its mayor (as would a more apt reason for bailing out of the case—admitting that the small city police force was in way over its head). City officials made much of the multiagency task force as a means of avoiding any conflict of interest, but the reality was that Biloxi police retained total control. Lynne believed the city should hand the case over to the FBI, or the sheriff's department, the Mississippi Highway Patrol—anyone else would do, so long as it removed the taint of bias, the suspicion of coverup.

"That's not gonna happen," Broussard told her. In fact, the FBI—Lynne's first choice to take over the case—was legally barred from assuming jurisdiction without evidence that a federal crime had been committed. Murder—even of a state court judge—is strictly within the purview of local authorities. The FBI could help, but that was all. Its role in the task force quickly faded to a token effort at best.

"If Blessey's innocent, I would think he'd want an objective investigation from outside," Lynne argued. "Otherwise, people will always say he covered it up, that it was a whitewash."[4]

"Not gonna happen," Broussard repeated. "It's their case, do or die."

So Lynne surprised him. "All right. Eric will take the lie detector test. In fact, all of us will, all the kids. But only on one condition: Gerald Blessey and the city council have to take a polygraph, too.

"All he has to do is answer two questions," Lynne continued. She had stayed up most of the night constructing just the right wording to ensnare someone who might have hired or sanctioned or even simply encouraged a killer, without witnessing the murder itself. "One: Do you know who killed Margaret and Vincent Sherry? And two: Do you have knowledge of any illegal activity on the Coast that could have contributed to their deaths?"

Silence followed. She didn't know what sort of reaction to expect—outrage, bafflement, ridicule. Instead, Broussard started laughing. Finally, all he said was, "Do you mind if I take this request to the mayor myself?" He sounded like he was planning to enjoy himself.

Lynne said sure.

Later that same day, Broussard called her back at the house. He was laughing again. "I guess Eric won't be taking that polygraph, Lynne, because when I took your request over to Biloxi, the chief of detectives brought it in to his honor, and he was told, 'I will not take a polygraph, I will not be questioned, and I will not be considered a suspect. Now get the hell out of my office.'"[5]

They both laughed about it then. Greg Broussard was the one cop on the case Lynne had begun to feel might actually accomplish something. He had started to share some of his findings with her, and she had opened up to him.

But a few days later, Broussard wasn't laughing when he called Lynne with the latest news. The polygraph request had backfired: He had been ordered off the case. Chief Deputy Sheriff Joe Price had called Broussard into his office and said Mayor Blessey wanted him off the task force. The demand had been relayed to the sheriff by Director of Public Safety George Saxon. Price said he had no choice— it was Biloxi's jurisdiction, a killing within the city limits. They would handle the investigation alone.[6]

Broussard told Lynne he would be working a separate inquiry for the sheriff on his own, but the days of cooperation were over. Worse, it looked like Buddy Wills would leave the case as well—in favor of Ric Kirk, the detective Vince and Margaret's neighbor swore had been driving the mysterious yellow Ford on the night of the murder. The case, Broussard told her, might never be solved.

"Don't they understand you're the only one over there we

trust?" Lynne said. "You're the only one the family will talk to."

"They may know it, Lynne," Broussard told her. "They just don't give a damn."

CHAPTER 8

B y November 1987, the Sherry task force had become a press release, a name to be invoked only when Biloxi officials felt the need to reassure their city. Publicly, the massive manpower of the task force never tired in its efforts to find the killers of Vincent and Margaret Sherry. Behind the scenes at the condemned elementary school, however, the investigation lay in tatters.

The Sherry children had returned home, waiting—with mixed hope and dread—for the next break in the case. But the task force had fallen apart, leaving the Biloxi police alone to solve the case. Cooperation had been iffy from the start anyway. The other law enforcement agencies on the Gulf Coast distrusted the department's integrity and competence, thanks to a long history of corruption and scandal. Most of the policemen there were competent and honest, but as an institution, the department had the worst reputation on the Coast, and that never seemed to change.

There were grievous errors from the beginning. Too many people had been allowed to tromp through the murder scene, disturbing potential evidence. Chuck Leger, who accompanied Pete Halat to the house, and Sandra Halat, who had preceded them, were never questioned in detail. Letters found in the Sherrys' mailbox were lost, Lynne learned when she tried to claim them. One of Vince's briefcases, holding papers and personal possessions, vanished after detectives inventoried it. Margaret's briefcase

was inexplicably released to a city councilwoman who had
been Margaret's ideological opposite. Other evidence was
misplaced or forgotten.

Judge Sherry had a note in one of his pants pockets,
discovered at the morgue. The slip of paper had a woman's
name on it, along with her out-of-state telephone number,
scrawled in Vince Sherry's handwriting. A logical step
would have been to call this person, to find out why Vince
thought her number so important he carried it the night he
died. Maybe it was meaningless, or maybe this woman
could solve the case. The only way to know would be to pick
up the telephone. It was that simple, and that basic.

No one did it.

Even worse was the matter of the yellow Fairmont.

A patrolman found it, quite by accident, on September
22—the same day Lynne and Leslie walked through their
parents' house. The Biloxi police were supposed to have
hunted this car throughout the city in vain. They concluded
it must have been driven out of town by the killer, and other
police departments were alerted. Then a Biloxi officer drove
to an apartment complex to take a routine theft report—a
man's Pontiac Firebird had been stolen, unrelated to the
Sherry case. When the cop arrived, there sat the Fairmont,
in the same lot the Firebird had occupied. The Ford had
been in plain view for the past eight days.

The apartment complex, the Golf View, stood less than a
half mile from the Sherry house, in an area supposedly
searched rigorously by the Biloxi police. Yet witnesses at the
complex confirmed the car had not moved for more than a
week—not since the day before the bodies were found. It
had been there all along.

Once discovered, Biloxi police evidence technicians examined the 1981-model Ford, anxious to make up for lost
time and to uncover some clue—a scrap of paper, a
crumpled receipt, a stray hair, or, ideally, some clean
fingerprints. The results were disappointingly meager.

Whoever stole the car had been careful to leave few traces
behind. They had added gas and driven about forty miles.
The dome light had been disabled—no lights inside when
the door opened, no chance of neighbors spying faces
inside. The horn cover had been removed from the steering

wheel. Police found no obvious tampering with the ignition.[1]

A computer check revealed the license plate on the Ford belonged to a 1975 Oldsmobile reported stolen three years earlier. A decal for September 1988 had been snipped from yet another license plate, metal backing and all, then glued onto the Oldsmobile plate to make it appear legal once it was attached to the Ford. Clearly, the car had been carefully prepared as a getaway car.

The department's crime-scene expert swept the car for hair and fibers with a special vacuum cleaner, then dusted for fingerprints. Two partial prints from someone's finger clung to the left rear door window, on the inside of the glass, with enough whorls visible for a definitive comparison—if they ever found a suspect to compare.[2]

But just when this evidence was ready for shipment to the FBI's lab in Washington, D.C., investigation of the yellow Ford was abruptly dropped. Someone—it remains unclear who—determined the timing of the Ford's theft ruled it out in the Sherry murders, assuming incorrectly it had been stolen *after* the killings, a grievous error that would go undetected for months.[3]

The fingerprint and hair and fiber evidence stayed in a locker at the Biloxi Police Department, even as Lynne Sposito repeatedly called to ask about the results. No one told her it had been ruled out—she was simply informed that the FBI's Washington lab had not yet sent its analysis to the city. She asked several more times throughout the fall, and every time she was told it would be just a few more weeks. News reporters—who had been informed of the supposedly pending tests during a press conference—were given the same line. It was not true. The evidence was never sent, the yellow Ford was returned to the dealer and sold— another testament to a floundering investigation, headed nowhere.

Investigative shortcomings aside, the Biloxi Police Department soon settled on a short list of suspects: Eric Sherry, whose refusal to submit unconditionally to the polygraph further fueled suspicions; and Diamond Betsy Inman, whose friend and cellmate had told investigators

Betsy had indeed wished to kill her former lawyer, and may have carried out her threats even while sitting in jail.[4]

Suspicions about Eric and Diamond Betsy both revolved around drugs—Eric's alleged small-time dealing and use of marijuana in Florida, and Diamond Betsy's big-time international smuggling of cocaine. The Biloxi authorities hadn't come up with a plausible motive or any evidence against Eric as yet, other than the adoption angle, his refusal of the polygraph, the questionable character of his friends, and a vague notion that someone supposedly mixed up with drugs could be capable of anything. They had a much better theory, if not better evidence, for Inman.

In a brief interview by telephone, Diamond Betsy's former cellmate, Barbara Anderson, told investigators Betsy had spoken of a drug-trafficking partner in Mississippi—Inman called him "Jew Boy"—who financed some of her drug buys. Jew Boy, Anderson said, had taken all of Diamond Betsy's property when she was arrested years before in Puerto Rico. The cellmate, who had become a paid informant working with police in Orlando, also said Betsy sometimes received financing for her drug ventures through Kentucky.

This resonated with what the Biloxi police knew about Vincent Sherry. Vince was from Kentucky, still had bank dealings there, still owned property there, and maintained a membership in the Kentucky bar. Vince's family, meanwhile, said he often had been mistaken for being Jewish. He even used Yiddish expressions sometimes. And Vince had taken possession of Diamond Betsy's motor home, sports car, Lincoln Continentals, and other property to cover his legal fees after her arrest in Puerto Rico.

Worse still for Vince's posthumous reputation, another informant had called newly elected Sheriff Larkin Smith and described a meeting he claimed to have attended between Diamond Betsy and Vince. The informant said the lawyer and his client discussed a quarter of a million dollars in cocaine Betsy had stashed. They also supposedly spoke of techniques to fly under radar while smuggling drugs, as well as jewelry and money Inman hid from the IRS.

All this gave investigators two new theories to work with: Either Diamond Betsy killed Vince for mishandling her case, or she killed him over drug deals gone sour. Perhaps it was a combination of the two. The viciousness of the twin killings began to make sense then. Drug smugglers often reacted violently to protect their interests—cocaine cartels killed whole families to make a point. Once investigators got the Sherrys' bank records from Lynne Sposito, they found Vince had recently made two large deposits in a bank back in his hometown of Bowling Green, Kentucky, totaling $100,000. Suspicions mounted further when a Florida investigator working on Inman's latest drug case reported that Diamond Betsy got financing for her drug deals from someone in Mississippi, through a bank in Kentucky.

"Are you prepared to accept that your father might be dirty?" Broussard asked Lynne during one phone call.

"Whatever the truth is, I'll accept it," Lynne answered. She had decided nothing—not even her father's reputation—was more important than finding the killers. "But tell me this: Even if my father was the dirtiest sonofabitch on the Coast, why'd they kill my mother?"

Broussard had no answer for that. It was a question that went to the heart of the case and these latest police theories—because Vince's possible involvement in criminal activity did not explain adequately why Margaret died with him. Clearly, she had been shot after Vince was gunned down. Clearly, she had not known she was in danger until the gunman entered her bedroom. The tableau at the house could not be explained any other way—the killer could have shot Vince, then left the house with Margaret unscathed. But he had not left with just one victim down. He had marched into the bedroom, ending Margaret's life with cold precision.

Perhaps with anyone else, the police would have assumed the wife died because she was into whatever her husband was doing. But not Margaret. No one believed she would be party to drug deals or any other crime, or that she would stand for knowing about her husband's involvement. If Vince was dirty—and, Broussard emphasized to Lynne, this was just an unproven theory—he no doubt kept it from Margaret.

Margaret had long ago proven she would sacrifice their marriage and Vince's liberty before she compromised her integrity. Everyone knew about the Charles Acevedo case. Six years earlier, when Margaret learned her husband had spirited guns out of Acevedo's home after the Biloxi gangster fatally shot his wife, Margaret threatened to report Vince to the authorities, then leave him, despite their devout Catholicism and its ban on divorce. Vince pleaded that he simply had protected his client from additional charges, and that none of the guns he had taken could possibly have been the weapon used to shoot Mrs. Acevedo. But Margaret, arms crossed and lips compressed into a thin, uncompromising line her family knew well, would have none of it. At such moments, she could assume an almost looming presence, her five-foot stature seeming to expand, her piercing blue eyes hard as stones. Give the guns over to the police and turn yourself in, she said. Or we're through.

No amount of arguing, shouting, or begging could move Margaret once she had staked out a position. She was Vince's only real match in a test of temper and will. In the end, he had no choice but to acquiesce, trudging to the police and suffering the ignominy of having to testify before a grand jury against his own client. Vince came within a breath of being indicted himself, but his cooperation saved him. In the eyes of the law, he had done the right thing, thanks to Margaret. But there would be those in Biloxi's underworld who would never quite trust Vincent Sherry again—and who had good reason to fear Margaret Sherry, Vince's conscience.

Even Pete Halat had asked Lynne about Acevedo. She and Dick had gone to Pete's house on their first night in Biloxi after the murders. Pete had taken them upstairs for a private talk, showing them a pistol he had bought the same day he found the bodies. He said he needed the protection after what he had seen happen to Vince and Margaret.

"What do you think of Charlie Acevedo as a suspect?" Halat had asked. (Acevedo, by then, was out of prison and tending bar in Biloxi.)

The Spositos had shrugged. Everyone knew Charles Acevedo did not think kindly thoughts about Vince Sherry. But that was ancient history.

"I'll listen to what you have to say about Dad," Lynne told Broussard. "But you'll never make me believe Mom did anything wrong. And you know, neither of them could have done anything bad enough to deserve what happened to them."

There was no way for Broussard to disagree. It was the kind of dispassionate analysis that he had come to expect—and respect—in Lynne, which is why he had begun to share investigative findings with her during regular telephone conversations. She, in turn, had used her powers as administrator of her parents' estate to get normally private tax returns, phone bills, bank records, credit histories, and other potentially revealing materials for the task force, making subpoenas and difficult records searches unnecessary. All she asked in return was a measure of candor. Broussard was happy to oblige. As the months went by, talking to Lynne Sposito seemed less and less like talking to the daughter of a murdered couple. Lynne had crossed some line, Broussard saw, whether she knew it or not. She had stopped talking like a victim, and started thinking like a cop.

But if Broussard was inclined to agree that the latest theories had holes in them, others at the Biloxi Police Department were excited at the new developments, despite the sort of doubts Lynne had raised. Public Safety Director George Saxon told the local press early in November that investigators were pursuing hot leads in Florida, one of which "we consider to be our best in the case." He provided no details, but, clearly, he was referring to Diamond Betsy and Eric Sherry—the only leads police had in Florida. This was one of his few opportunities since the murders were first announced to present some hopeful news, and Saxon seemed determined to make the best of it. "I am confident that this case will be solved eventually," Saxon predicted.[5]

And so, Greg Broussard and Buddy Wills were dispatched to Florida to pursue these leads. The city had rescinded its request that Sheriff's Investigator Broussard get off the task force, but the rift was only temporarily mended. In a few weeks, Broussard would be back out on his own, while the city police went their own way. The public remained carefully shielded from these back-room conflicts.

The results they brought back to Biloxi were less than satisfying. The informant, Barbara Anderson, who had sounded so promising on the telephone, provided a ram-

bling, often bizarre and incomprehensible story once the
detectives sat down with her in person. "God, I wish I
wasn't an alcoholic," she said, by way of explaining her
memory lapses, including her initial inability to recall who
Vince Sherry was. "I'm not gonna sit here and lie, I can't
remember. Like I said, I drink a lot."

Over the course of the interview with the increasingly
restive detectives, Anderson asked to be placed under
hypnosis, claimed Diamond Betsy tried to brainwash her,
complained repeatedly about her unsatisfactory love life,
and suggested Detective Wills babysit for her while she and
Investigator Broussard went out on a date.

The low point of their interview came when she finally
began to describe what she knew about the details of the
murders of Vincent and Margaret Sherry, and then revealed
the source of that meager information: a Biloxi Police
inspector helping to supervise the Sherry investigation. The
inspector, it turned out, had spoken to Anderson repeatedly
on the telephone. "He told me the whole thing," Anderson
informed the stunned investigators. Well, they asked, what
do you know about the murders from conversations with
Diamond Betsy? "Nothing," she said, then changed the
subject.

Barbara Anderson had no real information about the
murders, or about Vince Sherry for that matter, Wills and
Broussard realized. She barely knew his name, she knew
nothing about any criminal figures on the Coast, the sort of
people Diamond Betsy might have hired to do the job. She
appeared to be making her story up as she went along. And
what little she did know she had learned from another
policeman. As a witness, she was worse than useless—she'd
be a defense attorney's dream.[6]

The next day, the two detectives visited their prime
suspect, Diamond Betsy, in jail. It was a hopeless exercise
from the start. Inman, as bizarre as her back-stabbing friend
Barbara, solemnly told them she had found God during her
incarceration, and that she had nothing to do with murdering Vince and Margaret. The detectives knew Inman could
say anything she wanted, short of admitting to the murders,
and they had no way of challenging her. That was the
problem with an investigation based entirely on suspicions,
without supporting evidence. It left no room to rattle

suspects with an impressive assembly of damning facts, a favorite police tactic. They left Orlando right where they had started—empty-handed.

On the last day of their trip to Florida, Wills and Broussard traveled to Fort Walton Beach to check out their other prime suspect's claims of innocence. Eric Sherry had told them he had been home in Fort Walton on the day of the murders, and that he had canceled his plans for a trip to New Orleans and Biloxi. If this proved to be a lie, then the detectives would begin to focus much more closely on Eric.

Before the trip, they finally had persuaded Eric and his sister Lynne to agree to a polygraph test—without conditions. Eric had decided there was no reason he couldn't go through with it. Besides, the family had been unable to collect on Vince's and Margaret's life insurance because the Biloxi police had refused to assure the insurance company that the children were not suspects. Holding this over Eric's head, the police said they could do nothing to help unless he agreed to strap onto a polygraph machine. Meanwhile, mortgage payments on the Sherrys' house, their other bills, the funeral costs, and Leslie's college expenses were adding up. All of this weighed heavily on the family's finances, especially Lynne and Dick Sposito's, who bore the brunt of the costs.

"I'm gonna take it, Lynne," Eric finally declared. "You guys can't keep holding on much longer, and besides, this way, they won't have an excuse to keep saying I'm holding up the investigation. They can just get on with it and look for who really killed them." Lynne reluctantly agreed, and a date in early November was set for Eric to drive to Biloxi for a polygraph. Lynne had to hope the police would keep their promise not to reveal Eric's adoption.

But before the appointed time arrived, Wills and Broussard learned it might not be necessary. In Fort Walton Beach, they spoke to Eric's wife and, more important, his neighbors, who most likely could be counted on for an unvarnished account of Eric's movements. All confirmed Eric's story—they had seen him in Florida at the same time his parents were being killed. Eric had been home immediately before, during, and after the murders on September 14.[7] Just as he told police, he had canceled his planned trip to the Gulf Coast. The theory that he had come to Biloxi and killed his parents in anger over being adopted no longer worked. As far as Broussard and Wills were concerned, Eric could be taken off the suspect list.

When Eric showed up for the polygraph appointment a few days later, he was told to forget it. "You are not a suspect," Broussard told him.[8] Eric and Lynne were happy to hear he was off the list and, in short order, the insurance company paid off the Sherrys' policy. Finally, the case could get on the right track, Lynne hoped.

But as the Sherry family would later learn, others at the Biloxi Police Department would not so readily choose another course—or dismiss Eric Sherry as a suspect. Especially when it came time to defend their own conduct.

Still, George Saxon had to tell the news media that the Florida trip had failed to produce the hoped-for break in the case. Because Eric and Diamond Betsy had never been publicly declared suspects, Saxon did not mention them by name. He was also reluctant to proclaim the mission the abject failure that it was. He merely announced, "The trip was not in vain. It just didn't turn out the way we would have liked. The lead was not eliminated, but we will have to do more work on it than we had hoped for."[9]

A few weeks later, Broussard left the task force again, this time for good. The sheriff told him the Biloxi police brass wanted him ousted, this time because his higher sheriff's department salary had caused dissension among the lower-paid city policemen. Broussard believed this explanation to be a pretense, but the sheriff was adamant, though he told the investigator to continue working the case on his own.

The task force had been whittled down anyway, leaving only an overworked Buddy Wills with some occasional help. He also had been handed a stack of unrelated cases, sapping his ability to concentrate on the Sherry murders. Broussard preferred working alone anyway, and his severance from the Biloxi police cemented his relationship with Lynne. His one-man investigation had begun to veer off in new directions.

Two revelations had captured his attention. One was the realization that Margaret Sherry had been working with the FBI after all—and that the federal investigators were indeed pursuing a city corruption scandal, despite what the task force had been told. Lynne Sposito was not so far off the mark in seeing possible motives for murder there after all, Broussard concluded.

He realized this after he walked into the FBI's Gulf Coast office in Gulfport to meet with an agent and inadvertently spotted plans, drawings, and other materials related to Biloxi's massive waterfront redevelopment plan for the area of the city known as Point Cadet. There was no reason for the FBI to have accumulated that material unless it was investigating.

A decades-long slide into decay had left the Point Cadet waterfront a collection of old boats, ramshackle buildings, and aging docks, permeated with the aroma of rotting fish floating atop oily black waters. City visionaries argued this mess could be transformed into a perfect center for tourism, featuring a new marina and a shopping and restaurant district to complement Biloxi's natural physical beauty. This was Mayor Blessey's pet project, and it had been the latest target for Margaret Sherry. She had become convinced that redevelopment funds were being misused by city officials, and that all sorts of hidden and illegal schemes lay behind the waterfront project. She could have seriously hindered it with her ability to rally opposition in the community—as she had done a few months earlier by defeating a Blessey-backed bond issue—but with her death, opposition to the city's plans for its decrepit waterfront vanished.

The waterfront and alleged misuse of federal grants there had been the subject of Margaret's conversations with FBI Agent Royce Hignight. This had been part of her "work" for the FBI that she mentioned to family and friends. Hignight had concealed this from Biloxi officials for obvious reasons—they were his targets. Indeed, after Lynne had mentioned Margaret's work with the FBI during her first talk with police, Hignight had appeared at her door to gripe, "That was a covert investigation—until now."

At the same time Broussard learned of Margaret's work with the FBI, he received information from a completely different direction that seemed to tie into the case. The FBI was looking at a bizarre lonely-hearts scam. Personal ads were being used to bilk thousands of dollars from straight women and gay men throughout the U.S. and Canada. A convicted murderer doing life at the Louisiana State Penitentiary, Kirksey McCord Nix, ran the scam, employing a web of convicts, guards, and cronies on the outside to further his scheme. The FBI had found several informants among Nix's employees, one of whom had telephoned a woman named LaRa Sharpe. She was Nix's girlfriend and a senior partner in the scam. And this was the kicker, an FBI agent told Broussard: LaRa's phone number turned out to be the same as the Halat and Sherry law firm's. She worked there.

The FBI agents on the Coast thought the Sherry murder investigators might be interested in that little tidbit. What it meant, the FBI didn't know. Maybe, just maybe, it offered a motive for murder.

Back at his office, Broussard had a stack of old telephone bills and statements for the Halat and Sherry law firm. The bills were gathered up by the task force in hope that they might reveal the source of the threats against the Sherrys. Instead, they showed something entirely different.

"The first thing you're going to notice is a lot of calls from Tunica, Louisiana," Halat had told the officer who picked up the bills. "You know what's in Tunica?"[10]

When the officer shook his head, Halat said, "Angola. The Louisiana State Penitentiary at Angola." Then he explained how his client, Kirksey Nix, was incarcerated there, and that the calls were attorney-client conversations with him. Halat offered no more information, and the officer asked no questions. He just left with the bills.

When Broussard counted up the long-distance calls to and collect calls from Angola, he found three hundred forty-five of them between December 1986 and September 15, 1987, the day after Vince was killed. Quite a bit of talking between a law office and a convicted murderer who had long ago exhausted his appeals, Broussard mused—particularly when the lawyers practice in Mississippi and the convict is in Louisiana. Discounting weekends and holidays, the Halat and Sherry office averaged nearly two calls a day with Angola, almost all of them related to Nix. Million-dollar clients don't talk to their attorneys that much, Broussard would later say. Why would Kirksey McCord Nix?

CHAPTER 9

As autumn wore on and the killer remained free, Lynne Sposito became totally preoccupied with the case. She placed daily calls to Broussard, Wills, the FBI, whomever she could get hold of, trying to find out what was going on with the investigation. Shock had given way to obsession, and a fear that if she were less active, the Biloxi police would bury the truth forever. She could think of little else, talk about little else—all Lynne wanted to discuss was the case, the frustrating lack of progress, her endless speculations on motives and possible suspects. Work, home, even husband and children began to slip into the background, extras on a stage where the main drama was murder.

Lynne's family was understanding—most of the time. But now and then the kids wore that same glazed expression Lynne once adopted when her mother had spoken about corruption in Biloxi. As her husband and children looked on, Lynne was becoming Margaret Sherry, obsessed and unrelenting in her pursuit of justice.

A spare room upstairs at the house slowly disappeared beneath a mountain of newspaper clippings, notes she had jotted, and the voluminous records she had scooped up from her parents' house. She sifted through this material constantly, and more came in all the time—friends in Biloxi sent her more clippings, people called with tips and theories, several psychics claimed to have seen visions related to the murder. Lynne wrote it all down. Someday it could come in handy, she knew.

Late in November, the Biloxi police asked her to meet an officer in Paducah, Kentucky, where Vince had safety deposit boxes at two banks. Lynne wanted to jump at the

chance to participate in the investigation, yet this particular
trip seemed futile. She tried to tell them it was pointless—
one box had belonged to a long dead aunt, the other had
been Vince's mother's. The boxes were opened in the 1940s.
Neither had been used in years, as far as Lynne knew. Vince
had never gotten around to closing them out.

The Biloxi investigators—who still had Diamond Betsy
and her Mississippi-Kentucky connections in mind—said
they had to be sure. Who knew what might be in there?
Lynne couldn't be certain Vince hadn't put something in
the boxes recently. After all, the police reminded her, Vince
had gone to Kentucky for a bar association convention less
than a month before his murder. Perhaps he had gone to the
bank.

So Lynne agreed to meet them on November 20, to see
what secrets the safety deposit boxes held. When the keys
were turned and the boxes pulled from the wall, Lynne held
them upside down and shook. Only paint chips tumbled
out. Bank records showed that one of the boxes hadn't been
opened since 1974; the other had been untouched since
1981. The trip had been a waste of time.

Later, though, Lynne and Broussard spoke privately. The
sheriff's investigator did not know how much longer he
would be on the case—he had been turned down for
promotion and was considering leaving his department.
Before he left, though, he had some warnings to pass on to
Lynne.

"This could mean my job," he told her, "but the police in
Florida are going after Eric for drugs. They wouldn't be
doing it if not for Biloxi P.D. I personally think your family
has been through enough, so you might want to tell him to
clean up his act. I shouldn't be saying this to you, but it's a
question of morality versus legality. I just don't think it's
right."[1]

Lynne considered it for a moment, then said, "I really
appreciate this. Now I can be prepared. But there's not
much else I can do. I'm not going to warn him. Because if he
is involved, getting caught would be the only thing that
would stop him."

Broussard was speechless. If he had any doubts about
trusting Lynne with sensitive information before, they
vanished. She continued, "You know, I knew he was drink-

ing a lot, and I was really worried. Drugs and booze together will kill him."

She didn't mention it, but another factor lay behind her decision: Lynne wanted to maintain the trust of investigators working on the Sherry case. The FBI had begun talking to her, along with the sheriff and the newly elected D.A., a local football hero who had replaced a longtime political foe of Vince's. They had started telling her things, and they listened to her. But if it became known she had tipped off Eric about a drug investigation, her contacts would dry up. No one would trust her again.

Lynne, without realizing it, had reached a turning point, her obsession so complete that even her own brother's liberty had to take a backseat to finding the killer. She would not risk being cut off. The choice for her, in the end, wasn't even close.

"Thanks," she told Broussard again, "but I just can't tell him."

She pulled some papers out of her handbag, more records Broussard had requested. Then she mentioned Pete Halat, just in passing, something to do with difficulties she had encountered getting some records from the law office in order to settle the Sherry estate. And Broussard decided to give Lynne a second warning.

"Be careful of him, Lynne," Broussard said. "Be wary of your dealings with Pete Halat."[2]

"What do you mean?" Lynne wanted to know.

"Just be careful."

"Well, I need a little more than that. He's been pretty wonderful to us." Halat had helped with the funeral arrangements and the wake, his secretary had handled hundreds of personal thank-you notes to people who had attended the burial or sent flowers. And there was that incredible eulogy. "Why are you warning me about him?"

So Broussard explained about the scam, about Kirksey McCord Nix, about LaRa Sharpe and the hundreds of telephone calls between the law office and the prison at Angola.

It was Lynne's turn to be speechless. Broussard said the feds had known about the scam for months. "Nix has money going through your dad's law office. And at this point, we don't know if it's your dad or Pete or someone else who was doing it. That's why I wanted to get into the lock boxes, to see if there were large sums of money inside."[3]

"I told you they were empty," Lynne said, finally finding her voice. She was still trying to understand everything Broussard was saying. It seemed incredible: An imprisoned murderer was somehow making thousands of dollars, and he was tied to the law firm of Halat and Sherry.

"Well, we had to check," Broussard said. "Anyway, just be careful. We don't know exactly what's going on. It might have nothing to do with the murders. But it looks bad."

Lynne thought about it, still stunned. Then she asked, "Those phone calls to the prison, when were they made?"

"We got records from last December, up until September fifteen," Broussard said. "Nine, ten months before your mom and dad were killed."

"What about after?" Lynne said. "Were there more calls afterward?"

Broussard saw what she was getting at. If the calls stopped after Vince died, they would know he had been in touch with Nix. If not, then it was someone else in the law firm doing the talking. But the police had no phone records beyond the day of the murders. "We couldn't get them, at least not without a warrant," Broussard said. "The phone company took the position that anything after the murders was irrelevant. They wouldn't release them."

"I can get them," Lynne said. "As administrator of the estate, I'm entitled. And then we'll see."

Greg Broussard eventually shared his information about the scam with the Biloxi police, and in early December, two investigators, Buddy Wills and Ric Kirk, took the four-hour drive through densely wooded backcountry to the Louisiana State Penitentiary. Kirksey Nix awaited them in manacles, seated in a sparse visiting room. The convicted murderer— a notorious leader of the Dixie Mafia—immediately made his position clear.

"You gotta understand, even if I knew anything, I wouldn't tell you," Nix said, a tight smile on his jowly face. "I won't rat on anybody. I may have the person who did it taken out. But I'd never tell the police."[4]

Of course, this was all academic, he said. He was innocent. Yet he found talking about the case irresistible, and his comments suggested he knew more than he was admitting. "Judging from what I've heard," he said, "no more than three to four people would be involved, from the person who had the job done, to the person who pulled the trigger. Unless one of those people says something, it will never be solved." Investigators had been coming to a similar conclusion themselves—but how would Nix know that?

Nix also displayed detailed knowledge of the mechanics of the Sherry murders, going so far as to suggest the gunman probably escaped into the night by walking across the country club golf course across from the Sherrys' home. Biloxi investigators had also entertained this thought. Indeed, they had found one witness who, during a stroll with her husband and friends on the night of the murders, saw a man in a white shirt and dress slacks run behind a building and into a wooded area adjacent to the golf course and the Sherry home. The witness put the time she saw this man at just before 7 P.M.—which is about the time of Margaret Sherry's last phone call. The running man could easily have been involved in the killing. Unfortunately, the witness did not get a good look at his face. Two hundred fifty miles away in Angola, Louisiana, Nix managed to precisely mimic her account of the runner's movements—an account that had never been made public.[5]

How a fellow who had been locked up since 1971 could know the layout of the Sherrys' neighborhood would later strike some investigators as odd. Detective Kirk, however, summed up the conversation this way in his report: "Nothing was learned from Nix other than theories that we have all already discussed." Inexplicably, the Biloxi police decided pursuing Nix and his scam amounted to a dead end, just as they had done earlier with the yellow Ford Fairmont. Soon after the visit to Angola, the entire Sherry case and all the accompanying files were passed on to a new team of investigators at Biloxi P.D., who began retracing the original investigation from the beginning, developing their own theories. No one at the department pursued Nix further. No one questioned the girlfriend, LaRa, who had abruptly left the law firm. Nor did anyone question Pete Halat about all those odd phone calls.

Greg Broussard, with his one-man sheriff's investigation, wanted to pursue the subject, but he had no chance. Not long afterward, Broussard left the sheriff's department, ending his involvement with the Sherry case.

With Broussard out of the picture and the Biloxi police at a standstill or worse, Lynne sought help from the FBI. She called an agent in Jackson, Mississippi, she had spoken to before. He was sympathetic but noncommittal.

"We can't get involved with a murder investigation without an invitation from the local police, or evidence of a federal crime," the agent told her. "They haven't invited us, and there's no federal crime we know of."

This was an explanation Lynne had heard before—one she was sick of hearing. "What you're telling me is, I have to depend on a politically corrupt system, run by a man who hated my father and mother, to invite you to investigate? It's a Catch-22. They're not doing anything, and you *won't* do anything!"

"That's what I'm telling you," the agent agreed. "But there is another way. This case is beyond most small police departments anyway. They don't have the manpower or the expertise. But you could think about hiring your own investigator. Then something might shake loose."

"Hire my own detective?" The idea had never occurred to Lynne before. In a murder case, she had always supposed, you had to stick with the proper authorities, no matter how displeased you might be with the results.

"Yes," the agent said. "Why not? You bring us evidence of a federal crime, and we'll move in."

This off-the-cuff suggestion from an FBI agent became something of a revelation for Lynne. She could hire her own investigator to probe the areas she thought needed to be looked at. And if the case proved too big a job for one pair of hands, she would take on some of the investigating herself. Look what she had found out from Brett Robertson. She, not the police, had dug up phone records showing that the barrage of calls between the law office and the Louisiana prison continued for months after her father's death. Lynne began to relish the prospect of taking control. She realized she had wanted to plunge in all along.

And, that quickly, she decided. Lynne would see the murders solved—with or without the help of the police.

That decision would consume Lynne Sposito—not for the months she imagined, but for years. Before she was through, she would find her marriage shaken, her children in need of counseling, her home a virtual stranger's, her purse weighted down with guns and bullets—all from that one snap decision to take control. Yet the obsession could not be stopped once it was started—quitting was unthinkable. She would come to know more about Biloxi corruption and the Dixie Mafia than most policemen, more about Gulf Coast politics than most of the local pols.

But knowledge would be a long time coming. On that day in December, Lynne simply told her family—and promised herself—that she would not stop until the killers were caught and punished. They'd have to come after her before she'd give up.

CHAPTER 10

The threats began in the spring of 1988, six months after Vince and Margaret died.

By then, Lynne had talked to dozens of people on the Coast, interviewing her parents' friends, neighbors, council members, and more, trying to piece together what deadly truths her mother might have uncovered before dying. Like her mother, Lynne began speaking regularly with FBI agents, pushing for action and looking for help in finding a private detective. She asked uncomfortable questions about corruption in Biloxi, about the waterfront project, about who might profit from legalized gambling on the Coast—everything Margaret had tirelessly opposed. She appeared at city council meetings wearing a red dress, Margaret's trademark, taking notes.

Lynne took anonymous tips and passed them on to investigators, met furtively with strangers in dark restaurants, heard rumors about her father, his best friend, the mayor, the police. One source claimed Vince accepted stolen property in lieu of legal fees. Another source told her Pete Halat had spoken callously about Vince's death, supposedly saying, "Those are the breaks."[1] Yet another informant repeated a rumor that Pete and Vince had hatched a plot to kill Margaret together, so Halat could be mayor instead of Margaret. When Vince got cold feet, Pete killed them both, according to this rumor. Indeed, this groundless accusation had made the rounds so completely, Halat himself jokingly repeated it to the police when they came to interview him a second time.[2]

Lynne wrote it all down, passing much of it on to the FBI and the D.A. She felt it was only a matter of time before she found something of substance. And, apparently, she had begun to make someone nervous.

At first, they were just hang-up calls, silence on the other end of the phone: someone there, but saying nothing. This persisted for weeks, more irritating than ominous.

Then there was a call from a strange man who told Lynne as she stood in her kitchen that she and her family would be sorry if she did not stop looking for trouble in Biloxi.

"You'll be joining your parents if you don't wise up," another caller told her after a newspaper published her criticisms of the Sherry task force.

Yet another time, her son, Tommy, then fourteen years old, picked up the phone. "Tell your mother she won't make it through the night," the caller said.

"Come on over right now, let's rock and roll," Tommy shouted back, then slammed down the phone.

"Jesus Christ, Tom," Lynne exclaimed, rushing around the house locking the deadbolts and calling the police. No one appeared to accept Tommy's rash invitation, but it had been unnerving, a sudden feeling of vulnerability washing over Lynne. Risking her own safety was one thing. But she had kept a tight leash on her children. She did not want them exposed.

Lynne's response to the string of threats was to fire off a few clips at the shooting range, venting rage while improving her marksmanship. Dick began pricing home alarm systems. The kids had nightmares. Tommy's grades plunged. Lynne's brother Eric responded by granting an interview to a Jackson, Mississippi, newspaper. He declared that certain people in Biloxi knew who killed his parents and why, but were keeping silent.

"They were obviously going to lose some serious money by having an honest mayor and circuit judge," he said of the murderers, an undisguised slap at Gerald Blessey. "I have lost hope with the local police."[3]

The newspaper bannered the article across the top of its Sunday front page. Whatever reaction Eric Sherry sought to achieve from his incendiary statements, what he got was instant fury at Biloxi City Hall. According to a police report filed that same day by an investigator assigned to the murder case, Mayor Blessey had telephoned the department from Boston when he learned of the articles' contents, and told Director of Public Safety George Saxon to re-interview Eric Sherry and to get him to submit to a lie detector test. Saxon then passed on the request to the investigator. According to the report, the reason the mayor wanted to reopen what had been a closed line of inquiry against Eric was the newspaper article.[4]

Detectives were even sent to meet with the mayor's wife, Paige Gutierrez, in her Sun Room at home, so she could repeat for them a series of unsubstantiated (and later disproved) allegations about Eric, including the suggestion that he was a wife beater estranged from the rest of the Sherry family. Gutierrez also asked if the police could compare a recording of Eric's voice to some threats against the mayor's family that had been taped during a radio call-in show, to see if Eric might be the culprit.[5] Lynne eventually heard about this from sources within the police department. The direct involvement of the mayor and his wife only added to her conviction that they were out to get her family.

She had hoped all this turmoil would force some other agency to step in. But nothing happened. She began to despair of seeing the official police probe move forward, even as it focused more than ever on Eric Sherry.

It was during this state of siege on the family, with Lynne feeling threatened by people on both sides of the law, that a different sort of phone call came to the Sposito house in Raleigh, frightening in its own way, though it carried no threats. This call offered a promise—that, perhaps, the case of the murdered judge and mayoral candidate just might be solved after all.

After months of searching, Lynne had found a detective.

Her top choice for the job had come highly recommended by friends on the Coast, though he was alternately described as the finest investigator the state of Mississippi had ever seen, or as a virtual hit man for the police. He either possessed extraordinary ability and integrity, or he was unscrupulous and ruthless, a gun for hire. Given what she was up against in Biloxi, Lynne wasn't quite sure which vision of this detective—famous or infamous—she most needed. Perhaps a little of both.

Private detective Rex Armistead sounded like their best hope, but Lynne and Dick grew so concerned about his reputation—especially in light of the death threats she had been receiving—that they took precautions: Their son, Tommy, positioned himself in a neighbor's second-story window, covertly photographing the detective when he came to the Spositos' home for an interview. On the way back from picking him up at the Raleigh airport, Dick drove while Lynne rode in the backseat, her hand in her purse during the entire ride. Inside, her fingers were wrapped around a .357 Magnum, pointed through her handbag and the car seat, right at Armistead's back. She had put her other children in hiding, hugging them good-bye, then telling them she loved them and that she hoped to see them that night if all went well. And yet no one in the Sposito household questioned these precautions. That is what life had become for them. That is what the killers had accomplished, long after Margaret and Vince Sherry were buried: Lynne, Dick, and their children thought of themselves as targets.

Rex Armistead was a broad-shouldered, bald-headed man, middle-aged, trim and handsome, with piercing blue eyes and an expensive, well-tailored suit. A pair of thick gold jeweled rings flashed on one hand. A faint scar rippled one cheek, a long-ago brush with some enemy's bullet.

Years before, Harrison County's chief deputy sheriff, Joe Price, had worked as a criminal investigator for the Mississippi Highway Patrol with Armistead as his supervisor. They had gathered intelligence and pursued killers, pimps, and gamblers together on The Strip in Biloxi for many years. Later, Armistead had helped form the Regional Organized Crime Information Center, becoming its first director, tracking the Dixie Mafia and other career criminals for police agencies throughout the South. He had posed as a hit man in Georgia to help bust an heir to the Orkin pesticide fortune in an alleged murder-for-hire scheme. Not bad for a former constable, the monied son of a plantation owner in tiny Lula, Mississippi, about sixty miles south of Memphis.

But Lynne had also heard stories of him coercing and threatening suspects, along with rumors that he acted as a virtual assassin on behalf of law enforcement. One story had him cornering a Dixie Mafia killer in a ditch by the side of a highway as the fugitive tried to elude a roadblock. Confronted by Armistead, the crook threw down his gun and put up his hands. But Armistead supposedly leveled his gun at the fugitive and told him to pick his pistol up again. "You don't want to come out of that ditch without your gun now, do you?" Armistead told him, his own weapon cocked and ready.

Only the man's cries—"My gun's in the ditch, don't let him kill me!"—and the presence of a nearby television crew saved him, the convicted murderer would later claim.[6] Lynne suspected such stories were mere rumor, expanded to mythic proportions by years of retelling and embellishment. But she had heard a sufficient number of them from enough people to be concerned. Maybe there was something there. So they had taken what they considered to be prudent precautions—kids safe, camera snapping, gun poised.

Once in the house, seated in the living room, coffee served, Lynne's papers and notes spread out on the table, she decided to bring up her concerns. "I just want to say, right at the top, that everything about this investigation has to be open and aboveboard. I want to find the truth, but it has to be legal—there can't be any threats or coercion that would wreck the case. It has to stand up in court."

Armistead said nothing. Lynne finally spoke again to fill the uncomfortable silence. "I just had some concerns. I heard there might be some, ah, problems with you."

He laughed then, genuinely amused. "Okay. So you've heard some stories. Things have been blown way out of proportion. Let me just say this: I would never do anything that would endanger the prosecution of the people who killed your mother and father."

Lynne left it at that for the moment. The point had been made. In truth, meeting Armistead went a long way toward allaying her and Dick's concerns. As the three of them began to talk, his intelligence, his insights into the case, his commanding manner—all combined to put Lynne and Dick at ease. Most important to Lynne, he listened. He did not dismiss her suspicions. He had no agenda of his own, no political cronies to protect, no secrets to hide. It seemed he just wanted to find the truth. There was no other word for it: Rex Armistead was refreshing. After discussing Armistead's game plan to investigate the case, they found themselves doing something that no longer came easy after their dealings with the Biloxi police. They found themselves trusting the man.

Lynne made her priorities clear. She was worried, but not too concerned, about possible intrigue at the Halat and Sherry law office. She knew Pete would never hurt her father. As for Eric, she felt he had been pursued by the police out of desperation and, possibly, retaliation for the family's statements about the mayor. She knew he was innocent, and the police department's focus on his adoption as motive for murder was all the more despicable because it had been kept secret all these years. "I'd love to know how they found out about that one," Lynne said.

Finally, she told Armistead that the police had ignored what she considered the most promising avenue of inquiry: Margaret's crusade to expose corruption in the city.

"She was helping the FBI, so they killed her. And they threw in Dad for good measure. They assumed he knew what Mom knew, and that he would expose the killers if he lived."

Armistead nodded, listening, saying little, taking an occasional note, now and then posing a question. He was particularly interested in what Greg Broussard and Buddy Wills had told her of the investigation, and in the copies of police reports friends at the department had occasionally leaked her.

After Lynne laid out what she knew and what she suspected, Armistead held up a hand. By then, it was after midnight. The litter of Chinese take-out cartons and old cups of coffee were spread around them.

"Here's what I would propose as my game plan if I take the case," Armistead said. "I'll look at Eric first. From what you told me, I don't expect any problems there. We should clear him once and for all."

But if something did turn up involving Eric, he added, that would be it. His investigation would stop there. Lynne would have to accept it, and decide what to do—Armistead would pull no punches. Lynne nodded. The idea that Eric might be guilty was unthinkable, impossible. But she would not have trusted a detective who said any less.

"Once we rule out Eric," Armistead continued, "I want to check out Pete Halat." When he saw Lynne's faint look of surprise—she had expected him to say the mayor came next—Armistead held up his hand again.

"You always check out whoever finds the body, Lynne. It's routine. We don't know how far the Biloxi police went, if they went after him at all. So we start from scratch. And all those phone calls to Angola bear checking, too. Something's not right there—I've crossed paths with Kirksey Nix before."

He seemed particularly amused that the Biloxi police had actually visited Nix in prison—as if such a hardened criminal would have told them the truth about anything. "With him in the mix, there's no telling what might be involved," Armistead said. "We need to find out just what was going on in that law office, with your dad, with Pete, with Nix, with everyone.

"And when I get past Pete, then we go after Blessey. We find out what your mother had on him, what he might have stood to lose, and who else might have been worried enough to want to silence her. If there's something there, we'll find it."

As he investigated each suspect, Armistead said, he would assume they had hired a killer, rather than pulling the trigger themselves. The murders seemed professional, and neither Eric, Halat, nor Blessey should have been able to pull that off alone. So at the same time he went after those three, he would also search for a likely trigger man,

using contacts and informants he had maintained from his
police intelligence days.

Even with the paucity of physical evidence, this might not
be as impossible a task as it sounded, he said. Only a few
professional killers in this part of the country would have
taken the job, according to Armistead. Many hit men would
reject it because one of the victims was a judge, fearing the
intensive police investigation that would result. Others
would pass on shooting a grandmother in the head four
times. Put the two together, and the list of potential
suspects grew quite short, he declared.

Lynne raised her eyebrows, but Armistead said, "No,
believe it or not, these assholes have standards. There's
probably only two or three contract killers my sources know
of who would take the job." Someone with no fear, no
feelings, no honor, he said. A terrible man.

So that was the game plan: Prove her brother innocent,
resolve her gnawing doubts about Pete, then go after the
suspect she wanted pursued all along, had he not controlled
the very police department conducting the investigation.

There would be one other thing, Armistead said: Lynne
would have to help. She would have to continue traveling to
Biloxi, talking to people, giving interviews. She'd have to go
on the radio, ask for tips, make the rounds. "We'll need the
extra arms and legs."

Dick Sposito had to smile at this. Whether Armistead
knew it or not, he had just made his best selling point. He
made it sound as if Lynne would be a partner in the
investigation, exactly what she had envisioned.

"Good plan," she said, exchanging looks with Dick.
"When?"

As she had been warned, Armistead did not come cheap.
He could start right away, but he'd need fifty thousand
dollars. Results could take months, maybe longer, he said,
and the informants he dealt with expected money for their
help. Lynne said she'd have to talk it over with her husband
first, but, in truth, she already had decided.

After he left, and Tommy and the other kids returned, all
the precautions they'd taken, the bulge in her handbag, the
camera in the window, suddenly seemed silly. Lynne asked
Dick what he thought.

"What do I think? I think, finally, there's a cop on the Coast with some brains."

Later, Lynne sheepishly described for Armistead the precautions her family took for his visit. "I heard you were a hit man for the cops, Rex," Lynne explained.

Armistead looked at her mildly, but those cool, blue eyes never wavered from hers. "Listen to me. I've never shot anyone when it was not self-defense. I'm a Presbyterian and I have a strong conscience. And I sleep well."

Lynne laughed, and that was the end of the subject. She decided to trust Armistead, for better or worse. But many months later, Lynne once again heard the story of how Armistead ordered a cornered fugitive to pick up his gun so he might execute the man in mock self-defense. This time, though, Lynne heard the story from the convicted fugitive himself. And she just had to ask Armistead if it was true.

"That boy needed killing," Armistead replied with that same mild, noncommittal look of his.

"Rex!" Lynne said, shocked by his bland pronouncement. "That's a terrible thing to say."

"Well," Armistead responded, "he was a terrible man."

Lynne left it at that. She didn't want to know any more. And even if she did, it would not have mattered. If anyone was going to bring her parents' killer in, she had come to believe, it would be Rex Armistead.

CHAPTER 11

The lush air that blows in off the Gulf each spring has a cleansing tang to it, a taste of gritty brine that mixes perfectly with the magnolias and wild grasses. Parts of Biloxi take on the intensely green aspect of a rain forest at this time, profuse vistas of heartbreaking beauty, uncountable shades of green. New leaves shimmer darkly in the sunlight, tunnels of emerald shade enveloping winding country roads mere blocks from the ocean, a green curtain that masks at times even the coastal blight of The Strip. The air smells new.

At the city's southern edge, the green roads abruptly end at the coastal highway and its adjoining beach, swept clean of man's imprint, the season too young for the approaching onslaughts of heat and coconut butter and jet skis. In March and April, and in some lucky years, May, there are only thumbs of blank white sand jutting out into gentle waters a bare half-shade darker than the sky above, empty and shorn of summer's occupation.

This peaceful vista drew Lynne Sposito often, as it had Margaret Sherry before her, for long, mind-clearing walks early in the day, cool sand between her toes, each wave mimicking the sound of bacon sizzling, of Sunday morning in a household that no longer existed. At times, it seemed possible to close her eyes and forget she had been orphaned, to imagine her mother pacing there next to her, about to tell her what she needed to know.

But answers remained elusive. Her visits that spring to Biloxi to work with Rex Armistead had brought only doubt, confusion, and fear. So much had happened, she had learned so much, and yet the solution to her parents' murder seemed more remote than ever. All her assumptions seemed mistaken, even those about Gerald Blessey, though she was loathe to admit this. By the spring following her parents' murder, she did not know whom to suspect anymore, or whom to trust.

"That's easy to deal with," Rex Armistead had told her. "Don't trust anyone."

Lynne had embarked on a series of three extended trips to the Gulf Coast that spring, beginning with a visit to the Biloxi Police Department. A new "task force" had been announced with much fanfare in March 1988, a supposedly rejuvenated effort to take a fresh look at the investigation six months after the bodies were found.

This "task force" consisted almost exclusively of one very talented, mostly desk-bound police lieutenant with a weak bladder and a blood-sugar problem that at times mimicked narcolepsy. That was the task force: Lieutenant Mike Meaut, nicknamed "Rubber Ducky" within the department. He benefited from the part-time help of two other officers, but they were expected to keep up with their other duties and cases as well, so Meaut often was on his own. His official position as head of this nonexistent task force belied the reality of his true mission: cleaning up after the first task force's botched murder investigation.

Though her poor relations with the department brass continued, Lynne instinctively liked Mike Meaut. He was a beloved misfit at the department, caring and capable. They began sharing information, as she had done earlier with Greg Broussard. Lynne arranged to get copies of her parents' credit card receipts for him, and promised access to whatever else Meaut might need. In return, Meaut let Lynne sit in his office and read the autopsy reports on her mother and father. She had never seen them before, but felt she should—just to know.

When the time came, Lynne had to force herself to wade through the clinical descriptions of her parents' remains, how each organ was removed and weighed, the texture of their heart tissue, the color of their lungs, the contents of their stomachs—the routinely obscene protocols of dissection and analysis every post-mortem examination requires, thousands of times a day, throughout the nation. These reports are not designed for daughters and sons to read. They are for the initiates, for the insiders who have built up years of calloused immunity. Autopsy reports are cold things, laboratory experiments, deliberately devoid of humanity even as they carve up that which was human. Diagrams showed the damage inflicted by subsonic pieces of lead tearing through bone and skin and muscle of Vincent and Margaret Sherry. A dotted pencil line depicted the projectiles' paths, passing through crudely drawn figures of the human body. It made Lynne want to scream, seeing her mom and dad reduced to schematics, their bodies something to be calculated and weighed, like interesting specimens. But she read every word in those reports, then read them again, then made photocopies for her own files. The only thing worse than knowing, she told Meaut, was ignorance. She had to know everything. Throughout her reading, Meaut hovered over her in his fastidious way, hands clasped in front of him, a kindly Oliver Hardy, worried and endearing.

"Do you think you'll ever catch them?" Lynne asked when she was through. Her voice sounded hoarse.

Meaut looked sad but resolute—he was almost as preoccupied with solving the murders as Lynne. "I don't know, Lynne. Sometimes I think this case is going to kill me first. I go to bed thinking about it. I wake up thinking about it. It's going to kill me."

Over time, as Meaut came to trust Lynne, he let her know just how bad things had been when he inherited the case. Lynne finally learned the fingerprints, hair, and fibers from the yellow Ford had been shelved when the car was ruled out as the one used in the murders. Mike Meaut, however, had figured out that had been a terrible mistake—the car never should have been discounted. The Ford was last seen at the car dealership from which it was stolen on Friday evening, September 11. It was discovered missing Monday morning, September 14—twelve hours or more *before* the murders occurred that evening. It was noticed parked at the Golf View apartments on September 15, the day after the murder, and had not moved since. There is absolutely nothing about the timing that would rule out the Ford as the murderer's vehicle, Meaut concluded. Indeed, the timing of its theft was a perfect fit to the needs of a professional killer in town just long enough to do the job.[1] The car was worthless to a car thief, its resale value nil, its parts not worth stripping. Its only use would be as a getaway car.

So, six months late, Meaut sent the evidence to the FBI lab. The car had long ago been returned to the dealer and sold. Lynne was horrified. She had been told over and over the lab results were pending.

It got worse. A painstaking attempt ordered by Meaut to peel off the old month and year stickers that had been glued to the Ford's license plate by the killers yielded one fingerprint. Examined with much fanfare, it was revealed to be Lieutenant Bob Burris's, the department's evidence technician, a mistake made during examination of the plate.

The new task force leader also had learned officers failed to pursue a reluctant and fearful witness who had seen a man abandon the Ford in the apartment complex lot on the day after the murders. She should have been offered a look at mug shots and photo lineups, but never was. By the time Meaut got to her, her memory had faded.

No one had called the woman whose phone number was found in Vince's pants pocket during the autopsy, either. When one of Meaut's part-time partners finally did so six months after the fact, the woman said she was an old friend of the Sherrys. Vince had handled her divorce, and confided in her some months before the murder about threats on his life. But her memory had faded since then. She couldn't recall whom Vince had mentioned as the source of the threats.

The cop who called her was dumbfounded. "And no one from Biloxi P.D., or any other law-enforcement agency, has ever talked to you about this before?"

"No," the woman said. "No one."

Meaut had no choice but to retrace many of the steps already taken by the first task force, tying down such loose ends where he could. He interviewed the Sherrys' neighbor, Brett Robertson—the first time anyone from the department talked to him since Lynne and Vin first heard his story about the yellow Ford on the day of the wake. (The FBI secretly interviewed him shortly after Lynne told agents about him, however, followed by investigators from the district attorney's office.) Meaut also finally sought to clear up suspicions about Ric Kirk—the officer Robertson accused of driving the car that night. Kirk consented to a polygraph test and passed. Until then, Lynne had considered Kirk a legitimate suspect, but Meaut told her not to worry about him. Better she should worry about the fact that there were no viable suspects at all.

The new task force leader told Lynne he would welcome Rex Armistead's help. He'd gladly open the files to him, Meaut promised. "For what it's worth."

Lynne brought Rex Armistead to her parents' home that spring. They found the house much the way her parents had left it, although the den and bedroom had been painted and repaired, blood and bullet holes hidden behind new plaster and carpeting. Armistead had to rely on Lynne to describe the scene, the blood, the placement of the bodies. He had seen the police photographs of the scene already and drew some conclusions. For now, though, Lynne had to summon those images again, as she had while reading the autopsy reports. Sadly, this task got easier each time.[2]

They had come to the house with Lynne's new friends—Becky and John Field, who had known Vince and Margaret for years but had never met Lynne before the Sherrys died. John Field, the ex-Biloxi cop, had been the source of the ice cream message on the Sherrys' answering machine that the police briefly found so suspicious. Becky had introduced herself to Lynne for the first time at the funeral, offering her a place to stay any time she was on the Coast.

"You can't keep staying in hotels," Becky had said. "It isn't safe."

Lynne felt wary at first of trusting anyone in Biloxi, but Becky endeared herself by showing Lynne around her home this way: "Here's your room, here's where we keep the towels, and here's a three fifty-seven Magnum and two speed loaders to keep with you." She held out the weapon and bullets for Lynne as if they were no more extraordinary than a nice cup of tea. Becky Field's mix of motherly Southern charm and steely resolve caught Lynne completely off guard.

"Honey, John and I each keep a gun, one on each side of the bed," Becky explained. "Nothing's going to happen to you while you're staying with us."

(The pistol Becky gave her went to good use: Months later, this was the same weapon she kept trained on Rex Armistead during that tense ride from the airport.)

Walking through her parents' house, Armistead said the killer used a silencer. "There was no pillow. I've seen those foam bits at other crime scenes," he said. "Margaret was caught by surprise, though."

To prove this, he had carried from his car a bucket of sand and a homemade silencer, filled with foam rubber.

"You two go in the bedroom and shut the door," he told Lynne and Becky. "You'll hear what Margaret heard."

With the door closed behind them, Armistead set the bucket down in the den, where Vince had stood, and fired the .22-caliber Ruger he had brought for the occasion into the sand. Inside the bedroom, the two women heard a sound, distinct, but not too loud. It sounded just like a newspaper slapping down hard on a tabletop.

"Like Dad swatting flies," Lynne whispered. "He was always doing that. Mom never would have known they were shots." Three or four silent tears ran down her face. Becky watched her, waiting for more, but none came.

Afterward, Armistead explained why the foam-filled silencer apparently used in the murders was so unusual. Normally, steel wool or the small metal grommets used to attach snaps to clothing are preferred for silencers. They fit into baffles in the metal tube of the device, muffling the sound of the gunpowder igniting and propelling the bullet from the gun barrel. Foam worked quite efficiently at silencing the gunshot, too, but it could catch fire or clog the weapon as bits of foam came loose and flew out with each shot. That was why singed pieces of foam were scattered around Vince and Margaret when the police found them.

"Why use it, then?" Lynne asked. "Why not use the normal type?"

"This type of silencer has its advantages, too," Armistead said. Assembly came quick and easy—a soda can or plastic bottle could be used, stuffed with foam rubber, then taped to the barrel of the gun. The materials were easy to obtain, easy to dispose of, and completely legal, unlike a real silencer. Possession of foam and a can of root beer is no crime, yet such mundane items from a grocery store undoubtedly could be transformed into something deadly.

There was a name for such a foam-filled device, Armistead added: an "Angola Silencer." The name honored the Louisiana State Penitentiary at Angola, where inmates had shown a marked preference for the makeshift device.

Lynne had already heard of the prison, of course. Angola was where the Halat and Sherry law firm had exchanged so many telephone calls. It was the place Kirksey McCord Nix, Pete Halat's deadly client, called home.[3]

In May, Lynne Sposito met with Harrison County's newly elected district attorney, Glenn Cannon. A local football hero, he had replaced the former D.A., Cono Caranna, whose enmity with Vince had been common knowledge. Cannon assured Lynne he would undertake a more visible role in the murder investigation than his predecessor. John Field went to work for him as an investigator, and had explained to Cannon Lynne's still lingering concerns about the Biloxi Police Department. Cannon said he understood, and he agreed to withhold information from BPD when necessary.

Then the D.A. passed on a tip he had received about possible improprieties with the Sherrys' bank accounts. He urged Lynne to check it out. As administrator, she could examine bank records whenever she wished without arousing suspicion, while Cannon would need a subpoena.

Once again, Lynne assumed the role of investigator. She went to her parents' bank and asked to see records on their accounts. There it was on the computer printout: one account stood out, opened and closed on the same day.

"That's not unusual," someone in the accounts department said when she pointed it out. "Attorneys often open an account when they receive a settlement, then disburse it that same day."

"Oh, I understand that," Lynne said. "There's only one problem with that. This account was opened six months after my parents were dead and buried."

After a flurry of consultation, bank officials told Lynne the notation must have been a computer glitch. She didn't buy it—nor did she know what to make of it. The discrepancy was never resolved.

Lynne had already found bank statements in her mother's name, addressed to a Biloxi post office box—which turned out not to be her mother's. She also had learned her parents opened a new safety deposit box at their bank in May 1987—about the time the threats on their lives started. When she checked it, however, the box was empty. Lynne wondered: Had they neglected to put anything inside? Or had someone else emptied the box after they died? Was that why she could never find her parents' will?

After leaving the bank, Lynne went to her father's law office to ask Pete Halat what he thought. He wasn't in. Instead, she found Halat and Sherry's longtime secretary, Ann Kriss, at her desk, hard at work writing in a ledger book, copying information from a stack of canceled checks. Lynne glanced at the paperwork and saw Kirksey Nix's name at the top. Ann was copying the amounts from each check onto the ledger, which apparently was Nix's. Greg

Broussard's warning came back to her. She decided to ask a few questions, trying to seem casual.

"Isn't it easier to keep a ledger sheet at the same time you're writing the checks?" Lynne asked, working hard to sound innocent, barely interested.

"Oh, I did that," Lynne recalls Kriss saying. "But about three or four months ago, Kirksey wanted his ledger. And I asked Pete if I should make a copy, he said no, just send him the damn thing. Then he came out and he told me that I needed to redo the ledger sheets."

As Lynne would later remember the conversation, Kriss then said that, the funny thing is, the ledger she was completing would be inaccurate, because she was starting with a zero balance. "Kirksey has never had a zero balance," Lynne recalls Kriss saying. "He makes twenty-eight thousand dollars a year on this account."

"How in the hell does somebody earn twenty-eight thousand dollars a year in prison?" Lynne asked.

"I don't know," Kriss replied, as Lynne tells it. "And I don't want to know. The checks come in, I deposit it. I disburse them as he sees fit."[4]

Lynne decided not to press the issue. She needed to think about this, talk to Becky or Rex. Troubled, she prepared to leave the office, but Ann Kriss interrupted her farewells to answer the telephone as Lynne stood by.

"No, Pete's in Jackson," Kriss told the caller, as Lynne remembers it. "I'll tell him it's an emergency when he gets in."

When Kriss hung up, Lynne remembers her saying, "I hate that man. It's always an emergency with him."

"Who's that?" Lynne asked.

"Mike Gillich." Gillich was Biloxi's strip-joint king. Vince had befriended and worked for the old Dixie Mafia crony, while Margaret detested him, hoping to shut him down if elected mayor. Lynne wasn't sure what to think as she left.

The next day, Lynne returned to the Halat and Sherry office, her father's name still on the sign, causing a pang every time she read it. This time, Pete was in. Lynne said she wanted to discuss the dissolution of the law firm partnership, the building, the assets, the debts—all the issues she needed to resolve to settle the estate, and which she felt Halat was avoiding. Pete ushered her into his office, dismissing her concerns once again by saying, "We'll cross that bridge when we get to it."

Then, as Lynne recalls it, he said, "I understand you saw Ann working on a ledger sheet yesterday. I think I ought to explain that to you."

He told her Royce Hignight, the Sherrys' FBI agent neighbor, had come over recently and said Kirksey Nix was under investigation for running a fraud and scam ring out of prison. It was just as Broussard had told her months before. Halat said he had known nothing about it, but that the FBI apparently believed Nix was using the office to launder his scam profits. Hignight wanted Nix's ledger sheets, Halat said, which is why Kriss was working on them. Halat had promised to cooperate. In fact, he was so concerned about the allegations, he had immediately fired a letter off to Nix saying he would no longer represent him.[5]

"Well, then, why are you giving the FBI inaccurate information?" Lynne demanded, an edge to her voice.

"What do you mean?" Halat asked.

"Ann said it's inaccurate because you started with a zero balance, and that account never had a zero balance."

As Lynne recalls it, Halat became agitated then, a sudden fury that seemed far too extreme for the circumstances. He told her that he was just giving Hignight what he requested, nothing more. "He asked for 1985 forward and, Goddamn it, that is exactly what he is getting."

As Lynne sat in front of Pete's desk, he leaned toward her, face flushed. She remembers him pointing his finger at her, close to her face, and saying, "I'd better explain something to you. Kirksey Nix has been a client of mine since 1979. He is also a friend of mine. He is a friend of Mike Gillich's, and he used to work for Mike Gillich. Mike Gillich is a friend of mine. He always has been. He always will be. Do you understand what I'm saying to you, girl?"

Lynne felt as if her body temperature had dropped twenty degrees—she had not felt so afraid since she first learned her parents were dead. His pronouncement sounded to her like a threat, one more in a long line—though she hadn't expected it from her father's best friend. Halat gave her one more glare, then stalked off to the law library. Lynne just sat there for a while, then left the office. She never did get to ask Halat about that phantom bank account.[6]

Only that evening, after the shock had passed, did Lynne realize the significance of something Halat had told her during his tirade: Mike Gillich and Kirksey Nix knew one another. Mike Gillich, the sleaze merchant Margaret Sherry wanted to shut down, and Kirksey Nix, a murderer who might have been running dirty money through the Halat and Sherry law office, were connected. No one had ever told her that.

The conversation would carry Lynne Sposito and her personal quest for her parents' murderer in a new direction. She started questioning every cop she knew about Nix. Mike Gillich, she learned, was Nix's mentor, personal banker, the convict's most trusted friend. Gillich, in turn, sent to Halat's office some of the cash for Nix's trust fund. If Nix was involved with a scam in Biloxi, then so must Gillich be involved, Lynne would be told by more than one source.

And Pete Halat, Lynne recalled, had labeled both men friends.

When she phoned home and told Dick about this latest revelation, he said, "Well, what about the argument your dad and Mike Gillich had? Did Pete say any more about that?"

"What are you talking about?" Lynne asked. She knew nothing about any argument.

"The one Pete told us about."

Lynne remained baffled. "I don't remember that, Dick."

"It was when we went over Pete's house, the day after the bodies were found. He took us upstairs, showed us his new gun, asked about Charlie Acevedo. Remember?"

"Yeah, I remember that," Lynne said. "But I left the room right after that."

"Jesus," Dick exclaimed. "I was so out of it then, I didn't notice. I thought you knew. Pete told me that, about six months before the murder, your dad and Mike Gillich had some big argument. He asked if we thought Gillich might be a suspect."

"He wasn't then," Lynne said, pieces suddenly beginning to fall into place. "But he is now."[7]

Every assumption Lynne had made—about her parents, the police, Gerald Blessey, Pete Halat—all went out the window then. Because of these revelations, Lynne would undertake a crash course in Biloxi history in the coming months, taking her back two decades and beyond, to a time when a still-young lawyer named Vincent Sherry, and an even younger judge's son named Kirksey Nix, each chose to call Biloxi home—beginning a long and unlikely series of events that would inexorably draw the two men together.

Lynne would learn, too, that prison does not always stop a criminal's career. Sometimes it only makes him more ingenious.

Some time later, Rex Armistead called with a progress report. He had been carrying out his game plan: He had worked on Eric. He had worked on Pete Halat. He was supposed to investigate Mayor Blessey next.

"So where are we, Rex?" Lynne asked.

Armistead's next words would have shocked her at one time. Now she just felt numb.

"I can't get past Pete," Armistead said. "I can't get past Pete."

PART 2

Kirksey

Audacity . . . has to be part of any successful murder.
—James M. Cain, **Double Indemnity**

CHAPTER 12

I n a way, the outlaw men and women of the Dixie Mafia merely fulfilled history's mandate when they appeared in Biloxi with their dice and pistols loaded, their taste for rich living undeterred by their disdain for honest work. They were arrogant and amoral and the city embraced them as kindred spirits—at least until the bullets started flying, and the casualties of war spread beyond the ranks of mere criminals. Until then, though, the wise guys of the Dixie Mafia were just the latest incarnation of deeply rooted forces that had shaped this region with flare and brutality for nearly three hundred years. They knew it in their bones, if not from history books, and that was what drew them to this humid stretch of coast in the first place: Biloxi's long romance with confidence men and killers began long before there even *was* a Biloxi.

The biggest scam of all began only sixteen years after the French explorer Pierre Le Moyne, Sieur d'Iberville, first anchored in Biloxi's Back Bay in 1699 and claimed the region for King Louis XIV. A get-rich-quick con artist with the ironic name of John Law plastered thousands of posters throughout Europe, touting Louisiana and the Mississippi Gulf Coast as a veritable nirvana. As Law told it, the climate was unsurpassed, the natives uniformly friendly, the soil yielded untold abundance without benefit of till or spade, game practically posed before the hunter. His outrageous claims, endorsed by the French throne, drew thousands of hopeful settlers to pay him handsomely for the right to make unbearable voyages on inhumanly crowded ships, only to find death, disease, and the arduous life of taming a wilderness awaiting them. He was cursed by the settlers who found a very different New World than the one Law's broadsides described, even as he sat comfortably an ocean away, their gold in his bank. ·

In the century that followed, France, Spain, and Great Britain would each lay claim to the region at various times, and the settlers who managed to survive and create a community amidst these struggles routinely found themselves caught in the middle. Their solution became a Biloxi tradition: They turned to smuggling and piracy for a living, switching allegiances depending upon which sovereign had the upper hand, profiting by shrewdly serving all sides.

Early in the nineteenth century, when the new United States government asserted dominion over the region, Biloxi, along with five surrounding antebellum communities collectively known as the "Six Sisters," became rural ocean resorts for wealthy New Orleans residents. The scams continued: Vacationers who flocked to the Six Sisters were led to believe natural springs in the area spouted curative properties for everything from arthritis to yellow fever.

The region's first—and still legendary—outlaw hero, James Copeland, came along at about this time, terrorizing southern Mississippi and Alabama in the 1830s and 1840s. He promoted himself as a Robin Hood figure, even though his gang of thieves and killers would steal from anyone, rich or poor. Still, his violent and antiauthoritarian exploits made him a heroic figure to many on the Gulf Coast. He became a kind of role model for his distant Dixie Mafia successors, living hard and dangerously, bowing to no one, killing young and dying young—and amassing a fortune while he was at it. Treasure hunters still comb the Mississippi pine barrens in search of his gang's legendary cache of buried gold (reported at thirty thousand dollars in 1849, worth millions now).

Copeland started stealing at age twelve, burned the county courthouse to avoid indictment at age fourteen, ripped off anything he could resell—though he preferred horses and slaves—and looted and burned downtown Mobile. When Mississippi authorities closed in with a murder warrant, he employed a legal gambit his modern-day Dixie Mafia counterparts would mimic a century and a half later:

He turned himself over to lawmen in neighboring Alabama on a larceny charge, hoping he could serve a little prison time there, then bribe his way to freedom later. Instead, a Mississippi sheriff doggedly awaited his release, then escorted him back home on the murder indictment. Copeland hanged at age thirty-four—but only after he had dictated his memoirs to the sheriff, who penned a widely read biography of the killer, cementing the Copeland legend.[1] More than one Dixie Mafia killer would aspire to become the twentieth century's James Copeland.

At the start of the War for Southern Independence, as the Civil War is remembered in these parts, the Coast's moral ambiguity continued in full force. Yankee warships occupied the waters off Biloxi, maintaining a blockade—and enjoying regular deliveries of food, water, and New Orleans newspapers (including articles detailing Confederate troop movements) from cooperative local smugglers who professed loyalty to the Confederacy while pocketing Union cash. In the second year of the war, the mayor of Biloxi graciously surrendered his town to Union troops, who immediately were welcomed into the city's tourist-starved taverns, hotels, restaurants, and bordellos.

The turn of the century brought new methods of preserving and canning seafood, and Biloxi sought to recover from the Civil War and Reconstruction's devastation by becoming a center for harvesting the Gulf's abundant shrimp, oysters, and other seafood. The population exploded and the city began to take on its unique, other-than-Southern character as a flood of European immigrants came for the work, particularly from the region later known as Yugoslavia. They settled in modest, crowded neighborhoods near the canneries and wharves on the easternmost end of Biloxi, an area known as Point Cadet. Many years later, growing up "on the Point" would become a kind of badge of honor for successful men and women in Biloxi, an indication that you were a longtime resident with roots and an ability to pull yourself up from poverty. The Yugoslavian community would come to wield a great deal of power in the city through a potent good ol' boys' network; Pete Halat and Gerald Blessey both grew up on the Point, as did Mike Gillich.

When Mississippi declared itself dry in 1909 and Prohibition went into effect nationwide ten years later, many fishermen on the Point found running whiskey more profitable than hauling fish. With a decade's head start on the rest of the country, the Coast soon became the nation's premiere haven for bootleggers and rumrunners, outshining by some estimates even the Canadian border region. (This bootlegging industry stayed in place many years after federal Prohibition was repealed in 1933, as Mississippi state and local laws banning liquor remained in effect until the sixties.) Illegal casino gambling soon followed the whiskey, and local law enforcement began its long pattern of looking the other way—or actively accepting a slice of the profits in exchange for protecting crime.

The Pentagon's decision to train a half-million servicemen during World War II on the grounds of the former Biloxi Country Club provided the Gulf Coast with a tremendous fiscal boon—and the final ingredient needed to complete a recipe for lawlessness. Biloxi's mammoth Keesler Army Air Field (now Keesler Air Force Base) became the economic engine fueling a renaissance of gambling, bootlegging, prostitution, drug use, and other vice in Biloxi. The flood of homesick, Europe-bound servicemen offered a splendid opportunity to part young men from their paychecks. Even after the war, Keesler boasted a population of airmen in the tens of thousands, Biloxi's biggest employer and largest payroll by far, an irresistible target for the criminals of the then-fledgling Dixie Mafia.

The openness of the gambling grew breathtaking. There was no attempt to hide anything: By the fifties, virtually every drugstore, lunchroom, hotel, bus terminal, gas station, and grocery in Biloxi had illegal slot machines. One of the city's best hotels at the time had a full-fledged public casino. A survey by Air Force authorities in 1951 found in Harrison County, where Biloxi is the county seat, 1,257 slot machines, seventy-two organized blackjack games, fifty-five poker games, thirty-one dice tables, eleven wire services for off-track horse race betting, and ten roulette wheels—all of it illegal. There were more than three hundred joints devoted to illegal gambling in operation. In the absence of any regulation, cheating was rampant. The Air Force at the time estimated that, of its $4 million monthly payroll at Keesler, a half-million went to cover gambling losses.[2]

Soon servicemen began paying off their losses by stealing and fencing military gear, kiting bad checks, pawning their weapons and uniforms, and, in the case of two junior officers saddled with immense gambling debts, committing suicide. In 1951, a U.S. Senate hearing convened in Biloxi to examine those suicides, and the Senate investigators found criminal enterprises in Biloxi so open and fearless that it seemed as if the city was part of another, lawless country.[3]

To the senators' amazement, no one attempted to hide the impact that crime lords had on the city. The president of the First National Bank of Biloxi named, without a moment's hesitation, the biggest industry in Biloxi: "Gambling." The mayor and his police chief freely admitted extracting payoffs from the casino operators, but defended their $12.50 monthly protection fee on each slot machine (which amounted to nearly $200,000 a year) as a necessary source of revenue in an otherwise financially strapped town. They disguised this income in the city's books as disorderly conduct fines paid by fictitious people, whose names the chief would simply invent once a month to cover the rake.

Two days before this Senate hearing opened to a standing-room-only crowd in an old courtroom atop Biloxi's granite Post Office building, Harrison County Sheriff Laz Quave tried to short-circuit the controversy. He ordered his friends in illegal gambling to shut down. And the slot machines and card games did vanish—for about two months, which, not coincidentally, was all that remained of Sheriff Quave's term in office. After that, with the senators and the national spotlight gone and the problem declared solved, Biloxi's commitment to clean government vanished. The gambling business returned, bigger and better than ever.

In short order, neon signs appeared, advertising the action. Rows of striptease joints soon joined the mix, offering watered-down, overpriced booze along with blatantly promoted sex for hire. Buying a six-dollar cola in a champagne glass for a stripper got a lonely serviceman some insipid conversation and a brief crotch rub under the table. Twenty dollars more would cover oral sex in the confines of dark booths the club owners dubbed "passion pits." Fifty dollars bought fifteen minutes on dirty sheets and a lumpy bed in back of the strippers' stage, the dull thud of recorded dance music filtering through the clapboard walls. One club called its back room the "Honeymoon Suite."[4] Other club owners bought shares of clapboard motels so they could expand their horizontal operations, offering hourly rates.

The new sheriff presided over this gold-rush growth of vice, befriending the most notorious gamblers, pimps, robbers, and killers, exacting an even larger tithe for protecting or ignoring their crimes, even forming partnerships with some. He charged a fee for every slot machine, every card game, every prostitute, every case of illegal whiskey in his county. There was plenty to go around: In the process, he accumulated a mansion, luxury cars, and a half-serious reputation as the highest paid public official in America.[5]

The pattern of corruption continued well into the 1980s with a series of corrupt law-enforcement officials, a nightshift crew of policemen dubbed "Ali-Baba and his Forty Thieves," and a ready partnership between many cops and criminals on The Strip. Brief, occasional attempts at reform inevitably lacked public support, ending in failure.

And so The Strip was born, a mix of glitz, sleaze, and danger that proved irresistible to con artists and other assorted crooks, a concentration of crime of all kinds, nurtured by the police while the rest of Biloxi looked on. Or rather, looked away. Right next to the genteel Biloxi of Jefferson Davis, of antebellum mansions ensconced in oak groves overlooking the sea, of generous and mannerly, church-going Southerners, there sat this other city, this place of politicians bought and paid for, of greed merchants, of killers—a place where a kind of Darwinian anarchy ruled, survival of the most ruthless.

It was this other Biloxi, with its rich legacy of corruption, that fascinated and welcomed a certain young airman from Oklahoma by the name of Kirksey McCord Nix, Jr.

CHAPTER 13

Junior," as his friends called him, arrived at Keesler Air
Force Base in 1962 for a year-long tour. Kirksey Nix was
nineteen at the time, the year of his first arrest as an adult,
charged with larceny back home in Oklahoma City. He
posted twenty dollars bond, then split for Biloxi.

Nix's ambition then, as it had been throughout his
adolescence, was a simple one: to be an outlaw. As one of
his cousins described him, Nix found living within rules
intolerable. "He needed the challenge of beating the system
to keep him interested," the cousin explained. "He was too
smart, and too bored. And one thing led to another."[1]

Nix put it this way after earning a life sentence for
murder: "It started out as a game, and ended up not a
game."

Most of Junior Nix's friends on the street, even the
sharpest, most savvy of ripoff artists, found the dapper
young thug hard to figure. "You're not exactly the average
hoodlum," one of his many partners in crime, Bobby Joe
Faubion, once told him after they pulled a series of armed
robberies together in Oklahoma and Texas. Faubion, the
fugitive who later had the near-fatal encounter with Rex
Armistead, once said to Nix, "Hell, I steal 'cause I need the
moolah, but you, boy, you was born with a silver spoon in
your mouth." Nix had smirked at this. He liked cultivating
the image of rich boy gone bad.

And the image carried more than a little truth. Nix had
grown up with money, pampered by his parents, given cars
for his birthdays and enormous allowances in between,
bailed out of trouble endlessly. He looked the part as well.
Slim, handsome, with piercing blue eyes and wild brown

hair, Junior Nix was quick, bright, and well spoken back
then, as befitted the private military academies his parents
shipped him off to when his behavior became too outrageous at home.

He didn't need to steal. He enjoyed it, the power he felt
when his gun froze some rube in his tracks, the satisfaction
of scoring big, the police left wondering. Nothing matched
it. The food tasted better, the cars seemed shinier, the
women seemed to want him more.

Being an outlaw meant turning his back on a great deal,
however. The Nix family was prominent in Oklahoma. His
father, Kirksey Nix Sr., had been a well-known criminal
defense attorney who put himself through law school as a
janitor for the state House of Representatives. He was
elected to that same House two years later as a populist
legislator, becoming the youngest floor leader ever. He later
moved to the state Senate, then to the Oklahoma Court of
Criminal Appeals by the time Junior was thirteen, the
state's highest court for criminal cases. Kirksey Nix Sr.
eventually became chief judge there, where his political
career stalled—his intense ambition to become governor
frustrated by his liberal politics in a conservative state.

Junior Nix's mother, Patricia, was no less prominent than
her husband, one of the first women in the state to practice
law. She divorced Junior's father when Nix was two, then
married B.B. Kerr, a founder of Kerr-McGhee Oil Company and a member of one of the state's wealthiest, most
powerful families. Nix's new uncle was a U.S. Senator,
Robert Kerr.

Nix Sr. also remarried. Junior began shuttling between
his two parents and their new families, one in rural Eufaula
in mountain country, the other in Oklahoma City, each of
them monied and privileged, each intent on spoiling Nix.

As an attorney, Kirksey Nix Sr. had been the consum-
mate country lawyer, weaving a storyteller's spell over
juries and courtroom audiences—a gift his son inherited.
As a judge, he was known as a stickler for the rights of
defendants. But it was his father's days in the state Senate,
representing the rural mountain district in southeast Oklahoma where Junior was born, that the younger Nix remembers best.

Senator Nix owed his job and the votes that put him there to the state prison in McAlester, Oklahoma, a major source of employment for the district. The warden, the guards, and just about everyone else there—other than the prisoners—got their jobs through patronage, and Senator Nix was the man to see. The prison became his domain.

As a young child, Nix had walked through that penitentiary many times with his dad, playing and laughing in the halls, a little boy's lesson in how things work in an imperfect world. He seemed untroubled by the bars and confinement he witnessed there. Later in life, when his view of prison would come from the other side of the visitor's window, he observed, "I've never associated a stigma with prison. Everyone in it was nice to me."[2]

Judge Nix, prominent as he was, had some unsavory connections, in a way blazing a trail for his son. He was twice censured by the state bar association, once while in private practice, once while on the bench. More important for his son's future, Judge Nix vacationed in Biloxi, Mississippi, where he befriended an old-time Dixie Mafia gambler-swindler-thief by the name of Blackjack Powell. He also grew close to a young strip-club owner named Mike Gillich, going on fishing trips with him, frequenting his nightclubs and his illegal bingo and gambling hall. By the mid-sixties, Judge Nix began appearing in Mississippi Highway Patrol intelligence reports as a friend of career criminals—questionable associations for a state appellate court justice, though not a crime in itself. Later, Nix Jr. would befriend the same group of gamblers, con men, and thieves his father had come to know.[3]

"Go introduce yourself to Mike Gillich when you get to Biloxi," Nix's father told him before his son left for duty at Keesler Air Force Base. "If you need anything, or if you get in any trouble, go see Mr. Mike."[4]

The relationship that grew from that simple suggestion would span two decades, dozens of crimes, hundreds of thousands of dollars—and would draw Vincent and Margaret Sherry to their deaths.

Having quit high school and already suffering some minor legal scrapes as a juvenile, Junior Nix fled his home state by joining the Air National Guard, which trained him in electronics, then shipped him off to a year's active duty in Biloxi, Mississippi.

The allure of the gaming tables and the nightclubs quickly drew Nix to The Strip. His first foray was to introduce himself to Mike Gillich, who had four strip joints and a bingo hall at the time. Gillich's clubs offered drugs, prostitutes, and gambling, along with beer served up in spotty tumblers and striptease acts performed to scratchy recorded music. Nix spent his money freely, often hitting up Mr. Mike for loans when his wallet emptied before payday.

It didn't take long for Nix to figure out which side of the illegal gaming table held the most potential for profit. He went to work in several of the clubs, including Gillich's Golden Nugget, cheating marks at blackjack, poker, and three-card monte. He'd string them along with promises of setting them up with nonexistent women, letting them win a little, then cleaning them out. Gamblers foolish enough to get drunk while playing Nix woke up in an alley, pockets empty, body bruised. After closing, Nix got a percentage of the take. Later, he began selling speed in the bars, stealing cars, and setting up servicemen with hookers, then robbing them once they had arrived at the string of dingy motels that serviced The Strip. He always justified his conduct with a simple rationale: "You can't cheat an honest man." It became his credo and, eventually, his defense.

Nix served out his year of active duty with the military, managed to earn an honorable discharge, then became a regular in Biloxi's strip joints, forging contacts with other con men, thieves, and robbers who used the clubs as meeting places and clearinghouses for plotting crimes throughout the South. Between heists, the club owners carried messages, held loot, hid fugitives, fenced stolen property, and underwrote the expenses for this loose-knit band of criminals in exchange for a piece of the action.

And so the Dixie Mafia was born, conceived on The Strip in Biloxi, Mississippi, a throwback to another era, producing a pack of Dillingers, Clyde Barrows, and Bonnie Parkers at a time when the rest of the country had focused on Vietnam, on war protests, on civil rights marches and political assassinations. These criminals lived like men born in the time of Capone, not Kennedy and King.

"Dixie Mafia" was not a name the traveling criminals coined or used themselves, at least at first. They had no relationship to the Sicilian Mafia or its U.S. extensions other than a healthy respect for the turf controlled by New Orleans Mafia chieftain Carlos Marcello, and occasional business dealings with his organization or his East Coast counterparts. "Dixie Mafia" was a label invented either by a creative cop or a newspaper reporter who tired of the phrase "traveling criminals" sometime in the mid-sixties.[5] Either way, the name stuck. So much romance and fear came to be attached to it, its members, real and imagined, soon began bragging of being part of the dreaded Dixie Mafia, legitimizing the term, making fiction into fact.

But if bragging about Dixie Mafia connections worked on the street, it generally suited members' purposes to deny the existence of any such organization once arrested. And, in a way, they were right: They had no godfather or single leader, no continuing enterprises—just the common bonds of greed and ruthlessness, and their occasional cooperation on one-shot crimes of theft and violence.

There was one other difference between these criminals and their traditional Mafia namesake: Instead of being bound by the blood of family, they were bound by the blood of victims. Committing murder—preferably on behalf of another member of the brotherhood—was the best method of entering the Dixie Mafia's inner circle.

The Strip in Biloxi became one of the few places these characters could meet safely, and Mike Gillich became their anchor, keeping them in touch during their "expeditions," as Nix called them, feeding them information drawn from criminals throughout the South, Midwest, and Southwest. He conducted counterintelligence against the police, and received regular leaks from cops on his payroll. His word-of-mouth network was every bit as quick and accurate as a police teletype. More than once, phone records belonging to thieves and murderers—and sometimes murder victims—had a peculiar way of showing calls to Mike Gillich just before some terrible crime occurred. When the crooks trusted no one else, fearing betrayals or ripoffs, they trusted Gillich, universally known by the respectful nickname "Mr. Mike." He held their money, he knew where to find them when they were on the run. He kept his word, always.

"He runs the criminals' post office," one investigator told Lynne Sposito many years later. "He's their banker." And no one in the Dixie Mafia made more deposits and withdrawals in the Bank of Mr. Mike than Kirksey Nix.

Once Junior Nix hooked up with the Dixie Mafia, his criminal career took a more serious turn. In December 1965, when he was twenty-two, Nix got caught in Fort Smith, Arkansas, near the Oklahoma border, carrying illegal automatic weapons with phony registration. An old friend of his, Juanda Jones, ran a bordello there, and he was a frequent customer. He had taken a protective liking to Juanda's adolescent daughter, LaRa, who idolized Kirksey and, from age twelve on, had begged him on each visit to marry her. As an adult, LaRa would become much more to Nix than a child with a crush.

At the time of his arrest, Nix assured the police who pulled him over that he had just been visiting friends, nothing more. Fort Smith detectives suspected him of plotting an armed robbery in their city, but they could not prove it. He skated on the weapons charges with only a fifty-dollar fine, thanks to Judge Nix's influence in the neighboring state. He walked out of jail a short time later, LaRa rushing to hug her outlaw hero.

Junior's ability to elude charges through the power of his name and connections would continue for years: He was arrested four months later for transporting a prostitute in Tulsa, but prosecutors declined to file charges. The same thing happened in April 1966, when he was caught passing a bogus check—no charges filed, though the evidence against him was compelling. Nix remained free and fearless.

"That's the system," Nix would later say with a giggle.

In 1967, police suspected Nix, among others, of being involved somehow in killing a Biloxi gambler who was about to turn state's evidence against several Dixie Mafia members. No case was ever made against Junior, however, and questions still remain about just who left Harry Bennett's bullet-riddled body in an apartment complex parking lot.[6] It was the first gangland-style slaying in Biloxi in fifteen years—and the first in a long line of potential witnesses against the Dixie Mafia to be murdered. The floodgates opened with Bennett's death. In the next four years, more than twenty-five murders in six states were linked to a handful of Dixie Mafia figures well known on The Strip.

Nineteen sixty-seven was a busy year for Kirksey Nix Jr. On August 11, Nix, two other Dixie Mafia shooters, and a gangster out of Boston checked into the Shamrock Motel, a combination brothel and gambling house on the Mississippi-Tennessee line. The motel was run by another Dixie Mafia killer originally from Biloxi, Carl Douglas "Towhead" White, a close friend of Nix's who was serving prison time for bootlegging that summer.

An informant later claimed that White had telephoned Nix from jail, hiring him to kill the infamous Sheriff Buford Pusser of McNairy County, Tennessee, the flamboyant and corrupt lawman immortalized in the movie *Walking Tall*.

Not long before, Pusser had killed Towhead White's common-law wife, Louise Hathcock, after she pulled a gun on him at the Shamrock Motel during an arrest. White wanted revenge on Pusser, and he turned to Kirksey Nix for help.

One day after Nix appeared at the Shamrock Motel, someone telephoned Sheriff Pusser at home several hours before dawn. "There's a couple drunks going at it out on the edge of town," the caller said. "Someone's gonna get killed." The caller gave a location, and the sheriff said he'd take care of it.

Pusser got dressed and prepared to investigate. On the spur of the moment, his wife decided to ride along. Fighting drunks were nothing to worry about—she had been along for much worse.

But the call was a ruse, a lure to draw Sheriff Pusser into an ambush. He would later claim that Kirksey Nix and his crew had been waiting for him in a new Cadillac, parked out of sight behind a Methodist church on a country road. The big car raced up beside the sheriff, windows open and bristling with gun barrels. Pauline Pusser died instantly, shot in the head. But the sheriff, left for dead, survived his wounds, the lower half of his face virtually shot off by high-velocity, soft-nosed bullets.

Pusser's informants told him who was behind the shooting, and the sheriff eventually named Nix and White as the men he most wanted brought to justice. But he had no proof. No charges were ever filed in the case. This suited Pusser, however. He preferred a more personal revenge.[7]

In the next three years, four of the five men he named as his ambushers died violently—all but Nix. Investigators believed Pusser was behind at least some of this mayhem, if not all, and that Nix avoided further retribution only because he went to prison, and because Pusser, by then retired from law enforcement, died in an auto accident in 1974 before he could make his revenge complete.[8]

He may have tried, though: In May 1968, Nix brought a late-model Cadillac to Oklahoma City for his father. The car was registered to the wife of a Dixie Mafia strip-club owner from Biloxi named Dewey D'Angelo, a close friend of Nix's and the partner of the murdered Biloxi gambler Harry Bennett. After Judge Nix parked the Cadillac at the state capitol, the car exploded, sending wreckage flying hundreds of feet, nearly decapitating one passer-by. Though the car was obliterated, no one was hurt; Nix had parked the car an hour earlier and was safely in his office at the time of the explosion.

Neither of the Nixes came up with a reasonable explanation for the incident. Judge Nix claimed he bought the car from his son, but there were no papers to show any transaction, and it was still legally registered in Mississippi to D'Angelo's wife. Investigators eventually wrote the explosion off as an accident caused by a leaky welding tank Judge Nix had put in the trunk. That curious ruling came despite the fact that the judge swore the welding tank had been empty. Years later, Nix's partner in crime, Bobby Joe Faubion, would claim the Cadillac had been partial payment for Nix's role in the Pusser hit, and the explosion an attempt by the sheriff to even the score.

Nix avoided Tennessee after that, but he found ample opportunity for trouble elsewhere. In 1968, Nix had several run-ins with the law in Oklahoma, Atlanta, and Dallas. He was charged with assault with intent to murder, bribing an officer, narcotics possession, auto theft, use of a stolen credit card, threatening witnesses against him, possession of burglary tools, and illegal possession of police radios.

This last charge became a hallmark of Junior Nix—by scanning police frequencies, he could learn if he had tripped a silent alarm or had been reported during a break-in or robbery. With the emergency codes of a dozen different police departments committed to memory, he would know as soon as a patrol car was dispatched, leaving him ample time to get away. Nix, with his military training in electronics, had developed a habit of assembling an array of sophisticated devices to commit his crimes. When Dallas police raided an apartment he was using in November 1968, they found police radios, military-quality walkie-talkies, gas masks, lock picks, and police handcuffs, along with the usual assortment of rifles and handguns.

As in years past, Kirksey Nix continued to laugh off his legal troubles, telling his cronies he was invulnerable. "If I can't lie my way out, I'll buy my way out," the always flush Nix told one friend. "They'll never touch me."

Police investigators in five states had him pegged as a career criminal and Dixie Mafia heavyweight. Yet, despite this growing reputation, his five separate arrests in 1968 failed to keep him off the streets for more than a matter of days, sometimes hours. In four of the arrests, charges ranging in seriousness from reckless driving to assault with intent to murder were dismissed or, at most, resolved through payment of a nominal fine.

Only in a drug-possession and attempted bribery bust in Atlanta in December 1968 were formal charges pursued. Nix had tried to slip ten one-hundred-dollar bills to a policeman who pulled him over for a traffic violation, then found drugs in the car. And even then, he was released on minimal bail and immediately fled the state, becoming a fugitive, plotting new crimes.

On February 18, 1969, four heavily armed men in military fatigues, ski masks, and gloves stormed a trailer camp in Covington, Louisiana, across Lake Ponchartrain from New Orleans, near the Mississippi border. A group of Gypsies who ran a carnival had arrived for Mardi Gras, and they were rumored to have large amounts of cash on hand.

"Out, out, everyone out," one of the masked men shrieked. "Get your asses out here or we'll blow your fucking heads off."

The four marauders rousted the Gypsies from their

trailers, then bound all twenty-four men, women, and children together with one long iron chain looped around each of their necks, each person locked in place with a padlock. The victims were then herded, children sobbing, into a house next to the trailer court, where the gunmen forced open seven safes, taking more than twelve thousand dollars in cash, a bag full of jewelry, and other small valuables.

Margie George, the forty-four-year-old "Gypsy Queen" of the carnival, stubborn and shrieking, alone put up a fight, refusing to reveal the combination of one of the safes. One of the robbers responded by coolly planting a hatchet in her skull while several of her family members watched. Then, as she moaned and convulsed on the floor, another of the robbers shot her point-blank in the head with a .45-caliber automatic, spraying the living room with her blood, brain, and bone fragments. The crime would go down as the Dixie Mafia's most gruesome and gratuitously violent murder, as unnecessary as it was cold-blooded.

Two days later, police investigators acting on a tip rounded up a friend and crime partner of Kirksey Nix's, a Dixie Mafia burglar named Bobby Gail Gwinn.[9] A jug-eared thirty-seven-year-old loser with a flattened nose from too many fights, Gwinn initially denied being part of the Gypsy camp murder. But instead of leaving it at that and keeping his mouth shut, the panicked Gwinn also told police that he, Junior Nix, and three other men with long arrest records had been target-shooting at a trash dump near town sometime before the robbery. "We were pickin' off rats," he said. "That's all." The place he named lay a handful of miles from the trailer court where Margie George died.

Investigators searched the dump and picked up several spent bullet casings. Ballistics examiners then matched them to spent shells found at the trailer court murder scene. A Louisiana judge issued murder arrest warrants for five men, including Nix, the suspected ringleader. All were arrested a short time later, except Nix, who remained in hiding in Texas and on the Mississippi Gulf Coast.[10]

Nix decided on a James Copeland-like maneuver to extricate himself. On March 15, 1969, he returned to Atlanta and surrendered himself to the police on less serious charges. At the same time, he refused to waive extradition to Louisiana for trial in the Gypsy case, instead choosing to immediately plead guilty to the old charge of bribery he had been dodging since he fled Atlanta the previous winter.

This tactic ensured he would serve time in Georgia rather than being immediately transferred to Louisiana. He drew a two-year prison sentence, which, under liberal parole rules of the era, meant he would be out in ten months or less. Despite all his past arrests, this would go on record as Kirksey Nix's first felony conviction.

The decision to cop a plea in Atlanta turned out to be a fortuitous one. In October 1969, Nix's former friend and partner, Bobby Gail Gwinn, out on bail in the Gypsy murder case, was found shot to death by the side of a Louisiana highway—five days after promising to testify against Nix. He was last seen with a Texas killer and friend of Nix's, Stanley "Creeper" Cook, while both men were being questioned by Jefferson Parish sheriff's deputies in suburban New Orleans.[11]

With Gwinn gone, the Gypsy murder case fell apart for Louisiana prosecutors. The murder warrants were withdrawn. The killing of Margie George remains an open case to this day. Gwinn's murder was never solved either, though detectives suspected Nix had arranged it from the safety of a jail cell. That, too, would become a familiar pattern for Nix. There was no proof, however, and any hope that Creeper Cook might shed light on the subject vanished when he, too, was assassinated by a single shot from a high-powered rifle two years later.[12]

By autumn 1970, Nix walked out of prison in Georgia and into the arms of his fiancée, Sandra, an old friend from Oklahoma. He had put on some weight, and the boyish good looks had begun to fade, too much alcohol and amphetamines, too many late-night rounds at bordellos in Arkansas and Oklahoma where his name and bankroll were well known. His police mug shots after that time show a gradual decline—the chin receding and doubling, the eyes rimmed and red, the expression less cocky and more glazed with each passing arrest. His criminal creativity never dimmed, but Junior Nix soon exhausted his run of luck. The next time he was arrested would be his last.[13]

CHAPTER 14

Shortly after midnight on April 11, 1971—Easter Sunday—Marian Corso arose from bed in her one-story Lakefront home in New Orleans. She had been up late dyeing eggs with her sixteen-year-old daughter, preparing Easter baskets for her two younger children and her grandkids. Ready for sleep, she was about to turn out her bedside light when she realized she had forgotten a glass of water to wash down her evening medication. She walked to the kitchen.

As she poured some ice water, Marian noticed the back patio light had been left off, contrary to household custom. She flicked on the switch, and there they were: three men in her backyard, staring back at her through the window in the door, startled by the unexpected light.

They froze, the four of them, a long second or two, a frightened woman and three strangers, separated by seventy-five pounds of wood and a pane of glass. The man closest to her was painted with light, his young face twisted in surprise, his hair wild. As she yelled to her husband, "Frank, Frank! Come quick!," this man turned toward her, a cold expression piercing her through the door's window.

"Lady, be calm, and no one will get hurt. We're coming in," Kirksey Nix said.[1]

The job had been well planned, or so Nix thought. The Corsos owned a grocery store in the French Quarter and Frank Corso was known to be both rich and eccentric, wary of banks. He had been rumored to maintain large amounts of cash in the house, possibly from illegal book-making operations—false rumors, it turned out.

A hydraulic jack capable of exerting four tons of pressure

had been used to break in quietly, just a slight cracking sound as the doorjamb spread and the wood frame gave way. Telephone lines to the house had been tapped, then cut. Nix had disposable handcuffs in a satchel to secure the people in the house, and a walkie-talkie to maintain contact with his getaway driver, who was monitoring a police radio. But the plan relied upon one thing Nix no longer possessed —the element of surprise.

As Marian Corso screamed and ran from the room, Nix and his latest crime partners, a low-level Mafioso named Peter Frank Mule and Florida thug John C. Fulford, burst through the loosened door and into the kitchen. Frank Corso, awakened by his wife's shrieks, rushed from the bedroom at the same time, pajamas flapping, a pistol in hand. Eleven-year-old Susan Corso had run from her bedroom to see what was wrong. There followed a brief, terrible silence. Then Marian Corso heard Kirksey Nix shout, "I've got your child."

Before Marian could react, Corso, Nix, Fulford, and Mule faced off in the hallway connecting kitchen to bedrooms. The four men opened fire at once. Marian cowered in her bedroom door, bullets peppering the walls around her.

Nearly thirty shots flew before the battle ended. The other two children leapt from bed, running and screaming in the halls, somehow escaping injury while crossing the lines of fire. Only after the firing stopped did Marian realize Susan had hunkered in a chair, unhurt despite Nix's threat.

But Frank Corso fell heavily to the floor, struck by five bullets—though not before he put a .38-caliber slug into Nix's abdomen. As his attackers backed out of the kitchen and stumbled outside, Marian Corso scooped up her husband's gun and emptied the last two shots at the retreating criminals, striking the kitchen wall. Nix raised his gun and pointed it at her as he was half-carried, half-limped from the house. "Mamma, you're gonna get shot," Susan screamed, but to Marian's amazement, Nix never fired. She blinked, and they were gone.[2]

With their cohort slumped and bleeding, Fulford and Mule dragged Nix from the house to a dark blue Oldsmobile where a fourth accomplice, James Knight, waited behind the wheel. As they fled, they dropped Nix's 9-mm automatic pistol, the hydraulic jack, the bag with the handcuffs, and a sizable amount of Junior's type A blood—evidence that would combine later to bring them down. The reason why Nix had not shot Marian Corso became obvious as well. He had not been moved by compassion to hold his fire. The gun was jammed when police found it, an expended shell stuck in its ejection port.

The marauders sped through the empty streets to an apartment hideout, a place Nix had rented under the assumed name Accardo. Their plan lay in tatters. They could not risk alerting the New Orleans police by going to a local hospital, yet Nix's wound was too bad to ignore—he was slowly bleeding to death.

His new wife, Sandra Llewellyn Rutherford Nix, blond, waifish, and fearless, put towels on his wound and fed him orange popsicles, the only food Junior could keep down. She and Nix had met in Oklahoma a few years earlier. She was tough—tougher than her husband in many ways—raised in an orphanage, with no one but Nix and his family to provide any semblance of roots. Their brief marriage had been punctuated by prison and jail terms for each of them. Sandra was running some sort of photography business, while Nix divided his time between ski-mask robberies of New Orleans gamblers with Mule and Fulford, and periodically flying to Ecuador, where he had dreamed up a high-end scam to build a resort and casino on the environmentally sensitive Galapagos Islands. U.S. oil interests were investing heavily in the region at that time, and Nix harbored visions of fleecing money-laden oil workers in a tropical version of The Strip. He had been trying to close a deal with corrupt Ecuadoran officials when the Corso case cut his plan short.

Despite his constant infidelities and their relatively short periods of time living together, Sandra remained fiercely loyal to her husband. When his cohorts seemed about to abandon Junior, she fixed them with a deadly stare. "You've got to get him help," she told them. "Do it. Now."

Desperate to get Junior out of town, they turned to his old friend Creeper Cook in Dallas. Late that night, Cook arrived in New Orleans aboard a rented airplane. He picked up a still-bleeding, barely conscious Nix and returned to Dallas, with the wounded man alternately sucking ice chips and vomiting en route, barely able to speak. Sandra booked a commercial flight and arrived first, meeting the small plane at the airport, then driving Nix to the hospital.

Back in New Orleans, the failed burglary and shoot-out at the Corso home became front-page news. A home invasion in a middle-class neighborhood on Easter Sunday enraged the people of that staunchly Catholic city. The fifty-year-old grocer clung to life until five o'clock on the evening he was shot, then finally died of his wounds. Police saw the trail of blood leading out of the kitchen, and wondered if one of the killers had met a similar fate.

The Texas hospital, as a matter of routine in gunshot cases, called the authorities. When the Dallas police saw a teletyped bulletin on the Corso shooting, they called New Orleans P.D. to say Kirksey Nix had checked into a hospital there with a gunshot wound. The New Orleans police already knew of Nix: They had him under brief surveillance a few months earlier, along with Mule and Fulford, during an investigation of the ski-mask robberies of gamblers. All three became instant suspects in the Corso killing. An informant who knew them and had been to Nix's apartment confirmed the suspicions for police, then led them to the getaway driver, Knight.[3]

Knight confessed, agreeing to testify against his cohorts and completing the case for the police. With formal murder charges filed, Marian Corso identified the three men as the killers. The Dallas police marched into Nix's hospital room and chained him with leg irons to his bed until he could be shipped to Louisiana, Frank Corso's bullet still inside him.

Once there, he won a lengthy legal battle to keep the lead slug where it sat, lodged near his large intestine, affirming a legal principle that the state has no right to cut open a man in order to find evidence of a crime. Nix's cause had been helped when a team of court-appointed doctors said executing a search warrant for the bullet—with scalpels—might execute the man as well.

Jim Garrison, the district attorney who unsuccessfully prosecuted Clay Shaw for conspiring to kill President John Kennedy, delivered the opening statement in the trial, which had to be moved outside of New Orleans because of intensive media coverage. Several abortive escape attempts were made and failed. Corso's wife and family, as well as

the getaway driver, Knight, were kept in protective custody
for months, tribute to the Dixie Mafia's reputation for
eliminating witnesses. State troopers were assigned to guard
the judge on the case and the D.A. twenty-four hours a day
(the widow Corso eventually married one of them).

Nix's father, retired from his appellate court seat on full
disability shortly after Junior's arrest, joined his son's
defense team, as did his mother, Patricia Kerr. Father
protested son's innocence, though just a few years before, in
order to retain his judgeship, he had publicly branded
Junior a boy gone bad, defending himself against an
opponent's criticism. "They can't question my character,
ability, honesty, or performance of duty except by innuen-
do," Judge Nix had told the Oklahoma *Journal*. "The only
thing they can criticize me about is my son, who has not
lived with me for eighteen years. They have written him up
every time he's turned around. I sincerely regret the boy
didn't turn out as well as I had hoped."[4]

Junior Nix also proclaimed his innocence. He complained that police reports originally said the Corso killers
wore masks—suggesting that Marian Corso could not have
seen his face, and that her subsequent identification of the
murderers had been a police-concocted fable.

To explain the bullet in his gut, he accused a conveniently
dead Mafia hit man of shooting him for refusing to extend a
loan. He even produced the hit man's stroke-impaired
girlfriend to confirm the tale. The main problem with the
story was its inability to explain Nix's flight to Dallas. Why
flee when he had done nothing wrong? Why, the prosecutor
asked, hadn't Sandra Nix—who had died in a car crash
during Nix's trial—simply called the police and an ambu-
lance if he was an innocent shooting victim?

"She wasn't that type of person!" the hit man's girlfriend
exclaimed. "I think there is something wrong with a woman
calling the police any time."

The prosecution easily countered this defense, at least as
far as the jury was concerned. Not only did Marian Corso
identify the killers under oath (and deny the presence of
masks), but so did her daughter Susan. Police witnesses
produced the jack used to break down the Corsos' door,
linking it by receipts and a sales clerk's testimony to Peter
Mule. A map with pencil marks tracing the route to the

Corso home was found at the head of Nix's blood-stained bed in an apartment rented to Kirksey and Sandra "Accardo." Nix's blood type matched blood found in Corso's kitchen.

Nix's Dixie Mafia connections became clear when police searched his apartment: They found a trial transcript of a criminal case in Oklahoma against Nix's suspected partner in the Gypsy camp killing, Bill Clubb, and a copy of a confidential police file leaked to Nix about the "traveling criminals" Rex Armistead had helped write. There was even an issue of *Startling Detective* magazine with a long feature on the Gypsy camp murder in with Nix's things.

It played no role in his trial, but there was one other item found in Nix's apartment, innocuous-seeming at the time, though a different set of investigators puzzling over the Sherry murders fifteen years later would have found it all too significant had they bothered to look. Amidst gun parts and ammunition, the New Orleans police searching Kirksey Nix's apartment for clues in the Corso murder found a large piece of foam rubber.

In March 1972, just under one year after Corso died, Nix, Mule, and Fulford all were convicted of murder. Jurors and judge alike found the evidence in the case overwhelming. But the jury also found against capital punishment, and Nix and his accomplices each received a sentence of life in prison "at hard labor." Under Louisiana law at the time, the men could never receive parole; the sentence was "for the rest of their natural lives." Only a governor's pardon could set them free. A decade's worth of appeals accumulated in state and federal courts, twenty-four volumes in the Louisiana Supreme Court alone, to no avail.

Nix next went to Leavenworth to serve out a five-year federal prison term for being a felon in possession of a firearm, another old charge that finally caught up with him. He had already done six months for contempt of court for refusing to provide a sample of his handwriting.

After his federal time ran out, he shipped off to what had been one of the most infamous prisons in America, a bastion of nineteenth-century penal philosophy, where road gangs and guards on horseback remained everyday sights: the Louisiana State Penitentiary at Angola.

At age thirty-two, he entered for good this world of utter ruthlessness, where abuse, despair, and death awaited the weak, but where the strong and the clever could carve a special, privileged niche.

There was never any question where Kirksey McCord Nix would fit in this world. It took him time to realize it, but he had finally found a place where he felt at home, a place where he was *expected* to be an outlaw.

Yet, without ever perceiving the irony, Nix devoted his time there to finding a way out. He'd buy his freedom if he had to, he decided, through bribes, payoffs, whatever it took. The Louisiana penal system was notoriously corrupt. Pardons could be purchased with the right contacts and enough money. He set out to make that money.

Dedicated to this cause, Nix became a far more successful criminal from within prison than he ever was on the outside. He pioneered scams that began bringing in thousands of dollars, then hundreds of thousands. Using his Dixie Mafia contacts, he put an army to work for him, in and out of prison. Mike Gillich was there for him in Biloxi, and others throughout the South, the network he had forged in the Dixie Mafia.

And then there was Peter Halat and Vincent Sherry.

CHAPTER 15

Vince Sherry never wanted to move to Biloxi.

He despised what he had seen of the city in 1965, when he and his family lived within the protective embrace of Keesler Air Force Base. Outside the military reservation, the gambling, the corruption, The Strip and everything it represented—all the things that so enchanted Kirksey Nix when he had arrived two years earlier—persuaded Vince that the Gulf Coast was no place to raise a family.

During his time there as a military lawyer, Vince all but quarantined his children. He kept them on base whenever possible, away from what he called the "local ruffians"— defined as any child not living in Keesler's stock of red-brick ranch homes. Lynne and the other Sherry children could not even go on class trips because Vince refused to sign a waiver promising he would not sue the school if some harm befell his kids during the outing. "In Biloxi?" he asked. "You must be joking."

When Colonel Sherry transferred to Okinawa in 1967 to finish out his military career—a post some servicemen consider a hardship—Vince was overjoyed. The kids then grew up in the cloistered military community there. During vacations, Vince traveled throughout Asia. He studied and prepared for his doctorate in Vietnam, reading original documents in French dating back to the founding of that republic, haunting staid libraries and universities in a country unraveling with each passing day. He learned to speak Vietnamese, interviewing jurists and attorneys. He blithely traversed neighborhoods armed soldiers avoided, displaying a brand of fatalism about personal safety that sometimes bordered on the foolhardy, an almost Calvinist insistence that his fate had been decided long before and that nothing he did would hasten or delay his demise. One night driving with friends through Saigon, he insisted on switching on the dome light in their cab so he could read— even as gunfire could be heard nearby and his friends hugged the floorboards.

"If it's time for me to die, I'm not going to worry about it," Vince had said, silencing their pleas to extinguish the light. "If it's your time, it's your time."

After Okinawa, his military retirement plan had always been to move back to the lush green horse country of his adoptive hometown in Kentucky. Though he led people to believe otherwise, Vince had not lived his whole life there— he had been born in New York City, where he spent his childhood dodging an abusive father's fists. He had moved to Kentucky with his mother at age thirteen, declaring himself a Southerner and making his Yankee heritage his

most guarded secret. He loved Kentucky and wanted to
return.

But Margaret feared interference from their disapproving
mothers-in-law—neither liked her child's choice of spouse.
She suggested a return to Biloxi instead. She had not shared
Vince's distaste for the place, and it was a way of staying in
the South. She loved the ocean and the small-town feel—
apart from The Strip, much of Biloxi and the Mississippi
Gulf Coast seemed unsullied.

So the Sherrys settled in Biloxi for good in 1970, eventually buying a house in the Ancient Oaks section of town
near the Sunkist Country Club, a comfortable, tree-lined
enclave far removed from the sleaze and hustle of The Strip,
large, simple houses with big yards and fruit trees in back.
That same year, Lynne married Dick Sposito and moved
with him to Ohio. Eric and Vin continued grade school in
Biloxi while Leslie soon began kindergarten. Vince, meanwhile, at forty-one, began to wind down the final year of his
Air Force service, practicing military law at Keesler, then
entering private practice with one of Biloxi's largest law
firms. It was just as Margaret wanted. But then a curious
thing happened.

Margaret found herself increasingly appalled by the corruption around her. Though she never wavered in her love
for her adopted hometown, Margaret Sherry began to
despise the blurred lines of Biloxi government, the criminal
powers that carried such weight behind the scenes, the futile
attempts at reform, the essentially law-abiding majority
who seemed unable to shrug off the tyranny of a corrupt
few.

Vince, on the other hand, quickly overcame his repug-
nance for his new home. He became fascinated and be-
guiled by the characters he defended in court, who lived life
so hard and so fully, whose choices were so alien from his
own. They had no concept of conventional morality, he
found, though they seemed to live by their own code. They
were mysterious and cruel, like Vince's father, a man who
had married under an alias, and whose true identity was
revealed to his wife only when a brother appeared at the
door one day and asked for him by his true name. Once
found out, Vince's father had claimed he lived under a false
name because of undercover work he had done for the

government. But the family always suspected a shadier reason.

Now, half a lifetime later in Biloxi, Vincent Sherry found himself reveling in the uncertain moral landscape, happily and thoroughly at home in the same sort of environment that had so repulsed him when he was a child. He began spending more and more time with Biloxi's criminal elite, enjoying their companionship and secrets. Like his new city, Vince finally came to embody the same countervailing qualities that made Biloxi a place of contradiction—the man of high principle and ability who, nevertheless, was touched by and fascinated with the dark side.

In Biloxi, Vincent Jerome Sherry learned that he enjoyed the moral equivalent of juggling. To his credit, and his family's ultimate misfortune, he was all too good at it.

In short order, the bulk of Vince Sherry's law practice became the defense of the city's most notorious criminals. He would make his rounds at night, moving in and out of The Strip's various dives and haunts, a doctor of jurisprudence attending to the legal needs of an endless series of motley patients. He drove from courthouse to bar to illegal gambling casino to a doughnut shop to meet a stripper with legal troubles. The same man became a stalwart of the local Democratic Party, socializing by day with governors, federal judges, U.S. Senators, and Biloxi's elite. But he also enjoyed rubbing elbows with the city's underworld, inhaling the stale beer and tobacco atmosphere of some club on The Strip while a tired heroin addict removed her G-string to bad disco on a plywood stage. Vince even stored excess law books and case files in the cavernous warehouse on The Strip that housed two of Mike Gillich's clubs, the Golden Nugget and the Dream Room, and behind them, a variety of gambling and prostitution facilities. With a glowing introduction from Pete Halat, a lifelong friend of Gillich's, Vince came to enjoy an easy friendship with "Mr. Mike." Vince bailed Gillich's employees out of trouble time and again, his address book filled with their names and numbers.

Vince's work for Gillich most often involved getting work cards for the strip-joint owner's "girls." The cards were the city of Biloxi's gesture at keeping drug dealers, prostitutes and other assorted felons from working The Strip as bartenders, waitresses, and strippers—the idea being if you keep the criminals away, you keep the crime away too. Supposedly you couldn't get a work card from the Biloxi Police Department if you had a criminal record; clubs with cardless workers were supposed to be closed down, their owners arrested. It was a system observed more in the breach than in practice. Mr. Mike regularly hired Vince to obtain work cards regardless of a stripper's criminal past, and women with drug and prostitution records regularly went to work in Gillich's clubs.

Dick Sposito once asked Vince, "How can you hang out with these crooks, live the professional life you live, then go home and live your life the way you do with your family?"

"You just separate them," Vincent Sherry said. "It's that simple."

It was the sort of typical Vince comment Lynne Sposito would mentally replay time and again years later, wishing she could tell him, "It's never that simple, is it, Dad?"

If Vincent Sherry was a moral relativist, totally at ease with visiting a client at his illegal casino, dice tables and slot machines noisily in use, Margaret Sherry was another matter.

There were no shades of gray in Margaret's moral universe, just the absolutes of right and wrong, straight and crooked. She and Vince were something of an odd couple, he a lifelong Democrat (though he had been a George Wallace man), she an ultraconservative Republican opposed to even the most basic government programs. Margaret despised the criminals Vince brought home for dinner all the time, though she tolerated them as a necessary part of his business. On the other hand, she served as Vince's conscience at times, as she did with the Acevedo case, when she compelled him to turn over the guns he had removed from a client's home, despite potentially dire consequences.

Margaret shared the same poor roots as Vince, but unlike him, a closet Yankee, Margaret Smith was born in Louisiana, where her father had toiled in the oil fields, then later moved to Kentucky. The Smiths were far ahead of their time when it came to supporting the ambitions of their daughter, saving to put her through college. She and Vince met while undergraduates in Bowling Green. He stood her up on their first date, a Christmas party, apologizing the next day with the boxed candies of a Whitman Sampler. Vince made a habit of repeating that same gift every year throughout their courtship and marriage, the rectangular yellow box appearing before each Christmas without fail, an unspoken apology for the past year's transgressions.

Margaret's parents could never stand Vince. Her father told her to stop seeing him or get out. She chose the latter, moving to Detroit with her brother—later to be Eric Sherry's natural father. Vince courted Margaret with long, eloquent love letters, and she fell in love with his wit as much as anything else. For years, Margaret's parents virtually disowned her, even refusing to attend the wedding in 1950.

"They say you're the smart-ass from New York who came down to Kentucky to steal their baby," Margaret told Vince. Vince's mother was no better. "I don't want that Margaret at my funeral," she instructed Vince shortly before her death. By the time they settled in Biloxi and after twenty years of marriage, the rancor had cooled somewhat, but Lynne never had to guess why her mother had fought so adamantly against moving back to Kentucky.

In college, Margaret earned a dual degree in mathematics and art, then went to work for an architect in Washington. Vince joined the Air Force, serving at the Pentagon in Intelligence. Margaret became the breadwinner while Vince juggled military duty and law school.

Lynne remembers her mother as the calming influence in the family, while Vince was subject to terrible bouts of violence and temper, sometimes striking Margaret in the early days of their marriage. Lynne also remembers being knocked unconscious as a child for accidentally bumping her father while picking up a penny. Later, by way of apology, Vince came to Lynne as she lay in her room recovering, holding out a box and saying, "I bought you a corsage for Easter."

This was exactly the opposite of the Sherrys' public image, in which Margaret appeared to be the fire-breathing politician, and Vince the jovial everyman. Margaret Sherry was no doormat for Vince, however: She put up with a great deal, but she drew the line when necessary, fully capable of raging as loudly as her husband. Sometimes she refused to speak to him for days, walking by him, talking through him, until he began to feel like a wraith haunting his own home. He would in the end beg forgiveness, finding Margaret's silence too potent a weapon.

During one visit to Biloxi by Margaret's mother when Lynne was very young, Vince asked his wife what was for dinner. "Whatever you make," she replied lightly. He snapped out an open fist and struck her, lightning quick, right in front of Margaret's mother. He instantly regretted it, but said nothing. Margaret paled, but she, too, remained silent. When Vince left the room to take a nap—his bouts of anger always left him exhausted—Margaret followed a few minutes later.

Once they were alone, she pulled out the pistol she had just retrieved from the closet, and pointed it at Vince. "You apologize—in front of my mother," she said, "or I pull the trigger." He apologized. And he meant it.

Later in life, Lynne would come to believe that her father's sporadically abusive behavior owed as much to a medical condition as to the fact that Vince suffered at the hands of his own abusive father. Even as a young man, Vince had been stricken with high blood pressure and crippling headaches that would leave him alternately tense and irritable, or supine on the couch. As he approached middle age, a long-overdue diagnosis and new medication brought these conditions under control. Vince's violent temper faded after that, ending the intense swings between nurturing parent and belt-wielding terror. The youngest Sherry child, Leslie, would remember only a wonderful dad who doted on her in every way, and who never raised his hand in her life—though nothing would ever completely cure Vince's fiery temper and penchant for shouting in anger.

Despite the ragged memories, Lynne could always forgive her father. She always recalled Vince's attitude about his own father, whom he had forgiven in later life and welcomed into his home and family. "If nothing else," Vince once told her, "he gave me life. Who can ignore such a gift?"

Strangely, Vince and Margaret rarely battled over the most logical source of potential conflict between them—his representation of Biloxi's most notorious criminals and her desire to win the office of mayor, then put those same men out of business. On the contrary, Vince was Margaret's most ardent supporter when she decided to enter politics in 1981, eleven years after they settled in Biloxi, and he never wavered in that support. He had at first liked and supported Gerald Blessey, whose political philosophy more closely resembled his than Margaret's. But when she took him on, Vince got behind his wife, no questions asked. And when she announced she wanted to close down his friend Gillich, and the rest of The Strip, Vince just laughed. "If you want to shut them down," he said, "that's fine with me. You'll just make more work for a good defense attorney."

CHAPTER 16

Mike Gillich Jr. cut a curious figure for a crime boss. Humble in appearance and demeanor, Mr. Mike favored faded khakis and an untucked cotton shirt, a squarish pack of Lucky Strikes making the pocket over his heart bulge. He didn't carry a gun or flaunt his women. His favorite hangout was a doughnut shop. He refrained from boastful, loud talk, his mild hazel eyes slightly enlarged behind thick glasses, a paunch rounding out his stubby frame. He prospered by keeping a low profile, living as he always had lived—modestly.

His home lacked pretension, one-story and colorless, located in a fenced compound two blocks inland from The Strip, near one of his clubs, the Horseshoe Lounge, a bookie's haven later converted to strip shows. His first house on Point Cadet in the heart of Biloxi's Yugoslavian enclave was equally unpretentious, though the enormous white Cadillac parked out front, custom-converted into a pickup truck, belied the humble image a bit. The beachfront property Gillich owned and on which he placed his other strip clubs made him a wealthy man, at least on paper. Yet he rarely flaunted his money, except in the shiny new cars and pickup trucks he favored.

His only other display of wealth came with his frequent and generous gifts to the Catholic Church. He received regular thank-you notes from the nuns and priests he helped support. There also were ample, if unrecorded, campaign contributions over the years to politicians and lawmen, the sort of under-the-table payments that helped make certain Mr. Mike's business would continue smoothly even while his competitors suffered raids, arrests, shutdowns, and injunctions.

It didn't hurt that he was close to almost every corrupt lawman in town as well, always respectful and friendly, greeting good cops and bad alike with a polite "Hello, officer. Come in, have some coffee, have a drink. Have a seat." Some were amenable to other forms of hospitality—they knew about the bed in back, too.

Mike Gillich is that odd sort of success story Biloxi seems to have produced in great number, a man who rose à la Horatio Alger from humble origins, achieving wealth and status through his own hard, albeit illegal, work. For many years, he labored seven nights a week at his clubs, rising from bed around noon, returning home in the early morning hours after closing time. He never took vacations.

Born six months after the Great Depression began, Gillich was one year younger than Vince Sherry, though he looked older. Gillich started delivering ice for a living at age nine. He lived an undeniably hard life as a child, quitting school and going to work full-time after achieving a sixth-grade education and a threadbare mastery of the written word. This was a source of pride, however, not anguish: His completion of elementary school was more than either of his Yugoslavian immigrant parents had managed in the old country.

As a teenager, he bused tables, then tended bar at the Broadwater Beach Hotel, a long-lived Biloxi resort, legitimate if somewhat faded now, but boasting the Coast's grandest illegal casino in the time of Gillich's youth. It was tolerated—and patronized—by local law enforcement and mobsters alike. Gillich found his mentor at the Broadwater, a professional gambler and bookmaker, W. E. "Water Bill" Sanford. Water Bill looked as if he had just walked right off a riverboat, courtly in manner, merciless at the card table, possessed of a long, handsome face that gave away nothing its owner didn't intend.[1]

Water Bill's criminal contacts, his savvy, and his attitude about never cooperating with a police investigation made him a trusted member of Biloxi's criminal elite, shaping his protégé Gillich's attitudes and career. Mike Gillich might have lacked Water Bill's legendary charisma, but he inherited his many contacts. And the taciturn Mr. Mike's word became gold on The Strip, just like Water Bill's.

In the early sixties, Mike Gillich struck out on his own, using his years of savings to open his first club—featuring strip shows and a bingo hall. He found plentiful demand for his services: The out-of-town conventioneer, the local hood with flash money in his pocket, the Biloxi police chief—all turned up on Gillich's bar stool. In time, Vince Sherry would become a regular as well.

Biloxi was still wide open then, the illegal gambling undisguised, the prostitution all but advertised. It was a time when only one sort of business could thrive on that straight stretch of coastal highway, where a fraternity that would soon become the Dixie Mafia was beginning to nest. Gillich's bingo hall was topped by neon outside, an open advertisement. There is no question about his operation's illegality, but Gillich's club was just one of many, all engaged in the same blatantly crooked activities. Craps and cards were played in the back, next to the trick rooms. Informants told the FBI that Gillich had secret cameras over the prostitutes' beds, filming prominent men for purposes of blackmail. (This has never been proved, however.) In later years, Gillich opened a video store next to the club. A Biloxi policeman once stumbled on a bank of VCRs inside, churning out illegal copies of movies.[2]

Gillich pioneered a practice called "B-drinking" in his club, where the strippers, clad in a negligées or partially unclasped robes, would sidle up to patrons, cooing obsequious nothings. A waitress would then appear, asking, "Would you like to buy the lady a drink?" Conversation continued with a yes, ended with a refusal (though the next stripper in line would then try the same, a process that would continue five, six, or more times with different women until the rube finally said yes to a girl, or left). The strippers talked to customers as long as the flow of overpriced drinks continued—four dollars for about six cents' worth of Kool-Aid over cracked ice.

Each stripper kept track of her sales by collecting the swizzle sticks from every glass of Kool-Aid, which Gillich would count at the end of the night, doling out cash to each girl based upon her productivity. To the customers, each drink bought was worth about three or four minutes of purring, perhaps an occasional rub or pat, before the waitress reappeared and asked the man if he'd buy the lady another. More money led to more action in the back of the club or in the trick room, but even without escalating to actual acts of prostitution, the B-drinking earned tremendous profits—all in violation of city ordinances that banned the practice, but which were never enforced.

As the money poured in, Gillich eventually acquired more clubs—the Golden Nugget and the Dream Room, both located in the same huge complex that housed the bingo hall, and the Horseshoe a few blocks off The Strip. Over the years, he opened, closed, or held a part interest in several other joints, all similar in their seediness and use of striptease acts as fronts for B-drinking, prostitution, and gambling: the Tally Ho, the Jungle Club, the Mint, the Chez Joey, the Wits Inn, El Morocco, and several others, usually in partnership with one or more Dixie Mafia cronies.

Gillich co-owned one of the seedier joints, the Jungle Club, with a Dixie Mafia burglar and hit man, Henry Cook Salisbury. Known on the streets of Biloxi as Little Henry, Salisbury was notorious for his dapper, diminutive stature, his cruelty, and his willingness to kill for a pittance. He was eventually implicated in a plot to murder the police chief of Gulfport at the time, Larkin Smith, allegedly at the behest of another friend and confidant of Gillich's, the corrupt Sheriff Leroy Hobbs. (Smith would succeed Hobbs as sheriff, and would occupy the office at the time of the Sherry murders, while Hobbs went to prison.)[3]

Later, when Little Henry became terminally ill with

cancer while in prison, the charitable Mike Gillich sponsored him for humanitarian parole. Salisbury came home to die in lodgings paid for by Mr. Mike. Once Little Henry was in the ground, the already married Gillich took up with his widow, Frances. Gillich's wife, Marlene, much later divorced him on grounds of habitual cruelty.

Long known as the financier and middleman for the Dixie Mafia, Gillich nevertheless remained untouchable. Shrewdly, Gillich befriended and serviced corrupt members of Gulf Coast law enforcement and government, and for more than twenty-five years, he weathered every attempt to shut down vice on The Strip.

In 1968, the Mississippi Highway Patrol, under the direction of its chief investigator, Rex Armistead, arrested him for lewdness, then blockaded Gillich's Tally Ho with their patrol cars. Gillich outlasted the attempt to shut him down—as did every other strip-club owner in Biloxi.[4] The governor pulled back the patrols after receiving repeated complaints from politicians and business interests on the Coast who worried about lost tourist dollars. A lifelong friend of Gillich's, Justice of the Peace Roy Mattina, dismissed the lewdness charge the same year it was filed.

Gillich's influence with the judicial branch extended to others as well: When a Dixie Mafia burglar, Clifford Hugh Fuller, was arrested for assault with intent to commit murder, Mr. Mike appeared before his old friend Mattina, arguing on Fuller's behalf. Mattina unilaterally lowered the charges at Gillich's request, fined Fuller twenty-five dollars, then set him free. Representation from Mike Gillich could, in the right case before the right judge, accomplish more than any lawyer.

But if being on Gillich's good side had its benefits, anything could happen once his support withdrew. In December 1970, two years after Justice Mattina let him walk, police arrested Cliff Fuller in Georgia for armed robbery. Instead of falling back on his old criminals' support system, Fuller this time said he would cooperate in an investigation of the Dixie Mafia in exchange for leniency. The denouement surprised no one: A few weeks later, a shotgun cut Fuller in half, another Dixie Mafia witness eliminated. He had eaten lunch a few hours earlier with a

one-legged Dixie Mafia hit man named John Ransom, a
perennial presence near Dixie Mafia hits—and a close
friend of both Little Henry and Kirksey Nix. The murder
remains unsolved.

Two years later, another murder case revealed a tangled
web leading back to Mike Gillich and the peg-legged Ransom. William Mulvey and Tracy Johnson, two small-time
crooks, were murdered near Covington, Louisiana—the
scene five years earlier of the Gypsy camp murder. A man
who later confessed to helping with the murders fingered
two Biloxi thugs, friends of Gillich's and Nix's. Investigators learned that Gillich's protégé, Little Henry, had put out
the contract. And John Ransom was seen in the bar with
one of the killers shortly before the murders took place. But
no one was ever charged in the case.[5]

On the day they died, Mulvey and Johnson made several
phone calls from a motel. One of those calls was to Mike
Gillich's telephone. To this day, no one but Mike Gillich
knows why.

The Highway Patrol investigators returned to The Strip in
1972, reporting ten clubs, Gillich's among them, as havens
for vice. They identified Gillich in their intelligence reports
as "a known associate of many felons and fugitives."[6]

The report goaded the city of Biloxi into a reluctant but
well-publicized crackdown. Two hundred eighty-seven
charges were filed against the vice lords of The Strip, an
unprecedented attack by city prosecutors. More than half of
those charges were filed against employees of Gillich's
Golden Nugget and Dream Room.[7] The new mayor of that
era, Jeremiah O'Keefe, a war hero and local funeral home
magnate, reiterated the Gulf Coast politician's eternal
promise: to clean up The Strip.

And for a short while, he did. The clubs either shut down
or stuck to legitimate, if sleazy, business. But though
O'Keefe's police department appeared to get results for a
time, many of the arrests turned out to be mere showpieces.
Once the charges against Gillich and his cronies progressed
beyond the headlines and into court, many were dismissed
or dropped through a failure to prosecute. Many of the
dismissals came at the order of a newly appointed judge, the
youngest in Mississippi at the time, County Court Judge

Pete Halat, who found portions of the city's anti-B-drinking law unconstitutionally vague. It was during his time on the bench that Halat first became acquainted with Vince Sherry.

By the mid-seventies, the flurry of vice busts had ended, a return to business as usual, with more strip clubs fronting for prostitution and gambling than ever before. A new Biloxi police chief appointed by Mayor O'Keefe—later elected to the state legislature—befriended some of the vice lords, then ordered an end to the investigation of strip joints and gambling houses. In a series of scathing articles on Gulf Coast corruption, the capital city newspaper, the Jackson *Clarion Ledger,* savaged Biloxi in 1981, virtually indicting the entire community, arguing that nothing had changed in thirty years, that Biloxi sat in a time warp of speakeasies and gin mills. It was intensely embarrassing to Mississippi's second largest city. One article—reported as fact, not opinion—flatly stated "Biloxi, more than any area of the state, has ingrained social mores which render an already handicapped Police Department a virtual cripple—mores formed in a community where even churches are involved in gambling and there is a general acceptance of some vice because it enhances the town's reputation as a resort."

This was the Biloxi Gerald Blessey inherited when he took office as mayor in 1981, elected, like so many of his predecessors, on a vow to clean up his city. But this time, the politician seemed to keep his promise—mostly. The fortunes of the vice lords on The Strip really did change for the worse, after decades of immunity and profits. Under the Blessey administration, the city police department canceled its hands-off policy and launched undercover vice investigations. To no one's surprise, investigators found prostitution and other crime rampant in the strip joints. One by one, many of the joints were shut down as the city secured court injunctions against their illegal operations. This time, the joints stayed closed. Their empty shells stood as mute testimony to Biloxi's past, walls sagging like old cartons set out for the trashman.

By the end of 1986, only three strip joints still operated in Biloxi: the Horseshoe Lounge, the Golden Nugget, and the Dream Room. They were all Mike Gillich's joints. He had the vice business all to himself.

Many believed this monopoly showed official favoritism toward Mike Gillich, though city officials denied this. Critics saw many connections between Gillich and the Blessey administration. Mayor Blessey hired Gillich's daughter Tina fresh from law school as his administrative assistant. Blessey appointed Gillich's son-in-law to a city court judgeship. The city awarded Gillich's nephew Andrew a lucrative computer contract. Even the staid Biloxi law firm that gave Blessey his professional start as a young lawyer was tied by marriage to Gillich.[8]

Time after time, city prosecutors chosen by the mayor told patrolmen and detectives who went after Gillich that they lacked sufficient evidence to justify prosecution. Yet the investigators involved in probing the clubs swore they had uncovered exactly the same evidence against Gillich's joints as they had against his competitors, if not worse. Indeed, Gillich hired many of the same hookers put out of work by the other club shutdowns, expanding his hours and his shows, invulnerable as always.[9]

At least part of his ability to elude the police lay in an early warning system he devised to learn of upcoming raids. Federal prosecutors have alleged that Gillich's old friend Roy Mattina, who had moved from justice court to a seat on the Biloxi City Council, passed on tips about undercover police operations and raid plans.[10] Mattina, who regularly enjoyed coffee and doughnuts with Gillich at the Krispy Kreme on The Strip, would receive information from Biloxi police officials, then Gillich would give the hookers and gamblers the appropriate night off. The cops would show up at the Nugget or the Dream Room and find no hooking, no B-drinking, no gambling. And there would be Mike Gillich, smiling, nodding, yes-sirring the policemen, offering them anything they wanted. "When are you guys gonna learn?" Gillich would say. "I run a clean operation." Mattina later pleaded guilty to perjury for lying about the tips to a federal grand jury, but he was off the council by then, and Gillich had other sources of protection.[11]

On the few occasions police managed to earn a conviction against Gillich—as they did with an illegal gambling charge in 1973—Mr. Mike found a way out. A few years after the conviction, he walked into the courtroom of County Judge

Pete Halat, who expunged Gillich's record. Although he had been Gillich's friend most of his adult life—arguably a conflict of interest—Halat entered a court order that had the legal effect of wiping out any criminal conviction in Gillich's history.[12]

Gillich knew how to treat his friends. When Halat re-entered private practice in 1976, then took on Vince Sherry as his partner in 1981, Pete Halat found in Mike Gillich a ready source of legal business and referrals—starting with Kirksey McCord Nix.

CHAPTER 17

I have a new car, a Mercedes," Pete Halat said. He was slouching in the back of a Biloxi courtroom, watching a probation revocation hearing and jawing amiably with Biloxi Police Detective Gerald Forbes during lulls in the action. The car was fast, luxurious, a dream, Halat said. "It's really hot. You should see it."

Forbes nodded. Certain attorneys, he had noticed, loved to display their success in the form of flashy cars. Halat was no exception. The detective drove an old Ford himself, but he could appreciate a nice car when he saw one. After the hearing ended, he walked outside in time to watch Halat climb into the blue Mercedes. It was an older model sedan, a 1977, but in perfect condition, new paint and leather, a showy statement of prosperity.

Months later, Forbes saw the same car parked in the lot in front of the Golden Nugget. On a whim, the detective decided to run the tags through the police computer.

The car Pete Halat had been so proud of, Forbes learned, came back registered to Mike Gillich, though the address given was the post office box for the Halat and Sherry law firm. Halat had never owned the car—it was in Gillich's name even from the time Forbes had first seen it during the probation hearing in 1986. The detective knew the lawyer and the strip-club king were close, but letting a known crime figure provide you with a luxury vehicle seemed to the detective a bit much. Not illegal, certainly—though it couldn't help but make a cop suspicious.[1]

What Forbes could not know at the time was that the car did not really belong to Mike Gillich, either. Mr. Mike had simply agreed to do a friend a favor and put the title in his name. Halat's law firm had set it all up, and the real owner said the attorney could drive it whenever he wished.

The real owner was Kirksey Nix. The Mercedes was just one expensive purchase Pete Halat helped the convict make from behind Angola's prison walls. He also helped arrange for repainting the car, reupholstering it—he even drove the luxury sedan to Angola, Louisiana, with Gillich beside him, so Nix could look out from his cellblock window and see the car he coveted but could enjoy only vicariously. "My body might be in prison," he was fond of saying, "but I like to keep my mind on the streets."

When, years later, Pete Halat was forced to explain publicly why he drove a convicted murderer's Mercedes for two years, his reply came glib and guiltless:

"I'd much rather use his car than my car."[2]

If Vince Sherry was the gregarious scholar, Pete Halat, with his sharp features and nervous hands, was the man with connections. Smart, organized, and tough, Halat was the practical one, the man who made the partnership work. Vince might have known the law, but Halat brought in the business.

Pete's forte lay in knowing how to work his hometown. He knew which judges would issue favorable rulings, which cops and crooks made viable witnesses, and which ones could be counted on to cave in under pressure—priceless knowledge for a criminal defense attorney. Halat could be brilliant in the courtroom, capable of captivating a jury, a little smug, a little self-righteous, yet still convincing. He was one of a handful of lawyers in Biloxi you turned to when you were charged with some major felony. Most big drug cases on the Coast ended up defended by the Halat and Sherry law firm.

Though Halat was a Democrat, he became instrumental in Margaret Sherry's campaign for mayor in 1985, with the election bid managed from the law office. When she lost and became Mayor Blessey's personal nightmare, Halat sometimes accompanied her to city council meetings when she blasted administration policies.

One year after the election, it was Halat's friendship and influence with then-Mississippi Governor Bill Allain that earned Vince his appointment to the bench, infuriating Blessey, who had wanted someone else in the post, and who questioned the honesty and integrity of the state's newest jurist.

Almost everyone who knew Vince and Margaret Sherry and Pete Halat considered them close friends. Given this outward image, few people knew of the strain that had developed in the Sherrys' relationship with Pete Halat. Not even the Sherry children were aware of it. But it was there— a distrust both Margaret and Vince spoke of to a few select people. The detectives investigating the Sherry murders knew nothing of this. Halat denied it outright. And those who did know kept silent—for a while.

Even so, Pete Halat seemed the more hard-bitten of the two partners. Vince's devotion to Pete seemed complete, but some of his friends wondered if the reverse were true. Halat always griped that Vince behaved too kindly toward people who meant him ill. Someone slaps you in the face, and you say have a nice day, Pete would complain to Vince. Halat could never do that. He believed in hitting back. You don't survive in Biloxi if you're not willing to hit back.

A native Biloxian, born to the same Yugoslavian immigrant enclave that produced most of the close-knit good ol' boys who ran the city, Halat grew up poor, with a support system of half brothers and half sisters from his mother's several marriages—providing invaluable connections for Halat in later life.

The Halat family was friendly with the Gilliches as long as Halat could remember. An uncle of Halat's, a longtime bell captain at the Buena Vista Hotel near The Strip, was an old friend of Gillich's. Halat's father ran a little lounge just off The Strip, the International. Halat's mother worked

many years as secretary to one of the county's most legendary corrupt sheriffs, Eddie McDonnell, known for his ties
to the Dixie Mafia.

Pete worked his way through law school, then received a
political plum appointment to the bench in the 1970s, after
campaigning on behalf of the new governor. He became the
youngest county judge in Mississippi.

During his five-year tenure on the bench, he endeared
himself to Mr. Mike by becoming an obstacle to vice cases,
helping curb one of the many attempted crackdowns by his
dismissal of charges. In 1975, his last full year on the bench,
he expunged Gillich's record, briefly considered a run for
Mississippi Attorney General—the traditional stepping-
stone to the governor's mansion—then decided on the
more financially rewarding venue of criminal defense work.
He opened his own private practice, forming a partnership
with Mike Gillich's son-in-law, Keith Pisarich. There would
be time for politics later, Halat decided.

As he would for Vince Sherry, Mike Gillich became a
lucrative source of referrals for Halat. Pete represented
Gillich's friend Little Henry. Halat also defended various
strip clubs from closure.

In 1979, before Vince Sherry replaced Pisarich as Halat's
partner, Gillich provided a most important referral: He put
Halat and Kirksey Nix together by telephone. Nix had an
upcoming hearing before Louisiana's Board of Pardons—
an agency that would be the subject of a parole-buying
scandal a few years later. Nix had high hopes of having his
life sentence commuted at this hearing, and he was busy
lining up witnesses. He hired Halat to help.

While Halat undertook some legal work for Nix at this
time, it seemed minimal. There really was not much an
attorney in Mississippi could do for a convicted felon
serving time in Louisiana. Instead, Halat undertook a
variety of other jobs for Nix, safeguarding some of Nix's
income, assisting him in major purchases, and performing
other personal tasks.

Halat's wife, Sandra, an artist and real-estate agent,
worked with Halat to help Nix purchase a $60,000 home
with swimming pool in Ocean Springs, a picturesque coastal community across the bay from Biloxi. Halat's wife

found the house and helped negotiate the sale, then Halat served as trustee for the $48,000 mortgage Nix secured. Halat would later recall that Nix wanted to buy a home so his mother, an attorney, could be close to him while she worked on his pardon. Why he chose Ocean Springs, a two-hour drive from the pardon board in Baton Rouge, and more than four hours from Nix's cell in Angola, was never explained. Nor did Halat ever inquire where a lifer like Nix, whose job at Angola paid, literally, pennies an hour, found enough money to buy a house.

Halat next set up a trust fund for Nix, administered by his secretary, Ann Kriss. The $524 monthly mortgage payments came out of this fund and, when Nix's mother failed to make the move, rent payments from tenants living in the house were deposited in the account. Nix would also periodically direct Halat's secretary to send checks to different people—relatives, girlfriends, ex-convicts. At other times, strangers would appear in the law office, laying down cash to go into Nix's account, no questions asked or answered. Mike Gillich sent money over to the office as well for Junior Nix's account, again offering no explanation. And again, Halat asked for none. Repairs, upholstery, and maintenance for the Mercedes Halat drove also came out of the fund. According to a ledger maintained in Halat's office—the one Lynne had watched his secretary copy—the account received about $71,000 between January 1985 and May 1988.

Nix had stayed busy during his incarceration. He struck up a jailhouse romance with an old friend, Jan Newman, whom he had met in Atlanta a year before the Corso killing. Newman had attended Nix's sentencing in New Orleans with her ten-year-old daughter, Kellye Dawn, and later visited him in Leavenworth, then Angola. She eventually married Nix over the telephone. The marriage was later annulled, but Nix adopted Kellye as his stepdaughter, and stayed in touch with her, sending her gifts and letters. At about the same time Nix hired Pete Halat as his lawyer, he convinced Kellye's mother to move to Biloxi, where he arranged to support them through his trust account and with direct payments from his "second father," Mike Gillich.[3]

In 1980, just before Nix's pardon hearing, Newman and
Kellye were supposed to drive to Louisiana and deliver a
bribe to an associate of the governor to ensure Nix's
release.[4] Nix could almost smell freedom, but at around the
same time, an informant at Angola tipped off authorities in
Louisiana, warning Gene Fields, the former New Orleans
detective who helped bust Nix in the Corso killing, that Nix
was planning to deliver a suitcase of money to the governor
to buy his pardon. Fields got word to Marian Corso, who
immediately contacted the Louisiana governor, threatening
him with publicity and exposure if the still-infamous Nix
got out. The governor supposedly promised Nix would
never go free as long as he held office, and the pardon bid
failed.[5] But even with the pardon denied—the original
reason for Nix hiring Pete Halat—the lawyer continued to
work for Nix.

In 1983, when Kellye turned twenty-two and her mother
left the picture, Nix announced he had fallen in love with
his blond, voluptuous, chronically immature stepdaughter,
and he proposed marriage. Kellye was initially reluctant.
She already had a boyfriend to supply her with the cocaine
she increasingly desired. But she also had had two un-
wanted pregnancies and abortions because of him. When
she was arrested for drunken driving and drug possession
and she told Nix about her troubles during one of their daily
telephone conversations, he said, "I can have Pete Halat
take care of everything—if you marry me."

"Okay," Kellye answered. "Why not?" She had decided
she almost liked the idea of a husband in prison—she could
enjoy the benefits of his money and property, and still date,
party, do whatever she wanted.

When Nix told Halat about his marriage plans, the
lawyer, who would later characterize his relationship with
Nix as strictly professional, tried to talk him out of marrying his own stepdaughter. "Man, you got to be nuts," he told
the convict. Then he hopped in a car and drove with Mike
Gillich to Angola where, he would later claim, the strip-club
magnate and the defense attorney attempted to talk Nix out
of the marriage. Nix, however, was adamant.[6]

"I love her," Nix said. "I'm crazy in love with her."

In May 1983, Halat arranged Nix's second telephone

marriage. It is not clear who produced the license, but it contained a phony address for Nix, as well as phony blood tests for the bride and groom. The ceremony was bare bones, held in the chambers of a judge who was a friend of Halat's, with Pete as the only witness. The judge simply asked if Nix accepted Kellye as his wife, and if Kellye accepted Nix. Junior's voice crackled over the speaker-phone, "I do," and it was done.

Except, it wasn't quite done. Halat failed to file the marriage certificate for almost four years, keeping it in his office instead. The marriage did not become official until March 1987, when the certificate was filed with the clerk of Harrison County. Halat would later recall that Nix directed him to file it then, without explanation.

It was precisely that time that Nix's criminal enterprises began falling apart, with many of his associates, including Kellye, coming under scrutiny. The feds were onto his scam by then. But with the marriage made official, Nix seemingly had one less worry—a wife cannot be compelled to testify against her husband.

After the telephone nuptials, Halat continued to bail Kellye out of trouble: when she was picked up by the FBI in Baton Rouge; when some sheriff's deputies beat her badly after she drunkenly resisted arrest in mid-1984; and again during the Christmas holidays in 1984, when she was busted for cocaine possession. She was pregnant at the time of this last arrest, still inhaling the white powder. Used syringes were found in her apartment. Kirksey Nix's wife was a mess.

Once Halat arranged to bail her out over Christmas, Nix promised Kellye that everything would be taken care of. A few months later, the police lab reported back that the substance seized from Kellye at the time of her arrest had been baking soda, not cocaine.[7]

Kellye's chronically irresponsible behavior led to loud arguments and periodic estrangements with Nix. During one prolonged separation, a disgusted Nix invited another young woman to Biloxi—LaRa Sharpe, whose mother had run the Arkansas bordello Nix frequented as a free man, and who had harbored a childhood crush for him. Grown up now, buxom, with long blond hair so bleached it appeared white, LaRa came to the Coast in August 1985, and immediately took up residence in the Halat and Sherry law firm, working on Nix's case, as well as his extensive illegal enterprises.

Arrangements with LaRa showed just how accommodating Halat could be when it came to his client Kirksey. He never put LaRa on the payroll, but she had space in the office, a computer setup, and access to the phones, allowing her daily contact with Nix. She came and went as she pleased. She, like Kellye, drew generous support from Nix's never-empty trust fund. Halat also shared with LaRa a bank safe deposit box, which contained cash and jewelry, including a large diamond ring that had belonged to Nix's first wife, Sandra.

Though she apparently was never a paid member of his staff, Halat signed at least eleven sworn affidavits identifying LaRa as a paralegal in his employ. LaRa used these false sworn statements to visit Nix in Angola in private rooms reserved for legal conferences, rather than in the communal visiting areas where guards listened and watched. These documents enabled LaRa to smuggle in marijuana, nude photos of herself, and, most important, photos and papers to further Nix's lucrative prison scams—all thanks to documents signed by Kirksey's man in Biloxi, Peter Halat.

CHAPTER 18

Be my summer lover, the personal ad implored. *Cute, slim, seeks sincere, warm relationship. Willing to relocate for the summer or permanently if love blooms. I'm romantic, cuddly, shy and need someone special in my life.*
James Dickey couldn't have imagined a more appealing

advertisement, not if he had written it himself. The writer of this personal sought "a torrid summer affair that may change both our lives for the better," but also added, "looks and age are not as important as what's inside." Summer lover didn't even smoke.

At age fifty-four, divorced, with two grown children long gone from the house, Dickey had been feeling the cold gnaw of loneliness each night when he came home from work. He had just broken up with his live-in lover of seven years. There had been no warning, no argument, no hint of the relationship's end: Dickey had just returned from his reporter's desk at the San Jose *Mercury News* one evening to find an empty closet and a good-bye note on the kitchen table. Anger hit first, then depression, months of it, almost crippling. He toyed with the idea of suicide.

Then, idly scanning the personals, the long, thin columns of fine print one after another providing a testament to human desperation, he saw "Summer Lover." Something in that ad clicked for him, making him want to reach out from his sadness and apathy. He had never really considered seeking solace through the personals before. It seemed so melancholy and random, perhaps dangerous. The other personals he had read seemed alternately silly or grotesque, embarrassingly graphic or sickly sweet. But not this one. Someone out there had aimed right for him, uncannily on target. Why not give it a try?

Dickey penned a response, agonizing over the wording, wanting to get it just right. He, too, needed someone, maybe for the summer. Maybe more. And as far as he could tell, the author of that personal ad, Eddie Johnson, twenty-three-year-old gay white male, sounded just the answer to James Dickey's prayers.

He should have known better.

Dickey had come out of the closet nine years earlier, not long after his divorce. After that, he began covering gay issues for his newspaper, which, in the San Francisco Bay Area in which he lived and worked, quickly became a big beat. He considered himself a gay activist, educated and well-informed. As a journalist, he had heard about many kinds of scams—con games perpetrated on the elderly, on the terminally ill, on inexperienced investors and, yes, on lonely gay men. Hell, he had reported on that sort of thing before.

Yet Dickey still fell for it. Hard. Before he was done, Dickey's Visa card would be overdrawn, his bank credit exhausted. He refinanced his house, depleted his savings. He spent more than seventeen thousand dollars to bring Eddie to him, with nothing to show for it in the end but immense debts and that same empty closet and lonely house. And two thousand miles away, Kirksey McCord Nix moved seventeen thousand dollars closer to freedom.

But who could have known? The note Dickey had received in response to his letter seemed so convincing, so genuine and heartfelt. "Got your letter," Eddie had gushed. "It made my day."

There was a problem, though, Eddie wrote. Since his personal ad had run in the *Advocate,* a national gay magazine, his one remaining parent had died, then he'd been in a car accident. The wreck had led to some charges against him, and he had landed in what he called a "vocational program." He promised to call collect and explain everything to Dickey in more detail, urging him to be patient. That was his only initial request: not for money, just patience.

"Maybe we can add a little sunshine in each other's lives," Eddie wrote in his typed letter. "The summer is not over yet!"

The envelope had a Lubbock, Texas, post office box for a return address. Inside, a picture of a boyishly handsome young man with a glowing smile, wearing a university T-shirt bearing the logo "Central Michigan," beamed at Dickey. "I hope you like it," Eddie shyly added.

He called a few days later, as promised. His voice sounded young, hopeful, almost bubbly, despite his upsetting circumstances. Dickey was charmed.

Eddie said he was calling collect from the Shenandoah Ranch, where he had been sentenced to a rehabilitation program for first offenders. He hadn't just wrecked a car—he had been accused of stealing it. The charge was bogus, Eddie swore; he said he had permission to borrow the car. Unfortunately, the owner—either out of anger at the wreck or because he was scamming his insurance company—had reported it stolen. And Eddie now bore the consequences.

"They'll release me if someone will provide me a home and help getting a job," Eddie explained. "I can't wait to get out of here. It's all a mistake."

With Dickey promising to help any way he could, they agreed Eddie would come to California. Later, Eddie's supervisor at the ranch, Ben Dickerson, called. Eddie Johnson was different from the other inmates, Dickerson confided, his Texas accent gruff but his words kindly. "Eddie's a good boy," Dickerson said, "not like the other criminals we get here. He just needs some guidance." No one asked him for money, sealing the air of legitimacy. If they had, he would have said no.

Over the next several days, Dickey exchanged many calls with the ranch, which he learned was run by a quasi-public agency called FNW. The Texas number he called was always answered, "FNW," but the receptionist invariably said she'd have to take a message because Mr. Dickerson was busy. Dickerson would call back later in the day.

Eventually, Dickey agreed to wire $491 to pay for Eddie's airfare to California. He was directed to send it to Eddie's social worker, Martha White, which he did. Dickerson then called to give him the time Eddie's flight was to arrive in San Jose.

A few hours before arrival time, Dickerson called back. Unbeknownst to Dickey, the scam had kicked into a higher gear: Contrary to earlier promises, the owner of the wrecked car had filed formal theft charges. Eddie had been hauled to jail practically as he was boarding the plane, Dickey was told. "If you could just pay the fines, restitution, and court costs—another five hundred seventy-four dollars—Eddie can still come," Dickerson explained.

Then Eddie got on the phone and promised to pay back every penny. He sounded near tears. In the background, the institutional sounds of a jail could be heard, the clanging of metal doors shutting, the murmur of men confined like laboratory animals, impersonal and suffocating.

"Do you hear that?" Eddie whispered, weeping in earnest now. "I hate this place."

Dickey sent the money.

And so it went, one problem after another impeding Eddie's valiant attempts to get to San Jose, always plausible, always infuriating, always costing Dickey more. An incompetent travel agent landed the newly released Eddie in New Orleans instead of San Jose. Eddie then got into a scuffle with two young thugs while he awaited his flight. They wanted two diamond rings that had been his mother's, a weepy Eddie told Dickey. "I should never have taken them out to look at them," he said. "I was just thinking of my mom."

In the ensuing fight, several video game machines got damaged and one of the thugs dropped a baggie of marijuana. Now Eddie was locked up for drugs and criminal damage.

Through repeated conversations with New Orleans Airport Police Lieutenant Roy Garland, Dickey learned that Eddie had tested negative for drugs, but that the two thugs—both juveniles—had accused him of owning the pot. Worse, their parents were pressing charges against Eddie for contributing to their delinquency. Garland said it was all ridiculous and that he believed Eddie, but he had no choice in the matter. The system had taken over, and he had to arrest Eddie. The policeman had taken a liking to him, however, and he said he was protecting Eddie by keeping him in an airport immigration cell, rather than sending him to jail, where he would become a certain target for sexual assault. Dickey found himself thanking the lieutenant for his concern.

"Now, if you would just send his bond money, I can get Eddie on a plane to California tomorrow," Garland told him. "You'll get it back when this is all cleared up."

Two thousand dollars later, Eddie was supposed to be on his way. Instead, Lieutenant Garland called once again. Overnight, Eddie had been sexually attacked by a Haitian immigrant. Then a sobbing Eddie got on the phone, describing the open sores all over his assailant's body. He was terrified of contracting hepatitis or AIDS. Eddie had fought back, only to be charged with assault himself. More bond money would be required, or he'd never get out, he wept.

Garland said the new bond would be five thousand dollars. When Dickey began to protest, however, the police lieutenant quickly said, Don't worry, I can find another judge to lower it to twenty-eight hundred. Dickey was grateful. He sent the money.

More glitches followed as the trip from Lubbock to California took on Homeric proportions. Whenever Dickey objected to a requested payment, he would be told that if he stopped now, everything he had spent previously would be lost, and Eddie would land back in Lubbock where he had started. But one more payment, and you'll get everything back, they kept telling him. "Eddie will be safe in California," Dickerson said, "and you'll be repaid. The bail bonds will be released." Eddie promised to go to work and sell his mother's rings to repay him. Dickey couldn't say no, even when he began to suspect he was being taken. Whatever was happening, it was the system's fault. Poor Eddie needed help.

When his credit ran out and he had no more money to give, Dickey contacted a gay rights organization, looking for legal help for Eddie. They put him in touch with a lawyer in New Orleans, where Eddie was still trapped. The lawyer would do *pro bono* work in such cases.

But as Dickey spoke to the attorney and began describing the Eddie Johnson saga—articulating it aloud for the first time—he began to realize how insane it all sounded. The lawyer quietly confirmed his fears even as Dickey's gorge began to rise. There were no holding cells or police lieutenants at the New Orleans airport, the lawyer explained. Never had been. A few quick phone calls revealed more lies: There was no Lieutenant Garland in the New Orleans Police Department, no Shenandoah Ranch in Lubbock, and no FNW anywhere. The telephone number for FNW was simply a private answering service in Texas, which greeted calls in the manner it was paid to answer them, forwarding messages to an anonymous customer out of state.

When his phone bill came at the end of the month, the key to this bewildering puzzle spilled out on his kitchen table. Dickey saw no collect calls from Eddie in Texas and New Orleans, though there should have been dozens of such toll charges. Instead, he found a series of collect calls from somewhere called Tunica, Louisiana. The phone company told him the rest: the Tunica numbers on his bill belonged to pay phones at the Louisiana State Penitentiary at Angola. Any one of five thousand inmates could have telephoned him, posing as Eddie Johnson.

Dickey never heard from Eddie again. He reported his experience to the police, but no one was interested in hearing about Louisiana inmates preying on a gullible homosexual. So he ate his losses and got on with his life.

Dickey had no way of knowing it, but Kirksey Nix, whose range of disguised voices was beautifully practiced and astonishingly diverse, had been Eddie Johnson. He had also been Roy Garland. And Ben Dickerson. And just about everyone else Dickey had spoken to, except Martha White, who, phone records revealed, had been in New Orleans, not Texas, when speaking with Dickey. The money orders had been picked up by White, the wife of a criminal cohort of Nix's, and by the real Roy Garland, an Angola parolee, at Western Union offices in New Orleans and Biloxi, Mississippi. The recipient of a Western Union money order can pick it up anywhere in the world, it turned out, not just the Lubbock office where Dickey had directed his. The money then vanished, untraceable and clean. Martha White and Roy Garland were just two soldiers in an army Nix had assembled to fleece the Jim Dickeys of the world.

And there were thousands of other victims just like him, with more discovered every day.

"Whoever Eddie was," Dickey would later say, "he is very, very perceptive. He knew just what to say, just what to do, to hook me. And he really hooked me. They appealed to my desire to help someone else. They realized I am a rescuer by nature. I couldn't abandon it. And they knew that."[1]

In its 114-year history, the Angola penitentiary has borne a number of unflattering titles: It has been the nation's bloodiest prison, the nation's most brutal prison, the nation's most corrupt prison. Men have died of exhaustion, exposure, and starvation there, as concentration camp conditions wasted their bodies and destroyed their dignity. In its earliest days, guards with rifles and whips stood by as the convicts in their black and white stripes built levees on the malarial banks of the Mississippi, deadly epidemics of yellow fever sweeping through their ranks. The Angola cemetery is filled with crude crosses and headstones dating

back to that era—and from much more recent days—
etched with inmate numbers memorializing lonely graves
by the side of a prison road. A small picnic area was tacked
on to the cemetery at some point, so trustees could barbecue hamburgers with their families in full view of the
forgotten dead. That Kirksey Nix could survive and prosper
in such a place so long, bending to his will an institution
designed to punish and degrade, bears witness to his cun-
ning and strength and, most of all, to his persistence.
Thanks to him comes the newest addition to Angola's
bloody, corrupt reputation: The prison became home to the
nation's most lucrative inmate confidence scams.[2]

Even its name has a dark history: Angola was the region
of Africa from which slaves were forcibly exported to work
the land during its plantation days, before it was converted
to a prison. At eighteen thousand acres, Angola is now the
physically largest penitentiary in the nation. Surrounded on
three sides by a U-shaped section of the Mississippi River,
and on the fourth side by the Tunica wilderness, it is
virtually escape-proof—not because of its high walls (there
are none) or its imposing fences (simple chain-link topped
by barbed wire), but because there is nowhere to go from
there. Angola is isolated from civilization, a world unto
itself, with its own water supply, its own cattle, its own
crops, even a school, houses, and clapboard church for staff.
The nearest town, St. Francisville, with its shade trees and
wide porches, once home to John James Audubon, is more
than twenty miles distant. The only road to the prison from
St. Francisville ends at Angola's unimposing and gateless
front entrance, whose peeling brown guard shack and dusty
parking area resembles more than anything else an aged
rural service station.

The prisoners are confined in "camps" scattered throughout Angola—separate barrackslike, self-contained com-
pounds spread throughout the grounds instead of one
massive lockup for the fifty-two hundred prisoners. The cell
blocks grow inhumanly hot in summer, the inmates locked
inside lying on the concrete floors and dousing themselves
with buckets of water to survive the suffocating heat.

Behavioral problems are confined to Angola's extended
lockdown tiers, the modern version of solitary confinement,
where they are fed "the Loaf." The Loaf is a nutritionally

balanced meal—meat, vegetables, bread, starch, dessert—
liquefied in a blender, then baked into a dense square that
can be imbibed by hand, without need of potentially
dangerous utensils. Hard cases get water and the Loaf until
they learn to behave. Otherwise, they are kept twenty-three
hours a day inside their barren but constitutionally sized
and ventilated cells, a civilized, tortuous confinement. A
few meals of the Loaf accompanied by virtual sensory
deprivation, and most prisoners, even the psychopaths, are
ready to agree to anything.[3]

Such recent innovations aside, some things at Angola
have never changed. Stepping onto its grounds, once you
pass the deceptively charming flower gardens and white rail
fences near the main gate, is to plummet into another
century. Long lines of inmates dressed in stained blue
denim stiff with dried sweat, with hoes, spades, and picks
slung on their shoulders, still can be seen marching two
abreast into the fields to labor for two cents an hour, a sight
unchanged in fifty years. Guards on horseback cradling
shotguns, black leather boots and saddles creaking, still lope
alongside the work gangs, just as they have for decades.
Some guards still accept money, jewelry, or other forms of
payment to allow convicts to smuggle drugs, sell bootleg
alcohol, or, as in the case of Kirksey Nix, to conduct ever
widening criminal enterprises.

It was Nix's good fortune to enter Angola during a cycle
of reform, an era of extended inmate privileges, improved
medical care, and guaranteed constitutional rights. Nix's
genius lay in putting to use the resources he had at hand
within Angola. Unlike other convicts, who lay in their
bunks plotting their next big score as soon as they got out,
Nix chose not to wait. Prison would not impede Kirksey
Nix. As soon as he arrived, he took a quick survey: He had
access to the mail, to underpaid and easily coerced guards,
to a network of criminals on both sides of the prison fence,
and, most important, he had ready access to telephones.
The latest reforms at Angola guaranteed all inmates unlim-
ited access to phones for making calls related to their
criminal cases—legal calls, in prison parlance. Nix knew
the Halat and Sherry law firm would be the perfect vehicle
for getting him access to the phone whenever he wanted. All

he needed were the right victims. It didn't take long for him to choose that most vulnerable set of people—the lonely—as his targets.

In fairness, Junior did not conceive of the lonely-hearts scam that defrauded men like James Dickey. He merely raised it to an art form. The corrupt and pliant prison around him, so oppressive to most other inmates, nurtured Nix's criminal genius, making him creative and bold in ways he had never imagined as a free man.

Junior Nix learned the rudiments of the scam from an old friend who was awaiting him when he got to Angola. His one-time burglary partner and Dixie Mafia crony, Bobby Joe Faubion, had been in Angola since 1974, convicted of murder, then of kidnapping and shooting a state trooper. He had been arrested during a spectacular escape and flight that ended with Faubion in a ditch and Rex Armistead's pistol trained on his heart. He had already been sentenced to life in Mississippi for murdering a horse breeder there, but Louisiana held on to him, imprisoning Faubion without possibility of parole.

Faubion was known as "Fabian" at Angola, having changed the spelling of his last name years earlier to thwart police records searches. (Slight changes in names or birth dates can totally confound the literal world of police and courthouse file clerks. Fabian managed to be convicted as a first-time offender three times through this simple method.)

Fabian's nickname on the street was "Satin"—based, he claimed, on his old stage name from when he supposedly made a legitimate dollar singing the blues as Sonny Satin. Comrades say the moniker owed more to the satin-smooth delivery he used when lying, his story molding to the contours of a situation like a fine German sports car hugging the Autobahn. When it came to robbing, burgling, shooting, and stealing, Fabian turned out to be fairly incompetent—he had been caught time and again. But when it came to lying and conning, Bobby Joe Fabian had few equals. He worked the phones so often and so well to further his scams, he earned a new nickname at Angola: Mr. AT&T.

The scheme he used was simple and neat. He would respond to personal ads from women seeking male companionship, concocting a plausible reason why they should send him several hundred dollars so he could come visit them. Sometimes he would disguise his voice as a woman's and answer ads from men seeking girlfriends. For them, he would admit to being in a prison—albeit a woman's prison—spelling his name "Bobbie Jo" in correspondence, a good country girl's name. He collected pictures of inmates' girlfriends, or had associates on the street snap pictures of passers-by. Then he would have hundreds of copies made to send to the marks. As the inmates involved in the scams multiplied, they began trading the photos, keeping stacks of them in their cells, packs wrapped tight with rubber bands thick as a child's baseball card collection. Later, he published his own ads, then ripped off the respondents.

"You want to get in on a good thing, Junior?" Fabian asked Nix soon after he arrived at Angola. "We can partner up, make some serious moolah, ya see." Bobby Joe Fabian had a tendency to end every sentence with a "ya see."

"I see," Nix responded with a laugh. "Let's do it."

Nix had plenty of time to devote to perfecting the scam. His supposed sentence to hard labor for murdering Frank Corso went quickly by the wayside. He pestered the prison doctors with frequent sick calls, claiming his gunshot wound had left him in pain and incapable of any heavy duties. One of the prison doctors finally acquiesced and assigned him permanently to light duties—cleaning up the dormitories and other small tasks, which he quickly paid other convicts to handle. Nix's only hard labors at Angola went toward his newest criminal career.

Exactly when Nix began profiting from prison scams is unclear. He had some legitimate sources of income that helped him disguise his illegal profits—a life insurance policy that paid forty thousand dollars for his wife Sandra's death, and an inheritance when Judge Nix died in 1979. Clearly, though, a substantial income with no legitimate source began by the early 1980s, as he purchased his house on the Coast, a new Trans Am for Kellye Dawn, his Mercedes, a dune buggy, several other cars and motorcycles, and a houseful of imported furniture, all the while providing generous allowances—several thousand a month—to both Kellye and LaRa Sharpe. At the scams' height, Nix would later claim, his monthly *expenses* reached twelve thousand dollars.

Nix began scamming straight men looking for women at least as early as 1982.[4] By 1983, Nix hit upon homosexual lonely hearts as easier and more profitable victims for his con game. Not only did his gay "tricks," as he called scam victims, tend to be older and therefore to have more money, but if he was lucky enough to hit upon a victim who was still in the closet, he could later blackmail him with the threat of exposure. It also eliminated the need to pretend to be a woman. Nix and his fellow scammers collected stacks of photos of willowy young men to insert in their letters instead of female cheesecake—the photo of Eddie Johnson that James Dickey received was a particularly popular one, copied several thousand times.

By 1984, Nix had expanded his operations, employing confederates on the outside. He used free-world post office boxes, mail drops, and answering services to make contact with his tricks, then he would have them send money via Western Union. All he needed were helpers—"road dogs" in prison parlance—to make the pickups, to be his arms and legs. He had more than a dozen road dogs working for him, earning ten to fifteen percent of the cash they picked up, plus expenses. Other confederates helped him work the phones, posing as the policemen and social workers essential to lending the aura of authenticity to his scheme, freeing him from having to play all the characters.

Nix typed up elaborate scripts, distributing them to other inmates and to his free-world helpers. His information packets were professional in scope, containing complete dialogue suggestions for posing as policemen, lawyers, social workers, and relatives. The scripts provided suggested backup lies to use when tricks balked at a money request, and extensive biographies of young men and women, so Nix could remember the background of characters he was playing.

The scams also demanded elaborate cover-ups. Nix recruited other inmates to receive his mail in their names so he would not have to claim suspiciously huge quantities of letters himself. On other occasions, materials came to him disguised as thick packets of legal mail with return addresses of the Halat and Sherry law firm and other law

offices—Sometimes LaRa purloined envelopes and station-
ery with legal letterheads.[5] Other inmates hid his scripts and
papers for him, as well as notebooks stuffed with typed
sheets containing thousands of names, addresses, and
phone numbers for his tricks. Each entry had space for
Nix's frantic jottings as he recorded progress on each
individual victim. One read, "slow, but talked," another,
"Good prospect," while another entry reminded him,
"Needs call from ranch." One entry Nix penned stated, "So
easy, it's scary."[6]

On the outside, road dogs in Biloxi, Baton Rouge, and
New Orleans picked up, at a minimum, several thousand
dollars a week, extracting the ten or fifteen percent commission, then delivering the balance to one of several individu-
als: LaRa Sharpe, Mike Gillich, a variety of banks, and a
variety of attorneys' offices, including the law firm of Halat
and Sherry.[7]

Some of Nix's outside helpers made "three-ways" for
him, a type of phone call that greatly expanded his
scamming capabilities. He would make a single, supposedly
"legal" call to a scammer on the outside, who would then
use business telephone setups to link him through conference calls to his victims, one after another. That way, he did
not need to make multiple calls, arousing suspicion at the
prison, yet he could play a variety of characters for several
different tricks, without ever hanging up the phone. At the
same time, he could call his marks collect on a three-way,
and their bills would show the number and city of his
underlings on the outside, rather than the giveaway Tunica
phone exchange.

In time, Nix eliminated the need for an accomplice to
assist in patching through three-ways by buying personal
computers with custom-made voice-mail and telephone
switching programs—crafted by Mike Gillich's computer-
expert nephew, Andrew Gilich. Nix's ingenious computer
systems contained a dialing directory for hundreds of his
tricks. He could access the computer from a prison phone,
even though he called collect—the computer's voice-mail
would tell the operator it would accept the charges. Nix
could then command the computer to dial a victim or play
back his messages, all with coded access no one else could

touch. The computer served as the equivalent of a secretary. Nix's career-long penchant for gadgetry showed here, as it did in his pocket computers and autodialing devices concealed in wristwatches, which replaced his old bulky notebooks crammed with phone numbers. Instead of having to destroy papers during prison shakedowns, he could foil a search with one punch of a button, erasing his computer memory. He had backup minicomputers that other inmates held for him in case he had to purge the one he was holding. Nix left nothing to chance.[8]

Whether he used electronic gimmickry or human accomplices, one thing remained constant: The money poured in. He and Bobby Joe Fabian began sporting pounds of gaudy jewelry in the prison, as much as forty thousand dollars' worth each—big diamond rings, thick gold neck chains, gold bracelets, and imported wristwatches. Each of them had a dozen toadies to wait on them, some running errands, others acting as bodyguards. Inmates who might otherwise have targeted Nix for ripoff or worse hesitated when they heard of Nix's reputation, built through years of careful boasting about the Dixie Mafia, about shooting off Buford Pusser's face, and about killing Frank Corso and Pusser's wife. "Always go for the family," Nix would say with a grin. "That's how you really get to someone. Go for the family." He also enjoyed the protection of his old "fall partner" in the Corso case, Peter Mule, who had built his minor mob ties into a towering reputation at Angola, where inmates and guards alike called him "Uncle Peter." Everyone at Angola knew not to touch Kirksey Nix.

Nix's ostentatious displays of wealth showed just how profitable his scams could be. One parliamentary official in Canada alone lost $200,000 through fraud, then extortion. Another government employee in Canada, a legally blind man working on behalf of the disabled, lost thousands of dollars, then refused to make blackmail payments—only to be fired once the scammers exposed him. In Grand Junction, Colorado, a retired coal company manager squandered most of his life's savings—about $100,000—on a Nix creation named Billy Taylor. And a disabled postal worker in Kansas sent some $26,000 to his phantom would-be lover.

Such big-hit tricks were the exception, a cause for celebration on the cell block, as well as in Nix's house in Ocean Springs, which gradually became a hive of scam activities under the watchful direction of Kellye Dawn Newman Nix, then later LaRa Sharpe, then Nix's half-sister and her husband. Most of the victims ended up losing much less—anywhere from two hundred to five hundred dollars for "airfare." The lucky ones wised up after that first payment. Many others pumped thousands more into the scam, trying to help the poor young man they hoped to meet. And a few ended up in financial ruin.

But there was a weakness in his plan, as Nix often complained: the quality of his employees. He fretted constantly about informers, about people who ripped him off, about incompetents unable to convincingly scam tricks. To combat such human breakdowns, he always tried to bind his principal helpers to him through love, money, drugs, and, when all else failed, threats.

For a time, Kellye Dawn served as the most important cog in Nix's scam machine, with Nix bringing to bear all of these forms of persuasion to keep her in line. But eventually, Kellye's drug problems, the birth of her disabled daughter, Meagan, and her utter unreliability finally turned Nix in another direction. In the summer of 1985, with the scam picking up momentum, LaRa Sharpe supplanted Kellye as Nix's most trusted lieutenant, his new Number One. The scams began earning more than ever.

Just how much Kirksey Nix, Bobby Joe Fabian, and the other scammers working for them earned from their wire fraud scam may never be known. One of Nix's closest partners late in the scam—after Junior and Fabian had a parting of the ways—estimated the con game grossed some $800,000 in just two years.[9] The total earnings from 1982 on have never been ascertained. Nix would eventually claim to have personally profited by a half million dollars. Others estimated it as a multimillion-dollar enterprise—figures that more closely jibe with scrawled calculations prison guards once stumbled upon in one of Nix's datebooks. In any case, there is no question that his brilliantly conceived confidence racket was all too profitable, and that it was bringing Kirksey Nix ever closer to his goal: freedom, bought and paid for.

CHAPTER 19

Born Sheri Sharpe to a mother with as many aliases as Kirksey Nix had scams, LaRa was shaped by a youth spent in an Arkansas whorehouse frequented by the Dixie Mafia, with a madam for a mother and hookers for friends and role models. Her nickname had been "Punkin" as long as she could remember, a name she would continue using as an adult, even during scam communications—an odd incongruity, along with her sideline selling pink-packaged Mary Kay cosmetics.

LaRa fell in love with Kirksey Nix at age ten when he came to patronize the motel-bordello in which she lived at the time. He was the most handsome and interesting man she had ever met, kind, smart, brave. She admired his values: He taught her to hoot at Sergeant Friday and to root for the bad guys in *Dragnet*. Nix was heroic, bigger than life.

"I'm going to marry him someday," LaRa told mother.

"You could do worse," Mom replied.

LaRa grew up with the Dixie Mafia while it was at its zenith—before its members began killing one another or landing in prison. Most found their way to "Granny's," as LaRa's mother was commonly known. A few years after meeting Nix, Bobby Joe Fabian came by as well, staying a few days. Granny supplied him with a room, meals, clothes, and the favors of her working girls. Fabian was a fugitive murderer sought after by police in three states at the time.[1]

To no one's surprise, LaRa grew up to be something of a con artist herself, her résumé chock-full of phony qualifications. She embarked on a wide range of business ventures as a young adult, in fashion, art, food—all without formal training, all with big eyes and meager funds. All failed in time. Yet she possessed sufficient mastery of a variety of skills to land a job at age thirty managing a Chicago law office, which is where Nix found her when he tracked her down in the summer of 1985.

They had corresponded off and on for five years, exchanging occasional phone calls, though LaRa had not seen her dashing Kirksey since before the Corso murder. Still, she fondly remembered traveling with Nix, her sister, and brother-in-law to Biloxi when she was a child, so they could work in joints on The Strip. She eagerly kept in touch and, in 1985, she began assisting Nix's scams by phone and mail.

When LaRa and her husband separated that same year, the letters from Nix took on a romantic tone. She found the notion of a love affair with this prisoner compelling. Nix, she believed, was a genius. She knew nothing about the marriage to Kellye—Pete Halat had held on to the marriage certificate, the legality of the union remaining ambiguous. Somehow, Nix failed to mention it in his correspondence and phone calls.

"Come on down to the Coast," Nix suggested in one phone call in 1985. "You can live in my house rent free, and help me out. And when I get my pardon, we'll be together."

At the same time, Nix shunted Kellye off to Louisiana where she could be closer to him—he still professed to love her—yet out of the way of his scam. He needed someone smart and reliable and loyal to take her place. "You know I always loved you," he cooed to LaRa. "Please come."

With her own divorce pending, LaRa agreed. She moved with her two daughters, then aged ten and six, to the Ocean Springs house Nix had bought.

In August 1985, LaRa appeared at the law office of Halat and Sherry. Nix had arranged a special welcome for her. She was supposed to be working on Nix's pardon, but the mini-fiefdom she immediately established in the office's law library, where others were made to feel unwelcome and where she made endless three-way phone calls with the door shut, suggested very different activities. An idle personal computer, originally acquired for Margaret's mayoral campaign, soon became LaRa's as well.

Exactly what she was supposed to be accomplishing with Mississippi law books on a Louisiana murder case remained a mystery, but then, Halat's role in Nix's case was similarly mysterious. She told no one what she accomplished in those long hours in the law library.

LaRa visited Nix several times a month at Angola, both as a girlfriend and on far more private "legal visits"— thanks to the sworn affidavits Halat signed that falsely declared LaRa a paralegal in his employ. These legal visits became conduits for scam materials and other contraband.

Despite Halat's avowal that LaRa was his employee, she had no salaried job. At that time her only income was from the scams, which apparently was lucrative. One runner, an unemployed pool repairman named Robert Wright who picked up between one hundred and two hundred thousand dollars for Nix, made many of his deliveries to LaRa (with other drops to Mike Gillich and the Halat and Sherry law office).[2] This was more than enough to keep LaRa in groceries.

A handyman, Robbie Gant, originally recruited into the scam by LaRa to make fifty thousand dollars in pickups at Western Union, became her personal assistant, renting motel rooms for her under fictitious names so she could safely use the phones to call Nix's tricks. Other times, Gant chauffeured her in Nix's Mercedes up and down the Coast Highway as she stopped at phone booth after phone booth, feeding quarters into pay phones from a bulging canvas bank bag. They'd smoke a few joints of marijuana to get in the mood, then Robbie would put his feet up and wait in the car while Punkin got on the pay phone and became a policewoman, a social worker, a court employee—whatever it took to make an unsuspecting victim part with his money.[3]

Nix and LaRa used Gant for a variety of jobs, including faking hurricane damage to the Ocean Springs home for an insurance fraud and constructing a room-sized closet for LaRa's enormous array of dress clothes and work clothes, an entire chifforobe filled with lingerie, and custom racks filled with an army of shoes. Secreted in the closet was a shoe box crammed with bundles of bills, tens of thousands of dollars collected in the scams and destined to purchase Kirksey Nix's release.[4]

As reliable as LaRa proved to be for Nix's purposes, she

also was hot-tempered. One day she came home to the Ocean Springs house to find Kellye there, back from Louisiana, back in Nix's good graces, and back on the phone with Junior. LaRa raged at Kellye, ordering her rival off the phone and out of the house.

"This isn't your house, it's Kirk's," Wayne Henson, Nix's drug-running brother-in-law, told her, stepping between Kellye and the fuming Punkin. By this time in June 1986, Nix's half-sister Donna Henson and her husband, Wayne, had moved in and gone to work scamming, too. "He pays for the house. He pays for the phone. He says who comes and goes."

"Oh, really?" LaRa replied, stepping around Henson and ripping the phone from Kellye's hands and its cord from the wall, with Nix in mid-squawk on the other end of the line. "I guess we'll see about that."

She seized a hammer and methodically smashed each phone outlet in the house as the others looked on, too stunned or too frightened by the violence of LaRa's temper. Kellye cowered, figuring the hammer would be connecting with her skull next.

"I let him know that I could disrupt my telephone line if I wanted to," LaRa would later say in describing her conduct that day.[5] She knew where to hit Nix to make it hurt the most: No phones meant no scams.

LaRa then went to the safety deposit box she and Halat kept, cleaned it out, kept the cash—how much, no one knows, though she once claimed it was only three thousand dollars—then took the jewelry in the box to Pete Halat, including the large diamond ring that had been Sandra Nix's.

"I don't want it anymore," she announced to Halat after emptying the box. She handed him the jewelry. "If he wants it, he can keep it. Or if you want it, you can keep it. I'm getting out."[6]

It didn't take long for word to get back to Nix. He called her at a friend's house later that night. "I love you, Punkin," he pleaded. "I love those kids. Don't go."

"Stick it up your ass," LaRa replied.

But after a period of estrangement, Nix's whining and wheedling paid off. LaRa had been far too valuable to him to lose, doing more in a day than Kellye could manage in a month. He appealed to her as always, through her family: He loved LaRa's daughters, he loved her, they needed to plan a life together. How much of this LaRa really believed remains unclear—she began dating other men and living a suspiciously affluent life after that. But Nix didn't care. He had gotten what he wanted: LaRa agreed to stay on at the law office and to return to his arms. And his scams.

CHAPTER 20

Kirksey Nix's long run of luck dodging the law—ended, it seemed, by Frank Corso's bullet—had returned in force once he set foot on Angola's gritty, humid sprawl. His crimes inside the penitentiary soon outstripped anything he ever did on the outside, both in profit and audacity. No matter how things might go wrong, no matter how much the authorities might learn or how poorly one of his confederates performed, no one seemed able to touch him.

In retrospect, it seems inconceivable and outrageous that federal, state, and local authorities could have allowed him to continue scamming and enriching himself at others' expense for as long as he did. He was so open and obvious, his schemes exposed to law enforcement so many times, they could have shut him down years earlier. But the simple fact of the matter was, no one with the power to stop Nix, Inc., cared enough to act. He was a lifer, with no legal route to pardon or parole—essentially punishment-proof. Sentencing him to another ten years in the joint for fraud would be meaningless. He had only one lifetime to give.

And as for his victims, well, no one in law enforcement seemed to care much about them, either. Kirksey Nix had chosen his marks well. Older gays duped out of money while seeking liaisons with younger men didn't generate much sympathy in the ranks of Southern police agencies—a reaction Nix shrewdly banked upon.

Certainly there had been ample opportunity to bring him down. As early as April 1984, the FBI had uncontroverted proof of Nix's participation in the scams: a tape of Nix recruiting a friend to play the role of a halfway house director. Nix described in detail his scam technique, admitting he had made thousands of dollars defrauding innocent victims. The friend just happened to be an FBI informant.

"I've been writing these ol' lonely hearts," Nix explained in the taped conversation. "I gotta have somebody to talk to 'em on the phone about three minutes. . . . This is with a fruit, you know. The dude's role is to verify that he's providing the residence program for this person . . . but the plane fare has to be sent."

During the conversation, Nix griped about Kellye and her propensity for buying drugs with money reserved for their mammoth scam-related phone bills—Nix's lifeline, his telephone, had been shut off several times because of Kellye. Nix even confirmed his partnership with Bobby Joe Fabian for the FBI snitch: "I'm working with one now that's made as much as anybody . . . Old Fabian . . . I listened to him romance one the other night."[1]

A few months later, Nix called the same friend back and told him the scam continued better than ever, and asked that he pick up some money for him at Western Union. Then Nix instructed him to send the money to Peter Halat in Biloxi.[2]

With this information in hand, the FBI apparently launched an investigation, albeit a brief and ineffectual one, of the Angola scams. At the time, Kellye had been devoting several days a week to making pickups for Nix at Western Union offices in Baton Rouge, where she had moved in 1984 at Nix's insistence. One day, FBI agents descended on her as she arrived there. They brought Kellye to the FBI's Baton Rouge office and tried to sweat information out of her, threatening her with prosecution and prison.

But Kirksey Nix had prepared for this day. Kellye was still on good terms with him then, not yet addled by drugs and booze. "You don't know anything about anything," he had coached her repeatedly. "You don't know what they're talking about. And you want to talk to your lawyer. You call Pete. That's it."

"I don't know what you're talking about," Kellye parroted for the agents. "I want to talk to my lawyer."

"What are you charging her with?" Pete Halat asked once Kellye demanded the FBI call him.

"We're not charging her with anything at the moment," the agent said. "We're just holding her for investigation."

"Charge her with something and I'll come over and represent her," Halat demanded, "or let her go."

Kellye walked out a few minutes later.[3]

That night, Kellye later recalled, Halat telephoned her at home with a warning to pass on to Nix: "You'd better tell Kirksey he'd better leave those fags alone."[4]

Nix laughed off such warnings, as if he knew nothing more would come of that FBI inquiry. Nix's casual reaction turned out to be justified. For reasons as yet unexplained—either lack of evidence, lack of interest, or lack of sympathy for victims—the FBI backed off. All they had to do was monitor calls from the pay phones in Nix's area of the prison, then track down the victims. They could have nailed Nix with a reasonable effort. But they did nothing. And after a brief lull to make sure the FBI had lost interest, Nix gleefully expanded his telephone shell game.

"As long as we go after the fruits," he told Fabian, "they'll never touch us. People think they deserve it."

Nix would be proved correct time and again. When he scammed a former private detective out of a two-hundred-dollar plane fare, the victim provided the FBI and other authorities with extensive memos detailing his own investigation of the scam. He provided receipts, a series of scam-related personal ads in the *Advocate,* mail drops, and the names of Nix's road dogs, including LaRa's helper, Robbie Gant. In short, the victim handed over a complete case. But the result was just as Nix predicted:

"United States Attorney's Office, Muskogee, Oklahoma, has declined prosecution in this matter inasmuch as he does not feel the case can be successfully prosecuted . . . due to its lack of jury appeal," an FBI memo on the case says.

In other words, prosecutors decided jurors would be unlikely to sympathize with homosexual victims in the case

As in 1984, federal authorities had hard evidence of Nix's scamming, yet did nothing to stop Nix or protect the public.

There was so much in Nix's favor that his complacency is not all that hard to explain. More than mere lack of interest or homophobia on the part of law enforcement was at work. The small, cash-strapped jurisdiction that encompasses Angola—West Feliciana Parish—had a tiny district attorney's office, lacking resources to prosecute crimes at the immense prison. So the prison staff itself tried to deal with the scams by doling out punishments and withholding privileges. These attempts were desultory at best—casual corruption and the trading of favors enabled Nix and the more sophisticated scammers to elude them with ease.[5]

"The scams were legal in prison," Nix once said. "The guards knew, the wardens knew. It's like they approved."

LaRa, however, stumbled badly. In November 1986, with her false legal credentials from Pete Halat, she arrived to visit Nix in an attorney conference room. But prison officials, suspicious of LaRa's relationship with the lifer, searched her and her car and found marijuana and rolling papers. They also found in her purse a copy of a photograph of a young man in a tan suit and tie—another Eddie Johnson, whose image had been seized countless times from prisoners.

"Yes, it's mine," she told Angola's chief investigator, Captain D. K. Basco, when initially confronted with the photo. Then a few minutes later, she called the snapshot a plant. "I've never seen that photograph in my life."[6]

LaRa eventually pleaded guilty to a minor drug charge, ending her "paralegal" visits to Angola. But Nix suffered no consequences, nor did Halat for lying in LaRa's affidavits. Halat would later say LaRa stopped working out of the Halat and Sherry law office as a result of the November incident, and LaRa would swear she ended her participation in the scam even before that. Both claims would be contradicted in time by other witnesses and evidence.

Postal inspectors with jurisdiction to investigate mail fraud decided to make a run at Nix next, teaming up with prison officials to take on the scammers. In early 1987, they searched Nix and his in-prison cohorts, shaking down their

cells, seizing phone lists and other scam documents, even
yanking the phone and a pile of scraps of paper from Junior
as he made one of his supposed legal calls.

The inspectors and guards found they were overmatched,
however. Most of the incriminating entries were in code.
Nix merely smirked and hollered about his rights being
violated when the guards toted away a boxful of his belong-
ings. His latest scam partner, Arthur Mitchell, managed to
destroy many of the most sensitive documents, while Nix's
old partner in the Corso case, Peter Mule, held on to phone
lists, knowing the guards would leave him alone.

The guards did, however, manage to wrestle away from
Nix a script for part of the scam and, even more interesting,
one of his datebooks. Although there was a swastika embla-
zoned on the inside cover along with a white supremacy
slogan written in German, the book contained no Nazi
ravings—just extensive calculations for Nix's finances.
These included references to oil ventures, limited partnerships, real estate and resort investments, oil depletion
allowances, company cars, even wine investments. The
book did not make clear whether these were real investments, phony tax dodges created for his huge scam income,
or mere doodlings. In any case, the figures accompanying
these investments stated Nix had an annual income totaling
$746,000, and assets exceeding $2.4 million—boggling
figures for a man who made two cents an hour sweeping
prison floors. There were numerous references to Peter
Halat in this same journal, reflecting a constant exchange of
phone calls.

A search of Nix's locker turned up an unmailed, sealed
envelope, stamped and marked legal mail. Inside, prison
officials found 154 photographs of nude women, mostly of
LaRa Sharpe, large and self-assured, and Kellye Dawn
Newman Nix, trying to look sexy, but appearing more
pitiful, scared, and childlike than anything else. The photos,
investigators assumed, were for Nix's heterosexual scams.
The envelope was addressed to Peter Halat.[7]

"I have no idea if or why my name would come up with
that stuff," Halat said when questioned about the photos. "I
certainly have never received anything like that."[8]

When all the searches were done and the investigation

within the prison finished, no criminal charges were filed. The in-house disciplinary proceedings were so weak that the prison ended up returning Nix's datebook and other papers. Nix skated, as always.

Still, the spring of 1987 was a difficult time for Kirksey Nix. All the attention began to worry him. After years of refusing to bust the scam, the authorities were taking an uncomfortable interest. From speaking to LaRa, Robbie Gant, and other sources, he knew his web of victims and confederates had begun to unravel. His bagman in Biloxi, Robert Wright, had been questioned by the FBI. He had the unstable Kellye Dawn to worry about, and the explosive LaRa. Then there was Fabian, who had threatened to set up a rival scam after an angry blowup with Nix over money. Nix desperately wanted to plug any potential leaks, to eliminate any weak links. Someone, he decided, was talking. And they had to be silenced.

At about the same time, Nix also learned he had been beaten at his own game. He began to complain to his fellow inmates that hundreds of thousands of dollars he had squirreled away from his scam earnings had vanished—anywhere from a quarter to a half million dollars, bilked by someone on the outside he had trusted. The bounty he had accumulated to pay for his Louisiana pardon had been squandered without result.

The possibility that a trusted minion might have ripped him off, then covered his or her trail by informing on him, had Nix seething with rage. Whoever had done this to him, Nix assured his fellow inmates, would have to pay. He didn't care who it was. Whoever had stolen from him, whoever had ratted on him, had to die.

"One phone call," he bragged in the spring of 1987, "and it's done."[9]

In Biloxi that same spring, three hundred miles and a world away from Angola's barbed wire, Margaret Sherry told her daughter that she hoped some unnamed enemy wouldn't "come after my kids." That same month, she also told her son, Vin III, there was a contract on her life. And Judge Vincent Sherry spoke in open court of threats against his life—one from within the city, and one from out of state.

I know where it's coming from, Vince had said. *But I'll see myself in the pits of hell before I'll be afraid of these people.*

Three months later, in August 1987, a sixty-year-old ex-con, John Elbert Ransom, sought permission from his parole officer in Georgia to travel to Bowling Green, Kentucky, the Sherrys' old hometown. Ransom was well known to police in the South for decades for two main reasons: He had been a close friend of Kirksey Nix for many years, and he was supposedly the nation's only one-legged hit man.

He had lost his leg in a bar fight in 1950, blown off by a shotgun blast. An artificial leg gave him an almost imperceptible limp, though he still could move impossibly fast over short distances, producing a pistol almost magically in a hand that had been empty moments before. He was a gangly, Ichabod Crane figure with long, spindly fingers, enormous knuckles, and a prominent Adam's apple that bobbed like a fisherman's lure. His odd but essentially innocuous appearance and slow, gravelly but always refined diction belied his record—Ransom had been arrested fifteen times by 1970, when he first met Nix, charged with rape, burglary, robbery, assault, bootlegging, and other crimes. He had been suspected in a number of murders— usually involving the sudden and violent ends of men and women on the verge of bearing witness against Dixie Mafia figures. Ransom, invariably, was close by—though never close enough to be charged.

Nix and Ransom knew each other from The Strip in Biloxi, where the peg-legged killer was good friends with Mike Gillich's other protégé, Little Henry. Ransom visited Nix when he was imprisoned in Georgia back in the seventies, impersonating an attorney to gain access. They had been in a shootout with police together near Atlanta— Ransom got busted, Nix escaped—and later, after the Corso murder, Ransom tried to engineer Junior's escape while Nix was hospitalized in Dallas. Ransom even named his son Kirksey.

Once Nix settled into Angola, Ransom sent jewels and drugs to LaRa and Kellye for his friend, and made scam pickups in Atlanta through a crew of bagmen he had hired. He was always there for Nix when he needed help. They were in constant contact.

Late in the summer of 1987, Ransom told his parole officer he had to go to Kentucky to pay a relative's funeral bill. He offered no convincing reason why the personal check he eventually gave to the funeral home could not have been mailed instead of delivered in person. Still, Ransom got permission to cross state lines.

At the same time, Vincent and Margaret Sherry were preparing to leave Biloxi for Paducah, Kentucky, about three hours from Bowling Green. Vince was to attend the Kentucky Bar Association's annual convention.

If anyone had been threatening their lives or stalking the two of them, the trip to Kentucky would have been a perfect opportunity to strike. Away from Biloxi, their bodies would have been found in a town where they were relative strangers, where their deaths would generate far less publicity and investigative fervor. It didn't happen, of course: Margaret backed out at the last minute, so she could sew dresses for her daughter Leslie. Vince came home unscathed.

However, on the Halat and Sherry phone bills that month, Lynne Sposito would later find an unexplained collect telephone call from Paducah on August 28, made from a hotel pay phone there. Lynne believed the call was not from Vince Sherry—she remembered him using a calling card. Who else, then, Lynne wondered, had been in Kentucky then, and have reason to call the law firm, to ask, she imagined, "Where's the wife?"

A few days after that call was made, Charles Leger, the lawyer who went to work for Halat and Sherry after Vince accepted his judgeship, walked out of the office in downtown Biloxi and headed toward the parking lot. As he approached his car, a tall, thin man with a scarred or pocked face—Leger later wasn't sure which—beckoned to him.

"Where can I find Vince Sherry?" the man demanded, without greeting or nicety. Impassive and grim, the man towered over the slight Leger, who stared up at the stranger with alarm, saying nothing. Leger found himself mesmerized by the man's pale eyes, piercing, intent, utterly cold—the personification of evil, the lawyer would later say.

"Where can I find Vince?" the man repeated. He was blocking Leger's path now. Leger wondered how such a skinny man could project such menace.

"Well, he's probably in the courthouse," Leger finally stammered. "In Biloxi or Gulfport."

Without another word, the man stalked off. Leger noticed he had an odd limp, his right leg trailing stiffly, as if it didn't bend properly.

The face of that man haunted his dreams for the next year, though he wasn't sure why. He kept dreaming that man wanted to kill him. Long after he had forgotten the incident itself, the face pursued him at night, attached to that whipcord body, limping but moving with a spider's speed.[10]

A few weeks later, on September 14, 1987, a professional assassin strode into the home of Vincent and Margaret Sherry, leaving behind his bloody handiwork, to be discovered two days later by Pete Halat.

Shortly after the murders in Biloxi, after the pressure of the postal-prison investigation lifted in the fall of 1987, Kirksey Nix's inmate cronies noticed that he stopped complaining about missing money and got back to work.

Bobby Joe Fabian, angry over his share of the lost money, parted company with Nix for good, then tried to inform on him for scamming. No one listened, in part because no one in law enforcement wanted to pay the price for Fabian's cooperation—freedom for a murderer. So he decided to bide his time. Sooner or later, he'd have a chance to make another bid for freedom—and to take Kirksey Nix down at the same time. Fabian would say and do anything to find freedom.

Nix's scams were not quite in the clear, however. The memo and reports from the enterprising scam victim who conducted his own investigation had been passed around to various FBI offices. Finally, after six months, someone in the Jackson, Mississippi, FBI office decided to check out the scam helper, Robbie Gant. After learning from his mother that FBI agents were hunting for him, Gant turned himself in and spilled his guts, describing the whole scam and naming most of the principals, Nix and LaRa Sharpe chief among them. It was that easy.

Gant even telephoned LaRa Sharpe for the FBI, reaching her by calling the Halat and Sherry law office. Halat later claimed LaRa had stopped working there a year earlier—

after her dope bust at Angola—but Gant had no trouble reaching her through the law office. Halat's secretary was even expecting the call. And while the FBI tape recorder spun, capturing every word, LaRa told him not to panic, to keep quiet, and to lie about everything to the FBI, blaming it all on another Angola inmate—not Nix—if necessary. Money for an attorney would be provided him later, she promised.

"You just have to tell 'em that you didn't realize it was illegal. . . . When people stick together, then that's when they overcome things. Not when they fall apart, if you know what I mean."

This conversation occurred on October 23, 1987— exactly five weeks after Vince and Margaret Sherry were found murdered in their home.

Gant thought at the time he was bringing the great Kirksey Nix down. Not so. Nearly two more years would pass before any legal action would be taken to stop the scammers. And other than passing on a tip to Sheriff's Investigator Greg Broussard, who tried unsuccessfully to find answers in the Sherry case, nearly two years would pass before any real attempt was made to determine if a link existed between the scams and Mississippi's most notorious double homicide.

All the while, Nix kept making money and ruining lives. And the Sherry murders remained unsolved.

PART 3

Mississippi Mud

People do things for power that they would never do for money. . . . Power is something.

—*Arthur Mitchell, Kirksey Nix's scam protégé*

CHAPTER 21

"What do you mean, Rex?" Lynne Sposito asked. She had taken the call in her kitchen, the smell of fresh coffee and the dishwasher's watery hum providing an oddly homey counterpoint to the vocabulary of murder. But that was how Lynne's life went these days, the warm trappings of workaday life continually juxtaposed with the ammonia slap of a homicide investigation she had long since stopped idly observing, and had instead begun to live. It was late 1988, more than a year since her parents died. "What do you mean?" she demanded.

"Sposito, I can't get past Pete," Rex Armistead repeated. He had taken to calling Lynne by her last name—for him, a token of respect. "The plan was to clear Eric, then look at Halat, then check out Gerald Blessey. The problem is, I can't get past Pete Halat."

The explanation that followed brought back the same cold nausea Lynne felt months before, when Pete had told her about his friendship with Kirksey Nix and Mike Gillich. Nix, Gillich, LaRa Sharpe—all were tied to the law office, Armistead said. All were tied to Pete. There were the unexplained deliveries of money to the law office. Pete drove Nix's Mercedes, handled his money, and defended Nix's stepdaughter-wife. Now the circle was complete, Armistead said: Margaret was dead, and Halat was running for mayor.

"Your mom's death has worked out well for Pete," Armistead said. "And for men like Mike Gillich—who might have suffered in a Sherry administration."

After Lynne said good-bye to Armistead, agreeing to meet him in Biloxi later in the week, she called her friend Becky

Field, replaying the conversation for her. Becky said she
was not surprised to hear any of it. "A lot of little things
have been bothering me about Pete," she said.[1]

She had become Lynne's confidante and confessor in
recent months, the only person Lynne could comfortably
talk to about the case. Her husband and children were
supportive of her quest for the killers, Lynne knew that. But
she had seen the change in the way they looked at her in
unguarded moments, the distance her obsession had placed
between them, the resentment her family couldn't quite
hide at the time she spent away from being mother and wife.
But Becky understood the guilt, the anger, the helplessness
that consumed Lynne—and her need to try to make something happen. They spoke almost daily about the case,
comparing notes, sifting through bootleg copies of police
reports.

"I just find it hard to believe Pete's involved," Lynne told
her friend after speaking with Armistead. "Dad trusted
him. Mom and Dad never said anything bad about Pete.
Never."

"Lynne, except for Gerald Blessey, your parents didn't
badmouth people they didn't like," Becky reminded Lynne
pointedly. "They just didn't have anything to do with them
anymore. They just didn't say anything about them. What
were they saying about Pete before they died?"

"Nothing," Lynne said after a moment. "They hadn't
said a word about him in a long, long time."

At Rex Armistead's suggestion, Lynne and Becky spent
the fall and winter retracing the last days and hours of Vince
and Margaret, quizzing friends and colleagues about everything from the Sherrys' dinner plans to their occasional,
vague talk of threats.

When they weren't doing that, they staked out Mike
Gillich's nightclubs and his doughnut shop hangout on The
Strip, looking to see whom he met, recording license plates,
taking pictures. The police refused to do it, even after they
learned the prime suspect in a Texas contract killing with
similarities to the Sherry murders phoned Gillich's club
and several of his associates around the time of the murders.

One evening, a dark-colored car tailed Lynne and Becky as the two women left their stakeout of Gillich's club for the night. Armistead had taught Lynne to watch her rearview mirror constantly, and she soon spotted the tail. Lynne turned suddenly from the highway and floored the gas pedal, the dark car's headlights clinging to her rearview mirror as she glanced into the glare behind them—spying two heads silhouetted inside the pursuing car. Becky clung to the dashboard for balance, the Mazda's engine whining, Lynne's gun on the seat between them.

Months earlier, Armistead had insisted Lynne learn defensive driving, police style—the art of high-speed turns, one-hundred-eighty-degree reversals, and how to approach a suspicious parked vehicle from a siderear angle, so Lynne could have a clearer shot than whomever she was up against. When Lynne initially protested his long list of driving commandments, Armistead told her his professional paranoia had kept him alive nearly sixty years, whereas her parents, fatalists to the end, had ignored threats to their lives. "Now you're an orphan," Armistead had said. "Do you want your children to have to deal with that, too?" She had been upset with his bluntness then, but she grudgingly admitted he was right, and adhered to his lessons.

Now the detective's instructions were put to the test: Lynne led her pursuers on a screeching chase through Biloxi's Back Bay, seventy miles an hour on residential streets, running stop signs, leaning through turns, crunching over potholes with bone-jarring thumps as the car bottomed out on the asphalt. After a while—three minutes, five, ten, Lynne couldn't tell—she was aware of nothing but the roar of the Mazda's car engine, her fingers numb on the steering wheel, her eyes locked on dark streets she navigated. Finally, she felt Becky grab her and say, "We've lost them, Lynne. They're gone. You can slow down now." Becky said this three times before it registered, then Lynne eased up on the accelerator at last, coasting to a stop. She glanced over her shoulder at the empty street behind her, ears ringing, heart pounding. She looked at her friend. Becky's face in the dark car seemed so pale it glowed. Then they headed home.

Lynne never learned who followed them, or why, though they were certain that nothing good would have come of it had they been overtaken and stopped. Obviously, they had

touched a nerve. After that incident, Lynne and Becky
seldom bothered with covert stakeouts. When they wanted
to watch Gillich, they simply sauntered into the Krispy
Kreme and sat down in a neighboring booth, watching the
conversation dry up at Mr. Mike's table, exchanging expres-
sionless stares with their targets.

"This is damn dangerous," an uncomfortable Becky
Field whispered the first time they ventured into the hot-
grease smell of Gillich's turf. Lynne said nothing, but Becky
thought she saw the hint of a smile pass across her friend's
lips. Lynne was enjoying herself, Becky realized. And that
scared her just as much as anything else.

Later, Lynne interviewed a witness who saw a man in
business clothes running near the Sherry house on the night
of the murder but who could not identify the man, and
another witness who saw a similar man drive by in a pickup
truck a few blocks away.

Another witness, Dianne Harenski—the councilwoman
who was among the last to speak with Margaret—explained
to Lynne that all was not well between the Sherrys and Pete
Halat, despite his claims to the contrary.

"Your mother thought Pete was going to run against her
for mayor," Harenski said. "I remember Margaret telling
me time and time again, never trust Pete Halat. She
admired his mind, and she thought he could be a big help at
times, but she never trusted him."[2]

She was the first person to suggest the Halat–Sherry
friendship was not what Pete made it out to be—something
she told Lynne but had never mentioned to the police.
Worse still, Lynne obtained the Halat and Sherry phone
records for all of 1987, including the last three months the
Biloxi police had been unable to get. There were well over
one hundred calls to and from Angola in September,
October, November, and December—all after the murders.
Whatever had been going on between Nix and the law office
was still going on after Vince and Margaret were dead.

In January 1989, Pete Halat telephoned Lynne in Raleigh. She was concerned enough about him by then to
secretly tape-record the call, the ostensible purpose of
which was to discuss a bank loan of Eric's that Vince had
co-signed. Halat soon shifted the topic to news reports that
Lynne had hired Rex Armistead. Halat said he heard Lynne

paid the investigator $50,000, but she declined to confirm this.

"Fifty thousand sounds like a good number," he prodded, but Lynne did not bite. He added that he had never met Armistead and knew him by reputation only. "What I've never heard is him being disparaged as an investigator."

"I don't want any screwups," Lynne agreed.

"Well, I can tell you, I don't think the city of Biloxi is doing anything on the case now. . . . And I don't think they're *gonna* do anything—until I get in there in June." To Lynne, there seemed to be little outrage in Halat's voice over the city police department's inaction. If anything, he sounded a trifle amused. He was fully into his run for mayor by then, and seemed supremely confident of victory. Maybe Vince's and Margaret's murder had become nothing more than fodder for his campaign, Lynne thought.[3]

The conversation brought to mind an earlier one with Halat, which was merely hurtful at the time, but that now raised more questions in her mind. Three months after the murders, Halat had asked her if his son could buy Vince's old riding lawn mower. Lynne said no, she already had promised it to a task force investigator—if he solved the murders.

"Honey," she recalled Halat saying with a laugh, "You might as well put that out on the front lawn with a for-sale sign on it, because there ain't nobody going to solve this one."[4]

Lynne couldn't believe her father's best friend would say something so callous. Now she had to wonder just what he had meant. And another comment attributed to Halat in a Biloxi newspaper on the anniversary of the murders also took on an ominous new coloration: "Somebody is out there looking at us," he said, "and laughing about it."

Still, Lynne hadn't completely dropped her original suspicions in the case. She still hoped they were wrong about Halat, and that Margaret's old nemesis, Gerald Blessey, was involved instead. She kept finding reasons to fuel this hope. An old friend of her mother's told Lynne she, too, spoke with Margaret on the night of the murder. She had never told the police about this for fear of suffering Margaret's fate, but the woman's daughter, who had read about

Lynne's private investigation, prodded her into meeting with Lynne.

"When I told her I'd support her," the woman told Lynne, "Margaret said, 'That's great. We need to get that crooked, corrupt man out of city hall.'

"I said, 'Margaret! You can't say things like that without proof.'

"And she said, 'Don't you understand? I *have* the proof.' That's what your mother said. Right before she was murdered. She had the proof."

And there it was again—the suspicion Lynne harbored that the key to the murder was her mother's pursuit of wrongdoing in city hall, not at Pete Halat's office or Angola prison.

This belief was further bolstered when news broke that the FBI really did have a longstanding investigation of government corruption under way in Biloxi. Contrary to their past denials, agents had been examining many areas that had concerned Margaret after all, including alleged improprieties involving the city's waterfront project.

Mayor Blessey's outraged response to this assault on his administration's integrity was curious, further resurrecting Lynne's original suspicions: Once the existence of the investigation became public, he attacked the Sherrys. He accused the murdered couple and their FBI neighbor, Royce Hignight, of concocting the allegations to further their own, archconservative political agenda.

"Sherry was close to major underworld figures, especially in the drug-pushing business," Blessey proclaimed, challenging the murdered couple's integrity, then passing on what would later prove to be a false rumor: ". . . Mr. and Mrs. Sherry dined with known Mafia figures in New Orleans."[5]

The Sherry family responded to the mayor's odd attack on the defenseless dead by beginning their own barrage of public criticism of the Biloxi Police Department and Gerald Blessey. This, in turn, led to yet another renewed focus on Eric Sherry as a suspect.

On the one-year anniversary of the murders, Biloxi Director of Public Safety George Saxon—a few days after telling the press they had no viable suspects—publicly named Eric Sherry as a prime suspect in the murder of his parents.

Saxon referred to contradictions surrounding Eric's plans to come to the Coast at the time of the murders, even though investigators long ago had cleared up this confusion. He also criticized Eric for refusing a polygraph, despite Eric's having been told by detectives that it wasn't necessary.

"If he was truly innocent . . . he would demand a test to clear his name," Saxon told the television cameras, turning the presumption of innocence on its head. No other suspect would ever be publicly named in the case by the Biloxi police.

Saxon went on to harshly criticize Lynne for telling a reporter that the killer took Vince's appointment book. After keeping it secret for a year, Lynne mentioned it while being interviewed for a story on the one-year anniversary of the murders. The public safety director said he had wanted to keep the appointment book secret in order to debunk bogus confessions. Then, twisting the knife a little more, Saxon suggested the killer might have kept the book for the past year—a key piece of evidence if there were an arrest.

"But he's certainly destroyed it now," Saxon said, implying that Lynne had damaged the case that had become the center of her life.

It was a dubious theory—a professional killer would almost certainly have destroyed such a piece of incriminating evidence immediately. But Saxon's remark had the desired effect. More than anything, this notion that she could have inadvertently helped her parents' killers hurt Lynne deeply, consuming her with doubt. Then Saxon, a normally affable man who had admired and liked Margaret Sherry despite her poor relations with his boss, couldn't resist taking one last shot at his new archcritic. Lynne Sposito says she wants the case solved, Saxon quipped, but she apparently prefers to see her name in the news.

"They've been looking for an out since day one," Lynne responded. "Now they are trying to use me as an out."

Provoked and outraged, Lynne looked for any excuse to back off investigating Pete Halat, and to renew the hunt for evidence against Gerald Blessey and his police department.

"You don't know whether it is genuine ignorance or a very sloppy cover-up," she said in an interview with the capital city newspaper. "We are very frustrated."

Sometimes the warfare got to be too much for Lynne.

After Saxon's tirade on the anniversary of the murders, Lynne, in Biloxi for the occasion, disappeared from Becky's house without a word. Armistead and Becky, concerned for her safety, hunted her down at her parents' empty house. Lynne was in the master bedroom, sprawled face down on her mother's side of the bed, quiet sobs shaking her body.

"Don't you smell it, Becky?" Lynne asked, looking up at her friend.

"No, I don't, Lynne. What am I supposed to smell?"

"I can smell my mom on this bed." She inhaled deeply, sensing where no one else could the faint scent of talc and perfume and hairspray that was Margaret's—the complex and unique mixture of odors that we learn as children, pressed close to our parents, their power to summon memories across lifetimes never warning, never forgotten. "I feel close to her here. I feel at peace here."

It was the only time, before or since, Becky Field would remember Lynne saying she felt at peace over anything.

A month after the anniversary of the murders—and after Lynne and George Saxon had repeatedly dueled in news articles and television shows in Mississippi—Lynne received a call at her home in Raleigh.

"I've had some conversations with your mother," a soft-spoken woman named Sheri[6] told Lynne after introducing herself. She was calling long-distance from Biloxi, her voice high and thin, fear or uncertainty, Lynne wasn't sure which, making her speak haltingly.

"Yes, go on," she prodded. "When did you talk to Mom?"

"Ever since the murder," Sheri said. "I spoke to her last night. Margaret comes to me."

Oh, Christ. Not another one, Lynne thought. She had already been contacted by several psychics. There was the man in Kentucky who wanted anything metal Vince and Margaret had touched so he could pick up "mental images" from the Sherrys. Then there was the woman who swore she saw Vince, Pete Halat, and another man eating at a table in the Keesler Air Force Base officer's club when she suddenly "heard" one of the men at the table thinking, "You need to be killed. I'd like to shoot you in the head." The woman even relayed this information to the Biloxi police.

Now here was Sheri on the phone, timid and hesitant. She

said she didn't like the label "psychic." She just called her ability to speak with spirits and the dead "my gift."

"I don't pick my cases," Sheri said. "God picks them for me."

Lynne listened politely as Sheri explained she had never met Margaret or Vince in life, that she knew nothing about Biloxi politics or government, that she was just an ordinary homemaker—a "domestic engineer," she liked to say. But she had this gift, ever since she was a teenager, she claimed. Margaret had come to her the day after the bodies were found. It had been the first time she had seen a spirit, she said. Previously, she had only heard voices in the darkness.

"I have a ritual. I say, Do you walk in the white light of Christ? The spirits say, We do. I had just gone to bed when Margaret came to me. I thought I might be going crazy, because I have never seen a spirit before. But I wrote down what she said. And after that, it happened repeatedly. I started seeing Vince, too, but Margaret did most of the talking." Sheri groped for words here, then said, "She, like, dictated everything to me."

Sheri then informed Lynne matter-of-factly that her mother was the primary target in the murders, not Vince, and that it had something to do with what Margaret called "the rackets." She said Margaret had told her there was information hidden on the back of a picture in the house, and that it was important to the case. It could help them find the killers, Sheri said.

At this point, Lynne was ready to extricate herself from the conversation, politely if possible, rudely if necessary. But then Sheri silenced her by beginning to describe the murder itself, and by posing an odd question—odd enough to make Lynne listen a bit longer.

"I've seen it happen many times," Sheri said, "and there's one thing I've never understood. Don't your brothers live out of state? I thought I read that in some of the articles."

"Yes," Lynne said slowly. "That's right."

"And they weren't visiting or anything, right?"

"Right."

"Well, that's what doesn't make sense to me. I've seen the killing . . ."

Lynne, at this point, was saying to herself, Oh my God,

this is insane, why am I listening to this? But still she listened.

". . . and I see this hand reach out and it pushes open the bedroom door, and it fires at your mother and misses . . ."

Lynne began to grip the phone more tightly, her palms suddenly sweaty. Sheri was now describing, compellingly, a scene Lynne herself had pictured too many times, the detail so vivid. Too vivid. But of course, the papers reported that the killer missed Margaret twice, Lynne reminded herself. That's how this Sheri person knows this.

". . . and your mother's thinking in her mind, 'Oh my God, I'm never going to see my kids again, I'm never going to see my grandkids again.' And then she thinks, 'Where are The Boys? Where are The Boys?'"

Lynne was stunned, unable to believe what she just heard. She could not speak.

Sheri continued, lost in her own recollections, her voice puzzled, unaware of the impact she was having. "And that's what I don't understand. Why would she be wondering where your brothers are? They weren't supposed to be there. It just never made sense to me."

The Boys. Not Eric and Vincent III, not Margaret's sons. It was Meaux and Fritz, the two dachshunds the Sherrys loved so much, the ones found guarding the bodies with their little fangs bared. Only the Sherry kids and their best friends knew Vince and Margaret called those dogs The Boys. *Where are The Boys?* Margaret had thought at the last, hoping those dogs might somehow save her. Where had Sheri gotten that information? It couldn't just be a lucky guess, Lynne thought. Could it?

Sheri sounded like a complete flake to Lynne. But there she was, whispering her mother's last thoughts, *Where are The Boys?* Sheri didn't want money or fame, she had asked for nothing but anonymity—and for Lynne to listen.

"Tell me more about this picture, Sheri," Lynne finally said. "Tell me everything."

The picture, Sheri said, was supposed to have a man or a woman on it. It had been framed and in the Sherrys' house in Biloxi at the time of the murder. Margaret said something in back of it was important, and that Lynne needed to find it. That was why Sheri had called. Margaret told her to.

Still not certain what to believe, Lynne called Becky Field in Biloxi and told her what Sheri had said. Becky had a key and reluctantly agreed to go over and rummage around for it, feeling silly. It was a pretty vague description, so Lynne suggested she go though everything framed at the house. Becky called back later that evening.

"I couldn't find a thing," Becky said.

Lynne felt disappointed and relieved at the same time. But just to be thorough, she climbed the stairs to her office, where her files on the murder case had grown like cancer— and where she had collected a few treasures of her parents', some framed pictures and photos among them. Most of these had rested against a wall since Lynne had returned from the funeral. Now she flipped through them one by one. Halfway through the pile, she came to a framed front page from the Biloxi *Sun Herald*—June 5, 1985. The headlines and stories detailed Margaret's narrow loss to Gerald Blessey in the mayoral race. It had a particularly nice photo of Margaret, graceful in defeat, which is why Vince had gotten it framed and given it to his wife. Vince had also intended it to be a reminder for Margaret to try even harder in 1989. Lynne recalled seeing this picture after the murders, leaning against a stack of papers in the spare bedroom that served as her parents' library.

Lynne flipped over the frame. On the cardboard backing, she saw two parallel tears—the sort of marks that occur when masking tape is pulled off and the top layer of cardboard comes with it. The tears formed the shape of a large envelope, big enough to hold legal papers, the frame deep enough to hold quite a bundle of them. Unquestionably, something had been secreted there, secured with tape.

Inexplicably, Sheri had been right. Something had been behind a picture in the Sherrys' house. But someone had taken it. Maybe the same person, Lynne thought, who took her father's appointment book: the killer.

Still, she didn't want to jump to conclusions. Yes, it was an eerie fulfillment of Sheri's pronouncement, in a way. Yet the marks could have occurred innocently. Or something might have been hidden there once, but her parents could have removed it long before the murders.

It was only when she was standing in the kitchen the next day, talking to a friend, that she realized the significance of this find. She was explaining about Sheri and the picture when her friend picked it up and said, "Hey, Lynne, what's this?" She pointed out three reddish brown smudges, one on each side of the brushed aluminum frame, and one on the bottom. Lynne peered at the small splotches.

"Jesus Christ, it looks like dried blood," she gasped. As if someone with blood on their hands had gripped the frame and picked it up.

Lynne immediately called Armistead, who told her to call the district attorney's office on the Coast. After all the sniping in the press, they were not about to trust this find to the Biloxi police. That same day, Lynne shipped the picture off to the D.A., who arranged for a lab analysis. Lynne got the results a few days later: human blood. It was too small and deteriorated a sample to type and match, but it was human blood, nevertheless.

The killer had known to look behind that picture. No other explanation fit. The lab said he wore gloves, probably rubber, leaving small smudges of blood, probably Vince's. The gun had been in his mouth, no doubt spraying blood on the killer's gun hand. The picture had not been in the room with either body, so the killer had to have left the blood— and taken whatever was behind it.

After that, Lynne told Sheri to call her whenever she wanted. It wasn't easy for Lynne, but there was no denying Sheri seemed to be on to something. And so when Sheri called a month later with more information from Margaret, both Lynne and Becky wrote down what she said. According to Sheri, Margaret had mentioned something about "scams"—a word that, once again, brought Lynne up short. Then Sheri said a man whose name sounded like "Hicks" had been involved, and that Margaret and Vince died at the hands of a man whose name sounded like "John Rathman."

Sheri read from her journal, the next words—supposedly Margaret's—giving Lynne chills. They seemed so on the mark, so personal. "The time is near, the deal is close. Waterfront material. Scam . . .

"The detective is right. Eric is not guilty. Hugs and kisses. Becky, kiss the kids and the grandson. They were after me. My daughter is doing a fine job. Proud. John Rathman is the man."

Some of it made sense, some was hard to follow, but

Lynne didn't care. It was strangely thrilling to hear Sheri quoting Margaret—saying, it appeared to Lynne, that her private detective was on the right track, that answers were close, graspable, immediate. She kept telling herself it couldn't be real, that some odd little woman she had never met who called herself a domestic engineer could not possibly be talking with her dead mother. Yet Sheri had been right about the picture, and The Boys. Lynne had to admit part of her desperately wanted it to be true, all of it.

When she and Becky told Rex Armistead about their new source of information, he scoffed at Sheri, seizing on her country manner and nicknaming her "Goober Dust." If she did know anything, Sheri should be investigated as a suspect, he groused. "I don't believe in that shit," he growled. "I'm Presbyterian."

But as of October 13, 1988, the date Sheri imparted this new information, Lynne made sure they would look out for anyone connected to the case named Hicks or Rathman. Even Rex, who was dogging LaRa Sharpe's trail at the time, grudgingly agreed to that much.[8]

And Lynne would allow herself to believe one other thing: that, yes, her mother just might be proud of her if she could only see her now.

CHAPTER 22

The Biloxi police had been unable to find LaRa Sharpe, not in a year and a half of investigating the Sherry murders. It remains unclear just how hard they looked, if they looked at all. She had been tied to a prison scam, busted with pot at Angola, dated a convicted murderer, and lived in the murderer's house in Ocean Springs—all while she worked at the Halat and Sherry law firm. True, she said

she left the firm before the murders, but she still popped in
regularly. She had even sent flowers to the Sherry funeral
and baked a ham for the grieving friends and relatives—
signing her sympathy note from LaRa, her daughters, and
"Kirksey." Yet the Biloxi police and its vaunted Sherry task
force hadn't bothered to check out LaRa Sharpe.

It took Rex Armistead about three days to find her in
early 1989, and to begin following her off and on, certain
she would provide a key to the case. He confronted her after
a week of quiet watching and note taking, but instead of
reacting in fear, LaRa readily accepted his invitation to talk
and suggested they go to a seafood restaurant along Biloxi's
waterfront.

Once seated, Armistead wasted no time on small talk.
First, he told her he knew who killed the Sherrys and why—
attempting to bluff his way by saying he had evidence the
murders grew out of Kirksey Nix's prison scams. "And I
know both you and Pete are involved in it up to your
eyeballs, too," he said.

LaRa just shook her head and continued eating. She did
not seem upset. She seemed so at ease, she even kicked off
her shoes under the table, then tucked her feet under her as
she sat.

"Listen, LaRa," Armistead pressed on, "you have no idea
how dangerous a position you're in. You can either cooperate with the investigation and get some police protection, or
you'll go down with everyone else. And you will go down, I
promise you that—unless Kirksey decides to have you
killed first, just to shut you up."

"I don't know what you're talking about," LaRa said,
staring levelly at Armistead. She put her fork down. "It's
ridiculous. I liked Mr. Vince. He was a peach."

LaRa, it seemed, was no ordinary mark for Armistead's
intimidation tactics. Hardened and fearless—except when
it came to her two young daughters, Heather and
Amanda—she steadfastly denied knowledge of either
scams or murders, no matter how hard the detective
pressed. All she would cop to was recognizing Armistead's
name and bald head from stories she had heard during her
youth spent worshiping Nix and the other Dixie Mafia
heavies. "You're the guy they all used to hate," she said.
"You were always trying to bust them."

Even when Armistead suggested the police could arrange a new identity for cooperative witnesses who helped solve one of the South's biggest murder mysteries, LaRa Sharpe said no way.[1]

When they were through talking, the detective parted with LaRa in the restaurant parking lot, got in his car, and appeared to drive away. But he circled back and followed LaRa as she drove a few miles west on Highway 90, the waters of the Gulf a blue-black abyss to her left. Armistead watched as she pulled into a stained parking lot, spots of crankcase oil on asphalt reflecting murky rainbows of neon. LaRa hurried from her car and entered a warehouse-sized building, the thump of rock music briefly audible as the door opened.

After being accused of scamming and murdering Vincent and Margaret Sherry, LaRa Sharpe had made a beeline to the Golden Nugget and Armistead's old nemesis, Mike Gillich.

"This is the girl you need to talk to," Armistead told his friends at the Biloxi Police Department a short time later. George Saxon had welcomed his old colleague Armistead by then, teaming him with Mike Meaut and publicly smoothing things over with Lynne Sposito—once Armistead made it clear he was not pursuing Gerald Blessey as a suspect. Lynne still had doubts about the mayor and anger at the police, but the private detective was moving in other directions, and even Lynne had to admit that, rumors and emotions aside, no hard evidence against Blessey had ever surfaced.

At Armistead's suggestion, detectives questioned LaRa's most recent boyfriend, a Biloxi carpenter and boat builder named Michael J. Lofton. He and LaRa had met in a nightclub in early 1987, eventually moving in together. He gradually became concerned about her, however, as he learned of her involvement in scams with Kirksey Nix and an assortment of other unseemly characters. Once, in the summer of 1987, he recalled sitting in the car with one of LaRa's daughters for more than an hour while LaRa spoke on a pay phone with Nix. She had cried through most of the conversation, Lofton recalled. The air conditioner was going full blast in the car, so he didn't hear what she was saying—it was so hot the speedometer cable melted—but there was no mistaking how upset LaRa appeared. Her face was wet and red, eyes swollen, makeup running.

"She told me she had gotten tied in with something bad, and that she was trying to get out of it, but she couldn't," Lofton told the police. This caught the detectives' attention. Was she trying to get out of the scam? Or out of a murder plot? Lofton couldn't say.[2]

After much prodding, LaRa eventually agreed to speak to the police—with her lawyer present. In a lengthy and often heated interview at the Biloxi Police Department, six detectives asked her repeatedly about the murders, Pete Halat, Mike Gillich, and Kirksey Nix. Few of her answers seemed to satisfy her interrogators, but she seemed oblivious, insisting she agreed to come simply because she wanted to help any way she could to catch Vince's killer.

First, she claimed to be a part-time employee of Halat's—something both he and she would later contradict. She said she did most of her work for Pete, and had done very little for Vince—a statement LaRa later would also reverse when it suited her to do so.

As for relations between Nix and Halat, LaRa said they were friends as well as attorney and client. Halat "handled just about everything" when it came to Nix's business dealings, she said.

She knew that, LaRa said, because her job at Halat and Sherry required her to make frequent trips to Angola to see Nix and other inmates, and to carry paperwork between Halat and Nix. She admitted the paralegal credentials that gave her special visitation privileges were a ruse. The main purpose of her job at Halat and Sherry, she said, was to work on Kirksey Nix's case, with the goal of winning his freedom so they could settle down together. Before she became fed up with him, LaRa said, she would have done almost anything to help Nix.

"I was totally in love with this fellow," she said.

But, she insisted, she had always drawn the line at breaking the law for Nix. Suspecting the Biloxi detectives lacked hard information on her, she denied any knowledge about the Sherry murders, and she lied openly about her knowledge of the scams. She said she only had hints about what Nix was up to, "things that you just pick up in a conversation." Even when the investigators confronted her with some of Rex Armistead's findings—that she had used phony names and social security numbers for various telephones, then left bills chockfull of scam calls unpaid—she still denied any wrongdoing.

"I told him on more than one occasion, 'I don't want anything to do with anything illegal. I will not go to jail for anybody.' I've got two daughters who've got nobody but me . . . I'm the only one in my family who's never gone to jail. . . . I was raised in whorehouses and bars, and that's not the kind of life I wanted."

Gradually, her interrogators lost patience with LaRa's denials. When she described Mike Gillich as "about the nicest man that I think I've ever met," even the mellow Mike Meaut lost his temper at her lies. "We're talking about criminals, lady. We're talking about a man in Angola for murder, doing life. We're talking about Mike Gillich, a major crime figure here in Biloxi, not only here in Biloxi, but along the Coast. Nothing big moves through here without him knowing about it, or having his hand in it."

"Well, I was totally unaware of that," LaRa said mildly, shaking her white mane, her blue eyes locking on Meaut, unwavering, unblinking, the way a truthful person looks at you without effort, the way a liar looks for effect. She refused their offer of protection in exchange for information, and shook her head again when one detective suggested, "Vince might have come across something in this little group here that could've resulted in his death."

"The reason I'm here and came down willingly," LaRa said, "is I would like very much for whoever killed them to be caught." She made it clear she had no idea who that person could be.

Yet, when asked if Nix might be involved, LaRa gave a curiously tepid response: "Not to my knowledge."[3]

Four hours after LaRa's visit to the BPD ended, shortly after ten o'clock that night, an attorney from Oklahoma City named Beau Ann Williams pulled into the desolate Ramada Inn parking lot along the beachfront in Biloxi. Williams, Kirksey Nix's cousin, had just arrived in town to take depositions for a medical malpractice suit she had filed on behalf of Kellye's disabled daughter, Meagan. Nix had high hopes of cashing in on the little girl's misfortune, and he had hired his cousin and Pete Halat to handle the case.

As she parked Nix's Mercedes—Halat had given up use of the luxury car around the time he severed his formal attorney-client relationship with Nix—Williams noticed a black pickup truck pulling up behind her, honking. Mike Gillich hopped out and said, "I've got to talk to you."

Reluctantly, Beau Ann brought the strip-club magnate up to her room, where the normally taciturn Gillich, clearly upset, said, "LaRa is talking to them. She is driving them around town telling them everything. You have got to get word to Kirk." Then he handed her a note to deliver to Nix, which she later found to be incomprehensible. The only word she could be sure of was "LaRa."

Williams, who had been sleepy and eager to see Gillich leave, snapped to attention at these odd pronouncements. She didn't want to hear this, she didn't want this man's crumpled note. My God, she thought to herself, he thinks I am one of them. That I know what he's talking about.

Mike Gillich then began to talk about what he called "rumors going around"—rumors about his monopoly on strip clubs on the Coast, how Margaret Sherry had been investigating this monopoly, and how she had been ready to "blow the whistle on a whole bunch of folks—even if it burned Judge Sherry."

"The rumor is, that's why she was murdered," Gillich complained, throwing up his hands in disgust. The air conditioner roared in the claustrophobic confines of the motel room. "I've never ordered a hit on anyone."

As he spoke, Beau Ann grew increasingly fearful. It seemed clear Gillich believed LaRa was informing on him. And cousin Kirksey was somehow involved. "I got the impression," Beau Ann would later say, "that whatever Mrs. Sherry was exposing was a whole lot more than a strip-joint monopoly. . . . And that 'all these folks' meant people of position and power that could help him effect his keeping this monopoly."

As he left, Gillich made sure Beau Ann understood the urgency of his wishes. "You've got to get word to Kirk right away." When he was out of sight, Beau Ann wadded up the note and threw it away, fearful of getting involved.[4]

Four hours later, at about one in the morning, Beau Ann's

phone rang. A woman's voice she did not recognize and who did not identify herself told her to look outside her door in ten minutes. Instead, a thoroughly unnerved Beau Ann hung up the phone and called the hotel security guard, who came to her room and found a note stuck in the door frame.

The guard knocked and Williams opened the door a crack, leaving the security chain on. He handed the note through. Williams seemed extremely upset and nervous to him. The note shook so hard in her hand, the guard wondered how she could even read the words. The note said:

1. *I was questioned three hours.*
2. *Mostly V. and M. questions.*
3. *Not much Junior questions. Then later many.*
4. *Many questions Pete.*
5. *Mr. G. many questions.*
6. *Offered protection yesterday.*
7. *Today I said, "Leave me alone or take me in."*

(Give him my love, Punkin.)[5]

Whether Beau Ann guessed that V. and M. might refer to Vince and Margaret Sherry remains uncertain. Obviously, whoever wrote the note assumed the meaning would be clear, implying that the writer had discussed the subject with Nix enough for the meaning to be obvious. Beau Ann did know her cousin, whom she had grown up with, was commonly called Junior. And given her conversation with Mike Gillich a few hours earlier, she might have guessed who Mr. G. was. Certainly she knew cousin Kirksey called Halat "Pete"; for that matter, so did she, ever since he began serving as local counsel on the medical malpractice suit. Beau Ann did not, however, know LaRa Sharpe's nickname was "Punkin," so the source of the note remained a mystery to her, even as LaRa had sat in another room in the same hotel, awaiting Beau Ann's response. Her note, clearly, was intended to convince Nix she was not telling the police anything of significance, no matter what Mike Gillich believed. She told her lawyer to pass on a similar message to the police the next day: "I have nothing to say."

Armistead pursued LaRa for several more weeks, trying to convince her that Nix would have her killed unless she obtained police protection by coming clean on the scams and the murders. "They'll go after your kids," he told her, attempting to weaken her resolve by striking at her most sensitive point. LaRa remained unmoved. Lynne and Armistead would have given much to see that note from Punkin, or to talk to Beau Ann Williams about her meeting with Gillich, but they had no way of knowing about any of it.

Beau Ann Williams, meanwhile, hastily canceled her trip to see Nix and fled back to Oklahoma. She recalls throwing out both notes she received that night. When she finally drove to Angola two weeks later, she reluctantly passed on Gillich's message verbally, repeating his statement about LaRa talking to the authorities and telling them everything. Whatever everything was.

Nix's response was matter-of-fact and unconcerned, and the remarkable thing about it was how his mind seemed to work so much like Rex Armistead's. As if he was stating an unalterable law of physics, he said, "LaRa wouldn't do that. She has kids."[6]

The modest brick headquarters of the Jefferson Parish Sheriff's Department were not exactly what Lynne had expected when Rex Armistead suggested they drive to New Orleans, a city renowned for its garish splendor in everything from eating to music, sex to politics, crime to architecture. This place, though, seemed disappointingly ordinary, a squat, square building that could have sat happily in suburban New Jersey or Connecticut, were it not for the blast of humid Gulf air that enveloped Lynne in a warm, sweaty fist as she stepped from Armistead's Cadillac. No place else smelled or felt like this, a rich gumbo of brine, pollen, the spice of riotous greenery and overheated asphalt, a sweet hint of rot.

The Jefferson Parish sheriff's office was in the small suburb of Harvey, across the river from New Orleans' old-world sprawl. Nothing about this innocuous building suggested to Lynne that the key to solving her parents' murder awaited them inside.

Armistead had said simply that he wanted Lynne to meet

some old police buddies of his. He had heard they were working an informant who periodically passed information out of Kirksey Nix's domain, Angola prison. Their first attempt to break down Nix's organization through LaRa Sharpe had failed. So the next logical move, Armistead said, was to try and penetrate Nix's Angola turf, the place where the lifer felt safest.

"All of which," Lynne reminded her detective, "assumes that Pete and Nix and Gillich are involved, rather than Gerald Blessey. Maybe LaRa is telling the truth." Armistead just shook his head. He introduced her to Deputy Chief Gene Fields, who, seventeen years earlier, had been a sergeant with the New Orleans Police Department and helped bust Nix in the Corso murder case.

"We've got an informant at Angola who says he's heard some things about Nix and murders on the Coast," Fields said. Then he turned to Lynne. "The thing is, every informant has got a price. This one wants a shot at getting out of prison. Would you be willing to talk to the governor about getting clemency or a pardon for this man?"

Lynne thought about it a moment, her stomach beginning to churn. She reflexively wanted to say yes, whatever it takes—but then stopped herself. What if she helped turn loose something worse than the killers she pursued?

"If he's in for murder," she said slowly, "I don't know that I could do that. I don't want to help someone who put anybody else through what we've been through."

Fields held up his hands. "He's not in for murder."

"Well, then I don't have a problem with it, assuming it's good information, that it's credible and usable and leads to a prosecution. I'll talk to anyone he wants me to then."

A week or so later, Armistead drove alone to the Louisiana State Penitentiary at Angola to make contact with this informant and several other inmates, ending up, finally, with the man he had arrested—and nearly shot—twenty years before, a man who had been close to, but who now said he despised, Kirksey McCord Nix.

"Man, seein' you is like seein' my worst fuckin' nightmare," Bobby Joe Fabian exclaimed when he saw who was awaiting him inside a secure and private visiting room. "I got nothin' to say to y'all," he said, and turned to leave.

"Well, how about I go out there with you and thank you nice and loud for all your help?" Armistead said.

The color drained from Fabian's face then, at least what little there was in his pallid, fleshy cheeks. He sat down heavily. Armistead looked at the convict's flabby body, the gaudy jewelry, the red eyes of a substance abuser. He knew a beaten man when he saw one, and he didn't hesitate to twist the knife. Bobby Joe Fabian had a way of knowing things—and being in the middle of them.

"The children of Judge Sherry and his wife hired me to find their killer," Armistead said, then offered the same bluff he had tried on LaRa Sharpe. "Now, you can help me bring the killers down. Or you can go down with them."

It didn't take Bobby Joe Fabian very long to make his choice.[7]

CHAPTER 23

The call came to Becky Field's house one evening in April 1989. Lynne had returned to Biloxi to press the police about their idle investigation—a year and a half since the murders, no arrest in sight. She had always imagined a solution would come in days or weeks, not months or years. She had always assumed an arrest would come before the pain lost its edge, before her obsession destroyed her and her family—and before she had to strain, eyes closed, to summon the image of her parents' faces as she last saw them.

Now she was half-heartedly getting ready for a buffet fundraiser at the Holiday Inn for Pete Halat's mayoral campaign. Halat was locked in a tight race with a county supervisor for the Democratic nomination. He had campaigned on returning Biloxi to fiscal responsibility, improving basic services, cracking down on crime—the Margaret Sherry platform. One of his campaign promises included a vow to redouble efforts to solve the Sherry murders. Pete had asked Lynne to come to the fundraiser, and though she didn't particularly feel like it, she didn't want to arouse his suspicions by saying no. And she still harbored hopes that Rex Armistead would be proven wrong about Halat. Even if he was scamming with Nix, she kept telling herself, he would never hurt Dad. Maybe he would be a good mayor. Maybe he would help catch the real killers.

Then Armistead's telephone call from Angola changed everything. Becky handed Lynne the phone, sensing something momentous about to happen. She picked up an extension and listened in.

"I've got it, Sposito," the detective said. "I know who killed your mama and father."

Armistead's deep, flat, matter-of-fact voice froze her in Becky's office. "Kirksey, Pete, and some other inmates up here got together in the spring of eighty-seven for a meeting. They put a hit on your parents."

Lynne was too stunned to speak. She could only listen.

"This old boy here was working with Nix, he says they've been running scams for years, extorting homosexuals through the personal ads. They made hundreds of thousands of dollars, maybe more. Nix was saving it up to buy his pardon. And Pete, he was supposed to be holding the money."

Lynne closed her eyes, sensing where this was going.

"But then five hundred grand came up missing," Armistead continued. "That's when they had a meeting up here. Kirksey asked Pete what had happened. Pete supposedly blamed your dad. And they put out a contract, Sposito. Nix hired a man named John Ransom. He's a stone killer, a hit man out of Georgia, old-time Dixie Mafia. He's one of the few contract men who would kill a judge and a woman like that, just like I told you. The kicker is, your dad probably didn't take the money. The old boy I'm talking to here says he thinks Pete took it. Pete, and maybe LaRa, too."

Lynne could not begin to describe her feelings at these allegations. Years later, the word "stunned" would be the best she could do, along with nauseated and faint and so

angry she thought the top of her head would detach. She
had spent more than a year convinced that an innocent
man—Gerald Blessey—was behind the murder, and it was
not easy to admit she had been wrong. She was not stunned
to hear there had been a hit man—she had known this all
along. But to have the hit man's name, and to hear that he
had been hired because Pete Halat had blamed his best
friend for the theft of a criminal's loot, it was beyond
comprehension. Maybe beyond belief.

"How do you know this, Rex?" she asked, striving to
sound calm, but feeling as if her throat was almost too
constricted to speak. "Who told you?"

"Bobby Joe Fabian. He's an old Dixie Mafia criminal I
put in jail. He's got a life sentence for murder in Mississippi, and he's in here for kidnapping and shooting a state
trooper. He's been a criminal and a con man his whole life."

"Then how do you know anything he says is true?" Lynne
asked. She could not bring herself to accept this new theory
of the case. It was too horrible, far more cold-blooded than
anything she had ever imagined. "Why believe anything this
man says?"

"Sposito, how many front-row members of the First
Baptist Church do you know that have personal knowledge
of a contract killing? This is the kind of person we have to
deal with if we're going to get the truth."

Lynne had nothing to say to this. She knew from her dad's
work as a lawyer that an overwhelming number of witnesses
in criminal cases were criminals themselves. Who else is
present when crimes are plotted and carried out? Armistead
assured Lynne that nothing Fabian told him would be
accepted until some of it could be corroborated—a link
established between Nix and Ransom, for instance, or proof
that the meeting Fabian spoke of had taken place. But the
detective said he believed much of Fabian's story, and that
he felt confident the corroboration would be found.

"This is where the answers are," he said. "Fabian is one
of these people. He was in the middle of it. He knows if he
lies to me, I'll put *him* away for your parents' murder."

Lynne felt a sudden urge to run from it, almost wishing
she had never opened this up. Then she remembered what
Pete had told her right after the murders: "Drop it. You
can't bring back your parents. Put it behind you." The

memory made her remember her anger, that feeling of fury she could summon whenever she pictured her parents facing a killer's gun, or whenever she picked up a copy of the Jackson *Clarion Ledger* front page she had saved, from the day after the funeral, where an enormous picture of her sister Leslie's face, crumpled with grief, stared out at her. Now she had another image to make her furious: Pete Halat, face lined with apparent concern, telling her to back off an investigation that ended up leading to his doorstep. She took a deep breath. This is what she had sought: Answers. She asked Armistead, "What do we do next?"

"We take it to the police. And you must go to the fundraiser. Like nothing happened."

"You just told me my father's best friend may have set him up to be murdered," Lynne said, her words running together. "There's no way I can see him now."

"Oh yes there is," Armistead said, stern now, almost rebuking. "If you don't go, it'll arouse suspicion. We have one chance to prove this. If they figure out we're on to them, Fabian could be hit in a minute. You've got to put on a good front. You must go."

Reluctantly, Lynne agreed. Becky, meanwhile, had begun to rummage around for notes she had taken months earlier. She found them eventually, hurried jottings from October 1988—when Sheri the psychic had called with the names of Vince's and Margaret's killers.

"She told us it was John Rathman who pulled the trigger," Becky said. "And Rex just said it was John Ransom."

Lynne felt cold all over. She had focused on what Armistead had said about Pete, and hadn't given that much thought to the hit man. It was too much, an information overload. How could any of this be true?

"Sheri said Rathman and Hicks," Becky said, trying to sound matter of fact, the paper shaking in her hand. "Rathman and Hicks. Ransom and Nix. Damned if she wasn't just about right."

Pete Halat wore his high-wattage smile, basking in the show of support at his fundraiser, working the crowd of fifty or sixty people in the hotel conference room, shaking hands, snagging hors d'oeuvres, clapping backs. Vince had always

said Pete had charisma, that he could light up a room, that
he thrived on center stage. Lynne could see he had been
right: Pete looked like a candidate from central casting. The
gathering was enthusiastic, the people sensing that their
man was a winner, someone who could rescue Biloxi from
stagnation and bankruptcy and the cloud of investigations
and allegations that had crushed the Blessey administration
in the past year.

Halat's secretary, Ann Kriss, greeted Lynne at the door,
excited and flushed, as if her son was running for mayor, not
her boss. An old friend of Vince's and Margaret's clasped
Lynne's arm. "I wish this was your mamma's," he said,
quietly, wistfully. "But Pete will do his best."

Lynne found herself looking at the toes of her shoes. "I
hope to God you're right," she mumbled.

Nervous, frightened, and dubious of Bobby Joe Fabian's
story all at the same time, Lynne kept thinking of all the
good people at this gathering with such high hopes for the
future, banking on Halat. She wondered, would they be
feeling in a few weeks what I'm feeling now? Were they in
for a terrible disappointment and hurt if all this proved to
be true? She kept stealing looks at Halat, watching him greet
his supporters or exchange a word with his wife. He looked
no different than he always had. No evil revealed itself
lurking behind his eyes, no revelation gripped Lynne. She
remained as confused as ever by her mixed emotions about
him. She lingered a few minutes, then fled back to Becky's.

The next day, she received a collect phone call from
Bobby Joe Fabian. He wanted to speak with her in person.
Rex had said he might call, but she hadn't really expected
him to, at least not so soon. She accepted the charges and
listened as Fabian provided a more lengthy and colorful
version of Armistead's account, his slang sometimes impen-
etrable, but the meaning of the punchline of his tale
unmistakable.

"Pete told us your daddy had swung with the money,"
Fabian drawled. "I never believed it. I figured Pete had
swung with the do-re-mi, but Kirk said we had to do
something about it. You couldn't let yourself get ripped off
like that without someone payin' the price, ya see. So he
decides we have to reach out and touch someone."

The words, copped from a telephone company promotion

Margaret and Vince Sherry, one of Biloxi's most prominent and politically active couples, in 1986, one year before they were assassinated in their home.

The couple began courting in their college days.

As the twin coffins of Vincent and Margaret Sherry lay ready for burial, the police probe of their murders had already faltered—prompting daughter Lynne Sposito to act on her own.

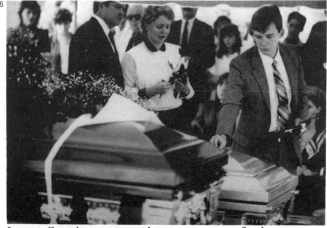

Lynne Sposito stares at long-stem roses for her parents as her brother, Vincent III, touches his mother's coffin in a final goodbye.

Vincent Sherry with his daughter Lynne in happier days, circa mid-1950s.

Vince and Margaret with their youngest daughter, Leslie, at homecoming in 1984.

Margaret and Lynne in 1956.

(*Below*) Margaret Sherry poses with "The Boys" during her 1981 campaign for Biloxi City Council.

(*Above*) Lynne and Margaret in the late 1970s, when Margaret first grew obsessed with cleaning up Biloxi's corruption.

12

Lynne and Dick Sposito, in the spring of 1987—a few months before the course of their lives would be altered forever by the assassination of Lynne's parents.

13

Margaret Sherry with son Eric in 1986. Biloxi police wrongly accused him of the murders, despite evidence showing his innocence.

Left to right, the Sposito children a few months before the murders: Beth, 7, Cathy, 16, Tommy, 12.

Lynne Sposito with her brother Vincent Sherry III, in 1993.

14

15

Investigators confer on the front lawn of the Sherry home while the murdered couple's son Eric sits beneath a tree a few hours after the bodies were found, September 16, 1987.

In November 1991, verdicts were reached, the toll showing in Lynne Sposito's face. "It's not over yet," she announced grimly. "When the people responsible . . . are awaiting their own death sentences, then we're done."

Mike Gillich—known in Biloxi as Mr. Mike—the king of Biloxi's tawdry strip.

18

19

Gillich's strip joints were long suspected as havens for crime and vice, but Mr. Mike's friendly ties to police and politicians helped keep them open.

20

Mug shot of young Kirksey McCord Nix Jr. as he rose in the ranks of the Dixie Mafia. Two decades later, he would be accused of engineering the Sherry murders.

21

John Ransom, the Dixie Mafia's notorious one-legged hit man, in 1970. Nix and Mike Gillich were accused of hiring Ransom to arrange the Sherry murders.

22

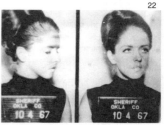

Sandra Rutherford Nix, Nix's first wife and a partner in crime, died in a car accident shortly before his 1975 life sentence.

Louisiana lifer Bobby Joe Fabian, in an August 1989 interview broadcast throughout Mississippi, accused Vince Sherry's best friend and law partner, Pete Halat, of participating in the murder plot.

23

24

LaRa Sharpe, Kirksey Nix's paramour, worked out of the Halat & Sherry law office and was a key player in Nix's massive wire-fraud scheme.

Kellye Dawn Newman Nix, Kirksey's stepdaughter turned wife, became a crucial witness in the Sherry case.

26

25

The Louisiana State Penitentiary at Angola in 1975, when Kirksey Nix began serving his life sentence—and engineering the massive and lucrative con games that ended with the Sherry murders.

Biloxi Mayor Pete Halat, flanked by his wife and son, proclaims his innocence after testifying before a federal grand jury. An entire city was paralyzed when its mayor was accused of murder.

Pete Halat became mayor just before allegations tying him to the Sherry murders surfaced. Though unproven, these highly publicized accusations cost him when he sought re-election in 1993.

Pete Halat, Vince Sherry's partner and best friend, has vehemently denied plotting with Nix to commit the murders. He has never been charged though he remains a subject of a continuing federal investigation.

and given a new and terrible meaning, chilled Lynne. It sounded all the more ominous delivered in the sweet tang of Fabian's molasses-slow drawl. She actually shivered at those words, an uncontrollable, brief shaking that moved down her body, neck, shoulders, arms, legs. They had to *reach out and touch someone.* That was how this man described the execution of her parents. This man, a lifer in prison, stealing hundreds of thousands of dollars with people who killed her mother and father—and he had reduced it all to the homilies of a television advertisement.

For the first time since Armistead called her from Angola, she began to believe—really believe—that the answer to the mystery had arrived, even if it came in the guise of a smooth-talking killer with ulterior motives and a gift for metaphor.

"I want to do what's right," Fabian told her. "And maybe then you can help me get a fair shake. That's all I ask."

When she hung up on Bobby Joe Fabian, Lynne went to the bathroom and threw up, heaving long after her stomach had emptied.

When Armistead returned from Louisiana, Lynne reluctantly accompanied him to see Lieutenant Mike Meaut in his basement office at the Biloxi Police Department. Armistead had insisted on following protocol and beginning with the department Lynne so distrusted. Meaut still constituted a task force of one investigating the Sherry murders— in between his other duties and cases. In truth, very little had been happening in the investigation, other than the interview with LaRa and her former boyfriend. Now Lynne watched Meaut's broad face sag and darken as Armistead laid out Bobby Joe Fabian's story linking Nix and Halat to the murders. Until that moment, Lynne had never heard the sagacious and eminently proper lieutenant use foul language.

"You've got to get the hell out of here," Meaut hissed when Armistead finished. "Don't you know I'm probably gonna be working for the murdering sonofabitch in three months. Take it to the sheriff. Take it to the D.A., the FBI. Anywhere, I don't care. Just take it the hell out of here."

Lynne felt a surge of genuine affection and respect for Lieutenant Meaut then. He was a man of principle, and she had been wrong to distrust him. Meaut had become red in the face as he spoke, and Lynne asked if he was all right. He shook his head and repeated something he had told her a year earlier: "This case is going to kill me, Lynne. Now go on."[2]

After leaving Meaut's office that day, Lynne asked her private detective where they would turn next.

"We've gone through proper channels," Armistead said with satisfaction. "Now we can take it where we want."

Lynne went to see the new district attorney, Joe Meadows, asking him to request federal help. Meadows had been appointed to replace local football-hero-turned-D.A. Glenn Cannon, whose attempts to help Lynne solve the case were cut short by his arrest for bankruptcy fraud, an old Coast pattern of political corruption. Meadows promised to ask the U.S. Attorney to step in.

Armistead, meanwhile, took his old Highway Patrol buddy Joe Price, the Harrison County chief deputy sheriff, and County Attorney Bobby Payne, an ex-cop turned prosecutor, to see Fabian. The convict met them in the chaplain's office at Angola, where Fabian was confident no one would spot him talking to the heat. Church was the last place anyone would think of looking for Bobby Joe.

Chain-smoking and sipping a warm, flat Coke, Fabian swore to the investigators that Halat had traveled to Angola in mid- to late March 1987—six months before the murders—to have an attorney-client visit with him, Nix, and a third inmate named Kenny Roy. At this meeting, according to Fabian, Halat shifted blame for the missing money to Vince Sherry, making him the "escape goat." The meeting should have been recorded in prison visitor logs, but Fabian said such corroborating evidence might be hard to find—the logs were easily tampered with and therefore were worthless, he swore.

"Peter come up with the deal that the judge swung with the money, ya see," Fabian explained. "And I tried to convince Kirksey that Peter Halat swung with the money and, ya see, he was just using this guy up, more or less. But Kirksey believes in Peter because they are like brothers."

Fabian then quoted Halat as saying, "You guys are in a position you can't let people fuck you over."

"I can get anything I want done to anybody," Nix

supposedly replied. "It ain't nothing but a phone call away."

To which Halat supposedly said, "That sounds good enough to me. And that's what has to be done."[3]

Fabian then claimed he assisted Nix in hiring the killer John Ransom. Fabian said he phoned Ransom and even haggled with him over the price for the contract. They settled on ten thousand dollars in cash and another twenty-five thousand in "crank"—methamphetamine—that Ransom could resell on his own.

One hour and twenty-five minutes after the Fabian interview began, Armistead, Price, and Payne left the chaplain's office. They had a convicted murderer's word, and little else to go on—but the pieces fit too well to ignore. It would be checked out, Price and Payne told Armistead.

Armistead called Lynne and told her the next step would be to try to corroborate Fabian's story. Though he would continue to help, they had to relinquish control to the authorities, he said. If they didn't, charges of conflict of interest and bias could be raised by the suspects down the line, he explained.

"It's in their hands now, Sposito. We have to wait."

The waiting did not come easily for Lynne. It had taken more than a month for Armistead and Lynne to persuade Joe Price to go see Fabian. The chief deputy seemed reluctant to Lynne to take on the popular mayoral candidate—perhaps, Lynne thought, because Price, who was running for sheriff himself, needed the same voters who supported Halat.

Price had also been unwilling to interrogate or surveil Gillich.

"He'd just lie to me," the silver-haired chief deputy had drawled, his pale blue eyes earnest, when Lynne begged him to talk to Mr. Mike. "He's the kind of person you get a call from in the middle of the night if he's got something to say.

"You're young, girl," he told Lynne with a wry smile. "You'll probably live to see this solved."

Once Price finally did see Fabian in May 1989, his visit, as far as Lynne could see, was followed by more inaction. By then, the two-year anniversary of the murders was just a few months away, and still nothing had been done about the allegations against Halat and Nix. Nix still scammed happily at Angola, and Halat was well on his way to winning city hall, where Blessey was retiring without running for a third term. Lynne finally decided to take matters in her own hands, unable to bear seeing Halat campaigning on Margaret Sherry's back, uttering what had been her promises of reform. She called a press conference.

"Contrary to the beliefs of many, a vote for Pete Halat is not a vote for Margaret Sherry," Lynne told a group of reporters gathered at her parents' house. "As a family, we are upset that this myth is being used for political gain."

This statement—the first public indication of any discord between the Sherry children and Vince's best friend—took the reporters, then the entire community, completely by surprise. The reporters knew Lynne was actively investigating her parents' murder, and they asked the obvious question: Had she uncovered something that caused her to speak out against Halat's candidacy? Lynne wouldn't say, though the implication behind her veiled remarks seemed clear. Instead, she deflected the pointed questions by comparing her desire for justice to the efforts of a famous Nazi hunter.

"I am a fanatic about this investigation," she announced. "I admit that I am obsessed with it, but I saw a movie the other night about Simon Wiesenthal, where he said, 'How, when I die, can I look in their eyes and say that I didn't love them enough not to find out who did this?' That's the way I feel. There's no way I'll ever stop this investigation, not till we have the people who have done this. . . . I just think about what my father must have felt with that gun stuck in his face, or those two shots that missed my mother, and the kind of fear she must have felt, and that anger gives me all the strength I need."

Halat seemed as shocked as everyone else by Lynne's press conference. It ended any semblance of cordial relations between them.

But the press conference turned out to be only a minor distraction in Biloxi's tumultuous political scene. That same week, Mayor Blessey and several other officials were indicted by a federal grand jury on fraud, conspiracy, and extortion charges. The FBI investigation Margaret Sherry had helped launch years earlier—of alleged misuse of public funds in the waterfront project—had finally led to formal charges. News reports on the existence of the investigation had already damaged Blessey's political career—despite the fact that he would eventually be acquitted of every charge against him. At the time of the indictment, however, the story dominated headlines and newscasts, eclipsing Lynne's press conference. Lynne found herself wishing it could be otherwise for the man she had once believed responsible for her parents' murder—not because she felt sorry for him, but because his misfortune was a distraction from the official homicide investigation.

In the end, her public comments did nothing but put Halat on guard: The investigators who went to talk to Fabian sat on their information while the election drew near. Lynne felt helpless—going public with explicit allegations could endanger the investigation and anger the men she now had to rely on to make an arrest. Silence, however, might mean Halat would become mayor. She could only hope something would happen before then.

But as Lynne watched from the sidelines, Pete Halat went on to win the Democratic primary. With a weak Republican opponent facing him in the general election in an overwhelmingly Democratic city, Halat seemed assured of victory. Lynne prayed for an arrest or an indictment, hounding the sheriff's department and Rex Armistead with phone calls and visits, without any apparent impact, other than sympathetic nods and assurances. Armistead counseled patience. "Joe's okay," he promised. "He would never play politics with the investigation."

As much as she wanted to press onward, all the old doubts still gnawed at Lynne. What if the investigation was stalled because Fabian had lied? What if Halat was innocent? Part of her hoped fervently this would turn out to be true. This hope briefly flared when she met a Biloxi teenager who turned her suspicions back toward an old target. The youth claimed to be part of a sophisticated burglary ring, and he swore he saw the ring's leader accept a briefcase full of money from Gerald Blessey in exchange for agreeing to assassinate Vincent and Margaret Sherry.

The teenager, whose mother had approached the police, then Lynne, at first sounded plausible. He mentioned certain details that seemed telling to Lynne. He correctly said, for instance, that the Sherry family had a home in Kentucky where papers were stored. He went on to say Margaret had secreted important evidence there, and that Blessey had ordered its retrieval as part of the murder contract.

"Maybe I was right all along, Rex," she excitedly told an openly dubious Armistead after talking to the boy. "There's something there. We've got to check it out."

"I'll talk to him, Sposito," Armistead agreed. "But don't get your hopes up. I don't believe it's going to check out."

And, in fact, the youth's story quickly fell apart as he spun an ever more ridiculous and lurid account. None of his details about the murder or the burglary ring proved true. Eventually, he ended up claiming that he witnessed the mayor and the hired killer sign a written "murder contract"—the boy's absurd fantasy of what a hired killing entailed. First they signed it, the teenaged burglar said, then they burned it. The boy could not even identify a photograph of Gerald Blessey. And when Dick Sposito traveled to Kentucky to check the old family home at Lynne's request, he found no sign Margaret had hidden anything there in recent years, or that anyone had searched the place. He even hauled back a trunk full of Margaret's old papers, none of which shed any light on the murders.

"I wanted so much to believe that boy," Lynne told Becky Field a week before election day, on yet another visit to Biloxi. "Now I'm not sure what to do."

In desperation, Lynne went to lunch that week at a Biloxi motel restaurant, where a law-enforcement convention was under way. She asked a television news reporter, Gurvir Dhindsa, to join her, choosing a conspicuous table near County Attorney Bobby Payne. Lynne made a show of whispering to Dhindsa and looking pointedly at Payne, who began to look concerned at Lynne's choice of luncheon companions.

Later, in an aside to the county attorney, she said, "I haven't told Gurvir anything about Bobby Joe." Before Payne could say anything to this assurance, she added a warning. "That might change if something doesn't start to happen."

Payne assured her things were happening behind the scenes. They were working hard on checking out Fabian's story. After that conversation, it seemed to Lynne that the investigation really did pick up pace. But it was too late to affect Pete Halat's march to city hall. He trounced his opponent in the June 1989 general election. Voters heard not a word about Bobby Joe Fabian. They saw only a chance at a fresh start with a new leader.

"This is Biloxi the way it can be, the way it should be," an ebullient Halat said in his victory speech. "This is the Biloxi that will work for all of us."

As he spoke, the investigation of Fabian's allegations crawled forward. Halat would hardly have his office furniture arranged in Biloxi's ornate mayor's office before he would be forced to fight for his political survival. And the city would find its hopes for a new, scandal-free administration dashed once again. It was, they realized, Biloxi the way it always had been—and, they feared, always would be.

CHAPTER 24

Two weeks after Pete Halat succeeded a wearied Gerald Blessey as mayor of Biloxi, two Harrison County investigators made the long drive from the Coast back to the Louisiana State Penitentiary at Angola. County Attorney Payne wanted a second go at Bobby Joe Fabian. With him was Randy Cook, a sheriff's captain assigned by Joe Price to take control of the Sherry murder probe. Cook would become a principal investigator in the case, the first in nearly two years to make actual progress.

Tall and lanky, with a long face and fine, sandy hair, Cook had that laconic, set-back-in-your-chair way of talking that suggested he'd be more comfortable in chaps than in the uniform pants with the single blue stripe he favored. Cook had worked briefly with the ill-fated first Sherry task force

early in the case, seeing firsthand how disorganized the
Biloxi-run investigation had been. Later, he had left the
sheriff's department for a brief and unsatisfying stint as
chief of security for a cruise ship line. He returned to the
sheriff's department on June 1, 1989. A cop most of his
adult life, Cook had missed the squad room badly, his
misery on the job mounting daily, until his wife and young
son finally begged him to go back to the sheriff's department. The day after his return, Joe Price handed him a
transcript of Fabian's first interview, with a file containing
John Ransom's photo and criminal history, shipped from
Georgia authorities.

"Have fun," Price told Cook, who hadn't even had time
to unbox his files. "You got your work cut out for you."

Cook and Payne arranged for a visiting room at Angola to
be cleared, still trying to keep Fabian's cooperation secret.
They wanted to fill in the holes he had left in his first
statement. But extracting details from Fabian proved a
frustrating and mostly unproductive task—a bad omen,
Cook knew. Fabian preferred to speak of his glory days with
the Dixie Mafia rather than the subject at hand, deftly
avoiding specific details when talking about the murders.

But Cook repeatedly pressed Fabian to replay the exact
discussion during the supposed meeting at Angola to plan
the murder of Vincent Sherry—the heart of his story.
Finally, Fabian sat back in his chair, flicked the ashes from
his ever-present cigarette, and said with that back-of-the-
throat, jailhouse voice of his, "Halat said something has to
be done. Nix says, yes, I'll take care of it. He will bite the
dust. That's the terminology they used, you know. Halat
said, all right, get with me on it."

Once the deal to hire John Ransom was in place, Fabian
said, "Ransom is supposed to have got in touch with Peter,
you know. To get the layout and stuff, the judge's house and
all that. Give him, you know, the inside on what he needs to
know to go in there, the best time . . . and so forth."

Here, Cook noticed something troubling: The story had
changed. In Fabian's first statement, he had Halat merely
shifting blame for the missing money onto his best friend.
Then Nix, Fabian, and Ransom had done the rest, with
Halat merely acquiescing. Now Fabian had Halat actively

encouraging Vince's murder: *Something has to be done. Get with me on it.* The first version made Halat out to be a contemptible Judas, but not a cold-blooded killer. Now Fabian made it sound like Pete wanted Vince dead all along.

Which was true? Cook couldn't tell. Maybe neither—the truth never changes, but lies invariably evolve. And Fabian admitted to being a world-class liar and con man.

"This dude," Fabian announced, attacking Halat even more vehemently than a month earlier, "is more of a crook than I am. I mean, he is more hungry than we are, ya see. He is wanting to, you know, get into everything. . . . He was bragging about how he is fixing all them cases and everything, making that money too, and about how he got the governor to appoint [Sherry] judge."

Fabian prattled on, nodding and grinning, puffing happily on his Camels. He ruminated on why Halat might have wanted both Vince and Margaret out of the way. "He could have been killing two birds with one stone. . . . He is eager, he is climbing the political ladder, you know."

"Did it get him anywhere that you know of?" Cook asked.

A fleshy grin split Fabian's pale, unshaven face. "Well, they tell me he is mayor now. . . . The next step will probably be governor, huh? Or Parchman, one."[1]

Parchman was the location of Mississippi's maximum security prison.

When Fabian finished this second rendition, Cook asked him to prove it. Any of it. But the convict just shook his head and said, "They covered their ass pretty good."

Still, just when it sounded like Fabian had no proof of anything, and Cook and Payne began to see him and this new line of inquiry as a waste of time, he would come up with something firm—and accurate. In between his rambling discourses on the Dixie Mafia, he provided information on LaRa Sharpe, explaining how Halat had helped her pass as a paralegal, getting her access to the prison's attorney-client room where she and Nix could exchange scam documents, and, according to Fabian, enjoy unofficial conjugal visits. There would have been no way for Fabian to know of Halat's false affidavits for LaRa unless he was privy to the scheme. Fabian wasn't all hot air, after all, Cook concluded.

He and Payne left a short time later, returning to Biloxi to chart a course of action. As he left the prison grounds, the sheriff's captain took in the work gangs headed to the farmland, the guards on horseback staring back at him with flat, uncurious expressions, the smell of dust and manure in the humid air. There was something about this place, a sense of utter corruption just below Angola's bucolic surface. You could see it in the way certain inmates sauntered as if they ran the prison, and in the whispered exchanges he had seen among some of the guards he passed, a feeling of things hidden and dark, as if they were the prisoners, not the men in blue denim marching to the fields.

"I could feel the hair on the back of my neck stand on end there," Cook told his companion as they drove back toward St. Francisville, passing through a green tunnel of oak and sycamore and Spanish moss, fresh, cool air cleansing the rank grit of Angola from the car's interior. "You spend a little time there, and you realize anything's possible."

Randy Cook found himself banging on LaRa Sharpe's door a few weeks after returning from Angola. A meeting with federal and state prosecutors was arranged where LaRa demanded immunity from prosecution in exchange for her help. She got it—then promptly denied any knowledge of the Sherry murders, just as she had done months before with Armistead and the Biloxi police.

LaRa did toss them a bone, however, this time admitting a small role in Nix's scams. But she insisted that she bailed out after a mere four months of helping Nix in his fraud operation, returning to law-abiding ways by late 1985. The prosecutors and investigators present for LaRa's latest statement believed little of it and, after a few hours more of useless interrogation, LaRa went on her way, the investigators no better off than they had been two months earlier, while LaRa enjoyed an infinitely better position, relaxed and jovial and immune.

The one contribution she made lay in her phone bills—stacks of them, thousands of dollars a month in calls, accumulated while she worked the scams for Nix. These bills proved invaluable. The sheer weight of phone calls between LaRa and the prison seemed impossibly huge—

2,666 calls, not counting four months' worth that LaRa had conveniently omitted from the packet of bills she handed over. The calls extended well into 1986, long after she claimed to have quit the scam and reduced her contact with Kirksey Nix. LaRa had provided evidence that undermined her own story.

She could have destroyed them instead of handing them over to Randy Cook and suffered no consequences. The phone company at that time destroyed long-distance records every few months to free up computer capacity. LaRa could have ditched the bills and been in the clear. Instead, she inadvertently convinced Cook she had lied.

The bills even provided a first bit of corroboration for Fabian's story. They showed numerous three-way calls between Angola, LaRa, and John Ransom, though there was no way of knowing what had been said in those conversations.

"What do you think?" one of the prosecutors asked Cook after LaRa had left.

"I think she's in it up to her neck," Cook said. "I think she knows we don't know anything, and she lied her ass off. She knows we can't prove anything." He paused, then added, "Yet."

Through most of July 1989, the revived Sherry investigation remained a closely held secret, a joint project of the D.A. and the sheriff, with backing from federal prosecutors in New Orleans. Although Lynne had continued to request it, the FBI had not joined the case.

Cook and his fellow investigators wanted to avoid tipping off the suspects they stalked, avoiding any publicity about a breakthrough in the Sherry murder case. Besides, there was the matter of Fabian's credibility: No one wanted to impugn, or even destroy, Mayor Pete Halat's reputation on the basis of unproven testimony from a convicted murderer.

Still, the Sherry investigation had been reduced to a simple straight line: Trying to corroborate—or disprove—Bobby Joe Fabian. The investigation no longer flew in dozens of unproductive directions, as it had under the Biloxi police Department's guidance. The problematic task force was history. Indeed, Cook and the others felt the

Biloxi Police had to be kept out of the loop. Pete Halat had
been sworn in as mayor that July. No one knew if the new
mayor had been tipped about Fabian—LaRa, certainly,
could not be trusted to remain silent—but telling Biloxi
P.D. would be tantamount to sending Halat a telegram.

Some parts of Fabian's story began to check out. Cook
spoke to a distant relative of his in Dallas, Cathy Warner,
who admitted acting as a go-between for Fabian and John
Ransom. She said she picked up scam money, which she
then sent to Halat.

At the same time, though, a review of the Nix ledger that
Halat had provided to the FBI showed no huge influx of
money as described by Fabian, no hundreds of thousands of
dollars in scam cash. The ledger showed only a total of
seventy-one thousand and change received between 1985
and mid-May 1988, an average of twenty-one thousand
dollars a year. Certainly a great deal of money for a convict,
Cook concluded, but not the scam wealth Fabian spoke of.
Bobby Joe explained it away, saying Halat would never keep
an accurate record because it could hang him.

Later in July, an agent from the Georgia Bureau of
Investigation called Cook with a startling development. A
man named Rodney Gaddy, six-foot-two and three hundred
pounds, had been shot in the head five times with a .22—a
professional killing, the body abandoned in rural Carroll
County, Georgia, not far from Atlanta, Agent Roy Olinger
told Cook. Three days later, on July 21, a tip led police to
John Ransom and another man, Donald Short. Olinger had
arrested them for the execution-style slaying.

Olinger later came across a note in Ransom's file that
stated photos and criminal records had been sent recently to
Cook's office.

"I figured you were looking at Ransom for something out
your way, and that you might want to know we picked him
up on a murder warrant," Olinger said.

Randy Cook could hardly believe this turn of events.
After the Sherry case had sat idle so long—almost two
years—Fabian talks about a killer named Ransom, and
suddenly he's booked for murder. The weapon used to kill
Gaddy was similar to the one used on the Sherrys, though in
this case, there had been no silencer. There were, however,

black smudges on Gaddy's hands, as if he had been holding the gun barrel when he was killed—just like Vince.

Cook told the Georgia agent about Fabian's story linking Ransom to the Sherry murders, and the two investigators met in Georgia the following week to search Ransom's home.

Expecting to arrive at some dark and dreary hovel on the outskirts of town, Cook instead found Ransom's house on a suburban street of ranch homes and minivans, kids' bikes on the sidewalk, the smell of charcoal barbecues in the air. Ransom's neighbors thought he worked in the salvage and pawnbroker business. His wife was a businesswoman, his daughter worked for the city of Smyrna. This was not the scene Cook had expected to behold at the home of the Dixie Mafia's notorious one-legged killer.

Yet, hidden in the crawl space beneath the Ransom house, the investigators found wrapped in cloth an unused silencer—professionally machined, the type that uses steel wool and metal grommets, not foam, to muffle gunshots. An assassin's weapon, with no purpose other than murder—merely possessing such a silencer is a crime. But it was different from the type used on the Sherrys, and so held little value for Cook. In Ransom's workshop, however, they found something more in keeping with the Sherry case: a roll of foam rubber. Later, attempts to match it to bits found in the Sherry home proved futile—there was no scientific method of comparison available. Besides, the roll was virginal, with no pieces cut out.

In Ransom's briefcase, Cook found a telephone and address book with LaRa Sharpe's number written inside. There was also a phony stock certificate from a scam Nix and Sharpe had put together, which involved the Halat and Sherry law firm.

"It's come full circle," Cook reported to Joe Price by telephone. "We have a definite link between Nix, Ransom, Halat, and LaRa—just like Fabian said there would be."

As word of the new break in the Sherry case spread through the Harrison County District Attorney's office, the sheriff's department, and other quarters—and to Rex Armistead and Lynne Sposito—someone leaked the story. A day after Cook arrived in Georgia, as he tried to arrange

an interview with Ransom, a news van from a Biloxi
television station pulled up at the courthouse in Newnan,
Georgia, where the murder suspect had been charged.
Overnight, the Mississippi press knew all about John Elbert
Ransom—and his possible role in the Sherry murders.

In the space of the next three days, newspapers in Biloxi
and in the capital city, Jackson, published articles with
headlines reading, "Georgia arrests may be break in Sherry
case," "Police have answers in Sherry case," and, most
alarming to Lynne Sposito and Bobby Joe Fabian, "Louisiana inmate gave police tip in Sherry case." In rapid
succession, the stories detailed Ransom's history as a contract killer, named Kirksey Nix as a suspect, then suggested
that inmate scams at the Angola prison lay at the heart of
the murders because convicts there believed Vince Sherry
had stolen their money. Clearly, someone with inside
knowledge of the investigation was blabbing. The only key
element missing from the stories was Fabian's name, and
the suspicion that the new mayor of Biloxi might have
somehow been involved in the murders.[2] The omissions
proved small comfort.

Fabian immediately called Lynne. "Are they trying to get
me killed?" he bellowed. "Do you think Kirksey and them
just might figure out who that Louisiana inmate is that's
done all the talkin'? I'm dead. I'm dead. I've got to have
protection, Lynne, or it's game over."

"Okay, okay, Bobby Joe. I'll get on it." Lynne immediately called the district attorney and Joe Price, and asked
them to arrange for Fabian's protection. Both men had been
quoted extensively in the press after the initial story on
Ransom broke, and Lynne had become thoroughly irritated
with them. Secrecy had been the investigators' only advan-
tage, allowing those who had gotten away with murder for
two years to remain complacent. Now Nix and Halat and
everyone else knew they were under investigation.

If she had known this would happen, Lynne realized, she
could have made it all public before the election. Now
Fabian's life was in danger for no good reason. She had
begun to develop an odd affection for the man and his
constant line of bull. More important, she needed him.
"You've got to do something about Bobby Joe," she told
Price. "He says he'll be killed, and I believe him."

Price promised to talk to the Angola warden and take care of things, mollifying Lynne somewhat, though she remained uneasy. Her fears were confirmed when Fabian called her the next day. With revelations about the case mounting in the press daily, Fabian remained vulnerable and frightened. He had been branded a snitch, yet he had gotten no help, he said.

"I don't know what I'm gonna do, Lynne. I think somebody wants me dead, so this whole thing'll go away. They don't want to deal with going after a mayor."

Lynne told him to calm down. She had been thinking about ways to keep Fabian safe. "Maybe I know someone who will want to deal with all this," Lynne said slowly. "I know someone who would love to talk to you."

The next day, August 1, Randy Cook called Price again from Georgia. He was finishing up, frustrated in his attempt to question Ransom. He started griping that he could get no further than small talk, but Price cut him off.

"You'd better hurry back, Randy," Price said. "All hell's breaking loose. Bobby Joe Fabian gave an interview to a television station. It's gonna be on the air tonight."

Fearing for the life of the key witness to her parents' murder, Lynne had turned to a television reporter she knew, Ed Bryson. He had reported on Margaret Sherry's election bid and, later, the murders. Lynne suggested Bryson could talk to Fabian, check out his story, and preserve it on videotape as a kind of insurance policy against attempts on his life. Instead, Bryson came back with what he considered the story of his career.

By the time Randy Cook returned home, the city of Biloxi had been transfixed by the extraordinary melodrama playing out on its television sets. Wearing sunglasses, smoking a cigarette, and chugging a can of Dr. Pepper, his features computer-scrambled but his accent unmistakable, Bobby Joe Fabian told his story on statewide TV. He repeated for the camera his key allegation—about a meeting at Angola between Nix, Halat, himself, and one other inmate, in which the murders of the Sherrys supposedly were planned.

"Peter Halat knew . . . that somebody was gonna die," Fabian drawled, pausing for dramatic effect. "And better Sherry than him."

The interview, broadcast by Station WLBT in Jackson then seen throughout the South in subsequent rebroadcasts, created a sensation—eclipsing all other news for days. Even the coincidentally timed start of the conspiracy trial of former mayor Gerald Blessey seemed tame by comparison. And Lynne Sposito had caused it all.

Fabian spilled everything—then Joe Price confirmed on the air that some of Fabian's story had checked out. This was crucial corroboration for Bryson, enabling him to report that the allegations against Halat carried some credibility.

Asked on camera if he had been involved in the Sherry murders, Halat calmly branded the allegation "preposterous," and labeled anyone who said otherwise a liar.

The story aired that same August night on the ten o'clock news—and then it took over every TV station, radio program, and newspaper in the state, then the region. City hall telephones jammed with calls from press organizations nationwide the next morning, network anchors, news magazines, and pulp tabloids vying for interviews Halat would not grant. In a matter of hours, everyone wanted a piece of the mayor accused of murder.

The decision to broadcast the story would remain a controversial one, subject to much second-guessing. Other press organizations might have investigated further and longer before airing or printing such an unproven accusation. Many would have sought corroboration of Fabian's account of a meeting at Angola to plan the Sherrys' demise. Still others might have waited to see if formal charges were filed before impugning a man's reputation. Halat, after all, had not been convicted of any crimes. He had not been arrested. He was, by law, an innocent man. Lives could be—had been—destroyed in a moment by unproven allegations spotlighted and amplified by the press. True, the broadcast that night did not say Fabian's allegations were true—merely that the police were investigating them. Still, the risk of unfairly tarring an innocent man remained enormous.

"Whatever happens," Lynne told her husband that night, after Becky Field described the newscast to her, "I feel sorry for Pete's wife and kids. They're going to suffer for this."

Yet she did not regret her decision to call Bryson. Fabian got his protection after the interview—in a hurry. And she had come too far to allow herself any regrets. Instead, she looked forward to receiving a videotape from Becky so she could watch Bryson's report and Pete Halat's response. Once again, she would watch Pete's eyes and look for truth.

The next day, Pete Halat called a press conference to denounce as irresponsible the news report of Fabian's allegations. He stood at a lectern before a packed audience in the city council chambers, tan, fit, his red power tie and dark suit immaculate, his eyes small behind wire-rim glasses, muscles jackhammering uncontrollably inside one cheek. At times bitterly sarcastic, other times plaintive—but never at a loss for words—Halat reiterated his denial of involvement in murders and scams, then fielded every question thrown at him for as long as the assembled reporters had questions to hurl. He re-enacted his discovery of the bodies (weaving in a few minor inconsistencies only Lynne Sposito, with her endless re-reading of police reports, would notice). He outlined his relationship with Kirksey Nix (minus some telling details, such as the telephone marriage he set up, the Mercedes he drove, the home he helped Nix purchase, and his trips to Angola with Mike Gillich). Halat said Fabian knew him only because he briefly represented the con man, who then used his knowledge of Halat to concoct a sensational story.

In all, Halat constructed a vehement defense of himself. Surrounded by the creamy white columns of the council chambers, the Confederate battle flag furled behind him, Halat gave a gutty, bravura performance even some of his detractors had to admire. His supporters, along with city hall workers, delivered him a standing ovation at the end.

"As far as the Sherry murder investigation is concerned," he avowed, "my life is an open book—legal, personal, or otherwise. . . . These reports were based upon statements made by a twice-convicted murderer . . . who has plainly said he hopes his statement will help expedite a transfer from Angola to Mississippi."

Here was the old trial lawyer's tactic: Accuse the accuser. He knew he could not lose such a credibility contest. Still, his occasionally tight smile, jittery demeanor, and dripping sarcasm undercut his message at times. When asked why police maintained heavy security during the press conference, an imperial Halat snapped, "Because I wanted them here." And when another reporter asked where he was on the night of the Sherry murders, he couldn't resist the wiseguy quip, "Where were you?" To some, he came across cold, concerned only with his fate, rather than with the truth about the murder of his best friend. Others seemed merely confused by the accusations. A city bewildered and still reeling from scandals left over from the previous mayoral administration now had to deal with yet another city government embroiled in controversy—and a far more sinister controversy, at that.

Despite his best efforts, Halat failed to put the story to rest. If anything, his fiery denials only made it that much more sensational. Follow-up stories began to appear detailing Halat's participation in the questionable marriage of Kellye Dawn and Kirksey Nix, the presence of LaRa Sharpe in Halat's office, the suspicion that the law office had received scam money, and the unusually large numbers of phone calls from Nix. Halat watched in amazement as the stories escalated, ever more damaging—all of it rooted in the word of a man whose lies were legendary, who admitted he made a living as a con man.

So Halat called another press conference five days after the first, and produced his own blockbuster. He had copies of the visitor logs from Angola, which showed nothing like the meeting Fabian had described with Nix, Halat, and company. According to those logs, the Sherry murder planning session never happened.

"Totally false and easily refutable allegations were made linking me to the planning and the assassinations of Vincent and Margaret Sherry," Halat railed. He said the logs were in the warden's office, within one hundred yards of the Bryson-Fabian interview. Failing to check them represented "the type of mistake that could only and should only be made by first-year journalism students."

He had been able to obtain this information in one hour, he claimed, yet a TV station intent on broadcasting Fabian's allegations had not even tried to get it.

". . . Outside of the allegations of Bobby Fabian, I stand before you accused of no crime, yet still having to defend my name."

The logs showed Halat had never jointly visited Fabian, Nix, and another inmate at Angola. Halat made a special point of emphasizing that they showed no visit by him to the prison in March 1987 (or any month in 1987), which is when Fabian claimed the Sherry murder planning session took place. And that meeting lay at the heart of Fabian's story.[3]

Yet, though the logs did tarnish Fabian's already dubious credibility, they did not entirely clear Halat. They showed Halat had scheduled an attorney-client meeting with Nix on December 3, 1986, arriving almost two hours late. No purpose for the visit was offered in the logs, and Halat chose not to dwell on this fact.

The logs also showed Halat had scheduled, then canceled at the last minute, a meeting with Fabian and another inmate on January 30, 1987. The cancellation came too late to stop the unwieldy visitation mechanism at the massive prison: Fabian was hauled to the visiting area anyway. Halat explained to the press that he had been retained by Fabian to examine the possibility of getting him transferred to Mississippi, which he soon determined would be impossible, making the meeting at Angola unnecessary.

Halat had scheduled a second visit with Nix, the logs also revealed, along with Peter Mule and another inmate, on February 23, 1987, at 1:30 P.M.—a meeting that would have been uncomfortably close in time and attendance to Fabian's recollection. But an anonymous scrawled notation on the log seemed to exonerate Halat here as well—indicating that the meeting was canceled by telephone at 1:25 P.M. Once again, though, the inmates he had arranged to see were hauled to the attorney-client visitor's bullpen in preparation for the visit, giving them a chance to mingle and talk—just as Fabian had said.

Still, as the mayor told it, the overall message of the prison logs proved him innocent and Fabian a liar. His eyes glittered behind his glasses when he asked one reporter, "What else do you need?"

Strangely, copies of the prison logs were not given to the

media until after the conference had ended—although they had been in hand in Biloxi since early that morning. The delay spared Halat from having to answer questions about two oddities that appeared in the log excerpts.

The first was a tiny handwritten notation on the log pages showing they had been photocopied on an earlier occasion by Harrison County Sheriff's Captain Randy Cook. The copies had been made August 3, the morning after Halat's first press conference and four days before the mayor sent his Biloxi chief of detectives to fetch them. Cook had driven to Angola to gather the logs before anyone else could meddle.

The other oddity appeared in log notations for the December 1986 meeting between Halat and Kirksey Nix. A notation indicated Halat had tried to bring someone with him to visit Nix: strip-club magnate and Dixie Mafia crony Mike Gillich. Gillich apparently tried to enter as a private investigator, but was turned away for lack of professional credentials. The significance of this notation eluded almost all of the reporters, as did another striking entry on the prison's front gate log, a separate record that showed Halat's entry to the Angola grounds for that December visit. That log listed a license number for Halat's car—a number that belonged to the Mercedes registered to Mike Gillich: Kirksey Nix's Mercedes.

And no one at the press conference thought to ask Pete Halat the question that puzzled Lynne Sposito when she reviewed the tape of the press conference: Why was Halat so adamant about denying being at Angola in March 1987?

True, March was the month Fabian claimed to have met with Nix and Halat to discuss killing Vince Sherry. But the convict had told this to only five people: Rex Armistead, Joe Price, Lynne Sposito, Bobby Payne, and Randy Cook. He never mentioned it in his televised interview with Ed Bryson. Lynne watched the tape three times to make sure before she told investigators what she had seen—once again noticing something where others had not. As far as anyone watching the now-infamous broadcast could tell, Bobby Joe Fabian never said when this supposed meeting took place. It could have been any time before the murders.

It was Pete Halat who brought up March 1987.

*   *   *

For Randy Cook, the prison logs also provided a revelation, but not the evidence of innocence Halat saw. He agreed with Fabian that the logs could be doctored or incomplete, blunting Halat's assertions of innocence. Cook himself once got on the prison grounds without showing up in the log books.

The revelation for Cook lay instead in that scribbled notation about Mike Gillich. It was the first time the crime lord's name had surfaced since Cook had become involved in the Sherry murder investigation. Fabian had never mentioned him. Yet here was Pete Halat, Biloxi's future mayor, visiting the notorious Nix with the equally notorious Mr. Mike in tow—in a Mercedes registered to Gillich.

In the wake of Pete Halat's press conferences, another, lower-key announcement was made. George Phillips, the veteran U.S. Attorney for the Southern District of Mississippi, announced that his office, along with the FBI, would join the resurgent investigation. A federal grand jury in Jackson would be convened to probe the case—the subpoenas were about to fly.

Almost overnight, Bobby Joe Fabian's revelation and heavy publicity did something Lynne Sposito's pleas had not accomplished in two years. At last, the agency she wanted all along to look at the murders, the FBI, was involved. In Raleigh, North Carolina, Lynne Sposito had one word to say when Becky Field called with the news: "Finally."

The publicity brought more than an end to inaction, however. An outbreak of conscience—or opportunism—gripped Angola. Prison officials had finally cracked down, creating a "scam tier" where Nix, Fabian, and his fellow con men were kept in special isolation, with mail, visitation, and phone privileges greatly curtailed. A federal judge monitoring prison conditions there had declared a "state of emergency." The inmates had even more time on their hands, and Randy Cook's number would be passed around among inmates as vividly as the scammers once had passed out pictures of fetching young men. This was one of the consequences of publicity Cook had most feared: Convicts looking for a break on their sentences suddenly wanted to help solve the Sherry murders—whether they had genuine information or not. And all of them called Cook.

The first witness to come forward after Fabian talked was indeed influenced by all the publicity Lynne had caused. But he did not come from prison or jail. To Randy Cook's amazement, the next key witness in the Sherry murder investigation came from within the office of Halat and Sherry. He had been there all along, and no one ever realized it.

CHAPTER 25

A nightmare plagued Charles Leger, clinging to his sleep like sweaty, twisted sheets. For months, a face swam in and out of focus as he slept, taunting and haunting the young attorney—the face of a stalker, intent on murder. He didn't know the name of the man who owned that face, but he knew he'd never forget it.

Then, in August 1989, he saw it again. Only this time, the face of a killer did not appear in his dreams. It floated into view on his television set. The face belonged to John Elbert Ransom. For the past year, Chuck Leger had been dreaming about the man investigators had just named as a suspect in the killing of Vincent and Margaret Sherry.

Leger would later swear the hair stood up on back of his neck when he saw that gaunt old man on television, shivers gripping him in the midst of summer. The memory came back to him then. He knew that face not just from his nightmares, but from his waking life, an unnerving encounter in downtown Biloxi—an encounter that occurred shortly before the Sherry murders. And it scared him to death.

After some hesitation—he knew his story sounded odd at best—Leger wrote to the district attorney. In short order, he was sitting down with Randy Cook, giving a statement under oath. A few weeks later, he became one of the first witnesses in the Sherry case to come before the new federal grand jury convened by U.S. Attorney Phillips.

In the summer of 1987, Chuck Leger had gone to work for Pete Halat, picking up the slack after Vince Sherry left the firm for the bench. A few months after joining the firm, he had driven with Pete that terrible day in September 1987, when Halat found the bodies of Vince and Margaret. Leger's nightmares began a short time later, he told Cook.

They were always the same: He would awake rigid and sweating, exhausted from fleeing a tall, gaunt man with sallow skin, scarred or wrinkled, and piercing, dead eyes.

At first, he could not remember where he first saw that face. Then it came to him—the encounter behind the law office a day or two, or at most, a week or two, before Vince and Margaret died.[1] The tall, lanky man had blocked Leger's path and demanded to know where to find Vince. When Leger suggested the courthouse, the man stared icily at him in silence, then stalked off, limping slightly, as if something were wrong with his right leg.

"Someday, that man's going to be arrested for something, and I'll see his face in the paper," Leger told a friend and fellow attorney after the nightmare had come to dominate his sleep. "Then I'll know who it was."

That prediction came to pass a few days after Bobby Joe Fabian's moment of fame, when a televised news report on the Sherry case included a photo of John Ransom, sitting handcuffed in a police car in Georgia.

"It's him. I've seen him—the man I've been dreaming about," Leger frantically told a friend of his, another attorney. He had described the dreams to this friend a year earlier.[2] "He's the one they think killed Vince."

Randy Cook might have found this whole story of nightmares hard to believe, given Leger's reliance on a two-year-old memory of a momentary encounter, filtered through the distorting gauze of dreams. Hard to believe, except for one thing: Leger not only had described Ransom with a limp, but he had named the correct leg, the right one. Leger distinctly remembered Ransom wearing some sort of boots, perhaps cowboy boots, and stepping down off a curb

awkwardly, as if something were wrong with his right foot.
The NCIC printout on Ransom was right there on Cook's
desk: Under identifying features, it showed Ransom's right
leg lost in shotgun blast, replaced by an artificial limb. At
that time, none of the news reports had mentioned
Ransom's wooden leg. Leger could not have known about it
unless he had seen the peg-legged killer himself, just as he
claimed.

Chuck Leger had provided a breakthrough in the case:
The hit man fingered by Bobby Joe Fabian had been in
Biloxi at the time of the murders, prowling about and
asking for one of the victims by name. There was no way
Fabian could be accused of fabricating this. It did not prove
Ransom a murderer, only that he had been in town at the
right time, and that he had some connection to the victims.
Still, it was powerful, damning testimony.

"It all sounds so bizarre and so incredible," Leger told
grand jurors within a month of sitting down with Cook.
"But if you ever look this man in the face, you will see what
I'm talking about. If he gives you this kind of look, it is like,
you know, a cold-blooded, I'm going to kill you kind of
look. And that is the way he looked at me."[3]

Chuck Leger's contribution to the case did not stop with
his remembrance of John Ransom. He also told Randy
Cook, and later, grand jurors, about LaRa Sharpe's suspicious use of the law office and telephones, how she took over
the law library and made him feel unwelcome there. LaRa
spent at least an hour on the telephone daily, he recalled—
with her presence in the law office continuing well into
1988. After she left, the office kept getting calls for an
attorney named LaRa—apparently she had posed as a
lawyer as well as a paralegal, Leger said.

"All I could ever see was that she was talking on the
phone and I thought, well, this is not productive. . . . She
seemed to have run of the office."[4]

Cook saw immediately that Leger's testimony put LaRa
Sharpe at Halat and Sherry long after she claimed to have
left the office, and long after she claimed to have parted
company with Nix and his scams. To secure her immunity
agreement, LaRa had vowed she had stopped working in

the law office by the end of 1986. Yet Leger had not gone to work there until May 1987, and he remembered LaRa being around for a full year after he started. Cook had caught LaRa in a crucial lie.[5]

Leger's recollections about his former employer, Pete Halat, seemed equally damning to Cook. When Halat became mayor, for example, Leger was supposed to inherit the office's case files, but he never could find the records on Kirksey Nix. Then one day late in July, Halat's secretary, Ann Kriss, who had moved to city hall with the new mayor a month earlier, showed up at the law office, looking for the Nix file. This would have been just after the first news stories appeared linking Ransom and Angola inmates to the murders, but before Bobby Joe Fabian appeared on the evening news with his stunning accusations against Pete. Kriss hunted down the Nix file, finding it in Pete's old office, then hauled the thick bundle back to city hall. Leger never did see what was in the file, nor did he know why Halat suddenly wanted it days before Fabian accused the mayor of murder.

"I don't know if he had been forewarned about an interview or whatever," Leger said. "But that was the Friday before the interview."

Then there was Leger's account of the morning Pete found Vince and Margaret dead in their home. To Cook's amazement, no one with the Biloxi Police Department had interviewed Leger in depth. No one had taken the time to find out that Leger's recollection of that morning differed dramatically from Pete Halat's. Cook hadn't even known Leger had been present until the lawyer told him—Halat had always made it sound as if he entered the house alone.

That morning in September 1987, as Leger had prepared to take a telephone deposition, Halat popped his head through the office door and asked what he was doing. After Leger told him, Halat replied, "Okay, let me know when you are done." No explanation, no sense of urgency, as Leger recalled it—just "see me when you are through." At this point, there was some general tension in the office, because the staff already knew Vince had not shown up for work.

Thirty or forty minutes later, Leger finished his deposition and reported to Halat, who said, "Let's go for a ride." Again, no explanation or hurry. Halat just issued the order, and they walked out to Kirksey Nix's blue Mercedes.

They drove for a while. Leger recalled that he had no idea where they were headed, but Halat seemed nervous, habitually rubbing his hands as he steered. Finally Halat said, "We have got a problem. No one has heard from Vince for at least two days. No one has seen him or Margaret."

They drove on in silence after that, ten tense minutes. At the house, instead of just knocking on the door, Pete chatted with a next-door neighbor, then shuffled around the cars parked in the Sherrys' driveway, trying to determine if they had moved recently. Throughout this inspection, Pete told the others not to touch anything, Leger recalled. At the same time, Leger started to rifle the mailbox to see when the Sherrys had last collected their mail. Again, Halat seemed concerned, calling out, "Don't touch anything!" As Leger told it, Halat issued these instructions before going into the house—*before* anyone should have known they had stumbled onto a crime scene, where fingerprints and other evidence could be crucial.

Leger next recalls Halat walking around the left side of the house, still without knocking or trying the door. Lynne Sposito would later question why Halat did that. A frequent visitor like Pete should have known the most direct way to the rear door off the den lay on the right side of the house. If he had walked that way, Halat would have come to that blood-streaked glass door, through which Vince lay clearly visible, clearly dead. But Halat did not do that.

Instead, Leger swore, Halat came running back to the front door. Leger had tried it, found the door unlocked, and yelped for Pete to come quick. As the dogs barked furiously inside, Pete pushed the door open all the way and, after gasping at the terrible odor rushing out at them, the two lawyers walked inside, Halat first, followed by Leger.[6]

As Leger stooped in the entryway to calm the frantic dogs, Halat walked a few steps inside, toward the kitchen-den area and out of Leger's line of vision. He returned almost immediately, pushing Leger outside and shutting the door behind them, panic and nausea etching his face. Leger remembers Halat crying out then, "Oh, God, no, not Vince. Not Vince, oh God, no, no. Not Vince."

When Leger saw the shock on Halat's face, drained of color, he asked what he had seen. Halat seemed on the verge of tears.

"Vince is dead," Leger recalls Halat saying. And then, without having come near the Sherrys' bedroom, Pete declared something else—something he should not have known. According to Leger, Halat announced, "Vince and Margaret are dead."

Randy Cook at first dismissed this part of the story as vaguely interesting, but not particularly useful. Halat could simply have drawn the obvious conclusion from the evidence at hand. He had not actually seen Margaret's body in the bedroom, but he could easily have assumed she had been killed. Then, in his grief and horror, he stated his suspicions as though they were fact as he stumbled out of the reeking house into the cauterizing sunlight of Gulf summer.

But then Cook started thinking about it, and he realized this only made sense because he had the benefit of hindsight, the knowledge that Margaret really was dead. On the morning of September 16, 1987, however, there had been no reason for such certainty. For all Halat knew, Margaret could have been kidnapped, or sitting gagged and tied up in a closet. She could have been lying unconscious, for that matter, in need of immediate medical attention. But Pete hadn't rushed inside to see if she needed help, an arguably reasonable reaction. No one had done that—because Pete said she was dead. To Cook, it raised serious questions. To Lynne Sposito, who spoke with Leger a short time after Cook, Pete's announcement seemed an admission of foreknowledge.

After he finished questioning Leger, Cook pulled out the box of files he had inherited from Biloxi. There it was: Pete Halat's initial statement, taken that same day, four hours after Halat first crept into the hot, stinking house. Halat had been very clear on the point: "I had no idea that Mrs. Sherry was in the house, but I did not, did not re-enter the house for reasons that I can't explain now."

It was a serious contradiction, based not on the word of a felon with ample reasons to lie, but an honest man, an associate of Halat's who, if anything, had reason to be grateful to the new mayor, not vindictive. Halat had ap-

pointed Leger to a city court judgeship, had given him a job,
helped him get started in private practice. Leger had given
this contradiction little thought at the time of the murders,
but over the years, he had begun having doubts about Pete.
Halat had seemed sincerely griefstricken when he emerged
from the house that morning, so overcome with horror. And
yet, there was that inexplicable declaration, Vince *and*
Margaret are dead.

"I keep thinking, was Pete acting that day?" Leger testified. "No, I'm thinking he wasn't acting. And I keep
thinking, was he acting? I don't know."'

CHAPTER 26

N ot long after Chuck Leger came forward, Randy Cook
received a new partner: FBI Special Agent Keith Bell.
A veteran bureau agent, Bell had returned years earlier
from duty in Los Angeles to his former home turf on the
Gulf Coast. He had been lobbying for months for an active
role in the Sherry murder investigation, battling his superiors' reluctance to commit federal involvement to a "local"
case. He had been as frustrated as Lynne Sposito with the
FBI's refusal to get involved. But with a multistate fraud
ring tied to the murder, and a potential conflict of interest
of epic proportions brewing in Biloxi city hall, the FBI
could no longer stay in the background. At the U.S.
Attorney's request, the silver-haired, professorial Bell
teamed up with Cook and the sheriff's department.

It was an unusual arrangement for the FBI, which does
not often mingle agents with local police agencies in such
close partnerships. But the combination proved an effective
one as the two investigators plowed into Bobby Joe Fabian's

tale and the mystery of the Sherry murders. An FBI agent for most of his adult life, Bell had investigated government payoffs, the Patty Hearst kidnapping, and, more recently, the corrupt former sheriff of Harrison County, Leroy Hobbs, a legendary figure with deep Dixie Mafia connections. Throughout his career, Bell had demonstrated endless patience in dealing with witnesses, particularly incarcerated ones, whose inevitable lies and shadings sooner or later irritated Cook. Bell would just smile and take them through the story one more time, eking out confessions. Randy Cook, on the other hand, could do things Keith Bell could not—such as tape-record witnesses, or trade information with other cops—simple but essential investigatory steps that the bureaucratic FBI and its web of regulations sometimes made impossible.

By the time Keith Bell joined the investigation, the case had taken on a manic rhythm all its own, with witnesses cropping up unexpectedly almost daily, sending the two investigators careening from Atlanta to Angola to Dallas, then back to the Coast. More than one hundred witnesses would be interviewed by the two-man team, covering ground the old task forces hadn't touched in two years of trying.

Early in October 1989, an FBI agent in Baton Rouge telephoned Bell with information on a wiry armed robber and heroin user named Robert Hallal. A three-time loser and escape artist, Hallal had served twelve years of a fifty-year sentence in Angola, much of it with Kirksey Nix. Hallal had scammed with Nix and was now claiming to have been offered a job upon his parole from prison in the summer of 1987.

The job: Kill a judge in Biloxi.

"We'll be out to see him tomorrow," Bell told the other agent.

They met with Hallal twenty miles from Angola, in the St. Francis Hotel, the FBI having arranged for his leaving the prison on a pretense. Hallal certainly looked the part of addict, convict, con man, and hit man. His forearm bore a crude tattoo of a bird. He wore his stringy hair slicked back, atop a face narrow and pallid, a mask of acne scars with eyes as gray and dull as ball bearings. The career criminal tried to sound earnest as he spoke in the unique, Brooklyn-meets-cypress-swamp accent of New Orleans, but all the while he surveyed his surroundings, as if measuring the distance between his chair and the locked hotel room door.

"I worked the scams with Junior for a year, in 1986," Hallal said. "My share was about fifty thousand dollars."

Hallal explained how he played various characters on the prison phone for Nix, then helped line up road dogs to pick up scam money. These confederates included his ex-wife, Patricia. With a smirk, Hallal added that she worked as a prostitute and ran an X-rated video store in the Mobile area. Nix had put her in touch with a "Mr. Mike" in Biloxi to help get her set up in the video business, Hallal said. "She'll back me up on this," he told the investigators. "Go talk to her."

He said he did not know for sure if Pete Halat knew about the scams, only that the lawyer's assistance had been essential. Halat's office repeatedly phoned Angola and left messages for Nix to call, Hallal said. This gave Junior crucial phone access. Monitoring at the prison was so poor, Nix easily made scam calls instead of dialing Halat, Hallal said.

By this point, Cook and Bell knew all about the homosexual scams. They had received a wealth of information from Louisiana authorities, who had just indicted Nix, LaRa Sharpe, Kellye Dawn, and twelve other inmates, guards, and road dogs, charging all with theft. Hallal's name had come up in that investigation, too, as had his wife's.

Hallal had worked the scam in Angola until he was paroled in May 1987. He promptly dumped his wife, then moved in with her landlady. Hallal lived off of credit cards belonging to the landlady's husband until he started scamming again for Nix on the outside. Then, in July 1987, Nix called with another sort of job offer.

"I'd like for you to knock someone off for me," Nix said, according to Hallal. "You know who my man is on the Gulf Coast, right? Go see Mr. Mike if you're interested."

Then Nix asked him to pick up eleven thousand dollars from his wife, Kellye, and deliver it to Mr. Mike, Hallal said. Kellye at that time was living in St. Francisville, near the prison. Nix didn't trust her to go to the Coast alone with the money, fearing she'd buy drugs with it instead. Hallal agreed, and with his girlfriend, they picked up Kellye and headed to Biloxi with the cash.

Once in Biloxi, they had trouble finding a hotel—Hallal said there was some sort of concert in town, and everything was booked. After driving up and down the beach, Hallal and his girlfriend ended up finding a room in one hotel, while Kellye stayed at another. He couldn't remember the names, though he described them in detail so Cook and Bell could try to find them. Kellye also showed him the Golden Nugget so he could find Mike Gillich later on. The investigators took careful note of all these seeming mundanities related by Hallal. They formed elements of the story that could be checked—reservation records, phone tolls—the specifics Bobby Joe Fabian so woefully lacked. Such detail would either corroborate Hallal, or prove him a liar.

The next day, according to Hallal, he went to see Mr. Mike, using a code name Nix provided, "Jimmy James." Cook and Bell exchanged a look at this. Cook remembers thinking, "Damn, here's an inmate actually telling us the truth for a change." It was that code name. "Jimmy James" was the alias used by one Donald Lester James, a Dixie Mafia killer with a long history on the Coast. Twenty years earlier, a gunman named Hugh Fuller had blasted James's home with a shotgun—the case in which Mike Gillich's friend, Justice of the Peace Roy Mattina, dismissed charges against Fuller. Six months later, James was dead, shot in front of an illegal gambling casino on The Strip, a murder that remains unsolved to this day. The thing was, Hallal had never been to the Coast before. You would have to be a cop—or a crook—with long roots in Biloxi to know James. Nix and Gillich, on the other hand, knew the late Jimmy James all too well.

"Okay, so you introduce yourself to Gillich as Jimmy James," Cook prodded. "Then what?"

According to Hallal, Gillich said, "Junior wants a judge killed."

When he replied, "I'm not interested in killing any judge," Gillich persisted, Hallal told the investigators. "Hear me out. Preparations will be taken care of. It won't be much of a problem for you because someone from Georgia will mail you a pistol with a silencer."

Cook and Bell exchanged another look. The gun from

Georgia could be the Ransom connection they were looking for. Or Hallal could have pulled this detail—along with a host of others—from news coverage of the case, adding it to his story because he guessed (correctly) that the investigators badly wanted evidence implicating John Ransom. The better the story, Hallal knew, the more likely he'd get a deal cutting his latest sentence of ninety-nine years for armed robbery.

Hallal still refused the job, he said. "I don't do judges." The name of the judge never came up, Hallal told Cook and Bell, nor was the wife mentioned as a target.

Hallal said he then delivered the eleven thousand dollars from Kellye, and bought another eleven thousand dollars' worth of narcotics from Gillich. He remained suspiciously vague when Bell asked where he had gotten that kind of money. A few months later, he said, he returned for another drug deal and ended up ripping off Gillich for eighteen thousand dollars by failing to make a promised delivery of heroin. Hallal said he never saw Gillich after that—for obvious reasons.[1]

Cook and Bell sent Hallal back to prison and began the arduous task of checking his story the next day. If only he had come out of the woodwork before Fabian, they ruminated, he would have cinched their case. But he popped up only after immense publicity about the case, with more than enough details available to concoct just such a tale.

But his story *did* check out. The investigators found a concert had filled hotels on the weekend of August 8, 1989. And records at the Buena Vista Hotel near The Strip showed Hallal's girlfriend, Alice Powers, stayed there August 8 and 9, using her cuckolded husband's American Express card.

At first they could not find a hotel in the area with a record of Kellye Nix, but a few weeks later, when Cook and Bell escorted Hallal to the grand jury, he pointed out a hotel on the beach they had missed. Records showed Kellye had stayed there that weekend, just as Hallal said.[2]

"Actual evidence," Cook remarked to Bell. "We haven't seen that too often."

Later, they tracked down Alice Powers, a reluctant witness at best. She backed up most of Hallal's story, confirming that he went to the Golden Nugget on The Strip during the trip to Biloxi. She denied witnessing any drug deals, however.[3]

Next, they interrogated Bob Wright, named by Hallal as one of Nix's chief scam operatives on the Gulf Coast. Wright had been questioned in vain two years earlier by other agents in the FBI's abortive Angola scam case. Now, though, he was ready to talk. Rotund, with a permanent squint and a rough-edged pirate's beard, Wright agreed to cooperate with the investigation in exchange for legal immunity. But unlike LaRa Sharpe, Wright spelled out in detail his extensive participation in the scam, as well as the substantial role of LaRa and others—more evidence that LaRa had been less than truthful with investigators. Wright recalled picking up as much as two hundred thousand dollars for Nix over a period of years, delivering most of it to Gillich, with some going to LaRa Sharpe and to Pete Halat's office. "Mr. Gillich counts money faster than the girl does at the bank," Wright quipped.

Wright swore he had no knowledge of the Sherry murders, although he did provide some crucial corroboration for Robert Hallal. He described a .22 caliber semiautomatic pistol with silencer attached—the same sort of weapon that had killed the Sherrys. Wright swore he saw such a gun in LaRa's camera bag in 1986 at the Ocean Springs house, that he had examined it and held it, and that Nix had asked him to testfire it, which he refused to do. The gun and its illegal silencer had appeared in Nix's Ocean Springs house shortly after LaRa drove four hours to meet John Ransom in a Jackson, Mississippi, motel room at two in the morning, her two young daughters in tow. She had made that oddly timed drive one day after visiting Nix in Angola. Wright said LaRa's mother later told him that LaRa had taken the gun to Mike Gillich.[4]

As far as Cook and Bell were concerned, this was the silenced gun from Georgia that Hallal had described. And if true, LaRa Sharpe was involved not just in scams, but in murder.

The last step the investigators faced in corroborating Hallal's story was verifying his participation in the scams, the only way of proving he had a relationship with Kirksey Nix. For that, Cook and Bell needed to question Hallal's ex-wife, Pat, in the Mobile area. They asked a sheriff's deputy there to track her down, and he called back within a few days, telling them to drive over to neighboring Alabama.

"Wait'll you see this place," their host deputy had said with a grin. "You'll think you're in the Best Little Whorehouse in Texas."

He escorted them not to the X-rated video store Hallal had described, but to an ordinary-looking house on Highway 90, in a rural area outside of town. Inside, as promised, Cook and Bell found a gaudily decorated lobby with a counter, a woman in a negligee behind it, and similarly attired ladies lounging about, surveying the two men in their suits and badges without apparent alarm. A sign in front indicated that Visa and Mastercard were accepted forms of payment.

They rounded up Pat, who quickly admitted to participating in Kirksey Nix's scams. She had been to the Nix house in Ocean Springs, she had picked up and delivered scam money, she knew all about LaRa, Bob Wright, and other players in the massive prison fraud.

"Bob Hallal is a lying sonofabitch," Pat told Cook and Bell. "But he told you the truth on this one."[5]

They left her where she was, assuring her that they had no intention of arresting her, but that she might be needed as a witness. Later, she was charged with scamming by Louisiana authorities.

And that was as far as the story could be checked. Hallal had scammed, he had gone to Biloxi in August, he had met someone at Gillich's strip club. Phone logs from 1986, 1987, and 1988 at Angola showed many messages for Kirksey Nix, telling him to call attorney Peter Halat, just as Hallal had predicted. The telephone records from the Powers home in Leesville showed a series of collect calls from a phone at Angola located in Nix's part of the prison—calls Hallal said Nix made before and after he was offered the murder contract, trying to convince him to take the job. Everything seemed to check out.[6]

What actually was said between Hallal, Nix, and Gillich could not be verified, however. There were no other witnesses. And even if there were, Bob Hallal's testimony did not tell Cook and Bell who murdered the Sherrys. They could put Kirksey Nix and Mike Gillich (but not John Ransom, Pete Halat, LaRa Sharpe, or, for that matter,

Bobby Joe Fabian) in a conspiracy to commit murder. But that conspiracy hadn't led anywhere. Hallal had turned down the job. He said he had no idea who actually did the killing. In essence, Cook and Bell had a case against murder conspirators whose plot failed to gel.

But then they got another call from the Georgia Bureau of Investigation, the agency that had first told them about John Ransom's arrest. Investigators there had a new witness, a friend of Ransom's who was talking to them. He was another convict with a story. And this one, Cook and Bell were told, just might solve the Sherry case—if it were true.

William O'Neal Rhodes had robbed banks, burgled houses, defrauded the government. He had taken corners in getaway cars on two tires and a few inches of rubber, just like in the movies. He was a forger and an escape artist—in short, a lifelong criminal. He'd done just about everything illegal he could think of, this side of murder.

In the spring of 1987, he was offered the chance to complete his résumé. All he had to do was go to Biloxi and drive a car. The man with one leg would do the rest.

Nearly three years passed before Bill Rhodes told this story to Randy Cook and Keith Bell. There was no way to verify what he said, no way to know if it was gospel or lies, even as he placed his hand on the Bible and swore to tell the truth. Like many a career criminal, he offered information for freedom, with all the doubts that such deals with the devil can carry. This was his story:

In March 1987, six months before the Sherry murders and well before Hallal was offered the contract, Rhodes drove to Biloxi at John Ransom's invitation. Ransom had been a friend and crime partner for twenty years, and they had already discussed "the job" in Atlanta, in person and on the phone with someone in Biloxi. Rhodes remained reluctant, however, fearing taking out a judge would create too much heat.

"Well, it's not a federal judge," Ransom supposedly said, his scrawny neck bobbing inside a turtleneck sweater, making Rhodes think of one of those felt-covered toy dogs with the perpetually nodding heads. His friend's painful, almost comical thinness, Rhodes knew, concealed a lumberjack's strength, his body all gristle and iron. As they spoke, they cruised around the night-dark streets of Biloxi in a Mercedes sedan, this baby-faced bank robber and the Dixie Mafia's most feared contract killer.

"It's a state circuit judge, that's all," Ransom was saying, leaning over the passenger's seat to talk to Rhodes in the back. A third man, dark-haired, in a natty gray suit and wire-rim glasses, drove in silence. "All you have to do," Ransom said, "is be the wheelman, and back my play. I'll be the one going in."

Here was the best part, Ransom added: "Someone with a lot of pull in Biloxi wants it done. You'll have the run of the town if you do it."

As for the motive for murder: The judge had supposedly screwed somebody out of nearly a half million dollars. Then a police investigation had begun, and the judge became the weak link. "He'll roll over on everyone," Ransom said. "He's got to go.

"The man will pay you twenty thousand to drive," Ransom continued. "I'm getting fifty to do the judge, and I'll give you ten of mine. Thirty thousand dollars."

Rhodes thought about it a minute. It sounded good. Too good. He suddenly had visions of his friend offering him the moon, then pumping a bullet into his head once the job was done. Maybe make it look like a shoot-out between him and the judge, so the cops could solve the crime on the spot. "You know, hell, I'd be getting almost as much as you," Rhodes challenged. "And you're pulling the trigger."

The hit man shook his head. "I don't know about that. I'm getting a hundred thousand."

Rhodes was confused. "I thought you said fifty."

At this, Rhodes told Cook and Bell, the well-dressed man driving the Mercedes spoke up for the first time, his silhouette dim in the glow of the dashboard lights. "No," the driver said, "the wife has to go, too."

It's going to be a double murder, Ransom chimed in, husband and wife, fifty thousand each. "She knows his business, so she has to die, too." It was simple, he said. It was business.

Bill Rhodes said he'd have to think about it.

As Rhodes tells it, the driver of the Mercedes then pulled something from his pocket and handed it to Ransom, who passed it on to Rhodes: five one-hundred dollar bills, crisp enough to still carry that unmistakable new-money smell. "A little traveling cash," Ransom said. "A little taste of things to come."

"Let me know what you decide," Rhodes recalls the hit man saying before they parted. Then they all got out of the car and shook hands. The man in the gray suit said he trusted Rhodes, because John Ransom's endorsement carried a lot of weight. Rhodes nodded, thinking the man had that same sharp-faced look of Al Davis, owner of the Los Angeles Raiders.

Rhodes made the long drive home to Atlanta then, knowing, for that kind of money, he'd eventually agree to take the job for his old partner Ransom. But he got arrested in Georgia for bank robbery a week later, and never got the chance.

He had kept silent for nearly three years after that, speaking up only when he saw a chance to use his story for profit. It never occurred to him to speak sooner, to stop the murder that had been set in motion *before* it happened. Bill Rhodes's mind just didn't work that way. "I'm a criminal," he explained simply. "That's what criminals do."[7]

Rhodes's account of a late March meeting in Biloxi jibed perfectly with Fabian's story of the meeting that same month in Angola. But one thing bothered Cook and Bell: Why the delay afterward? Why would the conspirators, who told Rhodes how anxious they were to get it done, wait from March until September to do the hit? "Why didn't they just get another driver and do it right away?" Cook asked.

"Simple," Rhodes said. "They were waiting to see if I ratted on them. They knew I was arrested. They probably figured I'd roll over on them to cut a deal. But I didn't. They waited awhile, then decided it was safe. The funny thing was, the reason I didn't have to talk was because this one time, I didn't do what they arrested me for. I was innocent. I figured I'd beat that bank robbery charge, and I did. I didn't have to roll over."

It made sense. In all, Cook and Bell were impressed with Bill Rhodes. He never mentioned Kirksey Nix's name in his story, but his account mirrored both Fabian's and Hallal's—the judge blamed for missing money, then targeted for murder. More important, Rhodes added a new element, something no one mentioned before. He said an investigation was under way at the time of the murders, that it was somehow tied to the missing money, and that its existence provided an additional motive to kill—fear that the judge would talk.

This provided important corroboration for Cook and Bell. Rhodes was right: At the time of his ride with John Ransom, the FBI and other agencies had begun investigating the scam. Kellye had already been interrogated, Bob Wright and Robbie Gant were under scrutiny, the law office had been identified as a tool of the scammers, if not a headquarters. Nix, LaRa, and the others knew all this. But Rhodes, who had nothing to do with the scam, would have no way of knowing an investigation was under way in 1987—unless someone on the inside had told him. It was something Rhodes could not have concocted from press accounts. It had never been reported.[8]

Furthermore, Rhodes's characterization of Vince as the "weak link" made sense to Cook and Bell. If Judge Sherry had known anything about the scams, either through participation or mere presence in the law office, Margaret would have made him talk, just as she had years before in the Charlie Acevedo case. And no one should have known that better that Pete Halat. It all fit, Cook and Bell decided.

There was one more point the investigators needed to nail down. Cook asked, "Did you get a name for the man driving the Mercedes, this guy who looked like Al Davis?"

"Yeah, but I just got his first name at the time," Rhodes claimed. "He was introduced to me as Pete."

One of the reasons William Rhodes had decided to come forward was his fear that John Ransom might try to cut a deal and finger him as a conspirator. So Rhodes decided to speak up first. He claimed Ransom had snitched on fellow criminals in exchange for leniency in the past, and had decades earlier been in the federal Witness Security Program. Cook and Bell verified this.

Now that they knew Ransom might be prone to cooperating with authorities, they pushed hard to talk to him, despite his previous denials. In January 1990, they set up a meeting in Georgia, where he was awaiting trial for the Rodney Gaddy murder. His defense attorney there attended, along with Kent McDaniel, the First Assistant U.S

Attorney in Jackson. McDaniel, an ex-cop turned prosecutor, was leading the investigation for his office, bringing Cook's and Bell's witnesses before each monthly meeting of the grand jury.

Ransom still denied involvement in the Sherry murders. But he mentioned traveling to Jackson in 1986 and being visited by LaRa Sharpe in the middle of the night at his motel. This led to an obvious question: What about the gun that appeared in LaRa's camera bag after you met in Jackson?

Before he could answer, Ransom's lawyer abruptly ended the interview. But then he pulled Kent McDaniel aside for a private conversation. When McDaniel returned, he told Cook and Bell what the attorney had said.

"He isn't ready to talk just yet," McDaniel said. "But apparently Ransom could tell us about that gun if he wants to. He told his lawyer he delivered a silenced twenty-two to LaRa Sharpe in 1986. The gun came out of Georgia."

Just as Bob Hallal had said. Ransom's lawyer had unwittingly corroborated a key witness in the case. There was still much to sort out, though. Why, for instance, had the plan shifted from Ransom doing the killing with Rhodes as backup, to Hallal being offered the starring role? And did Ransom end up pulling the trigger in the end, as Chuck Leger's testimony suggested? Cook and Bell couldn't be sure.

They just knew, finally, that they had a case.

CHAPTER 27

One of my greatest joys in life," Harrison County District Attorney Cono Caranna was telling Lynne Sposito, "was to turn your father completely white around the mouth—either because his blood pressure went too high, or because he had to drink a bottle of Maalox to calm himself down.

"I really never liked your parents."

Lynne blinked, too stunned to reply. Had she heard right? Sure, she knew this man and her father had been enemies. But who expected him to say so to her face? She managed to nod silently, gazing across a paper-strewn walnut desk at the large-boned man with iron gray hair facing her. The prosecutor barely paused, continuing his unflattering commentary, unaware Lynne had stiffened in her chair, her lips so compressed they seemed to disappear.

She had come to meet Caranna for the first time since his return to office in late 1989, ostensibly to discuss the Sherry murder investigation. Her previous dealings had been with District Attorney Glenn Cannon, who had unseated Caranna shortly after the murders only to be thrown out of office for bankruptcy fraud. Lynne had trusted Cannon. But Caranna had won his old office back in 1989, giving him jurisdiction in the Sherry murder case—if he wanted it.

Lynne had asked for the meeting, and Caranna let her know just how he felt about her parents. Vince had been charming, a brilliant networker. But at root, he was insincere, and even Machiavellian—qualities that probably got him killed, Caranna opined.

"He sucked up to me in person, yet he defamed me in the community," Caranna recalled. "He tried to give me a campaign contribution. I said, don't bother."

Margaret, on the other hand, had been sincere in Caranna's estimation, a true believer in what she did. The problem was, she never had an original thought in her life, Caranna said. Everything she said or did was in reaction to Gerald Blessey. Blessey, a political ally of Caranna's who hired him to represent the city after his ouster as D.A., was an honest man wrongly accused by Margaret and the feds, Caranna claimed. Nothing she had uncovered could possibly have been threatening enough to warrant her murder, he declared.

"She was cocked and loaded, but she misfired all the time. I once told Gerald that the most effective way to control her was not to say anything, because Margaret could never think of anything to say on her own."

Lynne remained silent, staring, hands bloodless and cold, clutched in her lap, too bewildered by the D.A.'s damning eulogy to get angry. She finally said, "Cono, I understand everything you've said. But what I don't understand is why you're saying it."

"Well, I wanted you to understand my position. As you may or may not know, I went to grade school with Pete Halat and Gerald Blessey. But if Pete was involved, I could still prosecute him. I don't believe Gerald had a thing to do with it, but if he did, I could prosecute him, too. My feelings about your parents would have nothing to do with it. I want their killers caught and punished just as much as you do. After all, this case is going to be mine eventually."[1]

Lynne realized then that Caranna had not been idly attacking her dead parents—he was trying to be honest with her. He knew she was aware of bad blood between him and her parents, and that he had grown up on Point Cadet, of Yugoslavian descent, just like Pete Halat. This was his way, however peculiar, of trying to put her at ease.

"I appreciate you leveling with me," Lynne said. She almost added that, candor aside, he remained the last person she wanted near the case. She knew from Cook and Bell that Caranna's role in the revived investigation was nil anyway—but that could change. He had the power. So she thought better of antagonizing him, and they parted civilly.

The odd meeting with Cono Caranna left Lynne shaken, however, once she considered the implications. Until then, she had naïvely believed it would be only a matter of time before the killers were brought to justice, now that a competent, outside investigation had replaced the city of Biloxi's ineffective efforts. She forgot that something else had to happen once the investigators concluded their work: The case had to go to court. There had to be indictments, a trial, convictions.

Lynne began to see these were not givens, regardless of what Randy Cook and Keith Bell might do. Not only had Cono Caranna expressed doubts about successfully prosecuting the killers in state court, where the crime of murder is almost always charged, but Lynne was starting to realize the U.S. Attorney, with power to take the case to federal court,[2] was less than enthusiastic as well. If the feds didn't act, Lynne knew, no one would.

She believed the investigation itself to be in good hands—that was not the problem. Lynne admired Cook's and Bell's dogged pursuit and had grown especially close to Keith Bell as she became a regular visitor to the FBI's modest offices in Gulfport, where three six-foot-high locked files sat in Bell's office filled with Sherry casework. Lynne told him of her encounters with Halat, her knowledge of Mike Gillich and her father's cases, all of which, Bell said, she would have to tell the grand jury later. Bell, in turn, kept Lynne updated on developments in the case. This give-and-take between investigator and victims' daughter—yet another unprecedented partnership in a thoroughly unique case—kept Lynne sane and able to function at home. She would not be relegated to the corner like most grieving relatives. She had to stay involved.

But a conflict had begun to brew between investigators and federal prosecutors, becoming apparent even to Lynne. The U.S. Attorney's Office and First Assistant Kent McDaniel had growing doubts about the case. The nature of the key witnesses—criminals, all—and the fact that the suspects included a sitting mayor, dictated a cautious approach, McDaniel explained to Lynne when she called to ask why no charges were filed months after Fabian testified before the grand jury.

"My role is devil's advocate," he said. "Someone has to sit here and pick the case apart, to make sure we get it nailed. Because we only get one shot at it."

If they moved prematurely and asked for an indictment too soon, the grand jury could vote against returning one, dealing a severe blow to the case. And if they got past that hurdle and went to trial with too little ammunition, they could be rewarded for their efforts with a chorus of not-guilties. The accused would go free, McDaniel told Lynne. The case would die.[3]

"I trust the investigators," she replied, "and they think they have a case. They know what they're doing."

"It's not ready," McDaniel told her repeatedly over the course of a year of federal investigation and grand jury testimony. "Every witness is tainted. They keep changing their stories. We'd lose."

McDaniel held back with Lynne. The truth was, he regularly left the grand jury in a rage. It was his job to present the witnesses to the jurors. He knew firsthand that every substantive witness in the case kept changing his or her story—Robert Hallal, Bill Rhodes, even Chuck Leger couldn't make up his mind if he thought Pete Halat was dirty or a saint. And each veer in a witness's story would provide defense lawyers a beachhead for attacking the prosecution's case at trial. "Maybe you'll send a Kirksey Nix back to prison with that," McDaniel said. "But what about a Mike Gillich, who's never been convicted of anything? What about Pete Halat?"

The reasons for prosecutorial hesitation seemed legitimate, but Lynne still found this attitude troubling. She knew the office under McDaniel's boss, U.S. Attorney George Phillips, took on other tough and iffy cases. Phillips had prosecuted dozens of corrupt officials in local and state government, from leaders in the Mississippi legislature to the sheriff of Harrison County to some sixty members of county boards of supervisors statewide. But the office had also been heavily criticized for a more recent case—the failed prosecution of Gerald Blessey. The former mayor of Biloxi had been totally exonerated, with jurors finding no evidence he misappropriated government funds, or did anything else wrong. After the verdict, the former mayor and his supporters excoriated Phillips for pursuing unprovable accusations. And though he made no apologies for tackling the Blessey case, the Republican U.S. Attorney in Jackson was not about to take on yet another Democratic mayor in Biloxi unless the case was nailed.

Lynne agonized over this, but the investigation had passed out of her hands, plodding through 1990 and into 1991. As the third anniversary of the murders approached without charges or arrests, she moved into another arena: She became a lobbyist. Senators, congressmen, White House officials, the Justice Department—all began hearing from Lynne Sposito, by mail, by phone, in person. All were encouraged to take an active interest in the Sherry case, and more than one listened. It didn't hurt that Mississippi's delegation of Republican senators and congressmen were well acquainted with Margaret Sherry. They didn't need much prompting to start making pointed phone calls to the office of George Phillips.

This made for an initially rocky relationship between

Lynne and the U.S. Attorney, but she wouldn't let that bother her. She had made up her mind that the killers of her parents would be brought to justice in federal court, the only venue in Mississippi she trusted. She didn't know whether or not there were political pressures dictating against prosecution of the case, but she would take no chances.

"If there are," she told Becky, "I damn well want to make sure there's just as much heat on the other side of the equation." The investigators, meanwhile, continued locking up testimony, gaining the cooperation of Nix's scam partners on the Coast and in Louisiana. The most important of these was Robbie Gant, LaRa's sometime lover who had made innumerable scam pickups—which Cook and Bell documented with receipts and Western Union money order records. Gant had worked for the FBI years before in the earlier, abortive scam investigation, only to be forgotten until Cook and Bell began their own probe. Then they dug out of FBI files the old tape of LaRa at the Halat and Sherry law office, talking to Gant about scams and how best to lie to the police, just one month after the murders. He also recalled being ordered by LaRa to deliver scam money to Mike Gillich. Cook and Bell realized Gant would be a gold mine when it came time to prove LaRa's extensive role in the scam, and her willingness to conspire with others to save Nix and herself.

Gant seemed puzzled, though, when the investigators came to talk to him. "What took you so long?" he asked. "I told the FBI all about this two years ago."

Roy Garland, the ex-Angola convict who played a fake New Orleans cop in Nix's scam, fell in line next when Cook and Bell came knocking on his door. He agreed to testify in exchange for immunity from prosecution, later estimating for the grand jury that he had picked up more than two hundred thousand dollars for Nix in the space of a year. Garland was followed by Nix's own half sister and brother-in-law, Donna and Wayne Henson, who provided additional corroboration for the scam case Cook and Bell were building, then added a bonus: They described several drug deals involving Nix, Gillich, and an old Dixie Mafia crony, Lenny Swetman, a Biloxi locksmith.

And, finally, Cook and Bell secured the cooperation of another crucial witness: Nix's stepdaughter turned wife, Kellye Dawn Newman Nix.

Kellye had been cooling her heels in a Louisiana jail for months on state scam charges when Cook and Bell went to see her. Half expecting Nix to have her killed to silence her, Kellye even wrote him a letter asking why he hadn't done so already. Then, instead of waiting to see what Nix would do, she cut a deal of her own, walking out of jail after serving ten months for theft, earning federal immunity for her testimony about the scams.

Flighty and irresponsible as she was, Kellye possessed a certain naïve charm Cook and Bell believed would make her an effective witness if the case ever got before a jury. She implicated Nix, Gillich, and LaRa in the scams, with her account of money pickups, deliveries, and secret calls from the "clean phone" at the Golden Nugget. She also corroborated Robert Hallal's story about driving to Biloxi in August to meet Gillich. She professed no knowledge about the Sherry murder contract itself, but Cook and Bell considered this testimony crucial, establishing a relationship between the two men that otherwise could not be proven. Mike Gillich, the investigators suspected, would claim he never met Bob Hallal.

Kellye also told them a few things about Pete Halat. She claimed he knew Nix was ripping off gay men as early as 1983, when the FBI first picked her up in its early scam investigation. She recalled Halat suggesting she pass on a warning to Nix: "Tell Kirksey to leave those fags alone." He mentioned that to her twice, Kellye swore. Yet he continued his association with Nix, and continued managing Nix's money—which by then was all scam money, Kellye said.

Her testimony about her questionable telephone marriage and Halat's representation of her in the mysterious disappearing cocaine case undermined the mayor's portrait of his relationship with Nix as totally innocent and professional. Kellye described more than one hundred fifty trips she made to the law office to pick up expense money from Halat, at Nix's direction, drawn from the trust account. During these visits, she often used Halat's legal calls to Nix as a pretext for speaking to her inmate husband-stepfather.

But Kellye could not say that Halat actually participated in the scams, or that he personally profited from them. She had no reason to believe Halat broke the law—only that he ignored Nix's law breaking.

"I think his only connection was that he knew where it [the money] came from, and he just didn't say anything," Kellye told the federal grand jury a few weeks after talking to Cook and Bell. "He was paid well for it."

At the same time, though, she did link Halat to what would have been an illegal scheme to get Nix out of prison. Nix explained the ultimate purpose of the scams to her this way, Kellye swore: Halat and Gillich knew someone with great political influence who, for a quarter-million-dollar bribe, could arrange Nix's parole.

"That is why he was working so hard—to get his freedom," Kellye said.

Even though most of Kellye's information concerned scamming, she and the other scammers were crucial. Proving the scam had become central to the overall murder probe. Whenever Cook and Bell sought a motive for the killings, they always came back to Nix's massive prison fraud operation: The Sherrys died either because the scammers believed Vince had ripped them off or because they feared Vince or Margaret would expose their crimes and destroy Nix's attempt to buy his way out of prison. They even considered the possibility that Margaret's loose talk about working with the FBI had gotten back to the scammers, who mistook her attack on Gerald Blessey for an assault on them.

"It was either revenge or coverup," Randy Cook would later say. "Or a little of both. And it all came back to those prison scams, the hundreds of thousands of dollars, maybe millions, that were being made at Angola."

But though the evidence supporting a case against the scammers had grown strong, the murder investigation still contained huge holes. One year after Bobby Joe Fabian first spilled his story, Cook and Bell remained unable to move beyond the time frame provided in Robert Hallal's testimony. They were frozen in August 1987, when, as Hallal told it, he had discussed the murder contract with Mike Gillich—a month before the killings. After that time, Cook and Bell had drawn blanks. The moment of the murder remained where it had been for two years, a blurred look at a yellow Ford Fairmont and a driver who resembled a hefty narcotics officer—a dead end.

CHAPTER 28

Unable to fill the gap any other way, the investigators returned to the place where their case had started: the Louisiana State Penitentiary at Angola. There they spoke with more inmates, trying to sift the self-serving lies from the genuine testimony, finding a bit of each.

Bobby Joe Fabian continued to massage his story to fit each new development, making himself look like more of a liar with each retelling. Another inmate, Harold Vincent, told a story remarkably similar to Fabian's, but when Cook and Bell brought him to Jackson for the grand jury, he began demanding parole and inserting new and preposterous details into his story, including a description of Margaret Sherry, whom he had never met, as being "like a mother to me." They quickly dropped Vincent from the witness list.

Cook and Bell next turned to convicted kidnapper Richard "Lobo" Durr, an Angola lifer with another remarkable story. Durr told the investigators that Robert Hallal had not rejected the Sherry murder contract after all, but had taken the job, with John Ransom as backup. "Bob Hallal admitted to me that he killed the Sherrys," Durr swore.

When it looked like Durr might be paroled in late 1987 or early 1988, Nix supposedly asked him to "clean house" for him by killing Hallal, Pete Halat, "Old Man Ransom," and "La La"—Nix's derogatory nickname for LaRa. "Nix said too many people knew his business," Durr claimed. But

Durr never got his parole, and so never cleaned house for Nix.

The most intriguing, if unprovable, part of Durr's story was his explanation of the motive for the Sherry murders. He, too, spoke of several hundred thousand dollars missing from Nix's scam earnings. But according to Durr, the money had been given to Pete Halat and LaRa Sharpe to pay Vince Sherry, who was supposed to use his judge's authority to have Nix transferred to Mississippi on some bogus writ. Once in Mississippi county jail, with far less security than Angola, Nix had escape plans in place.

"But the judge froze up," Durr said. "He didn't make the transfer."

Whether that was because Sherry double-crossed Nix, or because Halat or LaRa kept the money and blamed the judge, Durr couldn't say. Nix blamed Vince and, according to Durr, put out the contract on both Sherrys.

Cook and Bell were reluctant to accept Durr's story, even though elements of it appealed to them. Believing Durr meant discounting—and charging—Hallal, something they were not prepared to do. Yet some of Durr's story checked out: The investigators found correspondence in which Nix called LaRa "La La," one of those little details that Durr could not have invented on his own. And Gene Fields, the Jefferson Parish deputy chief sheriff who had helped bust Nix on the Corso case, had another tidbit. He uncovered an escape plot by an Angola inmate who had been transferred to a county jail in Louisiana. Crooks dressed as guards from Angola were going to sneak him out, but an informant revealed the plan first—and said it had been a test run for Nix. All Nix needed to complete the plan was a transfer out of Angola—just what Durr said Vince was to provide.

In the end, though, Cook and Bell decided not to rely upon Durr. He had no ties to the scam, no corroboration, no relationship with Nix. For the time being, at least, Durr would be held in reserve. If additional evidence pointed to Hallal as the real killer, Durr would become an important witness. Otherwise, he was just another inmate with a story.

Back in Biloxi, a cabbie named William Forehand popped up next, telling Randy Cook and Keith Bell that he recognized John Ransom's image on television as a fare he picked up and took to the Golden Nugget late one night in early September 1987, just before the murders. Ransom had a suspicious bulge in his coat pocket, possibly a gun, Forehand swore. After leaving the cab, Ransom walked into the strip club, then emerged five minutes later with Mike Gillich and Pete Halat. The three men climbed into a Mercedes, then left the Nugget's parking lot, the cab driver told Cook and Bell, then the grand jury. He recognized Halat because his aunt worked for him, Forehand swore.

His aunt was Ann Kriss, Halat's longtime secretary, he said.

Forehand thought little of this scene until two years later, when he saw Ransom on television, linked to the Sherry murders. Forehand had hesitated several months before coming forward—he was distrustful of the Biloxi police—but when he learned the FBI was involved, he decided to contact Keith Bell.

Like so many other witnesses, Forehand had a credibility problem: his unlikely explanation of how he remembered John Ransom after two years. Forehand admitted he would have forgotten, except for one thing. Instead of paying the five-dollar fare, Ransom pulled a wad of money from his pocket.

"He gave me two one-hundred-dollar bills," Forehand swore. "I said, 'Do you know what you have given me?' He said, 'Yes, you ain't never seen me before.'

"I told him, that's fine. As a cab driver, what else am I going to say to him? I'm not going to stand there and argue with the man. A two-hundred-dollar tip is a big tip in a taxicab. It is something you don't ever forget."[1]

Forehand offered to take a lie detector test to prove his truthfulness, but prosecutors never placed much stock in his story. They feared that personal concerns might have motivated Forehand to try to become invaluable to the police. But the real problem was that Cook, Bell, and Kent McDaniel found his story nonsensical. Who would believe Ransom could be so stupid?

An Angola guard, Marlene Hunter, surfaced next, describing a bizarre incident in late March 1987 allegedly involving Pete Halat. Hunter was fearful and reluctant

about coming forward. She had suffered a series of home
break-ins and threats since the incident. But she finally
pulled aside Randy Cook during one of his trips to Angola
and told him about it. At least at first, her story seemed to
represent devastating evidence against the Biloxi mayor.

Hunter claimed she was on duty in the section of the
prison where Nix was incarcerated on March 26, 1987,
when a man approached her who identified himself as Peter
Halat. He presented a bar association identification card,
then asked to see Nix. Hunter found this odd, because no
attorney-client visit had been scheduled. Normally, attorneys did not come directly to the prison housing areas to
meet clients. But she said it would be okay—if he signed the
visitation logbook.

"I'm an attorney and I don't have to sign," he replied,
according to Hunter.

"Then you can't enter."

Agitated, the man who said he was Pete Halat grabbed the
book, turned to the back, and signed on a page designated
for a much later date, Hunter told Cook. She let him pass
and he stayed with Nix for about an hour. Later, she
realized he not only signed in the wrong place, but had used
a phony name. More than two years later she saw Halat
giving his post-Fabian press conferences and heard him
deny visiting Angola in March 1987.

"I knew he was lying," Hunter told Cook.

Cook and Bell thought they had a witness that would
utterly discredit Halat. But the investigators' elation soon
faded when Angola officials dug out a three-year-old log
book and Hunter pointed out the signature she said Halat
put down in the back. The signature turned out to be from a
legitimate visitor and not in Halat's handwriting. Hunter's
insistence that this was the signature she remembered
destroyed her credibility as a witness. If she couldn't
remember the signature, how could they be sure she remembered Halat correctly?

Their trips to Angola always seemed to end in frustration,
leaving little to show for the effort. What the investigators
really wanted was a clean witness, someone outside the
sullen, what's-in-it-for-me world of Angola. They would
fantasize about it during their long drives, the one honest

witness that would convince Kent McDaniel—and perhaps themselves—that the case wasn't hopeless.

The odd thing about it was, they finally found such a witness—at Angola. They had gone to the warden's office, combing through the telephone logs, compiling information on Halat's endless contacts with Nix.

They also found the name of another attorney, another frequent caller to Nix: Beau Ann Williams, Nix's cousin in Oklahoma City. And with her, the case finally seemed to come together. She became the outside witness they had sought.

Beau Ann Williams provided a string of seemingly damning revelations in the case, first to Cook and Bell, then before the grand jury in Jackson where they rushed her after their interview.

First she recounted an odd telephone call she received in September 1987 from her cousin, in which he described in detail the Sherry murder scene, right down to Margaret holding something in her hand when her body was found—her earring. Nix told Beau Ann the killer had been welcomed as a friend, a telling bit of insider knowledge.

The call, as far as Williams could tell from her phone bills, came on September 15, 1987. That was one day after the murders—and one day *before* the bodies were found.

Williams also described her encounter with Mike Gillich in March 1989, the same night the Biloxi police first interrogated LaRa Sharpe. "He said . . . LaRa is talking to them and she is telling them everything. You have got to get word to Kirk." To Cook and Bell, this showed Gillich's consciousness of guilt—innocent men don't need to issue or receive such warnings.

Williams recalled being badly frightened by Gillich, who treated her like a confidante, "like I was one of them and I was to be entrusted with anything." Clearly, she said, Gillich feared LaRa would reveal his and Nix's involvement in murder. That's why he felt such urgency, Williams said.

Beau Ann also recalled her cousin's response to the message from Gillich about LaRa informing on him: "She wouldn't do that. She has kids."

"I took that to mean—and I took it to heart—that her kids' safety was in jeopardy if she talked."

Williams had firsthand knowledge of Nix's habit of threatening families and children. The two cousins had a falling out over the Meagan Nix malpractice suit— Williams won a half-million-dollar settlement to compensate the baby's birth defects, but Nix considered her fee too large. He also criticized her handling of custody arrangements for Meagan while Kellye was jailed. When Williams disagreed, he responded by threatening Beau Ann's daughter, Brook.

"How would you feel," Nix told her in one call, "if Brook all of a sudden one day could not walk or talk or function in this world. . . . That is a very real possibility."

Later, Nix made another threat: She had to follow orders, or Kellye would implicate her in the homosexual scam and the Sherry murders, using Beau Ann's phone calls and visits to Nix to concoct a story against her.

"My response to him," Williams said, "was 'Eat shit and die.'"

Finally, Williams related a troubling conversation she had with one of Nix's scammers—the testimony Cook and Bell had been hoping for.

In February 1989, she traveled South to work on the malpractice case. Former Angola inmate Arthur Mitchell, a scam partner of Nix's on both sides of the prison fence, had picked up Beau Ann at the New Orleans airport. He proudly told her he served as "Kirk's legs."

While they waited for a rental car, the subject of Pete Halat came up. He was working with Williams at that time on the malpractice case, at Nix's insistence. Mitchell told Beau Ann that there was "heat" on Halat, which Williams took to mean the police were investigating him.

"Well, I know Pete is denying responsibility for Sherry's murder," Williams recalled Mitchell saying. "But in a way, he is responsible . . . because he is the one that got him involved in all of this. When Judge Sherry wanted out, he couldn't get out, and Pete could not protect him."

Beau Ann drew the same conclusion from this as Cook and Bell. "My impression was that Pete had some prior knowledge that the Sherrys were going to be murdered. . . .

I believed that Kirk and Peter Halat were involved in something financial that got Judge Sherry murdered."

After that conversation with Mitchell, she stopped working with Halat on the malpractice case, she said. She even mentioned her concerns at the time to another lawyer involved in the malpractice case, who had since been elevated to the Mississippi Supreme Court.

To Cook and Bell, Beau Ann Williams seemed a godsend. She was a respected lawyer, with nothing to do with scams or plots, related by blood, not by choice, to Kirksey Nix. She was well spoken, well groomed, attractive—something that could not be said about most of their witnesses. And if Arthur Mitchell backed her up, Cook and Bell reported to the U.S. Attorney, their case would be close to complete.[2]

Arthur Mitchell would be the last Angola inmate to make Randy Cook and Keith Bell's list. A three-time loser with a string of armed robbery convictions and a substantial amount of his adult life invested in Angola, Mitchell unabashedly admitted that he considered Kirksey Nix a genius, his personal mentor. And he did, indeed, spin an interesting tale—once Cook and Bell made it clear he would go down on scam charges himself unless he cooperated. The threat carried added weight because Mitchell was out on parole at the time, and wanting to stay that way. But his story was not exactly what Cook and Bell had hoped for.

It began promisingly enough: One day in early to mid-1987, Kirksey Nix left their camp at Angola for an attorney-client visit, telling Mitchell on his way out that his scam-financed release finally was at hand. The visit, Mitchell said, was either with Halat or someone conveying a message from Halat. A few hours later, though, Nix returned bitter and angry.

"I just found out all that money I've been putting away for my pardon is gone," Nix announced. "Misplaced. Missing."

By Mitchell's estimate, Nix by that time had entrusted somewhere between two hundred and two hundred fifty thousand dollars in scam money to Pete Halat for the purpose of getting Nix out of prison, supposedly with Judge Sherry's help. Mitchell thought Nix would have both Sherry and Halat killed immediately.

Mitchell's story had all the right elements: He provided a logical motive for murder, he had Pete Halat involved with payoffs and scam money, and he had Vince in a position to be blamed when the money vanished. Mitchell even re-called Nix complaining bitterly about Margaret Sherry, calling her a "moral crusader" who irked Nix with her threats to shut down Mike Gillich. She posed a "delicate problem" that had to be "handled carefully," Mitchell said.

But from there, the contradictions began. Despite providing the setup for accusing Nix of murder, Mitchell swore his criminal mentor did not kill the Sherrys. Nix thought Vince would help him, Mitchell said, and he never stopped dealing with Halat, even after the money was lost. Mitchell never understood why Nix trusted Halat, but he did. Mitchell said Nix even sent him to meet Halat outside the Golden Nugget in Biloxi in 1988 so he could deliver a thousand dollars to the lawyer, with the promise of one hundred times that if he could engineer Nix's release. No matter how hard Cook and Bell pressed, Mitchell insisted Nix did not have the Sherrys killed.

Yet he admitted making the statement Beau Ann Williams recalled—that Halat got Sherry involved in the scams in some way, then was unable to protect the judge, leading to his murder. This statement implied Mitchell knew who had Sherrys killed—and why. But he would say no more.

In an odd way, Cook and Bell felt his insistence on Nix's innocence made Mitchell more believable. If he were lying, he could have given them Nix and Halat on a platter, telling the investigators whatever they wanted to hear. The truth is always messier, though—Mitchell provided key testimony, especially coupled with Beau Ann Williams's, but he didn't solve the case for them.

"I don't know who did it," Mitchell later told the grand jury. "I know . . . Halat has political aspirations to the extent that you can't understand. He is determined to be in high politics. People, you know—people do things for power that they won't do for money. If given a choice of winning the sweepstakes, that ten-million-dollar foolishness they have at Publishers Clearing House—if given a choice of winning that, or being governor, perhaps he would prefer being governor. Power is something."[3]

CHAPTER 29

Lynne Sposito got the news soon after Arthur Mitchell's appearance before the grand jury: The investigation was wrapping up. As far as Cook and Bell were concerned, it was time to seek indictments from the grand jury. They had enough evidence for conspiracy charges, though not the actual murder—the month before the killings and the identity of the triggerman still remained an evidentiary blank. They would make one more run at John Ransom and LaRa Sharpe to see if either would fill the gap. Then it would be in the hands of the U.S. Attorney. Lynne realized she had some more lobbying to do.

It had not been an easy time for the Sherry family. Lynne and her brother Vin had testified before the grand jury two months earlier, a disturbing and difficult experience. The telephone threats escalated, gruff voices promising Lynne she would never reach Jackson alive. While they were in Mississippi, the third anniversary of the murders passed, with the newspapers publishing lengthy stories on the case, headlines and photographs bringing back bitter memories.

Vin testified first, telling the twenty-five men and women of the grand jury about his visit to Biloxi on the Mother's Day before the murders, May 1987. Over dinner, his mother told him a contract had been put out on her life and Vince's. Margaret had implied that the source of the contract was Mike Gillich, but she never actually said that outright, and Vin could not swear to it—as much as he wished he could.

Lynne testified next, describing her mother's plans to go after Gillich's illegal operations if she became mayor, and her remarks to Lynne in May 1987 about threats. Lynne also spoke of her own dealings with Pete Halat. She described the conversation about the lawn mower three months after the murders, when Halat had asked if his son could buy it, then laughed at her response, predicting, "Ain't nobody going to solve this one."

She watched the grand jurors recoil at this story. "I can't believe he was saying that to me," she told them, skewering Halat, not hiding her hatred. "Three months after they were dead, when it was his best friend."

It wasn't the sort of testimony that would convict anyone, Lynne knew, just part of the vast mosaic the case had become. But if Pete were ever charged, she might have to face him in court and repeat much of this testimony. The prospect scared her—and thrilled her. At last, someone was listening, she told reporters when she emerged from the locked grand jury room.

The satisfaction she felt in Jackson was tempered, however, by the continued toll on her family. Once Halat had been elected mayor—and Lynne's role in the accusations against him became clear—she began to fear he would use his power to hurt her family, perhaps by having his police department renew investigation of Eric. They could even reveal his adoption, a final devastating inheritance for her brother, who was still struggling to recover from their parents' death. So Lynne decided to tell him first.[1]

Eric's normally dark complexion turned waxy white and he slumped to the floor, silent and shaking, when Lynne finally explained his adoption to him.

"What are you feeling, Eric?" Lynne asked, as she rushed to embrace him, fearing he would hate her for her acquiescence in this long secrecy. But it was not anger that gripped Eric.

"I feel just like I did when Mom and Dad died. I feel all alone. I feel so cold. I feel like I've lost everything."

If there were any lingering doubts about Eric's knowledge of his adoption being a motive for murder, this scene eliminated it once and for all, Lynne believed. No one could fake this, she remembers thinking at the time—that cold part of her that was always stepping back, gathering and analyzing evidence, even then. Even as she comforted her shaking brother, as upset and sincere as she was, a small part of her thought: I wish the Biloxi cops could see this. Then they'd know he was innocent.

"Now you know why the police were looking at you so hard," she said after a time. "They found out about the adoption, and they thought it might be a motive—that you found out and went crazy and killed them."

Eric looked up at her then and slowly nodded, the initial shock fading. "That actually makes sense," he said.

The final irony came a short time later. The Biloxi Police Department, responding to a news reporter's question, issued without explanation a terse statement saying Eric Sherry was no longer a suspect in his parents' murder. That was it: Case closed. The police had not intended to spring the adoption issue on him after all, Lynne realized, and Eric had been crushed for no good reason. It seemed to her then that her family might never recover from the murders and their aftermath.

Not even indictments and convictions of the killers could change that, Lynne began to see, though they offered the prospect of an ending, at least, perhaps a chance to heal. She looked forward to that moment, certain it would come. It would make the turmoil in her family, her brother's despair, the time she spent away from career and family, all worthwhile. It had to.

And then she got another call, a tip updating her on the case. The grand jury's two-year term was about to expire. There already had been two extensions, the maximum the law allowed. Lynne had expected to hear the U.S. Attorney would be asking for indictments before the grand jury dissolved. Instead, she learned prosecutors were balking, still questioning the evidence. Randy Cook and Keith Bell were confident in their case, but the prosecutors didn't share their sentiments, it seemed.

Lynne hung up and quickly called Kent McDaniel, who confirmed what she had heard: They were thinking of scrapping the last eighteen months of work and starting over again with a new grand jury. The evidence was too weak. There were problems proving the conspiracy. They didn't know who pulled the trigger. With a new grand jury, they could take up to another two years looking at the case. Maybe that would generate enough evidence.

"Or maybe the case will just die," Lynne replied. She had

intended her remark to be sarcastic and offhand, but McDaniel didn't take it that way. His reply froze Lynne.

"Maybe it will," he said. "Maybe it will."

The government's meticulously constructed account of scams and murder conspiracy had begun to unravel as lies and inconsistencies continued to tatter crucial witnesses. Even as they pressed for indictments, Randy Cook and Keith Bell had to admit their best witnesses had let them down.

Three weeks after testifying before the grand jury, Robert Hallal had escaped from the county jail in Mississippi where he had been housed temporarily. Six months passed before police in Daytona Beach, Florida, captured him after his girlfriend turned him in for beating her.

Shipped back to Mississippi in irons, Hallal admitted during an interrogation with Keith Bell that his original story contained some lies. In a July 1990 interview with the FBI agent, Hallal said he had lied about buying drugs from Mike Gillich, then ripping him off for eighteen thousand dollars. None of that happened. He also changed his story about the code name "Jimmy James" and said Gillich told him to use it, not Kirksey Nix, as he swore earlier.

By the time he came back before the grand jury five months later to correct his testimony, his story had changed again, further eroding his credibility. Now, Hallal claimed, he had done drug deals with Mike Gillich after all—they were just different from the ones he had lied about during his first testimony, and they occurred long *before* Gillich tried to hire him to murder a judge. Previously, Hallal had sworn he had never met Gillich until the day they discussed the murder contract, which is why he needed a code name to introduce himself to Gillich, and why he needed Kellye's help to find the Golden Nugget. Now none of that made sense.

Hallal also added another twist to his story, this one involving John Ransom, though previously he had vowed he knew nothing about the one-legged killer. Now he claimed to have returned to buy cocaine from Gillich in late August 1987, several weeks after their murder contract discussion. When he went to Gillich's video store to pick up the drugs, he saw a tall, thin, older man standing around. At the time, Hallal didn't know the man, but now, he swore, he realized it was John Ransom.

Had Hallal said all this at the outset, Cook and Bell would have been overjoyed. Now, though, it just sounded like a convict making up for his escape by spicing up his story.

He wasn't through yet. In February 1991, one month after his second grand jury appearance, Hallal tried to escape again, caught with a hacksaw and a rope of sheets while in the process of busting out. Threatened with new charges, he sweetened his story yet again, claiming Ransom had been present at the Golden Nugget when Mike Gillich offered the contract to murder a judge. Gillich introduced them, Hallal swore, and promised that Ransom would supply a clean gun and silencer if Hallal took the job.

"Why didn't you tell us this before?" Bell asked. In the past, Hallal always said he and Gillich were alone.

"I was afraid I'd be indicted for conspiracy if I mentioned my full involvement with these men," Hallal said.

Once again, his explanation didn't wash—during his last grand jury appearance, he had been given complete legal immunity. Anything he had said then could not have been used against him. There was no reason to lie.

On its face, his new testimony sounded fabulous—except for the fact that it meant Hallal had lied on four previous occasions when he described these same events. When Kent McDaniel heard the latest version, he threw up his hands. "Do you know what's going to happen to him on the witness stand?"

Keith Bell and Randy Cook knew—Hallal would be crucified. And he was their main way of linking Mike Gillich and Kirksey Nix to the murder conspiracy. They had no case without him.

There was one slight, bright spot. Hallal regained a shred of credibility when a totally unrelated, noncriminal witness—Becky Field's son—told investigators he too had seen Ransom in the Gillich video store, although it was a year earlier, in the summer of 1986. At the time, Greg Field had been an art student doing summer work air-brushing T-shirts in Gillich's souvenir store, between the Nugget and the video store. During a break, Field saw Gillich introduce a thin, older man in a trenchcoat to his son, Mike Gillich

III. The thin man seemed almost to clank slightly as he walked, and Field believed he was carrying a gun under his coat, if not an entire arsenal.

"If you ever need anything or anyone taken care of," Field recalled Gillich telling his son, "call this man."

Years later, Field recognized Ransom as the thin, clanking man when he came home from Purdue University to visit his parents, and his mother showed him some videotaped news clips on the Sherry case. He turned pale and shot out of his chair when he saw Ransom, telling his mother, "I've seen that man."

It helped. It proved Ransom had been in the video store, and that he had a close connection to Mike Gillich—something the nightclub owner would steadfastly deny. But it was a long way from rehabilitating the lies of Bob Hallal. His crucial testimony had become a morass.

As bad as the business with Hallal turned out, if that was all that had gone wrong, the damage would have been bearable and the indictments would have long ago been in hand. But the other main witness to the murder conspiracy, bank robber Bill Rhodes, also developed reverse amnesia, suddenly remembering details he previously omitted, undermining his credibility as well.

"Another one's gone squirrelly on us," Randy Cook griped as he and Bell drove to re-interview Rhodes in his Memphis federal prison cell.

Now he not only had discussed murder with John Ransom and Pete Halat, as he first claimed. Rhodes added several more trips to Biloxi to his story—and a face-to-face meeting with Mike Gillich.

He met Mr. Mike at Ransom's request at a doughnut shop on The Strip, Rhodes swore. Seated at his customary table, Gillich promised he would personally arrange a "clean" getaway car and a safe motel room for him and Ransom after the hit. Once the contract had been carried out and the Sherrys lay dead, Gillich promised to bring the money directly to Ransom and Rhodes at the motel.

The reason for this meeting with Gillich, Rhodes told Cook and Bell, was to allay his distrust of Halat and Ransom. Rhodes still feared he was being set up and would be killed after helping murder the Sherrys. But Mr. Mike's reputation as a stand-up guy among crooks was peerless. If Gillich made a promise, Rhodes said, he could count on it.

That made sense to Cook and Bell, but they had to pose the by now familiar question: "Why didn't you tell us this before?"

"Simple," Rhodes said. "I don't want to die, and I don't want my family killed. John Ransom, I'm not worried about. With him, killing is business. He'll come at you himself, maybe, but I can deal with that. Halat, I'm not afraid of either. He's a lawyer for them, that's all. He's not gonna kill anyone. But Gillich, him I'm afraid of. He can get things done. He would want payback."

Eventually, though, Rhodes said, he realized he would be a target whether he implicated Gillich directly or not. So why not tell the whole truth and help put the man away?

Cook and Bell found themselves believing Rhodes. There were no witnesses to back him up, no evidence other than his word. But his description of Gillich and of the Krispy Kreme in Biloxi seemed perfect, and his reason for lying—unlike Hallal's—made sense to the investigators. That was the way criminals thought—and Bill Rhodes made no bones about being a crook. "That's what I do," he said.

The parade of recanting witnesses never seemed to stop. In March 1990, Bobby Joe Fabian altered his testimony, too—not little additions and subtractions, but a total revamping of his account. His first story had launched a federal investigation, it had been broadcast nationwide, it had threatened to destroy Mayor Pete Halat. And now, Fabian admitted, much of his incendiary story had been a lie.

"I put a little yeast in it, ya see. I wanted to make sure you bought my story, so I could get out of here," Fabian told Cook and Bell. Then he hastily added, without a trace of irony, "Of course, I'm coming clean now. I want to do the right thing, nothing but the truth."

The occasion of Fabian's new bout of supposed candor did not owe to a sudden surge of conscience. He changed his story because Cook and Bell caught him in a lie: In February 1988, they learned, Fabian told Louisiana investigators that he knew nothing about the Sherry murders, and that he had never met Pete Halat. At the time, he was being

questioned about scams—the nascent investigation that
finally led to indictment of the scammers in Louisiana. Yet,
a year later, he claimed to have met with Halat and to have
planned the murder of the Sherrys with Nix.

"Why didn't you say that in 1988, Bobby?" Keith Bell
wanted to know. "You could have solved the case for us
back then just as easy."

"Well, ya see, I didn't want to open a can of worms back
then," Fabian said. "I was about to get parole, I thought,
and the last thing I wanted to do was to bring any of that
up."

Later, though, when it became clear he would never leave
Angola—that Pete Halat's efforts to get him released had
come up empty—he decided to come forward with a
partially true story. "I'm telling nothin' but the whole truth
this time," he promised.

And the truth was, Fabian said, he was never part of a
conspiracy to murder the Sherrys, and he had never haggled
with Ransom or sent him drugs and money to pay for the
murder. That was Fabian's "yeast."

"Okay, then how do you know Ransom had anything to
do with the hit?" Cook asked.

"'Cause he told me, ya see," Fabian responded. They had
been talking on the phone about a health insurance fraud
Fabian had worked on, and Ransom happened to mention
he planned to kill Pete Halat's law partner at the behest of
Nix and Halat. "He said he might hire someone else to do
it, he wasn't sure," Fabian added.

Cook and Bell didn't buy it. Ransom had operated for
twenty years without being caught next to a dead body. He
was not about to confess to the likes of Bobby Fabian about
his involvement in a murder contract, especially when
Bobby Joe had nothing to do with hiring him—and on a
prison phone, no less. It made no sense. But Fabian insisted
that was the way it happened.

As for the meeting at Angola with Pete Halat in which the
Sherry hit was supposedly plotted, Fabian had lied about
that, too. He had not been called to an attorney-client visit
with Pete Halat, as he previously swore. In his newly minted
account, Fabian had gone to the attorney visiting area for an
unrelated purpose (prison records backed him that much),
and simply barged in on a meeting between Nix and Halat.

When asked why he would do that, Fabian explained that Nix had been dodging a seventy-five-thousand-dollar scam debt to him for months, and this represented a chance to demand payment.

"I told you before, I'm not trying to rip you off, Bobby," Nix supposedly said after Fabian walked in. "Pete's got your money. It's just tied up. Tell him, Pete."

Halat supposedly said, "Yeah, Kirk's not trying to beat you out of the money. I've just got problems with my partner. As a matter of fact, I'm going to have him killed."

In this rendition, no one mentioned Judge Sherry "swinging with the money"—Fabian's infamous first accusation, rebroadcast and reprinted for months in the Mississippi media, the comment that made Halat sound like such a Judas. That, too, had been a lie.

This new statement Fabian attributed to Halat seemed as absurd as Ransom's supposed confession. Why would Pete Halat, an experienced criminal defense attorney, casually admit to a notorious con man that he planned to murder his partner? The answer: He wouldn't.

Cook and Bell knew, then, that Fabian was taking them for a ride. His whole story undoubtedly was concocted, a formulation of his genuine knowledge of scams, combined with secondhand information culled from the prison grapevine, news reports, and guesswork. The news broadcast that damaged Pete Halat's reputation had been based on lies, just as Halat had insisted all along. Fabian's only goal had been to get out of Angola and onto the streets, and he was going to keep trying new stories until he got his desired result—or until he was charged with perjury.

When Cook and Bell reported to federal prosecutors what Fabian had said, First Assistant Kent McDaniel had no choice but to bring him back before the grand jury to correct his previous testimony. The grand jurors were openly skeptical, questioning Fabian on a series of niggling details, even asking him how he came to be wearing fancy alligator boots.

"I bought them," Fabian shot back.

Even that, the grand jurors doubted. McDaniel decided then and there that Bobby Joe Fabian would not see the inside of a courtroom again—unless it was as a defendant.

The oddest part of all was that Cook and Bell still

believed the central premise of Bobby Joe Fabian's story, even though they considered him a liar. They still believed that Kirksey Nix, John Ransom, and possibly Pete Halat, along with others, were tied to the prison scams, and that those scams led to the murders of the Sherrys. Whether there actually was a meeting at Angola to plot that crime, or whether it was handled on the telephone, they might never know. Either way, there was too much evidence and too many other witnesses to dismiss the scam-to-murder theory.

"Just because a liar tells the story," Cook would later say, "doesn't mean the story is a lie."

And Fabian still remained a valuable resource. His knowledge of the scams was genuine, and Cook and Bell still sought him out when they needed help finding witnesses. Fabian remained useful, and this probably saved Bobby Joe from being prosecuted for perjury.

Still, the impact of Fabian's televised lies would hurt the case enormously. Defense attorneys inevitably would argue that all the other key witnesses in the case could have seen Fabian's false testimony, then concocted their own, similar stories, hoping they, too, could earn freedom with a lie. Everything in the case had been built upon a lie, they would argue, and it would be a difficult theory to rebut—because, strictly speaking, it was true.

"That's what Pete Halat keeps saying," Randy Cook observed morosely. "It's what I'd say if I were him, too."

CHAPTER 30

As lies continued to eat away at the foundations of the case, a day of decision approached. Before the end of May 1991, the U.S. Attorney would have to ask the grand jury for an indictment, witnesses' warts notwithstanding.

After May, the grand jury panel hearing the case would dissolve, its members sent home. Worse still, the five-year statute of limitations would run out on many of the scam charges if an indictment were not filed soon, making the case against the Sherrys' killers far harder to prove. Prosecutors would have to start over from scratch with a new grand jury and far less evidence—which, in practical terms, meant admitting the case against the killers of Vincent and Margaret Sherry was unprovable. There would never be an indictment.

Randy Cook and Keith Bell—and Lynne Sposito—knew this would be their last, best shot at getting a case into court. Already, nearly four years had passed since the murders, justice delayed far too long. Yet U.S. Attorney George Phillips and Kent McDaniel kept leaning the other way.

"We've got to have more," McDaniel kept saying. "I can't take this into court."

And so, with a few months left, Cook and Bell attempted once again to fill the one massive hole in their case that could make a difference—proof of who pulled the trigger. To do this, as they had known all along, they needed someone from the inner circle to cooperate. Someone who had been inside that house on Hickory Hill Circle on September 14, 1987. So once again they turned to John Elbert Ransom.

Ransom had proven to be a cipher. Cook first met him in August 1989, just after Fabian's news interview. Ransom refused to talk about the Sherrys then, but he and Cook had exchanged courtesies. Ransom was so convivial, Cook left feeling like he had just talked fishing with his grandad. But though they parted politely, Cook had said, "John, I hope to come back and charge you with capital murder."

"Well, I wish you luck, Captain Cook," Ransom said with a grin, his whipcord body swimming inside jail overalls. "If you can make your case, I'll see you in court."

Their second visit had been cut short by Ransom's lawyer when the topic of the gun and silencer came up. Now Ransom had been hauled from his Georgia prison to a Mississippi jail, subpoenaed by the grand jury. In the grand jury room, he asserted his right to remain silent, but Cook and Bell later found him in a mood to talk. It was a week before Christmas 1990, he was far from home and family, fighting bouts of pneumonia and other nagging ailments. For once, the feared John Ransom seemed vulnerable.

"Hello there, Captain Cook, Agent Bell," the respectful hit man murmured as they sat down at the visitor's table across from him. He always remembered names and titles.

"Hello, John. How are you?" Keith Bell asked.

Ransom just shook his head. He did not look well, skin sallow, eyes sunken. The confidence Cook had sensed in Ransom at their first visit two years earlier had been sapped from him by illness and incarceration.

Randy Cook looked him up and down and shook his head. "You're going to die in prison, John," he said sorrowfully.

"But it doesn't have to be that way," Bell added. "Not if you decide to help us."

Ransom's mood had changed. "Well, you know," he began, "I love my family. They could be in danger if I'm not careful. 'Cause I can't protect my family in here. And you can't protect my family."

Maybe we could work something out, Cook and Bell suggested, but Ransom shook his head. "I always told my family I didn't do this," he said. "And I don't want them to know I've been lying to them."

Ransom hesitated then, the silence stretching out, the clanging bustle of the jailhouse muffled in the background. Cook and Bell waited him out, saying nothing. Ransom sighed.

"I told them I would never kill a woman," he said. His hands were flat on the table, long fingers spread, eyes downcast. "I'm in here, and right now there's a man with a tie on walking around in Biloxi laughing at us, 'cause he'll probably never be indicted."[1]

There it was, the key to pushing Ransom over the edge: He was angry at the man in the tie. Cook and Bell had no doubt who this person appeared to be: They figured it was Mayor Pete Halat. Ransom showed all the signs of being ready to spill a story. A few more minutes, and they'd have what they needed. A confession. A star witness.

"Why're you so mad at the man in the tie, John?" Cook asked.

Just then, a deputy U.S. Marshal walked into the visiting

room, the question still hanging in the air, leaving Ransom no chance to answer. "Time to go," the marshal said. "He's got to come with me now."

Ransom fell silent, the mood broken. Keith Bell jumped up and pulled the marshal aside. Although this was a county jail, Ransom was in federal custody, and the marshals had responsibility for him. He was due to be shipped back to a federal facility, having completed his testimony before the grand jury. Bell explained to his fellow federal official that Ransom was an important witness in the Sherry case—and that they were in the midst of a delicate interrogation. Ransom was about to give up the most important double murder in the state, maybe the country, a sitting judge and his wife, Bell said. They just needed a little more time. "You understand?" Bell asked. The marshal nodded and left.

But three minutes later, he returned. "Okay, he's got to go. Now." The marshal would not listen to any further pleas from the investigators. "Maybe you guys get paid overtime," he said, "but I don't."

And with that, the marshal hauled his prisoner away. The moment was lost. Ransom was gone.

Later, they tried to pick up again where they had left off, but Ransom's position had changed. He had been returned to a federal prison in Georgia, close to home. He saw his family regularly, he was getting good medical care, he was feeling better, stronger. Even his legal prospects had improved: He had cut a deal on his murder case in Georgia, pleading to a reduced charge of involuntary manslaughter, garnering a mere twelve-year prison term when he previously faced a potential death sentence. Feeling good about his chances in Mississippi, he was not about to confess—though he readily agreed to speak with Cook, Bell, and Kent McDaniel one more time in March 1991.

The deal was simple: He'd tell them what he knew about the Sherry case. But they couldn't use it against him. If they accepted his story and he passed a lie detector test, he would get legal immunity and testify on the record.

With that agreed, Ransom admitted to arranging scam pickups for Nix, though he denied profiting from it, beyond recouping his expenses. He denied any involvement in the murders, and he denied knowing Mike Gillich.

He did, however, tell the investigators that he had re-

ceived a call from Nix in 1986. His old crime partner had
told Ransom about a friend "who wanted to meet Wilbur."
"Wilbur" was their slang term for a silenced pistol, Ransom
explained. He told the investigators that shortly after the
call, he purchased for Nix a .22-caliber Ruger—the same
type of weapon that killed the Sherrys—and then had it
threaded to accommodate a custom-made silencer. He
resold the completed Wilbur to Nix for six hundred dollars,
and delivered it, along with some jewelry, to LaRa Sharpe
during a post-midnight meeting at a motel in Jackson. What
happened to the gun next, Ransom couldn't or wouldn't
say.[2]

A month later, Ransom submitted to an FBI polygraph
test at his prison in Georgia. The polygrapher determined
he told the truth about delivering the Wilbur to LaRa.
Everything else, however, showed deception. When Ransom said he did not know Mike Gillich, the test showed him
to be a liar. And when he said he had no knowledge of or
participation in the Sherry murders, the test again revealed
deception.

"That's the only time I've seen John Ransom mad," Cook
later remarked. "He was furious. He thought he could beat
the machine. He just couldn't get over that he failed the test.
But he wouldn't change his story."[3]

Lie detector tests, though useful tools for investigators,
are not admissible in court, their reliability an open question, their measurement of heart rate, blood pressure, and
other involuntary bodily functions too blunt an instrument
for deciding questions of life and liberty. No jury would
ever hear about Ransom's mechanically interpreted deception. They were right back where they started—with a huge
hole in their case. So ended John Ransom's flirtation with
turning state's evidence. They would make several more
runs at him, but he would never again come close to a deal
with the prosecution.

No one was more incensed by the near-miss with John
Ransom than Lynne Sposito. The thought that he had been
on the verge of telling investigators what had happened
inside her parents' house on the night of the murders kept
her awake for weeks. She had done her own research on the
peg-legged killer, and she had found some odd connections
between her family and his. It turned out that his wife was

from Bowling Green, Kentucky, that she had gone to the same high school as Margaret Sherry, just three years behind Lynne's mom. Lynne found both their pictures in the same yearbook, an eerie confluence. The two women had lived three blocks apart at one time.

Lynne found herself thinking of John Ransom at the oddest times, imagining his lean, stooped form often while she was in church. Singing a certain hymn invariably brought him to mind, a song containing the line "Be not afraid . . . When you stare into the power of Hell, and death is at your side, know that I am with you." To Lynne, staring into the power of Hell was like staring at your executioner—like staring at John Ransom with his gun aimed at your face, his finger tightening on the trigger. Her mother had seen this visage of the grim reaper, Lynne believed, and her father.

Lynne eventually decided to write Ransom. She told him that her ill will toward him was not that great, that he had been an instrument of death, not the cause. Her greatest anger was reserved for other people, she wrote—people he could help bring to justice, if he had a mind to do so.

She asked for a chance to speak with Ransom, to explain herself, why she had done the things she had done, setting in motion events that eventually linked him to the Sherry murders. "Would your daughter have done any less for you if you were murdered?" Lynne asked him in her letter.

You say you are remaining silent because you can't bring yourself to admit your crimes to your family, Lynne wrote. *But wouldn't your daughter love you no matter what?*

I have questions only you can answer. Were my parents at peace? Or were they terrified at the end? I so badly need to understand why this had to happen.

Lynne Sposito never got any answers from John Ransom. She mailed the letter, then waited, still thinking of him at odd moments, still wondering. Still hoping.

Next to Ransom, the most coveted potential witness in the case remained LaRa Sharpe. So Cook and Bell tried one more time to convert her, too, though they had little hope of accomplishing anything. She had remained remarkably consistent for the last two years in voicing her denials.

Not that they hadn't tried. LaRa's immunity deal had

been revoked in April 1990 by Kent McDaniel, after the
investigators became convinced she had lied about her
participation in the scam, as well as the silenced .22
automatic from Georgia. LaRa maintained—to no avail—
that everyone else the investigators had talked to had lied
about her. With no immunity, she had officially become a
target and was soon charged by Louisiana authorities with
ninety counts of theft and other crimes related to
scamming. Cook and Bell hoped this might persuade LaRa
to rethink her story, but it had the opposite effect.

One day after McDaniel revoked her immunity, LaRa
gave a televised interview to a Biloxi news program, striking
back as best she could, accusing the U.S. Attorney, Cook,
and Bell of misconduct, of offering to pay her with freedom
and fifty thousand dollars if she would "frame" Pete Halat
and Mike Gillich.

"I would swear on my children's lives about the innocence of Peter Halat and Mike Gillich," she told the
cameras. She then immediately contradicted herself by
saying she had no way of knowing who killed the Sherrys.

A few months later, the investigators and McDaniel met
with LaRa and her new attorney to hammer out a new
immunity deal. This time, though, like Ransom, she would
have to submit to an FBI lie-detector test. If she passed,
LaRa would be assured of permanent immunity from
prosecution.

But LaRa told the same story to the polygrapher that she
always had told: She knew nothing about the Sherry murders, her involvement in the scams was minimal, Gillich
and Halat were innocent. The polygraph expert, with twenty years experience testing for the FBI, proclaimed LaRa
deceptive on every key point.

LaRa later hired her own polygraph expert, who made an
opposite finding. But it was too little too late. LaRa remained adamant about her denials, while the investigators
remained adamant in their disbelief. LaRa would stay a
target of the investigation, not a witness—assuming the
case ever got to court.

The FBI conducted one other polygraph test in the case,
this one in complete secrecy, with the U.S. Attorney's Office
promising to keep the results of the test—even its very

existence—confidential. Only the person who agreed to sit for the polygraph session would be able to release the results, if he chose to do so.

So far, he has not exercised that choice. The existence of the test has remained hidden from all but a handful. Not even Lynne Sposito learned of it, nor any of the man's political opponents. And so the people of Biloxi never learned their mayor had quietly submitted to a lie-detector examination—because Pete Halat never told them.

A year and a half earlier, Halat was anything but silent about lie detectors. He had been vehement about taking one if it helped rebut Bobby Fabian's allegations.

"If for some reason during the ongoing investigation, the sheriff's department, the U.S. Attorney's Office, or the FBI wants me to undergo a polygraph test," Halat had said at his first post-Fabian press conference, "we'll identify the best one in the United States of America and I'll submit to a polygraph test."

A year and a half later, Pete Halat's life had come under intense scrutiny. His wife and one of his adopted sons had been subpoenaed by the grand jury, as had his two secretaries. Other employees of Halat and Sherry had been questioned, Halat's movements and statements analyzed. He repeatedly fled from representatives of the national news media, including one network correspondent possessed of legendary persistence, whom he dodged by using the fire escape instead of city hall's conventional exits. On another occasion, Halat summoned the police chief and the director of public safety to a restaurant where he had been lunching with Mike Gillich's daughter, so he could be escorted safely away from a camera crew for a syndicated news program.

And despite confident pronouncements in public that he was innocent and would never be charged in the Sherry murders, Halat at one point telephoned Kent McDaniel with a worried request: "If you're going to indict me, please do me the courtesy of letting me turn myself in, instead of picking me up and handcuffing me."

"Sure, Pete," McDaniel replied. "I'll do you that courtesy."[4]

It was in this climate of intense investigative scrutiny that Halat agreed to take a polygraph. Given his statement at the press conference, he could hardly refuse.

But the results, the FBI polygraph expert said, mirrored Ransom's and Sharpe's: Halat was deceptive when asked about the Sherry murders.[5]

When told of the findings, the mayor of Biloxi stormed off, furious and grim.

Again, this provided no evidence that could be used against Halat—the tests would be inadmissible in court. They were not infallible. They proved nothing conclusively.

But Pete Halat, like the other suspects, remained under scrutiny in the Sherry investigation. His goal in taking the test remained unfulfilled. Bobby Joe Fabian, Cook and Bell told one another, might be a liar. But, they decided, he may not be alone.

CHAPTER 31

By early 1991, Randy Cook and Keith Bell felt they had gone as far as they could. They believed they knew who had conspired to kill the Sherrys, if not who pulled the trigger. There were a limited number of people who could provide that crucial information, who could say with certainty what happened inside the home of Vincent and Margaret Sherry on the night of September 14, 1987—and Cook and Bell had tried talking to them all. Absent some unexpected break or surprise witness—the getaway driver or gunman Ransom ended up hiring, if any—they had nowhere else to turn.

"We're one statement away from solving this thing once and for all," Cook observed. "That was true the day we talked to Fabian, and it's true today. We need someone who knows what happened inside that house. And we don't have him. . . . Or her."

And with that gloomy pronouncement, the prosecutors in

the U.S. Attorney's Office in Jackson found themselves left to puzzle out what to do with thousands of pages of reports and transcripts accumulated in a year and a half of questions and answers, lies and evasions. How, they kept asking themselves, do you charge a murder you can't prove?

First Assistant Kent McDaniel gave his boss this assessment: Cook and Bell had done a remarkable job amassing a huge body of evidence to prove the scams, and a modest amount of evidence to show who conspired to kill the Sherrys. But despite their best efforts, they had not proved any of the conspirators actually carried out the murder. Bob Hallal could have gone home after his meeting at the Golden Nugget, and Kirksey Nix, John Ransom, and Mike Gillich might have said, Let's forget the whole thing. Someone else could have killed the Sherrys.

They would be forced to bring a conspiracy case into court, McDaniel said, without any evidence of the actual murder. It would be legally permissible, but it was almost never done because the concept would be so alien to jurors: They would be asked to convict the suspects of conspiracy, even if they weren't sure who did the murdering. McDaniel wasn't even sure the grand jury—which traditionally rubber-stamps indictments requested by prosecutors—would buy this one. And if that was in doubt, how could they expect to persuade a trial jury, where the burden of proof would be so much greater?

"It certainly is a mess," U.S. Attorney George Phillips agreed. "Bound to give ulcers to whoever has to work with it."

But Phillips was not yet willing to pull the plug on the case. Too much energy and pain had been invested in it to stop now, he told his assistant. "Let's give it to Tucker. If anyone can pull it together, he can."

Thin and slightly rumpled, even when wearing freshly pressed pants and shirt, James B. Tucker had the droopy look of a basset and the deeply resonant voice of a born storyteller—qualities that helped camouflage the cutthroat instincts all good trial attorneys must possess.

Tucker was Phillips's top prosecutor, the chief of his criminal division, a twenty-two-year veteran of the Justice Department. Tucker had been involved in every major prosecutorial success in the office in recent years, as well as its biggest loss, the prosecution and exoneration of Gerald Blessey. Now he would have to try to close out one of the state's longest grand jury investigations ever, one that had received intense public scrutiny and that had generated enormous expectations for solving the Sherry murders.

Starting in the spring of 1991, Tucker spent the better part of a month locked in his office for eight, ten, sometimes twelve hours a day with a blizzard of paperwork from the case—computerized FBI summaries, police reports, grand jury transcripts, witness statements, legal pads scrawled with notes. He lugged bulging briefcases home with him at night, spewing the stuff on coffee tables and nightstands. Finally, he began writing a series of alternative proposed indictments for grand jurors' eventual consideration— putting together different charges, different statutes, different sets of defendants. Some left out the mayor of Biloxi, others included him as a defendant. Still others left out Mike Gillich or John Ransom, while others alleged scam charges against everyone, but murder-related conspiracies against only a few of the suspects.[1]

The problem Tucker kept running into was firmly tying the scam to the murders. Charging them in separate counts wouldn't work—the trial judge could easily decide that evidence about the scams was irrelevant to the murder case, and vice versa. If that happened, Tucker felt he had no chance to convict. But that problem evaporated if he could craft an indictment that made both the scam and the murder part of one massive conspiracy—a plot whose object was to defraud people of money to buy Kirksey Nix's way out of prison, and which led to a murder plot against the Sherrys when the buy-out money vanished. By charging such a dual conspiracy in one count of the indictment, even marginal evidence of involvement in the murder plot would convict a suspect—so long as the evidence of scamming remained strong.

There was a risk, though: Such an unusual indictment might be ruled illegal by an unfriendly judge or appeals court—and the whole case could be thrown out of court, perhaps for good. Still, Tucker became convinced this was their only shot at victory.[2]

One key element seemed to be missing, however: John

Ransom. For Tucker's approach to work, everyone named in the indictment had to be linked to both the scam and the murder plot. Cook and Bell had brought in plenty of testimony putting Ransom in the middle of the murder plans. But in searching through the reams of material the investigators had put together on the supposed trigger man, Tucker could find no usable testimony placing Ransom in the scam—other than Ransom's admissions, which he was barred from using by agreement, and Bobby Joe Fabian's word, which was useless.

"You need to get me some proof Ransom was involved in the scam," Tucker told Cook and Bell during a strategy meeting a few months before the grand jury's expiration deadline. "If Fabian's telling the truth about that, there must be someone else who can swear to it."

The request led Cook and Bell on one of the oddest episodes in the case, a fittingly bizarre ending to their investigation. Fabian once told them Ransom had help in the Atlanta area, someone who had made scam pickups for him, fetching money orders from Western Union. Fabian even claimed to have talked to the woman, but he only knew her first name: Peggy, but with an unusual spelling.

A measly lead at best, but they had to try to check it. Randy Cook dialed the Atlanta Police Department vice squad, then told the first detective he could get on the phone, "I'm looking for someone named Peggy and she spells her name funny." He felt silly—it was an impossible request.

Yet, without a moment's hesitation, the cop in Atlanta replied, "Oh, you mean Pegi Williams. P-E-G-I."

Cook could do little more than sputter. He had called a big-city police department with tens of thousands of suspects every year, and on the first try, he scored—just because Pegi Williams spells her first name a bit unusually.

"Yeah," the Atlanta detective continued. "I'm working two cases involving her. You want me to have her call you?"

Nothing had ever come so easily in this case. "Sure, have her call me. That would be great," he said, not believing for an instant he would ever hear from P-E-G-I Williams. It was too good to be true.

An hour later, at three o'clock on a slow Friday afternoon, the phone on Cook's file-strewn desk rang, and the long-distance operator asked him if he'd accept a collect call from Pegi Williams.

Surprised again, yet still figuring this would be a useless exercise, Cook took the call, then explained that he was investigating the Sherry murders in Biloxi, that John Ransom was a suspect, and that he was contacting her because he had learned she knew Ransom. When he finished, Williams remained silent. "You there?" Cook finally asked.

"Yes," the woman replied, saying nothing more. She sounded wary and tough, her response bitten off and spit out like a wad of tobacco. Cook decided to try to bluff her a bit—what did he have to lose?

"You picked up a bunch of money orders for John Ransom, didn't you?" he asked, not knowing if this was true or not, relying upon Fabian's dubious word.

"Yes," she said again, that same hard, monosyllabic reply—which, nevertheless, floored Cook.

"At Western Union?"

"Yeah, a couple times a day, six days a week," Pegi confessed morosely. "I've been dreading getting a call like this for years."

"Wait a minute," Cook said, cutting her off, trying not to shout. He put her on hold and reached Keith Bell at his office on a three-way call. "You gotta listen to this."

And with the two partners listening raptly on the line, Pegi Williams told them about scamming with John Ransom. Williams's husband, an ex-con, an old friend of Ransom's, and a printer by trade, had introduced Ransom to her sometime in 1985 or 1986. Ransom asked Pegi if she'd like to make some extra money—all she had to do was go to Western Union offices in the Atlanta area, pick up cash wired in her name, and give it to him. She could keep ten percent of everything she picked up.

"I said sure," Williams told Cook and Bell. She was a manicurist and a nude dancer at the time, and could always use a few extra bucks. "I didn't know where the money was coming from—I didn't know anything about any sex scam—but I can't say I wouldn't have done it anyway. It was easy money. I just never asked."

Six times a week, two, even three times a day, Pegi would go to Western Union to pick up the cash. She paid no attention to who sent the money—the less she knew, the better. Ransom would come to her apartment and pick it up later the same day. She said she did this for about two months. Usually, Ransom would tell her when to get the money. Now and then, though, she would get phone calls from people she knew only as "Junior" or "Bobby" who would tell her amounts and times to pick up the money.

Then one day, the amount Pegi picked up turned out to be less than Ransom anticipated. When he counted the cash and found it short, Ransom threatened her, accusing Pegi of stealing. At first she was more incensed than anything. But when she complained to her husband, he warned her not to make Ransom angry. "Don't mess with him. I did time with that man, and he is cold-blooded and dangerous. He'd kill you in a heartbeat," Pegi recalled her husband saying.

Pegi stopped making pickups after that, and she steered clear of John Ransom whenever she could. He still came around to visit her husband, however.

When she finished describing her role in the scam, Cook and Bell realized they had what they needed—a witness that put Ransom in the scam. The method of money pickups was unmistakable, and the calls from "Junior" and "Bobby" cinched it. Who else could it be but Junior Nix and Bobby Joe Fabian? And who else but someone involved would know Nix's nickname? Pegi put the scam money directly into Ransom's hands, just as Tucker had asked. Cook and Bell started talking about having her fly out that weekend to make the next session of the grand jury. But then she blurted out something else that at first made them doubt her sanity:

"And another thing, that sonofabitch ruined every phone book I ever had."

That quizzical remark brought the conversation to a standstill. "What do you mean?" Bell finally asked.

"I mean, he shot them full of holes out in back of our house. Uzis, machine guns, he'd test them out on our phone books. One time, he had a pistol with a silencer. An automatic. I watched him fire it."

Cook and Bell had stumbled onto an unexpected jackpot. One of them asked, "When would that have been? You seeing him with a silenced automatic?"

"Sometime after I stopped picking up the money. In 1986, I think," Pegi said. "Around then."

1986: The same year John Ransom delivered "Wilbur" to LaRa Sharpe at Kirksey Nix's request.

Pegi Williams's testimony before the grand jury the following Monday completed the conspiracy, at least so far as James Tucker envisioned it. She was not the last witness grand jurors would hear—she was just the last one to add anything substantial to the case.

After Pegi, the case came down to asking for an indictment, or starting over. The grand jury was about to expire. The statute of limitations on some of the scam allegations would soon lapse. By May 1991, it was indict or go home.

Even with the new witness, Kent McDaniel, James Tucker, and other prosecutors in the office voted for the latter. Keith Bell and Randy Cook pushed for indictments. U.S. Attorney George Phillips wanted to consider one more point of view before making a decision.

"I believe in Keith and Randy," Lynne Sposito told Phillips when he called to ask her opinion. "They've worked on this for a long time, and they would never want to do anything that would endanger the case. If they say it's ready, I've got to believe them."

She wanted everyone charged, if possible, Pete Halat more than anyone. For herself, for her family, for the city of Biloxi, some sort of outcome had to be reached, she said. "We can't just let it slip away. We can't just throw up our hands and say, We give up. You murderers get away with it this time."

She remained calm and reasoned, but Lynne wanted to shout, Go forward, take a chance, go for broke. She couldn't, though. Phillips had no legal or ethical obligation to consult her, and she was lucky he even extended her that courtesy. They had acknowledged her contribution to the case, what Phillips called her "grit and determination," and Lynne appreciated this. It had not always been so: At their first meeting, Phillips had accused Lynne of threatening his job with her constant lobbying in Washington, which had produced some pointed calls to his office from congressmen curious about delays in the case.

"I'm not threatening your job," Lynne had shot back. "I just want you to *do* your job."

Now, though, she made herself stay calm. "I think you

should take a safe course, file it however you have to so you'll have the best chance of winning. But you've got to do something. It's been so long. There has to be an ending to this."

"I understand, Lynne," Phillips said, sympathetic but not committing to anything.

"The people of Biloxi need to get past this," Lynne continued, her voice rising, then falling to a quiet, almost desperate plea. "And so does my family.

"And so do I."

There was one more person to hear from before Phillips made his decision. Fittingly, Pete Halat became the last witness to appear before the Sherry grand jury.

He testified for two and a half hours, accompanied by his wife and his attorney who, by law, had to wait outside the grand jury room. Afterward, he met the crush of cameras and newspeople on the courthouse steps in Jackson, once again proclaiming himself innocent and assuring the public that he would never be indicted. He did not mention his private encounter with the FBI polygraph machine, or his request to prosecutors that he be allowed to turn himself in, sans handcuffs, if he were indicted. Rather, he exuded for public display an angry confidence, just as he had for the past two years of suspicion and unproven accusation, insisting he was not a target of the grand jury that had just questioned him. He reminded all present that in America, everyone is innocent until proven otherwise, and therefore he was an innocent man.

"I can die right now and go before my maker, and I'm satisfied that I've told the truth about this case, which is something that can't be said for a lot of other people who testified."

The next day, May 15, 1991, Keith Bell and Randy Cook made the three-hour drive to Jackson, leaving the Coast before daybreak. They had prepared a summary of their entire investigation for the grand jury, recapping the highlights of the 117 witnesses who testified, starting back in August 1989 with Bobby Joe Fabian.

When the grand jury left for its lunch break, McDaniel and Tucker emerged looking glum, worrying that they might get a "no bill" vote—a refusal by the grand jurors to return an indictment. Cook and Bell had holed up in the tiny witness room next to the grand jury chamber, excluded from the discussions in which no one could participate but jurors, prosecutors, and, when summoned, witnesses.

"We still don't think you've got a case," McDaniel told Cook and Bell. "We may not ask them to vote."

"At this point," Cook pleaded, "let's let the system do its thing. Let them vote. If they say no bill, I'll go home."

McDaniel and Tucker remained unconvinced. They returned to their office and tinkered with the proposed indictments one more time, putting in one defendant, taking out another, all at the last minute. They finally settled on the version they thought would give them the best shot at victory. Then they went to Phillips with it. They handed it over, then gave him their recommendation: Hold off. They wanted to wait until they had enough evidence to be sure.

To their surprise, Phillips shook his head. "It's too late to turn back now. I think we've got enough to win," he told them simply. "Let's give it a shot, and see how it turns out."[3]

It turned out that the grand jurors found the case more convincing than the prosecutors had thought. Without a dissenting vote, they returned the indictment James Tucker and Kent McDaniel had brought before them: one count alleging Tucker's massive scam and murder conspiracy, another charging wire fraud, and two counts of traveling in interstate commerce with the intent of committing murder for hire.

The last two counts were a particularly ingenious creation of Tucker's because they required no proof that the Sherry murders even occurred—only that people crossed state lines to *discuss* murder for hire. It was tailor-made for the limited evidence in hand.

Cook and Bell were ecstatic at the news, though they could tell no one, not even Lynne. The indictments were sealed by court order until arrest warrants could be served on those charged.

But word that some sort of indictment in the Sherry case had been handed down spread through the courthouse, then the state, fueled by speculation that the mayor of Biloxi might be charged. Lynne Sposito got a call within minutes of the vote—a simple, declarative sentence from Kent McDaniel.

"Well, you got your indictment, Lynne."

It was the moment she had been awaiting almost four years. Someone finally was going to have to answer for striding into her parents' home and snuffing out their lives. Someone was going to have to pay for ruining her family. Dick and the children stood with her in the kitchen in Raleigh, watching, waiting. They had been certain she'd want to celebrate if good news came, but Lynne found she felt none of the relief she had long anticipated.

"We've still got to convict them," she said grimly as she hung up the phone, and any thoughts of celebration in the Sposito house vanished.

If anything, the uncertainty about exactly who and what had been charged in the still-secret indictment left her more anxious than ever. McDaniel wouldn't give her any details, and she could only wonder what would happen next. She was glad they hadn't dropped the case, certainly. But somehow she suspected that this long-awaited indictment would turn out to be less than a total victory.

Lynne was soon proved right. A few days later, with the indictment unsealed at a packed press conference, she had to try to hide her disappointment as reporters began calling her house for comment on its surprising—and confusing— contents.

Four people were charged: Kirksey Nix, Mike Gillich, John Ransom, and LaRa Sharpe. Pete Halat was not indicted. To Lynne, his absence from the case was a crushing blow, though she was not entirely surprised.

In the end, Phillips and his prosecutors decided, their best chance of winning was to keep Halat away from the defendants' table, where his reputation and standing might make a strong argument for acquittal—not only for himself, but for all the defendants. They felt certain evidence against Halat was lacking; what they did have would be held in reserve while the hunt for new witnesses continued.[4] The proposed indictments penned by Tucker that had named Halat got filed away, souvenirs that would never see daylight.

Their reasoning might have made sense inside the prosecutors' strategy meetings, but the indictment confused the

press and the public, which had long believed Bobby Joe
Fabian and his story implicating Halat to be the centerpiece
of the case. Yet the portion of the indictment dealing with
murder contained not a word from Fabian's story, focusing
instead on the convict Robert Hallal's testimony about
meeting Gillich and Ransom to discuss a hit on Judge
Sherry.

An even more glaring omission, one that was particularly
hurtful to Lynne, was the name of Margaret Sherry. The
complex, eight-page indictment didn't even mention her—
because Hallal had never mentioned her. Only the conspiracy to murder Vince was discussed. The indictment remained silent on the other alleged meeting to discuss
contract murder in Biloxi in 1987—the one described by
Bill Rhodes, who spoke of a plot against both Vince and
Margaret. Rhodes was left out because putting his account
in the indictment made no sense without charging Pete
Halat.

"It's like Mom didn't even exist," Lynne muttered as she
read the text of the indictment, faxed to her shortly after it
was unsealed. But to reporters, she forced herself to remain
upbeat, to say, "There will be more charges. . . . In all
honesty, I do believe that this is the beginning, not the end."

Mayor Halat sounded a very different note. Tuesday, May
21, 1991, the day the indictment was unsealed, was his day
of vindication, as he called it. He convened yet another
press conference in Biloxi to announce, among other things,
his intention to run for re-election. Then he excoriated the
news media for its unfair treatment of him, for propound-
ing a "preposterous and pathetic story" told by a "lying
thug." Among his opening words: "I told you so."

"The grand jury investigating this case for the past two
years did not name me because I was in no way involved in
any prison scam, or the plot to murder my friends the
Sherrys. That is what I told you the day you came to me
with the insulting suggestion that I was somehow involved.
That is what I told you for the past two years. That is what I
told you last week after I testified before the grand jury. And
that is—plain and simple—the truth."

The U.S. Attorney offered no comment other than the
obligatory expression of confidence in their case, whether

they felt it or not. They could not tell anyone who else they had seriously considered indicting.

Even so, Pete Halat's vindication had a bittersweet note to it. Instead of being named as a defendant, Halat became an unindicted co-conspirator. Though he would be spared the legal battle of his life, this designation meant he would have to endure continuing allegations that he participated in crimes. Without being formally charged, he nevertheless would remain a shadow defendant in the case—referred to as an alleged co-conspirator, but lacking the defendant's constitutional right to confront his accusers. To his lasting dissatisfaction, the absence of his name on the indictment did not remove Pete Halat from suspicion.

In Raleigh, Lynne pored over the facsimile copy of the indictment, its curled pages quivering in her hands. Reporters kept calling all day. She tried to sound sensible and serious when they asked the inevitable stupid question, *How do you feel?*, but later, when she read the press clippings Becky sent her, she cringed at her quotes, so pompous and formal.

Why didn't I tell them, How the hell do you think I feel? Lynne thought. These bastards killed my mom and dad and the damn indictment doesn't even mention Mom's name.

She felt anxious and raw, as if she had somehow failed to do something that might have added to the case, that could have made the indictment more powerful. It was so wordy and dense. It never said who actually killed Vince and Margaret. It didn't satisfy.

After her eighth or ninth reading of the thing, after talking it over with Dick and Becky and Rex Armistead, who was still monitoring the case, still working his sources, but who had no consolation to offer, she finally got Kent McDaniel on the telephone. If she wasn't celebrating, no one would.

"Okay," Lynne said. "So we've got an indictment. Now, when does it go to trial?

"And how can I help?"

PART 4

Down in the Pew

He's made deals with drug dealers, murderers and I don't know what all, in the dark of the night, when thieves prowl and bats fly. . . . Mr. Phillips, Sunday, you'll be in the choir singing pretty songs, trying to save souls, but you need to get down in the pew, and let somebody sing to you.

> —*Kirksey McCord Nix,*
> *on U.S. Attorney George Phillips*

No civilized man condones murder.
No civilized man condones crime.

> —*Wayne Mancuso,*
> *in Defending Nix, 1972*

CHAPTER 32

Nearly four years had passed since Vince and Margaret Sherry died. Lynne Sposito's thoughts had seldom focused elsewhere. And yet, she had dreamt of her parents only once. That one time, in her sleep, she saw her mother sitting at the kitchen table in Raleigh—just sitting there, calmly smiling. Even in her dream, Lynne had said to herself this could not be real. You can't be here.

"No, I'm here," Margaret told her.

That voice Lynne knew so well, strong and clear, just as it always had been, the gentle Kentucky lilt, a sound that evoked memories of walks on the beach and rum cake at Christmas. In her dream, Lynne reached out, almost touching her mother's hand, then stopped herself, fearing she would end the moment.

"No, it's okay," Margaret said. "I promise, I won't disappear."

So Lynne reached all the way across the table. She took her mother's hand in hers, warm and solid, a small woman's fingers gently curling around her own. The sensation felt so real, Lynne awoke with a jolt, disoriented, her hand still tingling with the touch of another's skin, searching the darkness for a moment, then realizing, with a freshness of anguish she had not felt in years, that her mother and father were dead. She tried diving back into sleep, to find her way back to that table, the late afternoon sun filtering in her kitchen and gently painting her mother, but it was not there. She could find neither Margaret, nor rest, just the ticking of her pulse in the pillow. She ended up trudging to the laundry room, an all-too-familiar insomniac's haven, where she began sorting whites from colors. Except when Lynne left town, the Sposito household had not had dirty clothes for four years.

The next morning at the breakfast table, before Lynne could mention the dream, her daughter Cathy said, "I dreamt about Grandma last night. She was talking to me, but I can't remember what she said." Lynne stopped what she was doing to listen as Cathy described the eeriest part of the dream: the earring. Cathy often slept with Margaret's earrings on—the gold ones she had died in. It gave her a link to her lost grandparents, she felt. When Cathy woke that morning, though, she felt something in her hand—one of the earrings. Somehow, in her sleep, she had removed one of the gold balls, closed its post, and awoke clutching it in a fist—a mirror image of how Margaret's body had been found, one earring on, the other in hand.

"It freaked me out so much, I threw it across the room," Cathy said.

When Lynne told her daughter she too had dreamt of Margaret that night, they tried to dismiss it as a coincidence of longing. But they couldn't. They weren't sure what it meant, but somehow their tandem dreams left them at peace with developments in the case. Lynne felt renewed confidence in the investigation, and in the belief that the killers, someday, would be identified, charged, and convicted. This new indictment, she kept telling herself, was just a first step. The dreams were a sign.

"It won't stop here," she told her family. "It can't."

The newly indicted suspects and their attorneys seemed to think otherwise.

Confident, even cocky, they derided the case against them at every turn, saying the government—unwittingly or willingly—had been scammed by lying inmates. After four years and three different task forces, the best the authorities could come up with was an indictment that didn't bother to say who murdered the Sherrys, or why. They made their indictment sound like the biggest con job of all.

Certainly Mike Gillich seemed supremely confident, free on bail, his strip joints still flouting the law, his strippers still selling themselves and collecting swizzle sticks to keep count, his cronies still gathering at the Krispy Kreme each night to speak out of the sides of their mouths over coffee and cigarettes. To the rest of Biloxi, Gillich's business-as-usual demeanor suggested nothing would ever change. Even his choice of attorney sent a message: the flamboyant and theatrical Albert Necaise, who, as district attorney two decades earlier in Biloxi, received reports of Gillich's law-breaking from his investigators, yet never filed a case against Mr. Mike.

When Gillich appeared for his arraignment on two earlier drug-trafficking indictments, he responded to the crush of news cameras and reporters surrounding the courthouse by extending the middle finger of his right hand, then proceeding to adjust his glasses with it, pick his nose with it, and otherwise wave it around in as obtrusive a fashion as possible.

Perhaps Gillich thought the obscene gestures would keep him off the evening news, but he was wrong. His crass message and display of contempt was replayed repeatedly statewide, cementing his image as a lowlife thug for all of Mississippi to see. Ever the class act, when television anchorwoman Gurvir Dhindsa shoved a microphone in his face and asked for a comment as Gillich emerged from the courthouse, he extended his middle digit once again, then belched loudly into the microphone. "That's some comment, Mr. Gillich," the bemused reporter responded. Mr. Mike burped again, then stalked off. It was the closest thing to an interview he would ever grant.

Unlike his silent benefactor, Kirksey Nix did not remain quiet while awaiting his day in court. He had been filing his own fruitless appeals in the Corso murder case for the better part of two decades, ignored by all. Now in the limelight, he delighted in peppering prosecutors and the courts with outrageous motions, objecting to everything from the rigid restrictions on his visitation privileges, to complaints that the cuisine at the Harrison County Jail amounted to cruel and unusual punishment.

Nix began granting a long string of press interviews, with reporters ascribing to him "refined manners, a wicked wit and a brilliant mind," and dubbing him the "dough-boy-shaped genius jailed for life."

His pudgy, balding image, the oddly tilted head, the habitual nod he affected when speaking, and the jowls and soft hands heavy with gold jewelry all became familiar sights on the evening news. The soft-spoken, middle-aged convict in the immaculate white jumpsuit and white Reeboks seemed hard to square with the handsome and wild Dixie Mafia killer jailed twenty years before in the Corso case.

He capitalized on public confusion about the ambiguous conspiracy charges, wondering aloud why the complex indictment neglected to name a murderer outright, or to mention where Mayor Pete Halat fit in, if he fit in at all.

Then he paid for his own polygraph test, which purported to show he told the truth when he denied knowledge of or involvement in the Sherry murders—finding he immediately released to the news media.

Although the government questioned the conclusions, methods, and reliability of the test, Nix pointed out that at least he had submitted to one. No one had ever polygraphed Bobby Joe Fabian, Robert Hallal, Bill Rhodes, or any of the government's other key witnesses, he complained, asking, "What are they afraid of?"[1]

Lynne saw the interview while visiting at Becky Field's house, mesmerized and disgusted by Nix's performance. He was so smug, she felt like punching him, pummeling him, wiping that smile off his face. He even made a direct plea to her, staring dramatically into the camera with fluttering eyelids and pouty expressions of sincerity.

"As the son of a judge giving an oath to the daughter of one, please know that I am totally innocent and in every way uninvolved in your parents' deaths," he said. "I understand your quest for their killer or killers—but it is not me."

Becky groaned. "Shut it off, Lynne. He's making me sick."

"No," Lynne said quietly. "I want to remember this. I want to remember it when I see his face on the day he's found guilty. Then I'll be the one smiling."

Lynne's anxiety mounted as the trial approached, set to begin just five months from the day of the indictment. Often, she felt useless and left out, unable to release her tension by contributing to the case.

But then, a few weeks before trial, the lawyers defending

Nix, Gillich, Sharpe, and Ransom had to divulge their witnesses to the prosecution. When McDaniel, Tucker, and their colleagues saw some unfamiliar names, they called Lynne for help. Her familiarity with her parents' friends and enemies, her newfound expertise in the history of the Dixie Mafia—and, they had to admit, her superior knowledge of the early police investigation of the murders—made Lynne a valuable resource to the prosecution.

One of the character witnesses on Mike Gillich's list particularly troubled them. With no idea who she was or what she might have to say, they turned to Lynne for help.

"What's her story?" Peter Barrett asked her. Barrett was one of two young prosecutors assigned by George Phillips to try the case.

Lynne laughed when she heard the name, overjoyed to be pitching in again at last. "Well, she's a very nice, very kind seventy-year-old lady," Lynne explained, "who just happens to be P. J. Martino's widow."

"Yes!" Barrett exclaimed. It was just the sort of information he needed to attack the witness. P. J. Martino, a bookie with ties to the New Orleans Mafia, had run a gambling operation at one of Gillich's clubs, the Horseshoe Lounge, protected—and patronized—in the seventies and early eighties by senior officials at the Biloxi Police Department.

Lynne had more to tell. Martino's widow had called her a few weeks earlier, concerned and upset about being a potential witness for Gillich. The woman had been close to friends of the Sherry family and had known Leslie Sherry all her life. "I wanted to talk to you about it," the woman told Lynne, "because I would never do anything to hurt you or Leslie, and if I say no, I won't testify, then I know I won't be hurting you."

"Well," Lynne had asked, "what do they want you to testify about?"

"I've been a neighbor of Mr. Mike for twenty-six years. The lawyers came and asked, as far as my dealings with him, do I know him to be honest and nonviolent? And I have to say yes. I've never seen him behave otherwise. And if they ask, as far as I know, is he capable of murder, I'd have to say no to that, too." The widow had paused for a moment, then added, "I really don't believe he could pull the trigger, Lynne."

"I don't think he could pull the trigger either," Lynne agreed. "That's why he hired to have it done."

The woman chucked grimly. "I know, I know. I'm sure he's in it up to his ass, honey. But I got to answer the questions honestly."

Certain that defense attorneys would claim she had interfered with a witness if she tried to tell this woman what to say or do, Lynne said simply, "You have to do what your conscience dictates."

But she had no problem relaying the entire conversation to Barrett. Lynne suggested he could use it to undermine any favorable testimony the woman might give Gillich.

"She's really very sweet, and I like her," Lynne told the prosecutor. "But I've come too far for that to matter now. If she hurts the case, get her on the stand and tear her apart."

CHAPTER 33

The trial convened in Hattiesburg, Mississippi, on September 30, 1991, four years and fourteen days after the bodies of Vincent and Margaret Sherry were discovered.

The small federal courthouse in Hattiesburg's modest downtown overflowed with members of the press and public, gripped by that same sort of sweaty excitement that permeates casino floors and race courses. Snack vendors set up shop on the sidewalk as if catering to a sporting event. Mobil television studios towered at the curb, microphone-toting reporters rehearsing lines for live broadcasts from the courthouse steps.

Inside the darkly paneled courtroom of U.S. District Judge Charles Pickering, the defendants assembled one by one, Mike Gillich uncustomarily wearing a tie and jacket,

John Ransom looking reedy and lost inside his own ill-fitting khaki leisure suit, and LaRa Sharpe sweeping into the courtroom in sunglasses, flowing white-blond hair, and her prim Sunday best, smiling and waving at the reporters. And Kirksey Nix, who had traded his prison whites for a striped shirt, red suspenders, and a bright, wide tie, was positively boisterous, mugging for the reporters, still smug and cocky, bushy eyebrows gyrating wildly, basking in the circus limelight of Mississippi's most notorious murder case. The first time he caught sight of Lynne Sposito in the gallery, Nix mouthed the words, *It's not me.* She grabbed Becky Field's hand so tightly when she saw this, Becky winced, but Lynne made no outward sign of recognition toward Nix, staring stonily through him, willing herself to ignore those fleshy lips hurling silent pleas in her direction.

Security precautions were unusually intense, with marshals posted on either side of the defendants' table, the courtroom protected by guards and a double battery of metal detectors. Attempted escapes, and attempts to kill the accused, were both feared, Lynne was told. The marshals' eyes never stopped scanning the courtroom and crowd, passing over her just as coldly as anyone else, as if she might pose a threat.

While awaiting the judge's opening gavel, the men, women, and children crowded together noisily in the hallway outside the courtroom, a mix of witnesses, attorneys, and supporters of the accused, mingling with ordinary citizens drawn to the courthouse in their free time. Together they formed a gauntlet through which everyone entering the courtroom had to pass, each witness, attorney, and spectator enduring furtive inspection and commentary. "Is he somebody?" was a common question hissed anonymously in the hall. As Lynne walked through the double doors of the courtroom, she could hear someone whisper knowledgeably, "That one in the red dress, she's one of the daughters."

It seemed everyone expected a dramatic resolution to the long-drawn-out case. It had captured the entire state's attention. At last, it seemed, a solution to the mystery of the Sherry murders was at hand.

But at the prosecution table, queasy stomachs and shaken confidence prevailed. The intense news coverage and unrealistically high expectations about the case made the prosecutors nervous because they felt no one understood what was really about to happen. The headlines kept screaming SHERRY MURDER TRIAL, but the prosecutors had no intention of even mentioning to jurors what happened inside the Sherry house on the day of the killings. They just wanted to talk about plots and conspiracies that may or may not have moved forward, meetings held a month or more before the murders. Their case was supposed to end there, dry and simple. But the press didn't seem to get it, and now the prosecutors wondered: Would the jury be equally confused, dissatisfied by a conspiracy in which the juicy details of murder were never discussed?

Problems with the prosecution's case had started long before—shortly after the grand jury issued its indictment. With few attorneys confident it could be won, the case had been passed around the U.S. Attorney's Office like an unwelcome relative. The veteran prosecutor James Tucker, who drew up the indictments, ended up not trying the case—as Lynne Sposito had been promised he would. A new team was assigned less than a month before trial, capable attorneys who nevertheless seemed unfamiliar with large blocks of evidence gathered by Randy Cook and Keith Bell.

Peter Barrett, a short, stout fighter renowned for his vigorous hand gestures and explosive, red-faced outbursts in court, had been pulled from the U.S. Attorney's Biloxi office and teamed with Al Jernigan, an experienced trial attorney with a quiet, jovial manner that offset Barrett's mercurial temper. They were dedicated to the case—Barrett, in particular, was one of the few attorneys in his office who seemed to be sure of victory—but they had to cram for the trial like students on a term paper. Lynne worried they had too little time to prepare adequately. Too often, in helping them with the witness list in the weeks before trial, Lynne had realized she knew things about the case that they didn't.

And it showed, once the bailiff silenced the courtroom with a bellowed command for order and Judge Pickering took the bench, instructing the attorneys to begin their opening statements. From the outset, the prosecutors seemed to be on the defensive, apologizing to the jury for their case's shortcomings even before they started presenting evidence. Barrett's opening remarks, in which he was supposed to forcefully preview their case, capturing the interest and curiosity of the jury, instead left jurors looking vaguely perplexed. Influenced perhaps by press coverage of the case, Barrett spent much of his time explaining what he *wouldn't* be able to prove.

"It's so very important for you to know what this case *isn't* about," Barrett told the jury, "because this case isn't about who pulled the trigger. It's not about who shot Vincent Sherry in the head. It's not about who shot Margaret Sherry in the head on September 14, 1987.

". . . There aren't going to be any silver bullets in this case. There aren't going to be any smoking guns in this case. You're not going to hear any of these defendants say on tape that he or she did all the things they are charged with."

The list of what the case wasn't went on for much of his presentation, followed by a confusing attempt to explain Nix's complex scam and its tenuous ties to the conspiracy to murder the Sherrys. Barrett closed, then, with a promise to the jurors, but even that was tinged with a qualifier: "It's going to be clear," he said. "And it's going to be close."

Not so, the battery of attorneys representing the four defendants told the jury, pouncing immediately on Barrett's soft pitch, showing all the confidence and certainty the prosecution seemed to lack. One by one, lawyers for each of the defendants rose in counterpoint before the jury, outlining their basic trial strategy, the same line Kirksey Nix had taken in his earlier televised interviews: The government's witnesses were liars all, more corrupt and venal than any of the defendants. Bobby Fabian, Robert Hallal, and Bill Rhodes lay at the heart of the government's case, and these admitted liars and con men knew nothing more about the murders than what they had garnered from newspapers and magazines and one another.

"You will find in this case that the scam being perpetrated here is a scam that is being run *on* the United States government," began Kirksey Nix's lead defense attorney, Jim Rose, the Mississippi Gulf Coast's most prominent criminal lawyer. A tall, fit, marathon runner in his early fifties, Rose stood at the court's podium, commanding attention, the epitome of righteous indignation. ". . . The witnesses who will testify for the government, each and every one of them, are looking for something. They are looking, you will find, for freedom. They are looking, you will find, for money. They are looking, you will find, for glory, or to solve what has been so far an unsolvable case. . . .

"There are no silver bullets, Mr. Barrett said. He also told you there is no smoking gun. Because there is no evidence whatsoever that those people are dead today as a result of anything these three men had to do."

Rose then decried the prosecution's case for sullying the image of a fine and upstanding citizen. He was not talking about Mike Gillich or LaRa Sharpe, and certainly not Kirksey Nix or John Ransom. He was talking about Vincent Sherry.

If you believe the prosecutors, Rose argued, if you conclude that Vince was killed for ripping off scam money from the killers, then you have to believe he was involved, too. That he was a criminal, like them. The problem was, no evidence supported this, he said. No one has ever been able to prove that Vince Sherry received one penny of scam money.

"It's all a lie," Rose said. "Every bit of it."

Lynne winced at this unexpected proclamation. Hearing Nix's lawyer defend her father seemed a cruel irony. Worse still, during a break, Rose approached her in the hallway, hand extended, solicitous and solemn, saying how much he had admired her father and his integrity. Lynne thanked him, barely biting back the comment she later hissed to Becky Field once Rose was out of earshot: "So why the hell are you defending the man who murdered him?" To Lynne, it seemed rank hypocrisy—though, at the same time, she remembered having the same sort of argument with her father many years before, Lynne complaining about his criminal clients, and Vince chiding that every accused man deserved a good defense. "If Dad were here," she ruefully admitted to Becky, "he'd be taking Jim Rose's side."

When his turn came, LaRa Sharpe's attorney, Michael Adelman, a soft-spoken Michigan native whose accent seemed out of place in a Mississippi courtroom, portrayed his client as a woman who made mistakes out of love for

Kirksey Nix, not greed. And those mistakes ended with helping Nix with his scams, Adelman said.

"LaRa Sharpe had nothing to do with the preparation, the planning, plotting, any type of conspiracy regarding the murders of Judge Vincent and Margaret Sherry," he declared.

Mike Gillich had a phalanx of four lawyers on his case, including his daughter, Tina, and his son-in-law and a former partner of Pete Halat, Keith Pisarich. (Tina Gillich eventually had to vacate the defense table, at Judge Pickering's direction, though she kept passing notes up to her colleagues throughout the proceedings.) But it was Gillich's lead counsel, Albert Necaise, the ex-district attorney, who rose up to deliver his attack on the government's case.

Necaise had the booming, drawling persona of the prototypical Southern lawyer, Fredric March in *Inherit the Wind*, protecting God and country from the devilment of evolution. Here, though, his task was to take the king of nude dancing, gambling, and prostitution on Biloxi's Strip and remake him into a God-fearing blue-collar hero whose respectable living was made in the "nightclub business," and whose only mistake was holding money for his good friend Kirksey Nix, no questions asked.

"Mike Gillich didn't have anything to do with bringing people, encouraging people, asking people to come to Mississippi to plan to kill Judge Vincent Sherry," Necaise thundered. "Not . . . Vincent Sherry, a man who had represented some of his employees, a man who had set in his place of business, a man that he knew."

The blustering Necaise also took a shot at Rex Armistead, just in case the government decided to call him and Bobby Fabian as witnesses. As part of their strategy, the prosecutors had encouraged this impression by listing five times as many witnesses as they intended to call, including Fabian. They had yet to reveal their abandonment of him as a witness, hoping the defense lawyers would waste time preparing to confront him and his ever-changing story. Necaise bit, declaring Armistead a "bounty hunter" who, in partnership with Fabian, concocted a lie-riddled solution to an unsolvable case so he could collect a handsome fee from the Sherry family. It sounded damning as Necaise said it at the beginning of the case, but later, when no evidence to support his contentions surfaced, Gillich's defense suffered.

Last came Rex Jones, the former county attorney appointed to represent John Ransom. With severely cut gray hair and a Clint Eastwood squint, Jones was, of all the defense attorneys, the most brief and to the point, plain-talking without theatrics or artifice. His task was to show someone other than Ransom had murdered the Sherrys—namely, the driver of the yellow Ford the night of the killings. Lynne Sposito's initial detective work in the case came back to haunt her here, as the defense sought to use it as proof to foil the prosecution. No way could that large bearded man spotted in the car that night be John Ransom, Jones said, looking toward his client. Everyone on the jury turned and saw the razor thin, balding man sitting in his leisure suit—"a wore out old man," as Jones described him. They had to wonder, why was the only talk about eyewitnesses to the murder coming from the defense?

Jones had another challenge for the prosecution, and again it harkened to something Lynne had done: the picture frame Sheri the psychic had helped her find, with the bloody smudges on it. It turned out that investigators had found a fingerprint on that frame that did not belong to Vince, Margaret, or any member of their family. That print had never been identified, Jones said, and it quite possibly belonged to the killer.

"And the proof in this case will show," Jones said, "by the FBI's own records, that John Ransom's fingerprint was not on there."

That meant someone else killed the Sherrys, Jones argued, hoping the jurors would agree, then disregard the law—which said conspirators in a murder plot could be found guilty even if the conspiracy failed and someone else did the killing. Jones believed the jury would never convict if it believed the real killers remained free.

Lynne felt her stomach begin a slow roll. Jones's remarks were the only ones that really upset her. The idea that her attempts to move the case forward could be used to aid the suspects galled her. She thought the prosecutors should try and stop this tactic, but they hadn't said a word.

"Isn't all that irrelevant, George?" she asked George

Phillips. "I thought the case stopped before the murder, that just the conspiracy was being proved. Now they're trying to prove someone else did the murder."

"Yeah," Phillips said, the grin on his face surprising Lynne. "Isn't it great?"

The defense had walked into a trap, he and his prosecutors believed. It wouldn't become apparent until the trial nearly ended—if at all. But early on, those comments by Rex Jones gave the prosecutors their first glimmer of hope.[1]

CHAPTER 34

The prosecutors led with their strength: the scam. They sought to discredit the defendants with a mountain of evidence showing Kirksey Nix and his cohorts had sat atop a multimillion-dollar empire of theft, fraud, and lies. Once established as professional liars, the defendants' pleas of innocence in the murder portion of the case would carry less weight. At least that was the theory.

And so, the first day of trial brought a parade of scam victims to the stand, capped by the emotional testimony of James Dickey, the California journalist who lost seventeen thousand dollars to Nix's fictional Eddie Johnson.

"I saw him as a young man, a boy, who was caught up in the system," Dickey said of his expensive and futile attempt to bring "Eddie" safely to California. "I thought . . . he was being possibly sent to prison for many, many years for something he was not really guilty of. I was bound and determined to rescue him from that, and it's my nature to be a rescuer.

"And he picked up on it. Whoever Eddie is, is very perceptive."

Nix grinned at this backhanded compliment. His lawyer

did not try hard to disprove the victims' testimony, largely because Nix did not care if he was found guilty of scamming. He was a lifer: Why not accept blame for his scams and just fight the murder charge? Maybe the jury would blame him for the scams and free the others.

The next day, jurors met the bearded and taciturn Robert Wright, the pool repairman who served as Nix's bagman in Biloxi. He testified about the dozens of times he fetched cash from Western Union for Nix, delivering it to LaRa, Gillich, and Pete Halat's office in exchange for a ten percent commission.

"It was easy money," he admitted.

He also introduced the first bit of information that suggested the defendants were planning a murder. He reiterated his grand jury testimony of a year earlier—that he had been shown a silenced .22-caliber pistol stowed in LaRa's camera bag at Nix's house in Ocean Springs, and that Nix asked him to test-fire it for him.

"I said no," Wright testified. "I had just been handed a loaded weapon I have never held. It was an illegal weapon."

But the bulk of Wright's testimony—like many of the prosecution's best witnesses—linked the defendants to scams, not murder. After Wright, Robbie Gant, the other scam delivery boy in Biloxi, gave testimony that put LaRa Sharpe—and the Halat and Sherry law office—in a leading role in the scam, his word backed by the FBI tape in which LaRa encouraged him to lie to authorities. But he had nothing at all to say about murders. And as the trial progressed, the contrast between the strength of the scam evidence and the ambiguities of the murder conspiracy only made matters worse for the prosecution, for it was here that some of the witnesses wavered.

Ex-Angola convict and Nix protégé Arthur Mitchell came next, the first witness who was expected to provide crucial details about the murder conspiracy. But when he was asked to describe discussions he had with Nix about the Sherrys, Mitchell looked at his friend at the defense table, then began to squirm. Lynne Sposito, sitting in the spectator area with Becky Field, saw the look on Mitchell's face, and gripped her friend's arm, sensing what was about to happen.

"Well, they were not really prolonged discussions," Mitchell muttered. "I know that, many times when we walk the yard, we discuss different things, many things." He paused, then reluctantly continued. "On one occasion, we were walking in the yard and he mentioned that, that they had been killed over here, you know, that they were discovered, killed over here."

Previously, Mitchell had described lengthy conversations in which Nix spoke of two hundred thousand dollars in missing scam money, and of the roles Pete Halat and Judge Sherry were supposed to play in buying him out of prison— all before the murders. Now, though, Mitchell barely remembered any discussions at all, and what he remembered occurred *after* the murders.

Assistant U.S. Attorney Al Jernigan, who was questioning Mitchell, shuffled papers at his table, buying time. But he had no choice but to push on. He tried another angle. "Do you remember what was said by Mr. Nix about the activities of Margaret Sherry in relationship to Mr. Gillich's business?"

Previously, Mitchell swore Nix had criticized Margaret for threatening to close Mike Gillich's clubs on The Strip. But again Mitchell altered his story.

"Not in direct relationship to Mr. Gillich's business," Mitchell replied. "But to everybody's business on The Strip. . . . She was like a moral crusader or something. She was against it."

It was an impossible characterization, because there were no other businesses like Gillich's on The Strip—he had the monopoly. But jurors did not know this.

Still, Mitchell's account, diluted as it was, startled Lynne. She was sitting in a middle row of the courtroom, furiously scribbling notes, as she did for all the witnesses, notebooks quickly filling with her neatly penciled longhand. "They must have really talked about her," she said to Becky. "That sums up Mom perfectly: She *was* a moral crusader."

Then something dawned on her, a point that wasn't really coming through in Jernigan's questioning, something the jury probably wouldn't notice—but which seemed suddenly clear to Lynne: "This man never met Mom," she said to Becky, "and neither did Kirksey Nix. But they know all about her. And that means someone, Pete or Gillich or LaRa, had to have been talking to them about Mom. And why would they do that unless . . ."

"Unless they were talking about getting rid of her," Becky finished in an excited whisper. "Lynne, that's what the prosecutors ought to be asking."

Lynne made a note to mention this to Peter Barrett during a break, but by the time she got to him, the trial had moved on to other points. It would be one of many frustrating moments in which Lynne wished she could stand up and start asking the questions herself.

Mitchell, meanwhile, continued his evasive ramblings, nervously deflecting questions, especially when asked about Mike Gillich or Pete Halat. Finally Judge Pickering sent the jury out so prosecutors could remind Mitchell of his previous testimony to the grand jury—and the penalty for perjury.

Chastened somewhat, Mitchell, with still obvious reluctance, then repeated most of what he had said earlier: He claimed Halat visited Nix in 1987—despite what the prison logs showed—after which Junior began complaining of the two hundred thousand dollars in scam money missing from Halat and Sherry's safekeeping.

With that, the prosecution established part of the motive for the murder conspiracy: Nix, his scam, and his plans for freedom had been ripped off.

Pete Halat, the unindicted co-conspirator, was implicated even further when Mitchell swore he delivered a thousand dollars to the lawyer while they stood outside Mike Gillich's nightclub one night in 1988. Mitchell said he relayed an offer from Nix to give him one hundred thousand dollars if Halat could buy his way out of prison.

But Mitchell balked when asked if Nix spoke with him about wanting the Sherrys dead before they were killed. Prison housing records suggested he and Nix had little or no opportunity to talk after the Sherry killings, so prosecutor Jernigan suggested it must have happened in advance.

"How could I discuss something like that before it happened unless—" Mitchell began to answer sarcastically, then stopped himself, spotting the trap the prosecutor had tried to lead him into.

"Well, if somebody was planning it, you could discuss it before it happened," Jernigan suggested with mock helpfulness, followed by a chorus of objections from the defense. But the point had been made.

On cross-examination, Mitchell gamely tried to undo any damage to his friend Nix. Oddly, though, by the time he was through, Mitchell's hostility to the prosecution, his obvious desire to help Nix rather than hurt him, ended up enhancing his credibility as a witness for the government. Everything negative Mitchell had to say about Nix seemed doubly believable, because it came so unwillingly.

Even so, his testimony fell far short of what the prosecution had hoped to elicit. Arthur Mitchell left the courtroom with the case clearly in jeopardy and the jury looking confused. Five days of trial with a half dozen witnesses had gone by, and there still was no evidence that directly proved a conspiracy to kill the Sherrys. Just scam testimony and vague innuendos. Lynne fidgeted in her seat, waiting for something substantive.

"If it keeps on like this," Becky told her worriedly, "they're not going to convict these people of jaywalking."

When the time came for Nix's wife and scam assistant, Kellye Dawn Newman Nix, to take the stand, both Lynne and the prosecutors feared she too would have a change of heart. It was bad enough that she was chronically unreliable. But even the stoutest-hearted person would have second thoughts after learning what happened to the previously scheduled witness.

Roy Garland, the ex-con who swore he picked up several hundred thousand dollars in scam money for Nix, was supposed to have preceded Kellye. But on the night before he was to testify, he was shot in the face with a blast from a twelve-gauge shotgun.

Suspicions flared that the shooting was an attempt to silence one witness and intimidate the rest. But Randy Cook and Keith Bell quickly determined Garland had been shot in a domestic dispute, having been caught sleeping with someone else's wife. Hospitalized in guarded condition, disfigured for life, Garland was dropped from the witness list, with little damage to the government's case— he would have spoken only about scams, not murder.

But with Kellye up next, scheduled to kick off the second week of trial, anything was possible. The investigators were certain Garland's shooting had nothing to do with the case, but rumors to the contrary were everywhere. Bell, seated at the U.S. Attorney's table with the prosecutors, and Cook, who baby-sat Kellye all morning and escorted her into the courtroom, had been certain she would try to flee. But she surprised them. "I'm not the same person I used to be," she told them flatly. "I'm trying to get my life back together, and I can't do that if I run. I just have to get past this."

And, it seemed, she really had changed. Looking well scrubbed and prim in an uncharacteristically school-marmish outfit, Kellye proved to be a devastatingly effective witness for the prosecution, remaining unrattled by her ex-husband's stares or the hostile cross-examination of the defense attorneys. This time, it was Kirksey who looked uncomfortable, spending much of her testimony staring down at his hands or looking mournfully at the young woman he inexplicably still loved. It was Kellye who made it clear that their entire life together had been riddled with lies—from the time she first met him at age eight, when he was courting her mother and making Kellye his stepdaughter, to their own bogus telephone marriage arranged by Pete Halat.

"Are you still married to him?" Peter Barrett asked.

"I'm not sure," she said, so naked a reply the prosecutor seemed at a loss for words for a moment. How many people don't know their own marital status? "The ceremony was performed in 1982," Kellye explained, "but Mr. Halat and Mr. Nix both lied to me."

When asked to define her relationship with Nix—the defense sought to make Kellye out to be a vengeful gold digger who feigned love in exchange for a generous allowance—she said with simple sincerity, "I was good to him because he was very good to me and my daughter.

"He was under the impression that I would fall in love with him in time," Kellye explained later in her testimony, again seemingly without guile, making no attempt to hide the fact that she profited from their relationship without being devoted to Nix. "That's what he was hoping for . . . I wanted to be in love with him like he was me, but I wasn't obsessed about him. There was a difference. That's what he told me, anyway, that he was crazy in love with me."

At the same time, Kellye said, Nix made her dependent on him by having Pete Halat continually bail her out of legal trouble, including the time when cocaine mailed to her by John Ransom was found to be baking powder after it was placed in a police evidence locker.

"Kirksey told me . . . that Mike Gillich and Peter Halat would take care of it, that they had friends at the police department."

Kellye provided a richly detailed portrait of the scam, starting with the three-way calls she made for her husband, sometimes to scam victims, sometimes to John Ransom, and once to LaRa, whom she overheard discussing a "trick" in Canada who had coughed up hundreds of thousands of dollars. She told jurors how Nix bought a sophisticated computer from Gillich's nephew that automatically put through three-way calls, enabling him to phone anywhere without the call being traced back to Angola. "It could do everything for him," she said. "Just like a secretary."

When asked to define Halat's relationship with Nix, Kellye provided crucial testimony about the goal of the scam—at the same time attributing less than pure intentions to the mayor of Biloxi. "I was told by Mr. Nix that Mr. Mike and Peter Halat knew someone political that could arrange to possibly get Mr. Nix out of prison for two hundred thousand to two hundred fifty thousand dollars."

This was perhaps Kellye's most important statement, because it matched the testimony of Arthur Mitchell, who had reluctantly spoken of two hundred thousand dollars in "buy-out money" entrusted to Halat—the money that later "came up missing."

Halat took another hit from Kellye, who accused him of continuing to accept money from Nix even though he knew the convict earned a living ripping off gay men.

"He just told me that I had better tell Kirksey he better leave the homosexuals alone," Kellye swore, in describing a 1983 conversation with Halat. "One other time, I overheard him on the telephone with Mr. Nix. It was later in eighty-three. Mr. Nix had been caught with some paperwork on him, some of the supposed trick's numbers on him. . . . And Mr. Halat jokingly said to him, 'Boy, I told you to leave those homosexuals alone. They are going to get you in trouble.' And he laughed about it."

Still, as bad as she made the defendants—and Pete

Halat—look, Kellye had little to say about the Sherrys. She offered only one bit of evidence pertaining to the murder plot. While jailed in Louisiana on scam charges, Kellye had sat in on a jailhouse meeting between Nix and his old lawyer, Wayne Mancuso, who had represented him on the Corso killing two decades earlier. While Kellye watched from across the small visiting room, the two men drew a map of Biloxi's Vieux Marche, focusing on the area directly behind the Halat and Sherry law office. They spoke in whispers—though Kellye could hear part of what was being said. Then Nix laughed, pointed to a spot and said, "That man just happened to be there that day. It was just a coincidence."

According to Kellye, Nix had been referring to John Ransom and his encounter behind the law office with the lawyer Charles Leger, just before the Sherry murders. If Kellye was to be believed, this represented a damning admission from Nix that the contract killer was in Biloxi at the time of the murders, looking for one of his victims.

After a full day of grueling testimony, Kellye Nix finally left the stand, gratefully leaving the courtroom behind, stepping into the crowded hallway. Lynne approached her there, already reconsidering her original unflattering estimation of the young woman. Kellye was not the drug-addled, money-grubbing, selfish girl-child Lynne had expected. Lynne had been ready to heap blame on her for being part of something that ended in her parents' death, but somehow she no longer saw Kellye that way. This woman appeared to be drug free, devoted to her daughter, anxious only for a fresh start and an escape from everything Nix represented. In her own way, Kellye seemed to be just another victim of Nix's lies, Lynne decided. If it was an act, she thought to herself, it was a good one.

"I just wanted to thank you for coming in here and telling the truth," she told Kellye. "I know it wasn't easy for you."

That was all she had wanted to say, but to Lynne's surprise, tears began to roll down Kellye's cheeks. Then, jostled by the people heading from the courtroom to the elevator, Kirskey Nix's wife embraced the daughter of Vincent and Margaret Sherry.

"I'm so sorry," Kellye whispered to Lynne, who had

stiffened in surprise. "I never knew what we were doing would end with your parents dead. I never knew. I would have done something if I knew."

As Kellye wept softly, Lynne slowly returned the embrace, hugging Kellye tight.

CHAPTER 35

The prosecution gradually built its case over the course of a month of testimony, recreating for jurors the slow steps Randy Cook and Keith Bell had taken in pursuing their investigation of the Sherry murders.

Witnesses recounted LaRa Sharpe's arrest at the prison, with scam materials on her. Money deliveries to LaRa, Gillich, and the law office were described. And Halat's faithful secretary Ann Kriss, anxious to champion her boss's cause, still revealed that Halat, in eight years of supposedly working as Nix's lawyer, had performed few lawyerly duties. The marriage to Kellye, and the closing on the house in Ocean Springs were all Kriss could recall.

Yet, throughout these first weeks of trial, John Ransom seemed almost forgotten, the hit man's name barely mentioned. While Nix took copious notes, exchanged winks with LaRa, and made faces at the witnesses, his old friend Ransom dozed at the defense table, his head tilted back, mouth open.

But that changed when Pegi Williams took the stand. Suddenly, Ransom snapped to attention.

By then using the last name Graham, having abandoned nude dancing in favor of a career as a manicurist, Pegi remained as brassy and taciturn as ever. She had stalked off a plane the night before, furious at being forced to fly to

Jackson from Atlanta on her day off, barely speaking to Randy Cook, who met her at the airport. "Take me to my hotel," and "I need a drink," were the only sentences she uttered before slamming her door shut on Cook. He left worrying she would vent her anger by harming the prosecution's case once she took the stand, and he warned Barrett and Jernigan to watch their step.

In court, though, Pegi dutifully faced off with Ransom, turning her testiness toward him, though on occasion, her fear of the man showed through when she found it hard to catch her breath under the intensity of his sallow stare.

She testified about her many money pickups at Western Union for Ransom, directed by the man she knew over the telephone as "Junior." She described Ransom's penchant for shooting up phone books as he test-fired his ever-changing arsenal of weapons. Then Pegi added an unexpected bonus for the government, a recollection she had never mentioned before.

As Ransom glared at her, Williams swore, "He told war stories. Things he had done in the past. . . . Murders that he was paid to do. . . . He said he went into a bar and stabbed a man in the heart and walked out with him as if the man was just drunk."

She also swore that on the many occasions she saw Ransom handle guns, he always wore gloves. Not only had Pegi created in a few sentences a portrait of a callous and boastful hit man, but she had driven a nail through his attorney's opening arguments about the framed picture Lynne had found. Of course Ransom's fingerprints weren't on it—he always wore gloves when he handled guns. That's what hit men did.

As Pegi's testimony drew to a close, Ransom started mimicking her by using his hand to make yakking motions, then shaking his head and rolling his eyes. More than anything, this seemed to unnerve Pegi. Weeping by the time the judge excused her, she fled the courtroom. But the hardened ex-stripper's tears turned to anger when a television cameraman tried to film her as she walked out of the courthouse. She decked him with a roundhouse swing of her heavy leather purse as a stunned Lynne Sposito and George Phillips looked on, mouths open.

* * *

Halat and Sherry's former legal associate, Charles Leger, soon followed, keeping John Ransom's name and activities in sharp focus, implicating him heavily in the murder plot.

Ransom stayed alert and agitated throughout Leger's time on the witness stand. Leger, nervous and small, watched as both Kirksey Nix and John Ransom shook their heads in tandem at him as he described his encounter behind the law offices with the accused Dixie Mafia hit man in September 1987.

"He stops me . . . and I had to be face to face with this man, no closer than maybe six inches and no farther than a foot," Leger said, recalling how he told Ransom that Vince Sherry was not in the office that day. As he testified, Leger avoided eye contact with Ransom, staying focused on the prosecutor questioning him. ". . . It was like he narrowed his eyes down on me. . . . And I felt almost as if I was pleading with him. . . . He stared down at me with a look like, I'm going to kill you. That kind of look."

Leger recalled then how Ransom finally stalked off, a rail thin figure in boots, possibly cowboy boots, who stepped off a curb in an awkward way, as if something were wrong with his right leg.

The defense lawyers tried to shake his story, mocking his account of how he dreamed about Ransom's face for many months before finally seeing his picture on television and connecting him to the Sherry murders. But Leger stuck to his story, pointing his finger at Ransom as the man he saw behind the law offices that day, although by this time— more than four years after the murders—he could only say it happened sometime in the two weeks before he and Pete Halat found the bodies. Previously, he had told investigators it could have been a day or two before.

As Leger finished describing his encounter with Ransom, Nix, who had been grimacing at the witness all day, scribbled a note on his legal pad and held it up to the witness, totally unnerving Leger. The note read: "Chuck, I know *you* killed Judge Sherry."

Afterward, with the jury cleared from the courtroom, Nix's apologies and vows that he had not intended his message as a threat were met with a stony response from Judge Pickering.

"There is no question in my mind that this is contempt of

court," the judge said, "and the only reason the court has not taken action in this regard is that I don't know what you do to a man who is serving a life sentence without parole."

Nix made an insincere swipe at apologizing, but it was clear he knew Pickering was right: contempt of court was nothing for a man who was never supposed to leave prison alive.

Chuck Leger's testimony had covered several crucial areas, including LaRa's suspicious activities at the law office, but when it came time to talk about Pete Halat, Leger seemed to have reconsidered his feelings about his former boss. He ended up commenting more favorably on Halat's actions and words than he had in the past. Peter Barrett had Leger briefly recount finding the bodies of Vince and Margaret, and Leger omitted all of the behavioral oddities he previously had ascribed to Halat that day—such as his command not to touch anything. Leger described that morning up until the point Pete Halat emerged from the back of the Sherrys' house and cried, "Oh God, no, not Vince. Oh God, no, not Vince." Then Leger stopped.

The prosecutor failed to ask his witness what Halat said next—how Pete seemed to know both Vince *and* Margaret were dead, without ever going into the bedroom where Margaret lay.

Lynne Sposito was furious when Leger left the courtroom, these questions unasked. To her, this could have been vital, damning evidence. "I can't believe you're letting Halat off so easily," she fumed to George Phillips.

"He's not on trial, Lynne," Phillips told her. "There's no point in tipping him off about everything we have. We need to keep some things in reserve. That will come later, after we get these guys."

Lynne was not mollified, though. She couldn't help thinking to herself, You mean, *if* you get these guys.

Still, if Leger's testimony dissatisfied Lynne, it infuriated John Ransom. Ransom had fixated on Leger's comment about cowboy boots.

"It's impossible for a man with a wooden leg to wear a cowboy boot," Ransom ranted to his lawyer in his stately Georgia accent, his six-foot-two, one-hundred-nineteen-pound frame quaking. "You can't pull it on over the prosthesis, no way."

Then, with the jury out of the room, Ransom personally addressed the court, asking the judge if he could perform a boot demonstration for the jury. But Judge Pickering said no, not unless Ransom took the witness stand to testify about it.

Ransom, grumbling, said he wouldn't do that. He feared taking the stand and being cross-examined about a host of other issues he had no desire to discuss before the jury— such as his criminal record.

The next day, however, Ransom appeared in court wearing a cowboy boot on his good foot, with the other boot half on, half off his wooden leg, dragging and flopping behind him. Furious, the judge ordered the marshals to remove the boot before jurors could see it, much to Ransom's and Nix's consternation.

"I just wanted to let everything hang out," Ransom quipped to his lawyer.

Things got worse for Ransom a short time later when he inadvertently undermined his image as the "wore-out old man" his lawyer wanted jurors to see.

It happened during a conference at the judge's bench, the lawyers huddled and whispering with Pickering. LaRa's lawyer, Mike Adelman, accidentally brushed against a light switch, extinguishing every light in the courtroom except for the red emergency exit lights at the doors.

With the courtroom plunged into darkness, a communal gasp rippled through the room, accompanied by the faint sound of rustling in the dark. Fumbling and embarrassed, Adelman switched the lights back on after three or four seconds, though it took a bit more time for the big fluorescent overheads to flicker back into life.

"If you'd kindly stay away from the wall, Mr. Adelman," the judge said dryly, once illumination had been restored, "I'd appreciate it."

"I'll do that, Judge," the lawyer said, abjectly enough to generate quiet laughter, breaking the tension. But most everyone else—lawyers, jurors, audience—noticed what had happened when the lights went out. All but five men had frozen in place: four marshals, who raced to the front of the bench to form a protective barrier between the judge and the rest of the courtroom, and John Ransom. Wooden leg and all, he had ducked under the defense table with astonishing speed, reflexively moving out of the line of fire. If anyone doubted the feasibility of a hit man with a wooden leg, they needed only to recall the image of Ransom crouching beneath the table, then rising up with a sheepish grin.

Beau Ann Williams, Nix's cousin, became the next witness to waver from a past account, replacing her accusatory testimony about Gillich, Nix, and Halat with milder recollections. Locked in, though, by her previous sworn testimony before the grand jury, Williams remained consistent when describing the actual words exchanged with the men on trial. But she put an entirely different interpretation on those conversations than she had in the past.

She re-created her odd encounter with Mike Gillich in her motel room on The Strip, when Gillich denied ordering a hit on the Sherrys and asked her to warn Nix that LaRa was talking to the police, telling them everything. But gone was the original spin she had put on this conversation—that Gillich seemed to be constructing a defense to crimes he had committed. Instead, she told the jury that Gillich seemed only to be responding to rumors, trying to put them to rest. And Mike Gillich, whom she had previously described to grand jurors as "scary as the devil," had become "a pleasant fellow" whom "I enjoyed talking to."

At the prosecution's prodding, Beau Ann Williams reluctantly described Nix's ominous response to Gillich's warning: "LaRa wouldn't do that. LaRa has kids." Though she told the grand jury she took this as a threat to LaRa's children, she told the trial jury that she saw it as a more innocuous comment. With leading questions from defense attorney Jim Rose guiding her along, she suggested Nix might have been referring to fears that LaRa had been leaking information to the other side in Meagan Nix's malpractice case. "She wouldn't screw up Meagan's case because she has her own kids," Williams said.

She also reversed her story about the timing of the phone call she had received from Nix when he told her about the Sherry murders. She had told the grand jury that the call occurred on September 15, the day before Halat found the bodies—timing that would virtually convict Kirksey Nix.

But she told the trial jury that the call came September 18, two days later, long after news about the murders broke.[1]

Williams went on to speak at length about her love of Kirksey, describing him as more than a cousin, calling him a friend who had taught her to drive at sixteen, who once had been "my Prince Charming." She provided an elaborate explanation and defense of the scams, how Nix had told her that they ripped off only evil homosexuals who wanted to prey on young, helpless boys. The scams were actually a way to protect these boys, Williams said, for whom Nix "felt a very keen bond," having been "abandoned emotionally" as a child himself by parents who shipped him off to boarding schools.

According to Williams, Nix told her, "It's not right to con someone unless they have an evil purpose."

This played perfectly into the "they deserved it" defense to scam charges being offered by the defendants. And it may well have been what he told his cousin. But if he did, he lied. Not a shred of evidence was ever produced that showed "young boys" were involved; all the letters and magazine articles that lured in scam victims described men in their twenties looking for companions. The evidence in the scam case was overwhelming on this point: Nix did not care whom he preyed upon. He had simply scammed his cousin with a skewed story, just like he scammed everyone else.

When asked about her talk with Nix's scam partner Arthur Mitchell, she again produced a subtly different version: "He said, 'Well, I know that Pete is denying responsibility for the Sherrys' murder. But in a way, he is responsible, because it was Pete that introduced Sherry to all those people, and when he wanted to get out, Pete could not help him.'"

Peter Barrett forced Williams to admit that, previously, she had quoted Mitchell as saying Pete "got him involved in all this"—far more suggestive than merely introducing Vince to some people. And she had also told the grand jury, "when Judge Sherry wanted out, he couldn't get out. And Pete couldn't protect him." The difference between "help" and "protect" was subtle, but telling.

Barrett did not, however, make clear to the jury the most crucial point of this testimony—that Williams previously

said this conversation with Mitchell occurred in February
1989, long before Bobby Joe Fabian went public, or had
even talked to Rex Armistead. There had been no public
allegations against Pete Halat at that time. Mitchell, then,
must have had another source for his information—an
inside source involved in the murders. And who else could
it have been but Kirksey Nix? It was yet another area that
infuriated Lynne, and left her doubting the likelihood of
convictions in the case.

Still, Barrett found a simple way to counter Williams's
praise of Nix and her dogged attempts to downplay threats
he had made against her in the past. The prosecutor asked:
A year ago, when you told the grand jury about those threats
from your "Prince Charming," you described your feelings
about Nix differently, didn't you?

Beau Ann Williams had no choice but to answer yes. "I
told my cousin to 'Eat shit and die.'"

After she was through testifying, Lynne had a chance to
speak with Beau Ann Williams in the hallway, as she had
done with Kellye earlier. Williams looked upset, and Lynne
asked if she was okay.

"You know, he's crazy," she recalls Williams saying, and
Lynne suddenly realized there might be a reason besides
familial loyalty for Beau Ann's change of heart. As Lynne
recalled it, Williams said, "He'd have my children killed."[2]

CHAPTER 36

Each time the prosecutors flipped through their papers,
looking for the name of their next witness, the defense
lawyers fervently hoped it would be Bobby Joe Fabian, the
man whose testimony they had so painstakingly prepared to

shred. But Fabian's name kept slipping to the bottom of the witness list—where it would stay, if the prosecution had its way. Barrett and Jernigan had decided the mainstays of their case would be Robert Hallal and Bill Rhodes, the men who said they had been offered the Sherry murder contract. The government would win or lose with their stories.

And so, seventeen days after the trial began, Robert Hallal took the stand, providing the first direct testimony jurors heard about a plot to murder the Sherrys. In the gallery, Lynne whispered to Becky, "Finally."

Smirking, slick-haired, pock-faced, and sarcastic, with flat, dark eyes incapable of warmth, Hallal was a lawyer's nightmare, the sort of witness jurors would need no excuses to dislike. He had an immense rap sheet, numerous escape attempts, a wealth of lies about the Sherrys behind him, and a ninety-nine-year sentence for two armed robberies ahead of him. The elusive Hallal was brought to the courthouse in double chains to prevent any further escapes. But the one believable quality about him was his profession: Hallal looked like a professional criminal. He looked like a killer.

"He is the average citizen's idea of the Mafia walking through the door," George Phillips whispered to Lynne.

"Worse," she answered.

Hallal had replaced Bobby Fabian as the star witness in the case. His testimony formed the basis for the murder-for-hire conspiracy contained in the indictment—the meeting he claimed to have attended in August at the Golden Nugget, in which he was offered the contract on Vince, along with a gun and silencer from Ransom. Because both he and Ransom would have crossed state lines to attend the meeting, Ransom's interstate travel itself also became a federal crime—again, based on Hallal's word.

"'Junior wants a judge knocked off,'" Hallal said, quoting Gillich at the meeting. "'. . . Junior thinks this judge ripped him off for a lot of money.'

"I said, 'I'm not interested in killing any judge.'"

Then he added, without a trace of irony, "If it wouldn't have been a judge, I probably would have taken the hit. But I didn't want to face that kind of heat from law enforcement for a judge being killed."

Asked directly if he were a hit man, Hallal asserted his

Fifth Amendment right against self-incrimination. Reminded that he had been granted full immunity, and that nothing he said could be used against him, Hallal still refused to answer the question.

Thoroughly contemptible in speech and manner, Hallal had tried to escape enough times, and lied and altered his story enough times, to make him completely unbelievable, the defense attorneys told one another. They seemed to take this almost as a given as they began cross-examining him. But an odd thing happened as they began to grill Hallal on the witness stand, a cross-examination that lasted eight hours over the course of two days of trial: Hallal began to sound more believable, not less.

It was a strange dynamic, one that frustrated the lawyers, even as Hallal smirked all the more. Instead of becoming tongue-tied when confronted with his inconsistencies, he always had a ready explanation, leaving the lawyers sputtering instead. Hallal said simply that he held back early on in the investigation because he feared he would have been indicted with everyone else if he talked too much. That's why he omitted the presence of Ransom in his first account of the meeting with Gillich at the Golden Nugget. If he had included Ransom, and it turned out later that Ransom carried out the hit, Hallal knew he would be in big trouble. So he got creative. He lied. But now he was telling the truth, Hallal swore.

The defense lawyers were unable to shake this story or its reasonable tone, though certainly it had its share of holes in it. The truth was, Hallal had continued to lie to the grand jury even after receiving legal immunity, when there was no chance of him being charged with anything. But the defense never made this clear. Rather than focusing on the spurious justification for his lies, they pounded Hallal with the lies themselves, pointing out every niggling contradiction—and thereby repeating over and over his most damaging testimony about Nix, Gillich, and Ransom.

After hours of this repetitive questioning, Jim Rose finally suggested lying came easily to Hallal, and that he had lied every time he testified, sweetening the pot to compensate for each of his escape attempts so he could stay on the good side of federal officials.

"All that is valid testimony," Hallal countered, with an

evil smile. "And I'm willing to take a polygraph test on that."

The defense lawyers jumped up and howled for a mistrial, but the judge denied their motions, saying the hostile and lengthy cross-examination had provoked Hallal's outburst. Hallal continued to grin; his "outburst" was as calculated as everything else he did. The judge instructed jurors to ignore the statement about the polygraph—promptly fixing it in their memories.

Each time the defense tried to disprove Hallal's testimony, he seemed to parry successfully. When his phone bill failed to show crucial toll calls from Nix and to Gillich— calls he claimed were related to the murder contract— Hallal accurately pointed to grand jury transcripts that showed he never actually said he used his home phone for those calls. Four years after the events in question, he said, was a long time, leaving him unsure what phone he had used. It had been his habit to use pay phones as a precaution, he added. Maybe that explained it.

He offered that same reasonable sort of explanation when he was criticized for providing different versions of conversations he claimed to have had with Gillich and Nix.

"As I have told you on several occasions," Hallal said slowly, infuriatingly, addressing Gillich's lead attorney, Albert Necaise, as if he were mentally impaired, "I can't recall verbatim, word for word, everything that was discussed. I'm sure no one in this courtroom could, four years ago, with any conversation they've had with anyone." Then, with his nearly black eyes slitted, he assured jurors that, "I know the essence of the conversation and I know why I went to Biloxi on that particular day."

Judge Pickering finally had to tell the lawyers to stop bickering with Hallal, suggesting the defense had forgotten the purpose of cross-examination. "It's not supposed to be to fix in the mind of the jury what the prosecution put on," he reminded Nix's lawyer, Jim Rose.

The net effect of this ineffective cross-examination and Hallal's surprisingly strong performance was that very real, very large discrepancies in his account ended up sounding like minor detail, unworthy of the jury's attention. Though the defense lawyers clearly felt otherwise, Hallal looked believable; the attorneys, meanwhile, came across as desperate and picky. Even Pickering, in an aside during a bench conference, made the unusual observation, "I find this witness to be very credible."[1]

Not long after Robert Hallal's testimony ended, a pleasant-looking man in his early forties sat down next to Lynne Sposito as she sat in the hallway, sipping some flat Coca-Cola from the vending machine in the courthouse lobby. The man looked at her for a long couple seconds, then said, "You must be Lynne."

Lynne stared back at the man, whom she had never seen before, then cautiously said yes. Smiling, he extended his hand and said, "I'm Bill Rhodes."

He had just arrived to testify about conspiracy and murder, but William Rhodes looked more like the sort of man you might meet at a neighbor's barbecue—no one you'd take on as a friend for life, perhaps, but someone you might chat with pleasantly enough while waiting in line for the hot dogs and fruit salad.

Lynne took his hand, too stunned to say anything. He seemed so—and there was no other word for it—ordinary. Just a guy, maybe even a nice guy, with short brown hair and a small round face, an easy smile. Yet here was a man who would have driven that yellow Ford if he had not been picked up for bank robbery first. Lynne was shaking hands with the man who said that, for thirty thousand dollars, he would have been John Ransom's wheelman, who would have helped kill her parents for Mike Gillich and Kirksey Nix and Pete Halat. What do you say to such a man, Lynne wondered? She didn't know whether to thank Bill Rhodes for his testimony, or to grab him by the shirt collar and shriek into his face, *Why didn't you say something in March 1987? Why didn't you save my parents' lives?*

What she ended up doing instead was making small talk. Nice to meet you, she stammered. How have you been? And Bill Rhodes reflected that the plumbing business really hadn't been going so well. "All I ever really knew how to do was rob banks," he said with a small shrug. "And I was never really very good at that, either. That's why I kept getting caught."

* * *

Although prosecutors had decided not to make Bill Rhodes's testimony key to their indictment, it did support their theory that Ransom, Gillich, and Nix—as well as Pete Halat—wanted the Sherrys dead. If the jury believed Rhodes, they would be more likely to believe Robert Hallal.

He certainly provided a sharp contrast to Hallal—no smirking, no sarcasm, just simple, genial answers as he coolly recounted a ride in Nix's Mercedes in March 1987, with Halat at the wheel and Ransom in the passenger seat, double murder the subject at hand.

Rhodes swore, as he had on previous occasions, that the two men—then later, Mike Gillich—offered him thirty thousand dollars to drive the car in the Sherry hit. Vince had to die because he had ripped someone off for as much as a half million dollars, Rhodes said.

"I said, well, you know, it's a judge. . . . I'll have to think about it."

When asked why a career criminal like himself would even hesitate at such a lucrative offer, Rhodes said, "You don't commit yourself to these people until you know whether you want to go through with it or not."

Alone among the witnesses, Bill Rhodes put the mayor of Biloxi—"the invisible defendant," as the Biloxi newspaper called him—squarely in the midst of the murder conspiracy. Rhodes didn't just attribute knowledge to Halat, he made him appear cold and vicious, even eager to eliminate his best friends for money and self-interest.

"No, she's got to die," Rhodes recalled Halat saying when the bank robber suggested Margaret might be spared. "We're under investigation, he's the weak link. She knows his business, she's got to go too."

The defense team attempted to attack Rhodes's testimony as hard as it hit Hallal, beginning with the fact that he had neglected, in his first grand jury appearance, to mention meeting with Gillich in the doughnut shop to discuss the murder contract. But the pattern set by Hallal continued: Rhodes blunted the attacks on his credibility even more smoothly.

"I didn't want to give that information because I was in fear of my life and my family's life. Because of his contacts," Rhodes explained. "I wasn't concerned about

Ransom. . . . I wasn't concerned about Pete Halat, because he [just] worked for the Dixie Mafia . . ."

Rhodes paused, then pointed to Gillich. "He's the man that can get something done. Mr. Gillich over there."

Then Rhodes surprised everyone, even the prosecution, by adding a new twist to the story, one that infuriated the defense but that it seemed helpless to contradict.

As he had sworn in the past, the witness explained how he had been unable to accept the murder contract from Gillich, Ransom, and Pete Halat because he was jailed in March 1987, shortly after his trip to Biloxi. He got out in November, after the murders—again consistent with his previous testimony. But the story had always ended there. Now Rhodes swore that within a few weeks of his release, Ransom met him and issued a warning.

"He was instructing me to keep my mouth shut," Rhodes recalled. ". . . And then he told me that he had carried the contract out."

This was a totally new and unexpected blow against the defense: John Ransom hadn't just planned the crime beforehand. Now, according to Rhodes, he confessed to carrying out the murders.

When the defense challenged his truthfulness on this and other points, Rhodes developed a disarmingly simple way of responding to attempts to sully his character: He agreed with them. When Ransom's attorney, Rex Jones, asked why there had to be so many meetings to discuss his driving the getaway car for the murders, Rhodes said he just couldn't make up his mind.

"I could tell them the first time that I wasn't interested," Jones said. "How about you?"

"No, sir," Rhodes said mildly. "I couldn't, because I am a criminal." Later, he added, "I've been a criminal all my life. I probably would have drove."

When the lawyers asked him if he illegally possessed weapons while on parole—hoping he would deny it so they could proclaim him a liar—Rhodes said, "Of course. All criminals do it, mostly. They don't think about, if you get busted you're going to jail, and stuff like that."

Rhodes, who had been nervous and uneasy while appearing before the grand jury, surprised prosecutors by coming across rock solid at trial, capturing jurors' attention, even charming them at times with his agreeable admission of criminality. The depths of the defense attorneys' desperation seemed to show when Nix's lawyer, Jim Rose, attempted to prove Rhodes did not know how to drive to Biloxi from Atlanta, as he claimed to have done to discuss the murder of the Sherrys. To do this, the defense confused Rhodes with an outdated map from 1957, which failed to show key highways and interstates—until Judge Pickering caught the deception, and prosecutors delightedly went over the route with Rhodes with a more contemporary atlas.

As strong as Rhodes's testimony sounded, the prosecution missed an opportunity to make it even more devastating. Sitting in the gallery, Lynne Sposito saw it, though. Rhodes's remark about the investigation suggested he told the truth. The scam was under investigation in March 1987, just as Rhodes said, though he had no way of knowing that—unless Halat or Ransom or one of the other conspirators had told him. The jurors had even heard evidence about this investigation earlier in the trial—the tape of LaRa coaching Robbie Gant to lie to the FBI had been part of that investigation.

It could have all been tied together, Lynne thought, along with Margaret's penchant for forcing Vince to do the right thing. March 1987 was also when Vince and Gillich supposedly argued. It was when Mike Lofton watched his girlfriend LaRa weep on the phone with Kirksey Nix, then admit to being involved in something bad she couldn't escape. March 1987 was the month Pete Halat filed the long-withheld marriage certificate for Kirksey and Kellye Nix—after which Kellye theoretically could refuse to testify against her husband. Things seemed to be coming to a head that month, a confluence of events that would be hard to write off to coincidence—it all fit. The following May, both Vince and Margaret spoke of death threats. Yet the jury was not hearing any of these things.

Again, Lynne felt like jumping up and asking the questions herself. But the moment passed. There was no follow-up to Rhodes's remark about an investigation. A few minutes later, the prosecution said, "No more questions."

The defense wisely steered clear of these points during its

cross-examination of Rhodes, choosing instead to attack the details of his account, hoping to show inconsistencies in his story, no matter how minute.

They attacked his description of Coast landmarks, suggesting law enforcement officials deliberately drove him through Biloxi on his way to testify before a special grand jury session so that he could spot Gulf Coast landmarks to bolster his testimony. Rhodes denied it, and police reports backed him up, stating that he described the landmarks well before his trip to the grand jury.

Undaunted, the defense got Rhodes to admit he had read a magazine article on the case published in April 1990—an article Bobby Joe Fabian had handed him while they spent a few days in the same county jail, brought together by grand jury subpoenas. The article erroneously described Halat as blond, and Rhodes had later testified that Halat's hair was blondish brown. In fact, Halat's hair is dark brown. Obviously, Rhodes had constructed his account from the incorrect article, the defense lawyers suggested.

They might have had something there—except that FBI reports on Rhodes's first statement in the case showed he had originally described Halat as having brown hair, though he had complained that the dimness of the light in the car made it hard to tell just what color it was.

They even attacked Rhodes for describing Halat as looking like the owner of the Los Angeles Raiders football team, Al Davis. The defense gave to the jury a picture of Davis to show a supposed lack of resemblance, but even if jurors agreed, Rhodes's account of driving in the dim car, barely seeing Halat's features, provided a ready excuse for errors in his description.

Rhodes's testimony infuriated John Ransom even more than Pegi Graham's or Chuck Leger's. At one point, when Rhodes was asked what Ransom did for a living, the witness said simply, "He was a contract killer."

Defense attorney Rex Jones leapt up and demanded a mistrial, but then a thin arm shot up, and Jones suddenly found himself thrown back into his seat by John Ransom. Again, the old man's strength and quickness were on display before the jury. Ransom then whispered privately with the judge. He wanted no mistrial. He wanted it all to hang out, he said.

Later, Ransom demanded the opportunity to conduct his own cross-examination of Rhodes, but finally relented, so long as his lawyer read a verbatim list of questions designed to show Rhodes did not know Ransom as well as he claimed. Ransom fancied himself a jailhouse lawyer the same as Nix, but the questions he insisted on did not have the effect he sought. To prove just how close they had been, Rhodes began to reel off a long list of crimes they had committed together, until finally the judge said, "I really think you are bringing some things out that could have an adverse effect on your case."

Ransom's cryptic reply: "What's good for the goose is good for the gander," but even Rex Jones had to admit that the only one being cooked by his client's questions was Ransom himself.

CHAPTER 37

Back in Biloxi, Mayor Pete Halat found William Rhodes's testimony infuriating.

"You can take Bill Rhodes's testimony and throw it out," he thundered. "If it were true, I wouldn't be sitting here. I'd be in the courtroom in Hattiesburg."

So far, the mayor had been forced into the role of spectator in the case, stewing in city hall, learning what had transpired in court from newspapers or from reports he received from Biloxi policemen attending the trial. He had watched as he was portrayed as a facilitator of the scams, his legal mail and legal calls usurped for illegal purposes, his unseemly use of Nix's Mercedes and his huge number of calls to the convict providing fodder for prosecutors.

But now Halat spoke out, releasing a written statement on the day of Rhodes's testimony, saying, "First of all, I do not have blondish brown hair, I do not wear glasses [as Rhodes claimed in his testimony] except to read, and I really don't think I look like Al Davis. . . .

"Justice is clearly not being served by my continued prosecution in the media," Halat said. And then, referring to another case that had captured national attention during the time of the trial, he added, "If Judge Clarence Thomas thinks he's been treated unfairly, he needs to come down here and look at this fairy tale.

". . . I hunger for the chance to repudiate the growing list of ludicrous and totally false allegations."[1]

Pete Halat soon got his chance. After William Rhodes walked off the witness stand, the government rested its case. The prosecutors felt a renewed hope—primarily because of the unexpected strength of Rhodes's and Hallal's testimony—though they were far from confident. They had merely gone from fearing they would lose to thinking they had worked their way into a toss-up.

In the fifth week of trial, the defense called Pete Halat to the stand as it began its attempt to rebut the prosecution's witnesses. The mayor finally got his opportunity to refute allegations against him under oath in open court—though he expressed regret that he could not face off directly with his chief accuser, Bobby Fabian. Even so, this date with the witness stand was what he had hungered for for years, he said.

Yet, the culmination of his two years of angry denials ended up seeming strangely muted. Oddly, he began to hedge on his previously vociferous proclamations of innocence the moment he sat down. When Jim Rose asked if Halat had ever suggested Kellye Nix needed to tell Kirksey "to leave those homosexuals alone," Halat replied:

"I do not recall having made that statement to Kellye Dawn Nix. And assuming that I would have made that statement, I would not have used the word 'homosexual,' which leads me to believe that I did not say that to Kellye Dawn Nix."

Instead of clearly denying it, Halat, in essence, said he didn't remember for sure—a tepid way of rebutting an allegation that went to the heart of whether or not he knowingly aided and profited from the scam.

Indeed, in her original statement to Keith Bell and Randy Cook, Kellye Nix used the word "fags" in quoting Halat, not "homosexuals." No one at either the defense or the prosecution table thought to ask Halat if that phrasing would be more like something he might have said.

Halat repeated this wishy-washy method of response for several key questions. Instead of denying meeting the ex-convict and scammer Arthur Mitchell, Halat said, "I don't have an independent recollection of having met Arthur Mitchell." He did, however, unequivocally deny meeting Mitchell at the Golden Nugget to discuss the one-hundred-thousand-dollar bounty Nix offered to get parole.

"Why would he have to convey that to me?" Halat asked, raising a sensible point. "I was talking on the telephone and writing letters to Kirksey Nix at that time."

Even when he had clear answers to make, Halat could not resist some lawyerly niggling, responding to questions with his own questions—which had the effect of making him appear unnecessarily evasive, even under the friendly examination of Jim Rose. When asked if he had any knowledge of Vince or himself being involved with hundreds of thousands of dollars of missing money, Halat responded: "Missing from where?"

Rose seemed perplexed by Halat's response—as if there were more than one allegation of missing money floating around in this case. He sputtered, "I—missing money."

"Neither Vince nor I were ever or have ever been involved in any missing money from any source whatsoever," Halat then answered. Even the defense attorneys grew exasperated with him for not answering so straightforwardly in the first place.

When asked by Assistant U.S. Attorney Al Jernigan if he had been to the Golden Nugget on a number of occasions, Halat asked, "What do you mean, 'a number of occasions'?"

"Tell me how many occasions you have been in and out of the Golden Nugget," Jernigan said.

"You used the word 'number,' I didn't," Halat griped.

"Mr. Halat, I'm not arguing with you."

"I'm not arguing with you, Al," Halat fired back. "I wouldn't say it's been a number of occasions." Then, contradicting himself, he put the number at eight visits.

When asked by Jernigan if he knew of any disagreement between Gillich and Margaret or Vince Sherry, Halat again equivocated, saying he did not understand the question. After several requests that Jernigan repeat the question, Halat rephrased the query himself, saying, "What do you mean by disagreement between *her* and Mike Gillich?" Either by mistake or design, Halat had removed Vince Sherry from the question. This was significant because Vince was the one who supposedly argued with Gillich, not Margaret.

But Jernigan didn't notice the discrepancy. He merely said, "How difficult is it to understand? You know what a disagreement is?"

"When was it supposed to have occurred?" Halat asked, still not answering. When Jernigan said it was shortly before the murder (actually, the argument with Vince supposedly came six months before), Halat answered, "I have no idea about that." Jernigan then moved on to another topic, letting Halat off the hook. Lacking the background Lynne Sposito had, the jury had no idea what had just happened. Lynne saw it, underlined the passage in her notes, and hoped she could get to prosecutors before it was too late. But she never had the chance.

Halat grew especially testy on the subject of LaRa Sharpe, who he swore was never an employee of Halat and Sherry. And yet, Jernigan said, you signed sworn affidavits stating LaRa was an employee, that she was your paralegal, even providing her social security number like any other paid employee, just so she could get legal visits with Nix at Angola. The prosecutor held up one of the affidavits. "Is it a false statement?" he asked.

Halat couldn't bring himself to admit the falsehood outright. He had to qualify it. *"Technically,* that's a false statement."

"You took an oath, did you not?" Jernigan pressed.

"I signed the affidavit in the presence of a notary public. . . . I did that as an accommodation to her so she could go in there."

"Basically, you disregarded the oath, then?" Jernigan asked, able to continue hammering at the issue, despite objections from the defense lawyers, because of Halat's evasiveness. Otherwise, the prosecutor would have been forced to move on to other subjects, and the jury might not have even noticed the issue. But now they hung on every word, watching one of the most heated exchanges of the trail.

Halat dug in further. "Say again?"

"You disregarded the oath?"

"I signed the affidavit."

The defense tried to cut it off again, but the judge again overruled the objection. "He has not answered," Pickering said.

So Jernigan asked him again if he disregarded his oath to tell the truth.

"I told you that technically—" Halat began.

"Yes or no, please," Jernigan interrupted. "Then you can explain."

"I disregarded the oath," Halat finally admitted. "Technically, Ms. Sharpe was not employed by me, I did that as an accommodation."

"So you feel like that as an accommodation, sometimes it's okay to disregard an oath?" Jernigan asked, closing the trap he had forced Halat to enter.

"No, I don't," Halat shot back, but the contradiction was obvious. "No, I don't."

He looked even worse when Jernigan asked him about Nix's trust fund, the twenty-one thousand dollars a year Nix put in there, on average, between 1985 and May 1988. "Did you ever seek to find out where Mr. Nix's money was coming from?"

"No, sir. No, sir."

"You were never curious as to where a man in prison at Angola was getting this kind of money?"

"I've already answered that question," Halat said.

"You weren't? That's right?"

"That's right."

The image of a defense attorney accepting without question inexplicable cash deliveries for a convicted murderer's account played to the most venal stereotypes of lawyers. Still, the sums involved were far less than the hundreds of thousands Arthur Mitchell, Bill Rhodes, and Kellye Nix had talked about. And Halat firmly denied any involvement with the scams when asked about them outright. If he had known the money was tainted—and he still didn't know that for sure—he never would have accepted it, Halat swore. The prosecution had no direct proof to the contrary.

On subjects related to the murder, Halat did not mince words. Without equivocation, he swore he never had met John Ransom or Bill Rhodes, and he certainly had never ridden around in a Mercedes with them. He swore he wore his bifocal glasses only when reading, not when driving—contrary to Rhodes's claims. When asked why he wore his glasses while addressing reporters at press conferences, Halat said he had them on because at each conference, he had read a prepared statement first. Rhodes got his story wrong, Halat said, proving the man a liar.

Halat also produced a picture showing he sported a bushy mustache in 1987, which he shaved only when he entered the race for mayor two years later—something Rhodes never mentioned in describing Halat. Halat had appeared on television clean-shaven, however, providing another chink in Rhodes's story, suggesting he got his information from news reports, not personal experience.

The government's cross-examination of Halat, eagerly anticipated by Lynne Sposito, ended abruptly, without ever getting into the discovery of the bodies of Vince and Margaret—or Halat's apparently contradictory actions and statements immediately afterward. No one asked how he seemed to know Margaret was dead without seeing her body, or how he seemed to know the time of death before anyone else did, or how he knew Bobby Fabian claimed to have met with him in March 1987 before that detail was ever made public. There was nothing about why he told Chuck Leger not to touch anything at the house just before finding the bodies. None of these questions were asked, and it infuriated Lynne, who had been exchanging angry stares with Halat ever since he walked into the courtroom, his wife at his side.

The last thing prosecutors asked Halat was whether he had dodged Biloxi police officers who wanted to interview him a second time about the murders.

"No, I am not aware of that," Halat said. Jernigan let it drop, and that was it. The defense was allowed to ask a few more questions, and Halat walked out of court, surprised at how quick and easy it had been, a mere five hours on the stand. He joked jovially with reporters afterward, refusing to walk a short distance to waiting TV cameras, telling them to move to him instead. "Let the mountains come to Mohammed," he declared with a smile. Lynne watched, stomach churning.

Oddly, though the newspapers reported the next day that Pete Halat had denied on the witness stand any involvement with the Sherry murders, no one actually asked him that question while he testified.

He had admitted that he scheduled a meeting with Kirksey Nix in late February 1987, but that he never made it to Angola then—implicitly denying allegations by Arthur Mitchell and Bobby Fabian, who said that meeting was a key planning session for the murder plot. Halat also was forced to admit that he had left Biloxi in Nix's Mercedes intending to go to Angola for that meeting—with Mike Gillich sitting beside him—but stopped in Baton Rouge to discuss Nix's case with Ossie Brown, an ex-D.A. whose wife served on the Louisiana Board of Paroles. When that meeting fell through, Halat swore, he canceled the Angola outing.[2]

But no one asked him outright, "Did you have anything to do with the murder of Vince and Margaret Sherry?" He had publicly denied it before, of course, and he undoubtedly would have done so again, but it seemed strange that no one thought to give him that chance, one more time, under oath.

One by one, the defendants took the witness stand next, mixing indignation and denial, striving to convince the jury that they were the truthtellers, not the prosecution's witnesses, each of whom was branded a liar.

Kirksey Nix, forty-eight years old by the time of his trial, his round, pale form decked out in white shirt, tie, and the flashy red suspenders he had worn throughout the trial, fervently denied any involvement in the Sherry murders, as he had done in the past. Unlike Halat's time on the stand, no one hesitated to ask him the question directly. He pronounced himself innocent—and then said the same for Gillich, Ransom, Sharpe, and Halat.

"I played no role," he boomed, "and I'll go to my grave believing none of these people here had any role in it."

Nix's testimony had been a long-awaited event. He had

been mouthing words to journalists throughout the trial,
with one reporter earning a scolding from the judge for
encouraging him by mouthing words back. Nix had repeatedly looked directly at Lynne, continuing to say silently,
"It's not me," over and over. Lynne forced herself to stare
back at him without flinching, even as Becky Field sat next
to her hissing "Sonofabitch."

Finally given his opportunity to address the jury directly,
Nix dramatically embellished every answer—earning more
rebukes from Judge Pickering and turning the already
excitable prosecutor Peter Barrett crimson.

Nix's game plan continued to be to absorb all the blame
for scamming, while at the same time swearing that the
other defendants had no part in it. Gillich and Ransom
were totally innocent, he said, and LaRa bailed out by
February 1986, conveniently in time to beat the five-year
statute of limitations on the May 1991 indictment. "She
told me, 'You can kiss my ass,'" he recalled, in describing
how LaRa left him and the scams.

As for himself, Nix readily admitted to scamming, conceding that he may have earned as much as a half-million
dollars in three years. It was easy money, he said, so easy it
proved irresistible. "I was fascinated. I couldn't believe it
and I couldn't stop. It was addictive."

He conceded another point in the prosecution case—that
he would have willingly used all the money he had scammed
in order to buy his way out of prison. He also admitted that
he enjoyed using his scam money to buy into houses, cars,
and other investments, even an Elvis Presley theme park
scheme that failed. When asked why a lifer with no hope of
parole would do such things, Nix grew wistful, and for one
of the few times during his day and a half of testimony, he
dropped his theatrical manner and seemed to reveal something about himself.

"People do their time in different ways. And I tried, I still
do I guess, to keep my mind and my thoughts, my ambitions, stuff like that, in the street. I still try to do things like I
was in the street, rather than just the prison scene, you
know, just to fold in, become institutionalized."

Nix remained good-natured and polite, if occasionally
sarcastic and always voluble, through most of his testimony.
His bitterness surfaced noticeably, however, when testifying

about Kellye Dawn, a woman he said he still loved, even though he maintained she had lied about him to elude jail. When asked why she would do that, yet not go all the way and link him directly to the Sherry murders, Nix smiled ruefully.

"She wanted out and she knows how not to oversalt the gold mine. She had a good teacher. . . . Me."

CHAPTER 38

Mike Gillich, whom Nix had described as his "second father," took the stand next, humble and soft-spoken, the sixty-one-year-old son of immigrants who, he swore, had given every paycheck he ever earned to his mother, right up until the day he got married.

Gillich swore he knew nothing of scams. Instead, guided by his attorney Albert Necaise, he painted a portrait of himself as a hardworking, hard-living man who gave generously to the Catholic Church, who left school at age nine to take his first job delivering ice, and who still worked seven days a week, twelve hours a day.

He only reluctantly admitted that he ran strip clubs for a living. When asked why his competitors were shut down while he remained open, he denied getting favors from city government in Biloxi, despite his ties to the city council and the offices of Mayors Blessey and Halat.

"Those other clubs were closed . . . because they violated the law. They had prostitution and sold narcotics in the clubs. They had trick rooms in the buildings. And they turned tricks in there and sold dope. And I never did that."

He swore he never took scam money deliveries, he never acted as Nix's banker, he never discussed murder with Bill Rhodes, he never met John Ransom. And the only time he met Bob Hallal was when the ex-con asked about buying Nix's Mercedes and a couple of video recorders. When Gillich declined to accept a credit card for the VCRs, Mr. Mike swore, Hallal said he'd be back with cash, but never returned.

"I have never seen that man again until I have seen him in this courtroom," Gillich vowed.

He called Hallal's account of meeting Ransom at the Golden Nugget a lie, as he did the account of Becky Field's son Greg, who swore he saw Gillich put his arm around Ransom one day and tell his son, "If anything or anybody needs taking care of, this is the man to call."

In his simple, earthy way, unassuming on the witness stand—at one point asking the prosecutor to read aloud from a document because "I don't read too good"—Gillich seemed at first to belie his image as the Dixie Mafia godfather. But he stumbled badly when he described his motel encounter with Beau Ann Williams and his supposed warning to Nix about LaRa talking to the police.

"That is a lie. There was . . . nothing about warning anyone about anything," he said. He had simply gone by to get the keys to the Mercedes Beau Ann had borrowed, and to tell Nix's cousin that his son, Mike III, would drive her to the airport in the morning.

"And we was sitting there talking . . . and then the conversation came up about the, the, the, Sherry murders," Gillich testified. He said he dismissed for Beau Ann's benefit two false rumors linking him to the murders, one that had him and Gerald Blessey arranging the hit, and another that put Gillich and Pete Halat behind the killings. "And I told her I ain't killed nobody. And I never have killed anybody or set a contract out on anybody."

"Who brought it up?" lawyer Necaise asked, and this is where Gillich made his mistake.

"She did," he swore. "And about Junior, and this and that. And I told her, I said, listen, don't worry about all that. There ain't nothing to that. I said, as a matter of fact, LaRa came by the club last night and telling me the police had been questioning her about the Sherry murders, and that I was a killer and that she was going to be in trouble, and somebody was going to kill her. And I told LaRa, I said, man, if that's what they are telling you, you ain't got no worry at all."

Gillich's rendition would have been a reasonable-sounding—and innocuous—version of Beau Ann's more ominous account of the conversation, except for one thing. The meeting in the motel between Beau Ann and Gillich occurred in March 1989—well before Bobby Joe Fabian had told anyone his story, long before any public discussion of Kirksey Nix's involvement in the Sherry killings surfaced, and long before anyone had accused Pete Halat and Mike Gillich of being involved in the murders. At the time of that meeting, Beau Ann Williams had no reason to bring up the subject. The second "rumor" Gillich said he was quashing, about him and Peter Halat arranging the murders, did not yet exist.

Later, in the rebuttal phase of the trial, the prosecution had a chance to disprove Gillich's claims that he was a law-abiding, truthful, God-fearing man whose strip clubs operated within the law. The chief of special investigations for the Biloxi Police Department, the chief of police for the city of Gulfport, and Mickey Ladner, a former highway patrol investigator now working for the Harrison County sheriff, all testified that Mike Gillich had a reputation for law-breaking and lying, his lack of felony convictions and his kindness to church and mother notwithstanding.

By law, the prosecution could go no further than that—they could only ask, What is Mike Gillich's reputation for being a law-abiding citizen? "Not good," the witnesses each said. But here, Gillich's lawyer, Albert Necaise, fell into a trap: Instead of leaving it at that, he could not resist going after these witnesses on cross-examination and, in the process, introducing much more damaging information through his own questioning.

If Gillich had such a reputation for being a terrible criminal, Necaise asked Mickey Ladner, why had he never been convicted of a felony? Ladner responded, "Just because a person is never arrested doesn't mean they are not criminals. It means that they are better than average and we just didn't get a chance to get them. I think a person with a long criminal history is just not a good criminal."

Necaise repeated his mistake with Tommy Moffett, the chief of special investigations who had been police chief in Biloxi at the time of the Sherry murders, only to be demoted by Pete Halat. When asked why there was no documentation of any wrongdoing by Gillich on file at the Biloxi PD, Moffett revealed that Mr. Mike's records were mysteriously missing from the department's files.

Necaise attempted to mock this assertion, sarcastically asking, "Is it easy to remove somebody's arrest record from the Biloxi Police Department?"

Moffett surprised him by saying, sorrowfully, "Yes, sir, it is easy."

Later, Moffett answered one of Necaise's questions by explaining that Gillich had been arrested in a prostitution case after an undercover investigation at his nightclub. When the lawyer tried to undermine this assertion by saying Gillich had never been prosecuted for this offense, Moffett replied that city prosecutors appointed by the mayor declined to take on a case against Gillich, even while identical evidence was used to go after other club owners. "We did the same thing with some other clubs earlier . . . and we closed probably twelve, fifteen clubs or more. . . . Sometimes decisions are made by people in the city that might be higher up."

And with that, Necaise managed to introduce into evidence a suggestion the prosecutors had not been able to get in on their own—evidence they had been specifically ordered to keep out. At Necaise's prodding, jurors were told that Mike Gillich and his strip joints benefited from a hands-off policy in the city of Biloxi, breaking the law with impunity, then having records of his offenses disappear and his record remain clear.

Mike Gillich's own defense attorney made him appear to be nothing less than the godfather of Biloxi.

LaRa Sharpe had a better time of it on the witness stand—at first. Very little evidence linking her to the murder plot had been introduced—just the "Wilbur" Bob Wright swore he saw in her camera bag. LaRa's main battle was to avoid conviction in the scam case.

Like Gillich, she was out of custody during the trial,

dressing fashionably in a different outfit every day, tossing her long blond hair as she entered the courthouse, her lawyer trudging at her side, laden with files. She smiled at Lynne Sposito one time, but the hateful stare Lynne returned ended any possibility of an exchange between them.

As in the past, LaRa swore that her involvement in the scams was minimal, while insisting Gillich and Halat had no role in the ripoffs at all. Like Nix, she embellished her answers whenever possible, trying to insert self-serving comments whether they applied to questions put to her or not. The judge repeatedly cautioned her to stop, with little effect. Each time, LaRa shot an apologetic look at jurors, who seemed less than impressed, either stonily staring back, or glancing away in embarrassment.

LaRa did make some admissions, however. She conceded that she had made scam-related phone calls to Nix from the law office, something she previously had denied. But again, she was careful to say Pete Halat knew nothing of this.

LaRa had an easier time on the witness stand than her lawyer expected. She was not confronted by testimony from Chuck Leger and other law-office employees, who knew LaRa had run of the Halat and Sherry office long after she claimed to have left. Nor was she confronted with her contradictory statements to the Biloxi police, in which she had denied any role in the scams and insisted she was a part-time employee of Halat and Sherry. And she was not asked to explain why her ex-boyfriend Mike Lofton, whom she said she met in June 1986—after she swore she had bailed out of the scams—knew all about her scam activities, and claimed to have witnessed them for the better part of a year.

Likewise, LaRa was not questioned intensively about the Sherry murders beyond the allegation that she had received a silenced pistol from John Ransom, which she heartily denied. The only gun she ever owned, she said, was a rusting old revolver Mike Gillich gave her for self-protection—an account buttressed by Gillich, LaRa's mother, and a carpet cleaner who spotted such a gun while working in Nix's house in Ocean Springs. That type of gun could not have been the murder weapon.

LaRa's denial of the Wilbur had an effect beyond sup-

porting her claims of innocence, however. It kept Ransom
from the witness stand, because he had told investigators
long ago that he had delivered the gun to LaRa. And though
that information had been offered with the promise that it
would not be used against him, there was one exception—if
he got up on the stand and denied delivering the gun. Then
prosecutors could introduce his earlier statement to show
he lied, which would surely lead to his conviction.

Before trial, during a meeting of lawyers and defendants
at the Harrison County Jail, Nix had tried to persuade LaRa
that she was mistaken in her recollection, that she had
received the silenced gun. If she were to admit it—with, of
course, an innocuous explanation about its disposition long
before the murders—then Ransom could testify. But LaRa
remained adamant: She had never gotten a silenced pistol
from John Ransom.

If Ransom testified anyway, he would have to contradict
her or change his story. Either way, prosecutors then would
be able to show at least one of them lied. Their fragile
defense would be doomed by the appearance they were
hiding something. Reluctantly, Ransom had to agree to stay
out of the witness chair. He would not be able to rebut Pegi
Graham or Bill Rhodes, nor could he make his cowboy boot
argument to the jury. Alone among the defendants, he
would remain silent, thanks to LaRa.

Instead of testifying, Ransom had to settle for having his
wife and daughter take the stand in his place. In simple,
believable fashion—far more effectively than the prosecutors would have liked—they swore that Ransom was with
them vacationing in Florida on the day he was supposed to
have met with Mike Gillich and Robert Hallal to discuss the
Sherry hit. They even produced vacation snapshots.

LaRa, meanwhile, might have been better off staying off
the stand herself. She fumbled badly when questioned
about the note she left for Beau Ann Williams. Asked to
relate its contents, she made the note sound like a series of
innocuous questions for the lawyer, left because LaRa was
confused and frightened by her encounter earlier that day
with the Biloxi police. Williams had testified she destroyed
the note, and LaRa must have thought her recollection of it
would go unchallenged. She said the note read, "What's

going on? Many questions about V. and M. Many questions about P.H. And many questions about JR." She could not explain why she would have used initials, or why she expected Beau Ann to understand what they meant. She said she left her motel room number on the note so Beau Ann could call her, but she never heard back.

LaRa said she was terrified because the police told her she would be murdered—an exaggeration at best. The police offered her protection. But it raised an interesting question—if there was a threat to her life suggested by police, it would have been from Nix and Gillich. Yet when prosecutor Barrett asked her about that, the inconsistency became clear: She denied having any fears of either man.

"I wasn't worried about anybody that I knew . . . I've never had a hint of danger from anyone but Kellye." Kellye Nix, LaRa Sharpe swore, had threatened her years before if she talked to the FBI.

The deception in LaRa's account became more clear a few days later, when, to everyone's surprise, the note she had left for Beau Ann Williams surfaced. She had not destroyed it after all. Robert Richardson, a meticulous individual who had worked as a motel security guard in 1989, had taken the note from Williams and filed it. When he read about LaRa's testimony in the newspaper, he called the authorities, and the note turned up still buried in the files at the motel where Richardson had left it.

In red ink and LaRa Sharpe's hand, the note was a numbered list:

1. *I was questioned three hours.*
2. *Mostly V. and M. questions.*
3. *Not much Junior questions. Then later, many.*
4. *Many questions Pete.*
5. *Mr. G. many questions.*
6. *Offered protection yesterday.*
7. *Today I said, "Leave me alone or take me in."*

(Give him my love,

Punkin)

The note, clearly, was not a scared set of questions to Beau Ann Williams—it was a report. There was no phone number. It was a message to Nix about the investigation—and a reassurance that LaRa would not be cooperating with the police.

The abbreviation of V and M—Vince and Margaret—proved that the topic of the Sherry murders had been discussed before by LaRa and Nix.

The security guard also made clear that Beau Ann Williams's reaction had not been the casual disinterest that Nix's cousin had described to the jury. The note had terrified her, he swore.

"She was very shaken, very upset. . . . [Her hand] was trembling. . . . I don't see how she could read it."

When the defendants finished testifying, their lawyers made a final attempt to blunt the prosecution's case. It was their worst mistake.

They brought in Brett Robertson—the Sherrys' neighbor whom Lynne had spoken to so many years before on the day of the wake. Robertson described how he saw the yellow Ford cruising the street on the night of the murders, and a man who strongly resembled Biloxi Police Officer Ric Kirk behind the wheel. The man could not have been John Ransom. And though investigators and polygraphs had cleared Kirk long before, the jurors didn't know that.

Then Robertson's friend, Mark Lamey, who had been visiting that evening, swore he saw not only Kirk in the car, but a second man in the Sherrys' yard. He also glimpsed this same man through the Sherrys' window, inside the house, he swore. Though he could not describe the man, he clearly was heavier than Ransom, Lamey said.

The defense sought to use this eyewitness testimony to undermine the entire conspiracy case—to suggest that someone else murdered the Sherrys.

But the prosecutors were jubilant at this testimony—this was the trap George Phillips had told Lynne about early in the trial. It opened the door for extensive rebuttal by the government, entitling prosecutors to introduce evidence that the defendants *were* involved in the murders. Because the conspiracy indictment ended in August, before the murders, they had been barred from doing this on their own initiative—until the defense opened the door. And the bonus was, unlike a murder case where the evidence must convince jurors beyond a reasonable doubt, this rebuttal portion of the case allowed them to present evidence about the murder without any burden of proof at all. All the little things Randy Cook and Keith Bell had put together that cast suspicion on the alleged murderers, but fell short of absolute proof, now became admissible. It was a gift.

And it made the difference in the case.[1]

First the prosecutors brought in Biloxi police evidence technician Robert Burris to explain the theft of the yellow Ford and how it appeared to be the getaway car in the murders. When it was found, he told the jury, the hub on the steering wheel covering the horn mechanism was missing. He also explained the modified license plate on the Ford, that it actually belonged to an Oldsmobile reported stolen in 1984.

The next witness, a resident of the St. Andrew's Apartments in Biloxi—owned by Mike Gillich's brother, Andrew—swore he saw that same Oldsmobile just before it was stolen. Gillich's brother was standing next to it, and inside sat Mike Gillich's close friend, the locksmith Lenny Swetman. The witness claimed he saw Swetman fiddling with the ignition of the Oldsmobile, the implication being that he stole the car—and its license plate.

Randy Cook then testified about what he saw when he arrested Swetman in a marijuana case a year earlier. Cook found the locksmith inside an old car, working on the steering column with the horn cover off. When Cook asked him what he was doing, Swetman explained that was how he started cars without having a key, by removing the horn mechanism and using a tool to manipulate the ignition from the inside—the same as the yellow Ford.

Former FBI agent and State Attorney General Investigator Ed O'Neill came next, casting doubt on the testimony of Brett Robertson and Mark Lamey. Three years earlier, he had interviewed both men about whom they saw in the yellow Ford and at the Sherry house on the night of the murders. In 1988, O'Neill found that Lamey could not identify photographs of Detective Ric Kirk—the man he now claimed he recognized. And Brett Robertson, at the

time of the interview, had helped put together a composite
drawing of the man he saw driving the yellow car—a clean-
shaven man. Ric Kirk at the time sported a mustache,
O'Neill said. And Lamey said at the time that Robertson's
composite looked like the man he saw as well. The testimony of Lamey and Robertson was thrown into doubt.

The prosecutors then compared a photograph of Lenny
Swetman to the composite. Peter Barrett wanted O'Neill to
say there was a striking resemblance. Defense attorneys
objected to this, and the judge sided with them, but it was
too late. The jury got the message: The government was
raising the possibility that Gillich's good friend Lenny
Swetman could have been the wheelman in the murders, not
Ric Kirk.

It was only insinuation: Lamey and Richardson never
claimed to have seen Swetman that night, nor is there any
evidence or testimony linking him to the crime. But this
possibility did fit with Bill Rhodes's testimony. Rhodes had
said Ransom wanted to hire his own wheelman quickly.
Otherwise, according to Rhodes, the people who wanted the
hit would pressure him to use someone local. Someone
close to Gillich.[2]

The last rebuttal witness for the prosecution was a
surprise addition to the list—a former Biloxi cop who had
contacted the U.S. Attorney a week earlier with startling
new information.

Mike Green, now a private investigator in Southern
California, had been an officer for the Biloxi P.D. until
1981, when he was demoted after trying to bust a gambling
operation at Gillich's Horseshoe Lounge. The police department he recalled had been a corrupt and distrustful
place, where training was scant, where a sergeant kept a
picture of the Ku Klux Klan's grand dragon on display over
his desk, where members of the Dixie Mafia befriended and
bribed cops, then enjoyed their protection in return.[3]

Most important, Mike Green recalled a meeting in the
summer of 1986 with Vince and Margaret Sherry. He had
come back to Biloxi to apply for the job of police chief,
hoping to reform the department he had left in disgust.

Vince and Margaret Sherry had met with him twice in the

law library at the Halat and Sherry office, Green said. He sought their advice on how to get the job, though Gerald Blessey—the Sherrys' nemesis—was mayor at the time. Green knew both the Sherrys well, knew Vince through service in the Air Force, and he trusted their advice.

When Margaret asked him what he would accomplish as chief, he said the first thing would be to clean up The Strip—the unfinished business he had left behind in 1981.

"I'm going to run for mayor again in 1989," he recalled Margaret telling him then. "This time, I expect to win. And when I do, I'm going to close the strip clubs down once and for all. I've been threatened already because of it, but I'm going to make it part of my platform anyway."[4]

Green said she did not identify the origin of the threats, but the implication was obvious—Mike Gillich owned the only joints in operation on The Strip then. He was Margaret's target for shut-down—making him the only logical source for the threats she spoke of.

One other comment stuck in Green's mind. While they spoke, Pete Halat had poked his head in the door, then entered the law library to get a book. Vince introduced him as his partner, Green and Pete exchanged hellos, then Halat walked back out. He left the door ajar.

A moment later, Margaret hissed, "Vince, make sure that door's closed," Green recalled, "I don't trust him."

This testimony contradicted what Pete Halat had said about his close and trusting relationship with the Sherrys. It left Lynne Sposito thunderstruck—she had never heard any of this before. Halat had sworn there were no bad feelings between Margaret and Gillich, and no plans to shut him down if she became mayor. Green—a man with no hidden agenda, no criminal charges to work off, no need for immunity, no stake in how this case turned out—called all that into question.

As Vince stood up and shut the door, Green recalled, Margaret looked at him and said, "I dislike that man, and one of these days, I am going to be able to put him and his criminal friends, including Mike Gillich, in prison."

Vince said nothing, Green testified. Pete Halat's friend and partner just stood at the door, nodding his head in sorrowful agreement.

CHAPTER 39

When she arrived in Hattiesburg, Lynne Sposito had no conception of just how tedious a criminal trial could be, trained as she was by television's hour-long proceedings, with their cliffhangers every fifteen minutes to accommodate commercials. Real trials can drag on interminably—six weeks for this one—the evidence revealed not with dramatic flair, but with the excruciating monotony of an assembly line.

Lynne attended nearly every minute, often with Becky at her side, other times alone. Dick was home working and taking care of the kids, all of them staying in touch by telephone, Lynne trying, but finding it hard, to focus on homelife while immersed in the trial.

Midway through the trial, her brother Eric joined her, celebrating his thirty-third birthday in court. Vin attended four days, but then he was asked to leave as a potential witness. Leslie stayed away. It was too painful, she said, and Lynne agreed.

Some of her best moments came in the hall outside the courtroom, where she often found a moment to chat with witnesses, something that inevitably drew jaundiced stares from one or two of the defense lawyers. Mostly, she just wanted to get a feel for the witnesses, to see if they seemed credible to her. That hug from Kellye Nix, the tears on her cheek—after that, she had no doubt Nix's stepdaughter-wife had told the truth. She got the same impression from Bill Rhodes.

Sometimes the encounters were not so pleasant, though. She daily withstood the pointed glances and muttered insults of Mike Gillich's many supporters attending the trial. "Watch out, you might catch something," one elderly relative of Gillich's kept warning whenever one of her group stood too close to Lynne or Becky Field. Lynne finally shot back, "I didn't put Mike Gillich here. He did that all by himself, and even if he's convicted, you'll still be able to see him, talk to him, visit him. I'll never be able to do that with my mom and dad. Never." Everyone in the hallway was staring by the time she had finished, her voice on the rise. They pretty much steered clear of Lynne after that.

Each day became a battle of nerves for her, but that was nothing new to Lynne. She had dropped four dress sizes since the day she had first learned of her parents' murder— all the anger, the extra work, the tension had, ironically enough, left her looking better and, she hated to admit, feeling better than she had in years. At age thirty-nine, she was a different person than she had been four years earlier: more cynical, more conservative, colder, far more bitter. But she was also fitter, more confident, self-assured.

During breaks, she would talk to the reporters who daily filled the two front rows in the courtroom, expressing confidence she didn't always feel. Later she would stand on the courthouse steps in her red dress—Margaret's favorite color—and give TV interviews before banks of cameras. She told them it would be nice to hear the jury endorse her and the government's theory in the case with guilty verdicts. But not even acquittals would stop the murder investigation now, she declared. If the conspiracy charges failed, there was still the possibility of murder charges in state court. "For those people still out there," she told one reporter, "can you hear the footsteps? Because we are coming."

In another interview, she explained why she had changed her views on capital punishment. "When it occurred to me that someone behind bars could have someone killed, I changed my mind," she explained, then added the deadpan kicker, eyes flat and lips pursed. "They'll never order another hit if they're dead."

Each evening, when the cameras and news vans had left and the jurors went to their hotel for the night, Lynne would make the long drive back to Biloxi, the gun holstered on the seat beside her, the Mazda topping the speed limit by forty mile margins. Still receiving occasional death threats, Lynne always tried to make it to the security of Becky's home by nightfall. The sixty miles between Biloxi and Hattiesburg are dark, rural, four lanes of blacktop through thick piney woods, a drive she did not relish.

Highway 49 is sparsely patrolled by the state police, but not entirely abandoned. One night toward the end of the trial, a highway patrolman pulled Lynne over for speeding on the road to Biloxi. She was alone. The trooper checked her license, then caught sight of the badge case she carried—her sheriff's commission. Then the name on the license registered: "You're one of the Sherry kids, aren't you?"

Lynne looked at the trooper, a big man, the customary ID tag missing from his shirt, expression and voice serious and neutral, neither friendly nor angry. Traffic was light, the road quiet, just an occasional burst of static from the patrol car radio, the creak of his thick leather gunbelt. It occurred to her that many in law enforcement supported her and her efforts in the case. And others could be in Mike Gillich's pocket. Not knowing what to expect, Lynne nodded.

"Oh, honey, I understand," he said, smiling then, handing her license back, his ticket book back in his pocket. "You're just trying to get back home before dark." He promised to call ahead to his fellow troopers down the road then, advising them who she was and that she could bust the speed limit. "You'll be okay," he promised.

Just before he turned away to return to his cruiser, he said one more thing. "Are they ever going to convict that sonofabitch down there? You know, your daddy was a friend of mine." Then he was gone before Lynne could think of an answer or ask his name.

Not everyone she encountered felt that way, certainly not in Biloxi. Pete Halat had his supporters—a majority of voters had elected him mayor, after all. And apart from questions of his guilt or innocence, there was Biloxi's long history of wearing moral blinders. While shopping one day, a businesswoman she had known for years asked Lynne why she insisted on stirring up trouble, causing investigations and trials that hurt Biloxi's image. "It's sewerage, honey, I know, but it's our sewerage," the woman complained. "If we want to swim in it, y'all ought to let us."

Now the conclusion of the trial was fast approaching and, as agonizingly slow as the past six weeks had been, the end somehow seemed abrupt and unexpected, even frightening to Lynne. Her existence for the past month and a half had been structured around this trial, getting up early, the drive to Hattiesburg, every gas station and landmark memorized to the point where she no longer even saw them anymore. Then the long day in court, banter with the reporters camouflaging gnawing doubts about the case, fueled by the cocky look on Kirksey Nix's face bobbing above those red suspenders, the way LaRa Sharpe smiled at the TV cameras when she trundled out of court, free on bail, convinced she would win. From talking to Keith Bell and Randy Cook—and from her own experience and investigations—she knew there was so much more evidence than what was being offered to the jury.

Just that day, Judge Pickering ruled that her brother Vin could not testify. His recollection that his mother told him there was a contract on her life, and that Mike Gillich was behind it, would be withheld. Telling that to the jury would break the rules on hearsay, the judge ruled. It would amount to using the words of Margaret Sherry to convict Mike Gillich without giving him the opportunity to face his accuser and cross-examine her.

"Mike Gillich made sure he'd never have to face her," Lynne hissed when she heard the judge's decision. "That's why he had her killed."

But the decision stood, grounded firmly in the law and in simple reality: Murder victims cannot testify—the murderer's ultimate protection.

And with that decision, the case ended. There would be no more witnesses.

Only closing arguments, the jury deliberations, and the verdict remained—the answer Lynne had awaited so long. Either there would be justice for her parents' murder, Lynne said to her friend Becky, or this whole trial Lynne had pressed for would turn out to be a gargantuan mistake. And Biloxi would continue to swim in its own sewerage.

One by one, the defense lawyers rose to pick apart the prosecution's case in their closing arguments, to remind the jurors of all the lies the government's witnesses had told, their varied stories, their desire for immunity that tainted their motives for testifying. The ugliness of the government witnesses was the key weakness in the prosecution's case, and all four lawyers hammered at it—they were criminals, robbers, hired killers.

As Ransom's lawyer, Rex Jones, put it, coopting one of Bobby Fabian's old expressions, "Convicts know that the only way they can get out of jail, when you are sitting there for a long time, you got to find something sensational. And you got to be able to reach out and touch someone that the government wants to touch. And if you do that, you get something for it."

It was that simple, an obvious principle, Jones said. Jones had the look of a lawyer more comfortable sitting at the prosecution table—which he had done for many years—but he seemed genuinely outraged at the case against his client. Both sides accepted the fact that this principle had motivated Bobby Fabian—the original force behind this case. Why else would he be absent from the trial? Accept this obvious principle, Jones argued, and you had to vote not guilty.

The government couldn't even get its story straight on a motive for the murder conspiracy, Jim Rose, Nix's lawyer, argued when his turn came. He derided prosecutors for presenting "a buffet of theories" in the case, unable to settle on any one. First the scam is the reason for the murders, then Margaret's opposition to Mike Gillich.

"If you don't like the turkey, you can get the roast beef," Rose chided. "If you don't like the mashed potatoes, you can get the potato salad or the okra. . . . If you don't like the fact that Vincent Sherry was the target of the scam people, then maybe you would like it better if Margaret Sherry is the target."

The defendants, meanwhile, had never been described so glowingly in their lives as they were in the defense team's closing remarks. LaRa Sharpe was motivated by love and friendship—then withdrew from a bad situation and should be rewarded with acquittal. Crimelord Mike Gillich had become "good-hearted Mike . . . who wouldn't be here today if his heart wasn't so big." John Ransom had "some trash in his life" but he didn't do this murder. He had an alibi, his wife and daughter. And Nix, finally, might be a scammer, but he was not a killer, not in this case, anyway. Besides, those scam victims lusting after "young boys" deserved what they got.

If anyone should be on trial, the defense argued, it was a Biloxi policeman driving a yellow Ford.

Finally, the four lawyers pointed to an empty chair at the defense table: the invisible defendant. It was, perhaps, one of their most compelling arguments.

"Either Pete Halat ought to be sitting here in one of these chairs, or the government don't believe William Rhodes," Albert Necaise said, making the U.S. Attorney pay for his strategy of not trying to charge Halat. "One of the two. They can't have their cake and eat it, too."

It was one of the last comments made in the case by the defense. It was the first thing any of the defense lawyers said that Lynne Sposito agreed with. She, too, thought Pete Halat should be in that chair.

Assistant U.S. Attorney Peter Barrett had a simple response. There was no buffet of theories, he said. There was one theory: Witness after witness swore that scam money went to Mike Gillich and Peter Halat, and that a big chunk of that scam money came up missing. To save their own necks from a dangerous man like Kirksey Nix—who had dangerous friends like John Ransom—Gillich and Halat needed a fall guy, Barrett said. And that was Vince Sherry. That was why Vince had died—to cover their tracks.

And why Margaret Sherry? Well, look what happened because she died along with her husband, Barrett said. "Mike Gillich . . . can go on with his B-drinking, he can go on with his scams, he can go on with his drug dealings. . . . Go on with the corruption of the political process. Go about his business of [ensuring] the ascendancy of Pete Halat to the mayor's office in Biloxi, an office that Peter Halat lusted for and Mike Gillich desperately needed to control."

Margaret's death was a bonus, Barrett argued, one that gave city hall to Pete Halat and Mike Gillich. It was two for the price of one.

And after this scathing indictment of nondefendant Pete Halat, Barrett turned to that empty chair the defense lawyers had complained about and said, "There is one more thing you need to remember. We take investigations one step at a time."

The jury went out on a humid Thursday evening, charged with sorting through stacks of phone bills, prison records, tape recordings, and weeks of sometimes conflicting and always complex testimony. They deliberated through the weekend, sequestered by night in a Hattiesburg motel. Hours and days dragged by.

Then, at 3:30 Monday afternoon, after thirty-four hours locked in the jury room, in a courthouse emptied for Veterans Day, the foreman of the jury sent out a note. The bailiff charged with safeguarding the jurors' privacy began summoning the lawyers to the courthouse. Word soon reached the reporters camped outside, and a crowd began to gather on the steps of the locked federal building: a decision had been reached.

In a house in Hattiesburg, Lynne Sposito, Becky Field, and U.S. Attorney George Phillips had just poured coffee when the phone rang. They had stayed close by, sensing a resolution might be imminent after a long three days and nights. The call was simple and uninformative: Come to the courthouse. The jury says it's done deliberating. That was it. Only those eight women and four men on the jury knew what decision had been reached. Not even the judge would know until everyone had assembled in court.

"I don't want the coffee now," Becky said, staring at the full cup in front of her. "I'm too nervous."

The others agreed. Phillips, who did not smoke, bummed a cigarette from her and fumbled to light it. Lynne found herself unable to speak, other than to mumble, "Oh my God," over and over, "what if it's a hung jury? What if they're not guilty?" She hadn't felt this out of control in four years. She kept imagining the way Kirksey Nix's face would look if a not-guilty verdict was read. Or maybe they were unable to reach a verdict, and they'd have to go through it all over again. That might be even worse.

The three of them piled into Phillips's Trooper and headed for the courthouse, tense and silent. Lynne and Becky had grown close to Phillips, his rocky start with Lynne forgotten, his country-lawyer manner winning her over in time. They all looked rumpled, Lynne's hair wild,

Phillips without a tie, the cigarette burning uselessly in his ashtray.

After driving a few blocks, Phillips fished around for a cassette, then popped it in the stereo. To Lynne and Becky's surprise, "Amazing Grace" filled the car. Silent tears started running after a few verses, first down Lynne's face, then Becky's, and finally George Phillips's. Then they all began to sing the hymn along with the tape, the only words uttered during that five-minute drive to court.

When they pulled to a stop and Phillips turned the ignition key off, silencing the music, Lynne just wiped her eyes, unable to speak. Becky looked at her and said, "That's what they played at Vince and Margaret's funeral. My father's, too."

Phillips nodded, then said, "Yep, and at that wonderful man, my father's, too."

Then he bent to check the small gun in his ankle holster—he too had received his share of threats—and the mood broke. Phillips asked, "Are you ready to run the gauntlet?" With Lynne's nod, they walked toward the press of reporters and into the courthouse, Lynne flashing a thumbs-up even as she fought back more tears.

An hour-long wait crawled by as each of the attorneys made their way to court. Members of the press finally got permission to enter the locked courthouse, and the friends and relatives of the defendants began taking their seats in the courtroom, whispering as if they were in a library. Outside, Peter Barrett kept pacing in a back hallway, muttering, "We've got 'em, I just know we've got the sonsabitches." The other prosecutors looked less certain. Keith Bell was there too, looking kind and impassive as always. Lynne remained silent, fearful and uncertain, trying to take it all in. The defendants sat uneasily at their table, Nix and Ransom in custody, Gillich and Sharpe arriving on their own, wondering if this would be their last day of freedom, or the first of many to come.

Finally, at 5:45 P.M. on November 11, 1991, more than four years after the Sherrys died in their homes, Judge Pickering asked the jury if they had reached a verdict. They had, the foreman said. There would be no hung jury. Everyone in the courtroom grew still, waiting.

Lynne's thoughts were a jumble. She was barely able to sit still. This was her moment, when the years of sorrow and obsession would either pay off—or lead nowhere. Her stomach churned and she closed her eyes, trying to imagine her mother's voice or her father's laugh, but she could not do it. It was Kirksey Nix's guttural laugh that stuck in her mind instead, jabbing at her, his lips mouthing words at her. She found herself pleading silently to the jury to do the right thing. Please, please, she chanted to herself. Please.

The clerk stood to read the verdicts, the ancient ritual. The first count in the indictment—the all-important conspiracy charge that combined the scam and murder for hire—would come first, before the others. Kirksey Nix, John Ransom, Mike Gillich, and LaRa Sharpe all stood and faced forward, awaiting their fates. Kirksey Nix, the man obsessed with finding freedom, and Lynne Sposito, equally obsessed with finding her parents' killer, each held their breath.

"Guilty," the clerk read.

In count one, all four defendants were guilty as charged. Not even the wails of LaRa's children or the gasp from Mike Gillich's row of relatives could dim the relief—and, yes, she had to admit, the joy—Lynne felt when she heard that word.

CHAPTER 40

Six months of bickering and recriminations followed the verdict, as defense lawyers tried to delay sentencing by accusing the government—and Lynne Sposito—of all sorts of misconduct. Everything from political manipulation of the justice system to suborning perjury was claimed, each charge requiring a hearing and a ruling.

One by one, Judge Pickering threw out each argument, finally telling the attorneys to get ready for sentencing in March 1992. He would allow no more delays.

As the day approached, the length of the potential sentences confronting the defendants remained uncertain, in part because of the way the jury had decided the case. The verdict was unquestionably a victory for the prosecution, but it was not a complete rout because not every defendant was convicted of every charge in the indictment.

All four defendants were convicted in the most serious count, the conspiracy charge that merged the scam with the murder-for-hire plot. And all four were convicted of wire fraud—the actual scamming.

But of the two remaining counts in the indictment—which involved interstate travel with intent to commit murder for hire—the results were mixed. Nix and Gillich were convicted of count three, inducing Robert Hallal to cross state lines for murder for hire. Ransom, however, was acquitted on this count. And all three men were acquitted of count four, interstate travel by John Ransom for murder for hire on August 8 and 9, 1987. (LaRa Sharpe had not been charged in these last two counts.)

"I can't reason how the jury can reach a verdict about Nix and Gillich, yet find Ransom not guilty," lawyer Jim Rose said after the verdict. He and his colleagues said it seemed inconsistent, and that the jury must have been "confused." Either Robert Hallal was telling the truth and they're all guilty, or he's lying and they're all innocent.

"It makes no sense," attorney Rose said.

Pete Halat put an even more dramatic spin on the verdicts: He pronounced himself "vindicated." Because Ransom was found innocent of taking a trip to Biloxi to discuss murder for hire, Halat concluded that the jury must have disbelieved Bill Rhodes—the prime link between the mayor and the murders.

"I feel vindicated to the extent that the jury didn't believe anything Bill Rhodes said," Halat told reporters.

The jurors had a simple answer for all this: They were not confused, several said in news interviews. They believed Bill Rhodes. And the only reason they acquitted Ransom was because the government put the wrong dates in its indictment. The indictment said John Ransom traveled across state lines with intent to commit murder for hire on August 8 and 9—days that Ransom's family convincingly swore he was vacationing in Florida, not plotting murder in Biloxi. The jurors had no doubt that Ransom was involved—that's why he was convicted in the conspiracy—but for those two particular days in the indictment, he was in the clear. And the fact that portions of Hallal's story seemed untrue did not persuade jurors that they should discard everything he said. They felt that on key points, he had been consistent throughout.

As for Bill Rhodes, one juror said, it was Pete Halat who was confused. "He testified about January and February, and the date on the indictment was August, when Rhodes was in jail. . . . As a whole, I believe Rhodes. I believed his ingredients, not his spices. That was said in the jury room."

Their belief in Rhodes had not greatly contributed to the case, however, because of the way the indictment was written: his testimony did not apply to those last two counts of murder for hire. Several of the jurors told prosecutors afterward that they would have convicted Pete Halat if he had been among the defendants.[1]

When the day set aside for sentencing finally arrived—March 12, 1992—Lynne returned to Mississippi, accompanied by her sister, Leslie. Her two brothers sent letters but did not come.

At home, while Dick was at work, Lynne's children were safeguarded by a former Navy Seal commando, a co-worker of Lynne's at her clinic who had agreed to move into the Spositos' spare room. The former Seal acted as combination tenant, nanny, and bodyguard. He took the kids everywhere, stood guard after the occasional threatening phone call, helped keep the rebellious Tommy in line. A heavy-duty lock had to be installed on the door to his room, however—to keep all his guns safe. It is testament to the effect a murder can have on a family that all this seemed a comfort, not a terror. Lynne felt safer than she had in years, knowing he was there.

People had already packed the courtroom when Lynne and Leslie arrived, accompanied by John and Becky Field. Both the Sherry children wore red dresses in honor of their mother's favorite color, a show of support for the prosecution and a silent plea for justice for their parents.

They found themselves greatly outnumbered. The Gillich family had advertised on cable television and in newspapers, pleading for letters of support. They deluged the court with testimonials and petitions for Mr. Mike, more than five hundred signatures attesting to the good character and generosity of their favorite strip joint operator. Catholic nuns, a school principal, the general manager of Barq's Root Beer Company of Biloxi, even the bishop of Biloxi, the Most Reverend Joseph Howze—the man who had conducted the funeral Mass for Vincent and Margaret Sherry— wrote the court on Gillich's behalf, joining the painstakingly penned missives from Gillich's strippers describing what a prince their boss could be.

Bishop Howze's letter was the only one that really hurt the family, detailing as it did Gillich's generous contributions to the church, sympathizing with the burden on his family, and calling for leniency because "I am sure the ordeals Mr. Gillich has endured thus far have made him contrite and repentant." The names of those other good Catholics, Vince and Margaret Sherry, did not appear in the bishop's letter, nor did it acknowledge the suffering of the Sherry family. Lynne called the Biloxi *Sun Herald* in a rage, begging a reporter there to write about this testimonial, but an article never appeared.

In the face of this onslaught, the four Sherry children wrote their own letters to Judge Pickering, struggling to find words for sentiments they had never before fully articulated. No one had ever so baldly asked them to describe, as the U.S. Attorney had asked, just how they had been affected by the deaths of their parents.

The question overwhelmed. Vin Sherry took refuge in sarcasm: "I hear the good citizens of Biloxi have rallied behind Mr. Gillich in his time of need," he wrote. "Community leaders like him are the rock on which Biloxi is built, or at least the stuff that grows under it. . . . What people don't realize is that there is a little-known city ordinance that gives immunity to strip-club owners who tithe."

But mixed in with the bitterness, Vin Sherry III also spoke of the new peephole in his front door and the burglar alarm he had installed, the pointless fistfights he kept getting into, part of the impotent rage that eats at him, that leaves him punching holes in the walls of his home. His therapist, he wrote, says he suffers from post-traumatic stress syndrome, just like combat veterans.

Eric Sherry wrote of being alienated from the city he once loved, of the horror of being suspected of killing his own parents, the grief for his seven-year-old son who needs counseling and who can't sleep alone at night because he fears "the bad men" who killed his grandparents might come for him next.

Leslie Sherry, in an eloquent letter reminiscent of her father's writings, explained how her parents never saw her graduate college or earn her master's degree. Her father will not give her away at her wedding, she told the judge, nor will her mother hold and cuddle the grandchildren that someday will come. She recalled how her parents taught her critical thinking and self-reliance—to know she could achieve anything if she worked hard enough. This, more than anything, drove her to go on with her studies and her life after they died, she told Pickering.

"It is quite a shame," she wrote, "that often by the time we are old enough to appreciate such 'words of wisdom,' those who passed them on to us are no longer around to thank."

All the Sherry children asked the judge to treat the defendants sternly, to hold them fully responsible for their actions. No amount of charitable acts could confer absolution for murder, they wrote.

"If we can keep another family from going through this by standing up and saying, this is wrong and must be made as right as it can be, then we have done the job that was assigned to us all on September 14, 1987," Lynne wrote in her letter to the judge. "Nothing can bring my parents back, but knowing that the people responsible for their deaths do have to answer to someone in this lifetime gives a sense of peace to us all." Even as she penned the words, Lynne could only hope this was true. Peace seemed farther off than ever.

In court on the day of sentencing, Lynne, Leslie, and their two friends, John and Becky Field, sat on one row in back of the prosecution table. The other side of the courtroom filled with the supporters of Mike Gillich. LaRa Sharpe had her two teenaged daughters there for her. John Ransom was absent, sick with pneumonia. Kirksey Nix, heavier than ever, head nodding crookedly, eyebrows bushy, had no one but his lawyers.

Assistant U.S. Attorney Peter Barrett surprised the defense by arguing that the law allowed a life sentence, at least for Nix and Gillich—something the prosecution hadn't mentioned before. The judge rejected this, however, saying federal sentencing guidelines adopted in recent years tied his hands and limited him to a maximum of five years on each count in the indictment. He made it clear, however, that this did not mean he agreed with defense claims that someone else killed the Sherrys.

"I do believe that, by a preponderance of the evidence, that the murder took place as a result of the conspiracy," Pickering ruled—a prerequisite for imposing the maximum sentence. When Gillich's son-in-law/attorney Keith Pisarich began loudly objecting to this finding, the judge cautioned him to lower his voice, then repeated his finding in even plainer terms. "The court feels that the murder of the Sherrys was a result of the conspiracy charged in count one."

With that said, each defendant had the chance to speak before sentencing. LaRa Sharpe presented her two daughters, one of whom read a tearful letter to the court, pleading for probation. The judge declined this suggestion, but found that LaRa's role in the murder conspiracy had been nil—so far as the prosecution proved at trial. The evidence proved only that she was a scammer, he said. Pickering then sentenced her to one year and one week in prison, to be followed by three years probation and counseling. She left the courtroom arm in arm with her daughters, granted a month's leave before she had to report to prison. "I hope I don't see you again," the judge said.

"You won't see me again," LaRa promised.

Mike Gillich remained mute when his turn came. He wore a badly rumpled brown suit, looking exhausted and unshaven. He had been placed in custody six months earlier—the moment the guilty verdict was read—and his first-ever stint in jail at age sixty-one had worn heavily on him. His temporary lodgings were overcrowded, and there was no bed for him. Mr. Mike had been reduced to sleeping on a jail-cell floor. His lawyers pointed to all the letters on Gillich's behalf and asked for mercy, but Mr. Mike personally had nothing to say.

Judge Pickering remained unmoved by the testimonials. Gillich may have been a charitable man, the judge said, but his part in the conspiracy cost the Sherrys their lives.

Convicted on three counts, Gillich received a five-year term for each, stacked one on the other—a total sentence of fifteen years, with a one-hundred-thousand-dollar fine as well.

Marshals immediately hauled Gillich from the courtroom to a holding cell. As he left, he waved and offered a weak smile to his family and supporters, who fled the room shortly thereafter. Lynne idly watched them go, unable to completely suppress a grim smile. An elderly woman, Lucille Schenk, a longtime backer of Gillich's, suddenly leaned toward Lynne, leered, and screeched belligerently, "What are you lookin' at?"

Lynne said nothing, but John Field muttered, "Not much."

The court was mostly empty when Nix's turn came. Unlike his patron, Kirksey Nix found the podium irresistible. It would be his one final platform before sentence was passed.

Reciting poetry, rambling about lies and innocence, Nix admitted to scamming, then denied all else. "Like the woman in Macy's basement who shopped till she dropped, I did scams with a frenzy," he said. "But somewhere in the dark of the night . . . the killers of Vincent and Margaret Sherry still lurk. . . . This case is not solved."

"Mike Gillich is an innocent man," he said, trying to shoulder blame one more time. Then he looked directly at Lynne, saying, "Judge Sherry and Councilwoman Sherry deserve more. . . . A political assassination occurred. . . . It is textbook Machiavellian to blame the criminal element. . . . The killers are out there. The people should not think the Sherry case is solved. I know it is not."

Lynne stared back at him, fascinated and repulsed at the same time, wondering if she would ever feel relief, if this process would ever be finished.

When Nix was through with his lengthy statement, Judge

Pickering spoke. "Mr. Nix, you are quite eloquent. . . . The court observes that it is unfortunate for you, and unfortunate for society, that a man with the talents and abilities you have would dedicate himself to crime."

"No one regrets it more than me," Nix said, still standing at the podium, wearing his red suspenders and tassled loafers for the last time.

"You kept your mind on the street, even while your body was in prison," the judge said, quoting Nix's own testimony. "The Sherry family must live with the consequences of that."

With that, the judge passed sentence. Nix received a fifteen-year term as well, to begin only after his life sentence was completed, if ever. That way, if he should ever be pardoned or paroled in Louisiana, he would still have fifteen years of federal time ahead of him. Then the marshals led Nix from the room. The judge left next, then the lawyers gathered their boxes of papers and briefcases and filed out. It was over.

(Recovered from his pneumonia, John Ransom came to court a week later offering to solve the case with his own investigation if given three months in the field. The judge declined this odd offer from the Dixie Mafia's feared hit man. He gave Ransom a ten-year sentence instead, stacked on his twelve-year sentence in Georgia. At his age—sixty-five—and considering his poor health, this amounted to a death sentence, his lawyer argued, pleading for leniency. But the judge said Ransom deserved no such consideration.)

The end seemed almost anticlimactic to Lynne. Six months had passed since the trial, and the ebullience she had felt then had long since faded. She felt no relief, just exhaustion. "Let's get the hell out of here," she said to Becky after the sentencing. There would be no celebration.

In the glow of the guilty verdicts the previous fall, George Phillips had vowed to reporters, "We're gonna work this case until I either die or go out of office, one of the two. We're never gonna stop the investigation until we are certain we had solved the murders of Vince and Margaret Sherry."

At the time, it seemed like a new break in the case was

imminent. Someone would crack, and they'd have their murder case cold. Now that he was convicted, John Ransom would change his tune and confess. Or Mike Gillich, facing prison for the first time in his life, would roll over and say who pulled the trigger. Or maybe Lenny Swetman, facing a drug indictment with Nix and Gillich, would cooperate.

But six months had gone by, sentence had been passed, and the investigation was no closer to a final solution than before. The defendants had maintained their innocence. Lynne wanted to know what happened. All the confident predictions had led nowhere, she said. If these men were guilty, they had nothing to gain from insisting on their innocence, and everything to gain from telling the truth, she reasoned. And yet they still said the government had it all wrong, that someone else did the killing.

Well, the prosecutors told her now, the defendants all thought they had a shot at a successful appeal: They're convinced the combination scam-murder conspiracy was unconstitutional, and they still expect to win a new trial. Maybe, George Phillips told Lynne, when the appeals were resolved and the convictions affirmed, they might start hearing a different story. But that was years off, he conceded. And suddenly, that "first step" Peter Barrett spoke of started sounding like the only step to Lynne. She had confidently told reporters six months earlier that the killers should listen for footsteps, the investigators were coming—but now she wasn't so sure. The case remained far from solved, as far as she was concerned. They had the conspirators. But did they have the killers?

"They keep talking about footsteps," Pete Halat observed. "They're never going to completely solve this case until those footsteps turn in a different direction."[2]

As she emerged from the courtroom after sentencing, Lynne was asked when she would finally pronounce her ordeal ended. Hadn't she had enough? one reporter wanted to know. As discouraged as she felt, Lynne had a ready answer.

"When the people that cold-bloodedly murdered my parents are awaiting their own death penalty on a state charge, then we're done."

Lynne Sposito is waiting still.

EPILOGUE

*I have a firm belief in the hereafter, and I expect to
see Mom and Dad someday. And I can't bear the
thought of not being able to tell them I did
everything I could to bring their killers to justice.*

—*Lynne Sposito*

*As a young man, I laid waste my life, and I regret it
every day. But I have never done anything so
despicable as the nightmare Mr. Fabian has set upon
the good families of the Gulf Coast.*

—*Kirksey McCord Nix*

Biloxi, 1993

The impasse in the Sherry investigation remains, a case
partially solved, an odd sort of murder. People have
been jailed for conspiring to kill, yet no one has been
charged with the actual killing. This curious outcome has
left no one satisfied—not the accused, not the investigators,
not the prosecutors, and certainly not Lynne Sposito.

After the sentencing, Lynne returned to Raleigh, returned
to her family, returned to work. But every few days found
her back on the telephone, talking to George Phillips or
Keith Bell, sifting through her files, talking to potential
witnesses, wondering if Step Two would come.

"I can't let it drop," she continually told her husband.

"I'd never ask you to," he always answered.

A month after the sentencing, Kirksey Nix, Mike Gillich, and the locksmith Lenny Swetman went on trial for trafficking in marijuana. Nix allegedly underwrote the purchase of ninety-one pounds of pot while in prison, with Gillich middling the deal, and Swetman arranging for its storage. The trial, a simple four-day affair, had little resemblance to the complexities and contradictions of the scam-murder case, and it ended in clear-cut convictions. Gillich received a five-year sentence for his role, stacked on top of his existing fifteen-year prison term—a twenty-year total that meant he too almost certainly would die in prison before earning his release. Mr. Mike's only hope remained his appeal.

Nix, meanwhile, had ten years added to his term in the Sherry case, giving him a total of twenty-five years of federal prison time to serve should he somehow survive his no-parole sentence in Louisiana. He began penning massive filings to the federal appeals court in New Orleans—as he had been doing for years with his old conviction in the Corso case.

Lenny Swetman netted a five-year term on the marijuana charges. But when approached by federal authorities, neither he nor the other defendants offered to provide any information about the Sherry murders. Once again, they all said they had nothing to say, other than to protest their innocence. Lynne hadn't even bothered to attend the trial. She knew the investigation was going nowhere while both sides awaited the outcome of the appeals.

In June 1993, more than a year after sentencing, the Fifth Circuit Court of Appeals made its decision: It upheld all the convictions, finding no merit in any of the defense claims.

Lynne eagerly awaited news of a breakthrough from Keith Bell or George Phillips. Surely someone would talk now, she hoped. But again she was disappointed: All attempts to get cooperation from the defendants failed. Gillich and Ransom still had nothing to say, and the prosecutors couldn't offer Nix anything that would matter to him even if he did want to talk. Besides, all were pursuing the next stage of appeals, to the U.S. Supreme Court. And LaRa Sharpe, by the time of the appeal, had served her sentence and was out on parole, remarried and starting a gourmet salsa business in Alabama. She had no reason to talk to anyone.

Meanwhile, yet another indictment came down, this one charging Mike Gillich and two cohorts with attempting to bribe a witness—the scammer Robbie Gant—with twenty thousand dollars to alter his testimony in Mr. Mike's favor. This time, the prosecution did not have to depend upon the ambiguous testimony of immunized criminals to prove their case. The bribery attempt was captured on tape—including recordings of phone calls Gillich made from prison phones at the federal penitentiary in Pennsylvania where he had been serving his sentence.

"Mr. Gillich is looking at a potentially lengthy prison sentence," FBI Agent Keith Bell told Lynne after the indictments came down.

"Yes, maybe so, but will it help solve the murder case?" Lynne asked.

After a long silence, Bell said, "I can't say that it will. Mr. Gillich has made a living all his life by not talking."

The murder investigation had come down to this, Lynne was told: Either Mike Gillich or John Ransom would change their minds and stories, or the case would remain unsolved. And they would never know what went on in her parents' house on the night of the murder.

There was another possibility, of course, the one Pete Halat and Kirksey Nix both tirelessly offered: Either the investigators would turn their footsteps in a new direction —toward new suspects and new theories—or the case would never be solved. Kirksey Nix, who for years said he knew no more about the identity of the Sherry killers than the guy in the bar or the barbershop, now hints that he does have some ideas on who the killers are—ammunition he is saving should his constant appeals ever prevail.[1]

So what is the truth in the Sherry murders?

The first truth—a matter of law—is that Kirksey Nix, John Ransom, Mike Gillich, and LaRa Sharpe were convicted of a conspiracy that included attempting to hire a killer to murder Vincent Sherry. That conspiracy, the judge who heard all the evidence ruled, led directly to the murders of both Vince and Margaret. To that extent, the case is

solved: A plot behind the killings had been established. But
who pulled the trigger, who else might be involved, and
exactly why it had to happen—all that remains unanswered.

Which leads to the second truth in this case: Peter Halat
is an innocent man in the eyes of the law. He has never been
charged with a crime, much less convicted, and any testimony at the trial or the grand jury that suggests otherwise is
nothing more than talk.

Yet it is possible to weigh the evidence against him, to see
how it matches up with his adamant and consistent denials
of wrongdoing. In his press conferences, Halat asked for just
such an evaluation, certain it would reveal his innocence.
So what does it show?

The evidence is compelling that the Halat and Sherry law
office, phones, library, and even Halat's own sworn affidavits were used to further Kirksey Nix's scams. Halat's entire
relationship with Nix invites questions—the telephone
marriage with Kellye, the registration of Nix's Mercedes in
Gillich's name with the law office's address, the unusual
trust fund. Even Rex Jones, John Ransom's lawyer, said he
never heard of a lawyer's trust fund like Nix's. And in all the
nine years Halat served as Kirksey Nix's lawyer, he never
represented the convict in a single criminal case, Halat's
specialty.

"Halat's lucky," Jones said after the trial.[2]

But just because the office was used by scammers does not
mean Halat knowingly participated in scams. Only Kellye
Dawn Newman Nix's testimony suggests Halat knew what
Nix was doing. No investigation has ever turned up evidence that Halat—or Vince Sherry—profited from any
illicit income. For that matter, no one has located any
evidence of where the missing scam money went—or if it
ever existed at all. There is only the word of convicts to
attest to that.

Of course, the same can be said—and was said—in
defense of Mike Gillich. There was no documentary evidence he ever profited from the scams, either, only the
testimony of convicts and bagmen who said they delivered
money to him. Yet that testimony was enough to send
Gillich to prison.

The evidence of Halat's alleged involvement in the

murder-for-hire conspiracy is even more scant. Bill Rhodes swore Halat and John Ransom tried to hire him for the job. No other witness implicated Vince Sherry's best friend in the murder, except for the discredited Bobby Fabian.

Anything else that might be used as evidence of Halat's involvement in murder is circumstantial at best. There are his comments at the wake—his seeming knowledge of the time of death before he should have known—and his alleged behavior at the house when the bodies were found. There is the testimony that Vince and Margaret no longer trusted him. And there is the fact that he knew, before the information was made public, that the meeting at Angola to discuss the murders described by Fabian supposedly occurred in March 1987.

But none of this is sufficient evidence to charge a man with murder—no more than Nix, Gillich, or Ransom could be charged with the actual killing.

As for the conspiracy case, Pete Halat is now in the clear. If there is a Step Two, it won't be a replay of that charge. The statute of limitations has lapsed on the scam and most other elements of the conspiracy. And even if it hadn't, the decision not to name Halat in that first indictment was far more irrevocable than Lynne Sposito was ever told. She has since learned that charging Halat with the same case brought two years earlier against Nix and company would violate Halat's right to a speedy trial. There would have to be new evidence or new witnesses to justify charging Pete Halat.

Halat, meanwhile, harbors deep grievances against journalists and prosecutors. He has suffered innumerable accusations without ever being charged with a crime, and he argues forcefully about the unfairness of this, and the cruel pressures it has exerted on his wife and children. He has said he will write his own book on the case to set the record straight. "It's the only way the truth will be told."

Kirksey Nix also says he is writing a book, ensconced again at Angola, a place that has been his home for nearly twenty years, where the former chieftain of the Dixie Mafia is accorded the respect and fear he believes he deserves.

It is an easier place for him now: In the summer of 1993, the extreme restrictions of the special tier created for scammers were relaxed. He has better access to phones and visitors and attorneys now. He swears he no longer scams. Instead, he paints with acrylics. Some say he is good at it.

Those who know him say he has not changed though, that he remains as ruthless as ever, a born killer behind his folksy, rotund, gray-haired façade. A year earlier, while Nix still resided at the Harrison County Jail near Biloxi, Randy Cook was tipped off by a U.S. Customs investigator about an escape supposedly being planned by Nix and two drug traffickers in the jail. Two men on the outside named by Customs were stopped with police radios and camping equipment shortly before the escape was supposed to come down. Nix was placed in lockdown, his movements restricted and supervised. When his cell was searched, jail guards found a short piece of rope made from braided pieces of torn sheet, painstakingly bound together in a tight, thick, strong cord.

Inmates have a word for such a piece of rope, Cook says: It is a strangle cord.[3]

Nix, however, swears he has never hurt anyone who didn't try to hurt him first. He is still hoping for freedom, still penning his appeals. It is what Kirksey Nix lives for. It is what anyone consigned to life to a place like Angola would do, though few have the tools Nix possesses. He is tireless and cruel and single-minded, and the arguments he crafts always contain convincers that make you wonder— all with one goal in mind. That's why he scammed, that's why he trafficked in drugs, that's why he conspired to kill Vince and Margaret Sherry. To put himself back in the streets.

So he can start all over again.

Lynne Sposito returned to Biloxi in June 1993, first to attend the appeals hearing in New Orleans, then to observe the mayoral elections on the Coast. After all the turmoil, Pete Halat was running for a second term in office.

Six years had passed since Lynne had lost her parents. She no longer makes regular trips to Biloxi, though she speaks regularly with Becky Field. She still has her files, she still stays in touch with Keith Bell, Rex Armistead checks in with her now and then, and, once in a while, Sheri the psychic passes on some eerie new pronouncement. Bobby

Fabian, out of Angola and in protective custody in a federal prison, calls often, cajoling Lynne, still hoping to buy his release with information.

Still, Lynne and her husband, Dick, have tried to rediscover a semblance of normalcy back in Raleigh. Her oldest daughter, Cathy, is finishing college now. Her son, Tommy, remains troubled, struggling to graduate from high school, then running into legal trouble of his own. Beth, seven years old at the time of the murders, has become a teenager, an accomplished equestrian, her memories of her grandparents dim. When she first plunged into the investigation of her parents' murder, Lynne wanted to teach her children about doing the right thing, about standing up to evil. But now she is not so sure she likes having a little girl who knows what a .22 Ruger looks like, who can talk knowledgeably about conspiracies and autopsies. Who understands death.

Sometimes Lynne flips through the notes she began taking after the murders, keeping certain things fresh in mind, rediscovering the anger and fear she felt at various moments. These notes are captioned only by the month in which they were written, not the year. "I never thought it would take more than one year for the case to be over," she observes ruefully. "Now I have to wonder if it will ever be over."

Lately, days, sometimes even weeks, can pass without her thinking about the case. The reporters have stopped calling; the case is old news now, and she is no longer a celebrity. If she misses the attention, she gives no hint of it. Lynne still thinks of John Ransom when she listens to that certain hymn in church, and at night, when the house is quiet, she still can imagine her mother speaking in veiled terms about threats and fears for her children's safety. Lynne still berates herself for not asking her mom to explain that remark, still agonizes over the missed hints, the feeling that her parents knew what was coming, and that she would know too, if she had only asked.

Her trip in June 1993 to the Gulf Coast brought it all back, as always, memories riding the thick, humid air, forcing her to drive by the empty house on Hickory Hill Circle, to visit the cemetery, to park in front of the Golden Nugget and wonder.

To Lynne's amazement, she found Biloxi had come full

circle since its heyday in the 1950s, when illegal gambling
had flourished and magazine writers portrayed it as
America's Riviera. Something called dockside gambling
had come to Mississippi in 1992, and Biloxi—along with
the neighboring towns on the Coast—had become home to
a fleet of ersatz riverboats permanently anchored a few
inches offshore, each of them housing a Las Vegas-style
casino. It was everything Margaret Sherry had warned
against: The one-armed bandits, the poker games, the
blackjack—all were back in Biloxi, only this time it was
legal. Suddenly, the crowds were back, the hotels were
booked, the tourists again flocked to Biloxi—not to mention the servicemen and other locals who came to the docks
to blow their paychecks, moths lured to the neon flame, just
like the old days.

Gambling had transformed the city. Her mother would
have fought tirelessly against it, another reason, Lynne was
sure, that Margaret had to die along with Vince. Without
her opposition, the gambling law had cleared the state
legislature and a local referendum, changing the face of
Biloxi for good.

By the time of the mayoral election, the benefits—as well
as the problems—associated with big-time legalized gambling had become apparent. On the plus side, years of city
budget deficits—a financial picture so bleak that Pete Halat
seemed a year earlier to be headed for certain defeat—had
turned around. Tax receipts from the casinos had given
Biloxi a multimillion-dollar surplus, for which Halat was
quick to take credit. Unemployment has been cut in half as
jobs opened up at the casinos. Gambling seemed a rousing
success, part of a nationwide trend to bolster ailing econo-
mies with the industry of greed.

But with the gains came losses. Crime was rising. The
shrimpers who had once been the backbone of the Gulf
economy were being pushed out. Beachfront real estate was
being snapped up by gambling interests. Traffic, for the first
time in memory, posed a problem. Landmarks were being
paved over into parking lots for gamblers with cash in their
pockets. Development threatened to rage out of control
along the beachfront, with little or no controls by the city.
The Strip was being remade, even as downtown Biloxi
remained a ghost town. A few men and corporations grew

rich, but the impoverished, potholed side of Biloxi away from the beachfront saw few tangible benefits to the gambling. Many wondered if they'd made a mistake.

The Gillich family prospered, though. After Mr. Mike was convicted on drug charges, the federal government seized his beloved Golden Nugget and the attached Dream Room, video store, and souvenir shop, labeling them illegal havens for drug dealing. But the same law that allowed authorities to seize the property also required the U.S. Attorney to give Gillich and his family the first shot at repurchasing it—which they did, for four hundred thousand dollars (and the promise not to reopen a strip joint there). The price paid by the Gillich family was only three quarters of the Nugget's appraised value—and the appraisal had been done before legalized gambling inflated the value of many waterfront properties like the Nugget.[4]

The family still operates the nearby Horseshoe Lounge, which was not seized. The girls there still sidle up to customers and the waitresses hawk overpriced soft drinks with swizzle sticks. The Gilliches have opened two new strip joints as well, Gentlemen's Paradise and the El Morocco Lounge, a name copped from a once notorious Dixie Mafia haunt of decades past. As of 1993, the Gilliches still had the strip joint monopoly in Biloxi, even with Mr. Mike languishing in prison. The new joints honor his time-tested precepts: They are dark and sleazy, with expensive drinks and loud, tinny music, and business has never been better.

The election itself was remarkable for what wasn't said. The allegations against Pete Halat were seldom an open topic of discussion in the three-way race for mayor. His relationship with men who conspired to kill his best friend somehow never came up. Once the trial ended, the local press studiously ignored the issue, sensitive to previous allegations of bias leveled by Halat. His opponents were mum on the issue.

Yet the Sherry killings undeniably became the subtext of the election. An anonymous graffiti artist scrawled the word "killer" on Halat's campaign signs, even on the window of his storefront election headquarters. His opponents' supporters spoke of banging on doors to solicit votes and having people say, "I'd put your sign in my yard, but the last time I did that, the person running for mayor got mur-

dered." Anonymous flyers reiterating testimony that implicated Halat were circulated citywide, infuriating the incumbent mayor, who then wrote his opponents to say he knew
who was responsible. "They will be dealt with at the
appropriate time and in the appropriate manner," Halat
promised, without explaining further.

Whether he liked it or not, fairly or unfairly, the election
had become a forum on whether or not the people of Biloxi
believed Pete Halat might have had a hand in the murder of
the Sherrys, his innocence under the law notwithstanding.

On June 8, the same day Kirksey Nix and his fellow
defendants argued their appeal in New Orleans, the people
of Biloxi passed judgment on Pete Halat. It was a narrow
decision: They turned their mayor out of office by fourteen
votes out of some 8,500 ballots cast.

For the first time since Reconstruction, Biloxi elected a
Republican mayor and a Republican majority to the city
council. Watching the returns in city hall, Halat, unshaven
and weary, teared up as the results were tallied late that
evening, then fled the room, making no comment.[5]

To his utter astonishment, Pete Halat had lost even
Biloxi's Ward 7, his home ward, one he had expected to
capture easily. It made the difference in the election.

But then, another politician had once called Ward 7
home. She had lived there, campaigned there, won a council
seat there. And, finally, Margaret Sherry had died there.

Lynne Sposito had spent a few hours greeting people and
chatting outside polling places earlier on election day. It was
a way of feeling close to her mother, who had lived for such
occasions, thriving on them. Lynne had just returned from
hearing the appeal in New Orleans, and it struck her then
that her efforts—and of all the others involved with the
case—had achieved a measure of justice after all. It was not
the outcome she once had hoped for, it was a
compromise—something her father would have understood
and embraced. Perhaps, someday, it would seem like
enough to Lynne, too.

After a while, an elderly friend of Lynne's parents approached as she stood in the late afternoon sunlight, a cool
breeze beginning to push through the moist air, working its
way in from the Gulf. As he got closer, Lynne saw tears
running down the man's face. Then he pulled a wrinkled

piece of paper from his pocket. To Lynne's amazement, it was a Margaret-Sherry-for-mayor bumper sticker—from 1985.

"This should have been your mom's re-election," the man said, hugging Lynne.

And she, too, felt the tears come.

POSTSCRIPT

After a long period of little progress, the Sherry murder investigation—still pursued by FBI Agent Keith Bell and federal prosecutors, with Lynne Sposito constantly urging them on—has picked up steam again. To everyone's surprise, just when Lynne was ready to give up hope, Mike Gillich, taciturn, uncooperative and for years insisting upon his innocence, reversed himself and agreed to testify for the government.

A combination of pressures finally humbled Mr. Mike: His and the other defendants' appeal to the U.S. Supreme Court failed; he was facing even more prison time from the new bribery charges; and he was told others close to him might also be targeted in the bribery case should he remain uncooperative. And so he reluctantly proffered what he knew, then sat for a polygraph test as others had before him.

This time, prosecutors were satisfied with the results. In February 1994, they dropped the bribery case against Gillich without public explanation. Still, it was clear what had happened: They struck a deal. Gillich would testify in secret before a new federal grand jury.

Though they will not publicly comment on the case, federal prosecutors believe Gillich's story bolsters every allegation they made at trial. His testimony will allow them to identify and charge the men, along with all of their accomplices, who shot Margaret and Vince Sherry—even those already convicted in the first trial. Although John Ransom was involved, as prosecutors charged at trial, investigators now believe others may have pulled the trigger. A suspected hit man in Texas and a former associate of Gillich now doing time for drug trafficking are suspects.

Lynne, who obsessively tracks developments in the case, has been led to believe that Gillich's story implicates all those previously charged and convicted as well as several others, former mayor Pete Halat among them. Yet prosecutors remain cautious in pursuing new charges, scraping and searching for every bit of corroboration they can find before filing new charges. And, thanks to Gillich's new loquaciousness, they have found some: Investigators have uncovered ballistics evidence from a 1987 test firing of the suspected murder weapon—a Nix and Ransom trademark, eerily reminiscent of evidence uncovered in the Gypsy camp killings twenty years before the Sherrys died.

In exchange for testimony, prosecutors have promised to seek leniency for Mike Gillich, not only for potential cases, but on his current prison term as well. In the end, he is likely to walk, a shockingly lenient concession to Biloxi's kingpin that anyone who might be implicated by Gillich could argue provides powerful motivation for Mr. Mike to fabricate a story pleasing to the feds' ears, just as Bobby Joe Fabian did before him.

This concern has staved off a resolution of the case, much to Lynne's frustration. She had hoped George Phillips would seek new indictments before leaving office, but by November 1994, two years after the first verdicts, nothing had happened. President Clinton finally installed a new U.S. Attorney in Jackson; Phillips—and his promise to Lynne to never drop the case—were gone.

The new head prosecutor, Brad Pigott, has met with Lynne and assures her his office remains committed. Not taking any chances, Lynne has turned to the new Republican-controlled Congress and Margaret Sherry's old friend and political ally, Trent Lott, who has taken the powerful position of Senate Whip, and who immediately began pressuring the Justice Department to act in the case. Senior officials at the Justice Department, even Attorney General Janet Reno herself, have taken an interest in the case. If new indictments come, Lynne has been told, they will come before the end of 1995, employing powerful organized crime laws that carry hefty sentences. Still, there are no promises.

Lynne is as close to content as she has been in seven years. The new developments in the case have thrilled her, though the old frustration and fear remains. Her hope has been made brittle by past disappointments. After all this time, patience still comes hard to Lynne.

"The people who did this to my parents have had seven years to walk free in the sun, an opportunity that was not afforded Mom and Dad," she says. "I don't know if my family will ever recover from this. At this point, I really don't see how we can. But I see the light at the end of the tunnel. It's going to happen. There's going to be an end.

"And then maybe we can get on with our lives."

NOTES

CHAPTER 1

1. This account is drawn from the author's interviews of Lynne Sposito and Eric Sherry.

2. From the author's interview with Lynne Sposito. Sposito recalls the conversation taking place sometime in mid- to late May 1987.

3. The conversation portrayed here is based solely on the recollections of Lynne Sposito. Pete Halat refused repeated requests from the author—in person and in writing—for an interview. The substance of the conversation as related by Lynne closely resembles accounts Halat provided to police and in public forums. There are, however, here and throughout the book, potentially crucial discrepancies between Lynne's recollection of Halat's statements to her and his subsequent accounts.

4. Again, this account is based solely on Lynne Sposito's recollection of a telephone conversation with Pete Halat. It resembles some of his public statements, with some variations.

5. Based solely on Lynne Sposito's recollection of the conversation with Halat, who refused the author's interview requests.

6. Lynne Sposito's suspicions about Mayor Blessey were based solely on the political enmity between her mother and the mayor, and on her assumptions about information Margaret Sherry claimed to have passed on to the FBI—not on any actual evidence. Though perhaps understandable, Lynne's suspicions were misplaced. No credible evidence

ever surfaced to link Gerald Blessey to the murders. Quite the opposite: Evidence in the case points elsewhere. Despite Lynne's urgings, no investigative agency ever considered Gerald Blessey a suspect in the Sherry murders.

CHAPTER 2

1. From testimony before the Armed Services Committee on October 22, 1951, at hearings chaired by Sen. Lester Hunt of Wyoming.

2. The officials charged included Sheriff Leroy Hobbs, accused of drug trafficking and other crimes, District Attorney Glen Cannon, indicted for bankruptcy fraud, City Councilman Roy Mattina, charged with perjury, and Mayor Gerald Blessey, accused of misappropriation of federal funds. All were convicted but Blessey, who was acquitted of every charge against him.

3. From the author's interviews with Eric Sherry and Lynne Sposito. As previously stated, Pete Halat declined to be interviewed by the author.

4. From the author's interviews with Lynne Sposito and Eric Sherry.

CHAPTER 3

1. Details of the murder scene, the method of killing, and the wounds to the Sherrys were drawn from the autopsy reports on Vincent and Margaret Sherry; from the crime scene synopsis dated September 23, 1987, by Detective Kevin Ladnier, Biloxi P.D. Case No. 87-30529; the investigative report dated September 21, 1987 by Detective Otto E. Wills, same case number; the untitled report dated September 16, 1987 by Lt. Robert Burris; and the author's interviews with Biloxi Police Detective Gerald Forbes and Lt. Richard O'Bannon. The police and the coroner initially found only two wounds in Vincent Sherry, though a second autopsy revealed a third wound that had been so close to one of the others as to have been obscured. The second autopsy was performed because nine empty shell casings were found in the house, but only eight bullets had been accounted for.

2. From the Biloxi Dept. of Public Safety statement of witness/complainant, a transcript of the tape-recorded interview of Peter Halat on September 16, 1987, by detectives Buddy Wills and Ric Kirk.

3. As recalled by former Harrison County Sheriff's Investigator Greg Broussard, in an interview with the author. Broussard was assigned to a multiagency task force investigating the Sherry murders. He and Biloxi Police Detective Otto "Buddy" Wills became the primary investigators in the case after the initial flurry of activity in the week following the murder.

CHAPTER 4

1. From the transcript of a tape-recorded interview of Leslie Sherry by the Biloxi Dept. of Public Safety on September 17, 1987.

2. From the transcript of a taped interview with Eric Sherry, dated September 17, 1987, by the Biloxi Dept. of Public Safety; police reports contained in Biloxi Police Dept. Case No. 87-30529; and the author's interviews with Eric Sherry, Lynne Sposito, and Greg Broussard.

3. This account is based on the recollections of Lynne Sposito, corroborated by Greg Broussard. It is neither corroborated or contradicted by police reports on the interview with Sposito, which do not mention the adoption issue but make clear that much was discussed while the tape recorder was switched off.

CHAPTER 5

1. From a transcript of proceedings on May 12, 1987, in Biloxi Circuit Court in the case of State vs. Troy James, Cause No. 5079.

2. This account is based on the recollection and notes of Lynne Sposito. Robertson told the same story to FBI agents four days later, according to FBI summary reports on the Sherry murder case. He repeated the story again to Biloxi Police Lt. Mike Meaut, as reflected in Meaut's "Confidential Report for Insp. Payne" dated April 7, 1988.

3. Detective Ric Kirk was never seriously viewed by

police investigators as a suspect in the case, a conclusion
with which Lynne Sposito eventually concurred. No evidence ever surfaced tying him to the crime, or to those
ultimately charged with conspiracy to kill the Sherrys.
Nevertheless, the Sherry family spent months fearing the
Biloxi police as a result of Robertson's claims, and the fact
that the yellow Ford he described would be identified by
police as the getaway vehicle compounded their fears.
However, it now seems certain that Robertson was wrong
about whom he described as the driver of the car. Ric Kirk
eventually volunteered to clear his name by submitting to a
polygraph test conducted by an outside, disinterested police
agency. He passed the test.

4. From the author's interviews with Lynne Sposito.

CHAPTER 6

1. From the author's interview with Lynne Sposito.
Harrison County Medical Examiner Steve Delahoussey's
recollection and notes confirmed Lynne's account. Halat
would not respond to written and oral requests about this
rendition of events.

2. According to Margaret Sherry's friend and the former
president of the Biloxi City Council, Dianne Harenski, who
says she was shown the list by Margaret.

CHAPTER 7

1. From the author's interviews with Lynne Sposito and
Greg Broussard.

2. "Vince Sherry had a questionable background,"
Sheriff's Investigator Greg Broussard wrote in his report
that day, summing up the discussion at the end-of-the-day
task force meeting less than thirty-six hours after the bodies
were found. "Sherry and Halat [were] always seeming to
represent known crime figures on the Coast." In weeks and
months to come, investigators would speculate in their
reports that Vince might have even been in partnership with
one of these crime figures, though evidence to support this
supposition never appeared.

3. The preceding account is drawn from the author's
interviews with Lynne Sposito, Eric Sherry, and Greg

Broussard, and from police reports describing investigators' discussions with Eric and Lynne.

4. In a December 1992 letter to the author, Gerald Blessey declined to be interviewed or to answer most questions posed by the author. However, he vigorously denied that there was any bias in the murder investigation because the task force included a variety of agencies other than the Biloxi Police Department. "The suggestion that the investigation was 'politically biased' is an absurdity, contradicted by the overwhelming weight of the evidence for anyone who really cared about learning the truth," Blessey wrote.

5. From the author's interviews with Greg Broussard and Lynne Sposito.

6. From the handwritten notes of Investigator Greg Broussard, dated October 26, 1987, filed in the Harrison County Sheriff's Office as the "Sherry Homicide Case," no file number. The note reads: "0830 met w/Chief Price. Advised that Blessey demanded me to be off the case. Price was advised by Saxon." Broussard confirmed these events in an interview with the author.

CHAPTER 8

1. The intact ignition system and the lack of hot-wiring probably meant a key had been used, the police initially theorized. Investigators knew that the car dealer still had its set of keys for the car. The logical conclusion: a copy of the ignition key had been made, perhaps when someone took the car for a test drive. Making a wax impression of the key would have been a simple matter for a thief, requiring but a few seconds out of the car salesman's sight. Yet months would pass before investigators thought to ask if any of the car dealer's salesmen remembered taking the Ford out for a spin with a prospective customer. By the time police got around to asking, memories had long since faded—more investigative bungling.

2. Finding usable latent fingerprints on the suspected getaway car did not represent a breakthrough in the case. The fingerprints of an unknown, nameless person are worthless without a suspect—police have to have something in hand to compare, a name and a face and a known

pair of prints extracted from the inked fingers of a person with a prior criminal record. Some states have computer systems that can match unknown prints to known criminals whose fingerprints are on file. Financially strapped Mississippi has no such system, however. Pulling criminal files at random by hand, hoping to find a match, would be a hopeless, massively time-consuming exercise in futility. For all they knew, the culprit had never been fingerprinted before.

3. From the Biloxi Police Department report dated March 10, 1988, by Lt. Mike Meaut, Case No. 87-30529. Meaut, who assumed responsibility for the Sherry murders as head of a second "task force" in March 1988, wrote: "On the Fairmont, Insp. Williams reported that the investigation into it was suspended because it was considered not to have played a part in the murders. The reasoning for this was 'the time frame of the murders and the first time the car was noticed was not right.'" Meaut concluded that this had been a misjudgment, and that the Ford was, indeed, a valuable potential link to the killers, which he began to pursue intensively.

4. Several other suspects were getting a secondary look as well, notably a mysterious fellow who called himself Bates who arrived in town claiming to be a writer researching a book about organized crime. Bates had appeared in the Biloxi area shortly before the murder, then disappeared shortly afterward, skipping out with a leased Mercedes and leaving behind a rented house he had masked with heavily tinted windows and muted lights so no one could see inside. His identity and previous address proved to be phony. Detectives considered him a possible hit man, and began to research his movements. Still, Eric and Diamond Betsy remained priority targets of the investigation. For all the police knew, one of them could have hired Bates to do the dirty work on Hickory Hill Circle. Bates turned out to be a mere con man from Kentucky, disappointed investigators eventually learned.

5. From "Police work Sherry leads in Florida," by Gene Swearingen, Biloxi *Sun Herald,* November 6, 1987.

6. From the transcript of a tape-recorded interview of Barbara Anderson on November 4, 1987, at her home in

Orlando, by detectives Greg Broussard and Buddy Wills, and from a report filed by Wills on November 17, 1987, under Biloxi P.D. Case No. 87-30529.

7. From Wills's November 17, 1987, report, and from the author's interview with Greg Broussard.

8. From the author's interviews with Eric Sherry and Greg Broussard.

9. From "Sherry murder case investigators lose one lead, pick up another," Biloxi *Sun Herald,* November 11, 1987.

10. From statements by Pete Halat in an August 1989 press conference.

CHAPTER 9

1. From the author's interviews with Lynne Sposito and Greg Broussard. Lynne had promised Broussard she would not reveal the source of this tip—she identified him merely as a member of law enforcement. Broussard, however, confirmed that he had provided the warning.

2. From the author's interviews with Lynne Sposito and Greg Broussard.

3. Ibid.

4. From a December 5, 1987, police report filed by Investigator Ric Kirk.

5. Ibid.

CHAPTER 10

1. From an April 4, 1988, report by Biloxi Police Lt. Mike Meaut, on a conversation with a confidential informant.

2. From the transcript of a taped Biloxi police interview with Pete Halat on January 26, 1988, at Halat's office.

3. From "Son says someone on Coast knows who killed Sherrys and why," Jackson (Mississippi) *Clarion Ledger,* May 23, 1988.

4. From the report by Lt. Mike Meaut, dated May 23, 1988, in Biloxi Police Dept. Case No. 87-30529. In a letter to the author, Gerald Blessey, who declined to be interviewed in person, stated that investigative decisions in the Sherry case "were done, not by the direction of the mayor or any other elected official, but by good law enforcement

practice and judgment. I can tell you that there has never been any retaliation of any kind, before, during or after this investigation by me against the Sherry family or any other person."

5. According to the May 26, 1988, Biloxi Police Dept. report by Lt. Mike Meaut, in Case No. 87-30529.

6. As told by convicted murderer Bobby Joe Faubion. Armistead has denied any improprieties in his investigative techniques, a contention supported by several law-enforcement officials, including his former colleague, Harrison County Sheriff Joe Price.

CHAPTER 11

1. According to the March 1988 report by Lt. Mike Meaut. An FBI interview of a different witness at the car dealer puts the yellow Fairmont on the lot as late as Monday afternoon, September 14—a day on which a car lot employee said he twice locked the car and rolled up its driver's window, only to find it lowered later. The same employee told the FBI that he noticed the car missing the next day, Tuesday, September 15. Because the murder took place on the evening of September 14, the times noted by the FBI's witness, though different than the Biloxi Police Department's information, still allow time for the car to have been used in the murders.

2. Another day, Lt. Mike Meaut came by to show them photos of the scene. He was supposed to have screened out any pictures that included the bodies, but he missed a few in the big stack of color snapshots. Lynne blanched at the sight as she flipped through the thick stack of photos, but said nothing until her sister, Leslie, who had accompanied them to the house, left the room.

"You probably didn't mean to show me these," she said calmly, revealing the shots of her father's bloated, disfigured corpse that she had kept pressed against her side. Meaut wouldn't stop apologizing. Armistead was furious. But Lynne couldn't stop looking, saying, "It's really not as bad as I thought it would be."

3. The preceding account of the visit to the house is drawn from the author's interviews with Lynne Sposito and

John and Becky Field, and from Biloxi police reports on investigative findings at the murder scene. Rex Armistead declined to be interviewed.

4. This conversation is based upon the recollections of Lynne Sposito—an account she provided the author, to newspaper reporter Gene Swearingen for the August 5, 1989, edition of the Biloxi *Sun Herald,* as well as in her sworn testimony before a federal grand jury in Jackson, Mississippi, on September 18, 1990. The conversation, according to Sposito, took place May 16, 1988.

Ann Kriss did not corroborate this account for the author, though she admits re-creating the ledger on Nix's account in approximately the time frame Sposito recalls. In the August 1989 newspaper article, Kriss was questioned by the reporter, and quoted as saying, "I don't have any recollection of that [conversation with Sposito]. I can't deny I made that statement, but I don't have any recollection of it." Kriss denies preparing an inaccurate record—just a partial one, beginning with the year 1985. The account dated back to 1979, the only time there had been an actual zero balance. She also questioned Sposito's ability to remember conversations more than a year after they occurred.

However, Sposito apparently relayed her account of this conversation shortly after it occurred. A Biloxi police report dated May 26, 1988, shows that Sposito told both the FBI and the police that Ann Kriss had produced "doctored books" on Kirksey Nix's accounts.

5. The basic facts of Hignight's visit to Halat, his statements about the scam, and the request for the ledgers is based on Halat's sworn testimony, and, unlike other portions of this conversation with Lynne Sposito, is not in dispute. The letter to Nix in which Halat says he will no longer represent the convict was dated May 13, 1988—four days before this conversation between Sposito and Halat. However, testimony from Beau Ann Williams, Nix's cousin and an attorney, as well as other records, show Halat did maintain contact with Nix after this date, and continued to work on legal matters for Nix's wife and stepdaughter.

6. This May 17, 1988, encounter with Halat is based primarily on the account provided by Lynne Sposito, to the

author and before a federal grand jury in sworn testimony. Halat, in comments published in the Biloxi *Sun Herald* on September 16, 1990, disputed Sposito's recollections, though more in tone than in substance. He was quoted as saying that he may have said something about Nix and Gillich being friends and clients of his, but that he would not have related this to Lynne in any threatening way. "Her recollection doesn't correctly characterize the conversation that we had, which doesn't surprise me," the paper quoted Halat as saying. Sposito's account is supported somewhat, however, by the statement of a secretary who once worked in the Halat and Sherry law office, who told the FBI, in a report dated November 9, 1990, that she recalled that Lynne and Halat argued loudly for about twenty minutes in Halat's office one day, long after the murders. She recalled Lynne leaving looking furious, and Halat slamming the door behind her.

7. From the author's interviews with Lynne and Dick Sposito.

CHAPTER 12

1. From the *Encyclopedia of Southern Culture,* Vol. 4, Charles Reagan Wilson and William Ferris, eds. (New York: Doubleday, 1989), and *The Mississipi Gulf Coast: Portrait of a People,* Charles L. Sullivan (Northridge, CA: Windsor Publications, 1985). The book on Copeland by Sheriff J. R. S. Pitts was entitled *The Confessions of James Copeland,* and was later republished in 1980 under the title *Life and Confessions of the Noted Outlaw James Copeland.*

2. With gambling causing a crisis on the air base, one senator asked Keesler's commander why he had not simply ordered gambling establishments off limits to Air Force personnel. The general responded that he had considered such a move, but decided against it. Gambling was so rampant throughout the community, he said, that such an order would virtually quarantine the base. None of the troops would ever be able to leave without being airlifted out, then parachuted into some remote area away from the one-armed bandits and croupiers, the general testified before the Senate.

3. Sen. Lester Hunt, Democrat of Wyoming, convened

the hearing on behalf of the Armed Services Committee on October 22, 1951.

4. The rampant prostitution in Biloxi strip clubs in the sixties, seventies, and eighties is detailed in numerous investigative reports by the Mississippi Highway Patrol and other law-enforcement agencies, as well as in the news media—in particular, in a series of copyrighted articles published in the Jackson (Miss.) *Clarion-Ledger,* March 23–26, 1981, entitled "Mississippi Gulf Coast: Wide Open and Wicked," by W. Stevens Ricks and Stephanie Saul. A particularly detailed account of sex-for-hire in several Biloxi nightclubs circa 1970 is contained in a document entitled "Memorandum to Albert Necaise, District Attorney, from Gene Evans, Investigator, District Attorney's Office," reporting on his undercover visits to strip joints on February 1, 1972.

5. This sheriff, Eddie McDonnell, with his bulbous, quivering nose and blustery manner (later to become chief deputy sheriff under a corrupt successor), became the prototype for Biloxi law enforcement at its worst, fearless and corrupt. He was sheriff for two nonconsecutive terms in the fifties and sixties. He once threatened to jail a group of state alcohol commission agents—and their boss, the governor—for busting a gambling operation in which he had a secret share.

Later, he addressed a convention of policemen in Biloxi, regaling them with a tale about his latest meeting in the Mississippi capital. The governor had summoned him to Jackson to threaten him with the National Guard—which the governor ultimately deployed to help close down gambling houses and bordellos McDonnell protected. As was his habit then, McDonnell wore an expensively tailored suit on his stocky frame, gaudy in color, an equally gaudy diamond stickpin glittering on his lapel. "And where the hell does a sheriff get off wearing a diamond that big?" the governor railed, as McDonnell told it.

"That's what I'm trying to tell you, gov!" the sheriff replied, jumping to his feet. "If you'd just leave me alone, we'll all be wearing 'em."

The aura of corruption in Biloxi was so complete then, Sheriff McDonnell felt comfortable recounting this story to three hundred lawmen gathered on the Mississippi Coast.

He was met with laughter and applause. Biloxi was never more wide open.

CHAPTER 13

1. From the author's interview with Beau Ann Williams, Nix's first cousin and lifelong friend, and a practicing attorney in Oklahoma City.

2. From the Dallas *Morning News,* "Trial set in judge's slaying. Man allegedly killing from prison," by Jason Berry, September 29, 1991. The information on State Senator Nix is based on the reporter's interview with Nix.

3. From copies of Mississippi Highway Patrol intelligence reports retained by Harrison County Sheriff Joe Price, who was an investigator with the MHP in the sixties and seventies, involved in several investigations of crime on The Strip in Biloxi. Powell, also known as Jack Powers and Donald Baugh, had a seven-state criminal record for burglary, theft, possession of gambling devices, liquor violations, swindling, forgery, and grand larceny. His associates, according to MHP reports, included the most notorious Dixie Mafia killers, drug smugglers, and armed robbers, along with Judge Nix. Information on Judge Nix's association with Mike Gillich is drawn from thesworn testimony of Gillich and Kirksey Nix Jr.

4. From the sworn testimony of Kirksey McCord Nix Jr. and Mike Gillich Jr., in *U.S. vs. Nix, Gillich, Ransom and Sharpe,* Criminal Case No. S91–40, in the U.S. District Court for the Southern District of Mississippi.

5. Law-enforcement sources and early press accounts alternately credit a crime commission in Dallas, a Houston newspaper reporter, and the director of a Southern-based regional criminal intelligence network with coining the term "Dixie Mafia." All sources agree that the criminals themselves did not begin referring to themselves as Dixie Mafia until after the press popularized the term. Harrison County Sheriff Joe Price, who was investigating crime on The Strip since the 1960s, gives credit for coining the term to Rex Armistead, the former chief investigator of the Mississippi Highway Patrol.

6. Nix denies his involvement in the murder. Bennett was a partner in an illegal Biloxi gambling club with a close

friend of Nix's, a Dixie Mafia nightclub operator and drug dealer named Dewey D'Angelo. The rigged gambling house was closed down by federal agents; Bennett was killed six days before he was to go on trial. Nix skipped on his rent for a Biloxi apartment two days before the killing. He was sought for questioning in the case, but this was short-circuited when James Blackwell, another Dixie Mafia nightclub operator, convicted felon, and good friend of Nix's, was arrested for the Bennett murder along with a gambler named Aris Toles Diamonicus, commonly known on The Strip as Art Diamond. Nix later denied any involvement.

A convicted felon had told police that Blackwell and Diamond had tried to hire him to kill Bennett because the gambler was talking to federal investigators in order to cut a deal in his own case. The ex-con later told Blackwell's defense lawyer that his story was a lie, and that yet another bar owner on the Coast—rivalries erupted on The Strip constantly—had forced him to falsely accuse Blackwell and Diamond. The lawyer, Robert Adam, revealed this change in the witness's story on the first day of Blackwell's trial; that night, Adam's house was consumed in a fire and he was killed, along with two of his children. A mistrial was declared, and the case against Blackwell and Diamond was never pursued further.

The labyrinth of the Bennett case continued, however. A burglar and escaped convict with no connections to the Dixie Mafia eventually confessed to the killing after he was arrested in Florida for shooting it out with policemen there while robbing a hamburger stand. Later, the burglar, Harold Diddlemeyer, recanted his confession, claiming he constructed it from news accounts so he would be extradited to Mississippi, where he felt he had a better chance at a lenient sentence. He said he felt comfortable doing this because he knew he had evidence to prove his innocence. But despite a witness who put him out of state at the time of the Bennett killing, and a police-administered lie detector test that showed him to be truthful in asserting he did not commit the murder, Diddlemeyer was convicted. He is still serving a life sentence at the Mississippi State Penitentiary at Parchman.

(The preceding account is drawn from the Harrison County Sheriff's Department files on the murder of Harry

Bennett and the confession and trial of Harold Diddlemeyer; from the author's interviews with Harrison County Sheriff Joe Price and Captain Randy Cook; and from "Bennett slaying: What was the motive for murder?" by Gene Swearingen, Biloxi *Sun Herald,* September 11, 1990.)

7. The account of the shooting and Nix's alleged involvement is drawn from multiple sources: the author's interviews with Harrison County Sheriff Joe Price, Jefferson Parish Deputy Chief Sheriff Gene Fields, and convicted felon and former Biloxi policeman Harvey Felsher, a friend of Nix's; *The State Line Mob,* W. R. Morris (Nashville, TN: Rutledge Hill Press, 1990); and "Hit List," Biloxi *Sun Herald,* September 15, 1990.

8. Though Nix admits a relationship with White, he denies involvement in the Pusser shooting. He has never been charged in that crime, though numerous inmates who served time with Nix have told investigators that Nix often boasted of killing Buford Pusser.

The men Pusser named as his wife's killers were Nix, a Boston-based Mafioso named Carmin R. Gagliardi, and two Dixie Mafia cronies, Gary Elbert McDaniel and George Albert McGann. Towhead White hired Nix, who then picked his accomplices, according to Pusser. Allegedly, Nix made the phone call that lured Pusser into the ambush, and the Cadillac used in the crime supposedly was the same one that later exploded in Oklahoma City. Gagliardi's body was found two years later, riddled with bullets in Boston Harbor. McDaniel, under indictment for conspiring to kill a Mississippi prosecutor, was found shot in the head and back, floating face down in the Sabine River in Texas in March 1969. McGann was shot three times through the heart and back in Lubbock, Texas, in September 1970. And Towhead White died in April 1969, shot in the head outside a motel with another man's wife.

Pusser was never charged in any of these killings; all but one of them are officially unsolved. Police admit that the deaths of such notorious gangsters provoked little enthusiasm in pursuing their killers. In the case of Towhead White, another man, Barry "Junior" Smith, confessed to the shooting, but claimed he acted in self-defense during a confrontation outside the motel. Smith eventually was exonerated, although evidence showed White had been shot by a gunman on the motel roof, not on ground level, as Smith had claimed. Pusser's authorized biographer, W. R. Morris, reports in his 1990 book, *The State Line Mob,* that Pusser had hired Smith to set up the murder, and that another assassin had been employed to do the shooting from the rooftop while Smith acted as the fall guy.

9. Police records and news accounts from that period show Gwinn had been busted the previous year with Nix after an aborted burglary attempt and a high-speed police chase in Oklahoma. The pair skated on the charges in classic Nix style: a $150 fine apiece.

10. Louisiana warrants were issued for five Dixie Mafia cohorts: Nix; Gwinn; a small-time thief named Charles Christian; a hulking Biloxi drug-smuggler and Dixie Mafia enforcer named William Mansker Clubb; and a diminutive Oklahoma armed robber and thief named Charles Floyd Yandell. All of the men were friends of Nix. Three of the five—Nix, Gwinn, and Christian—along with five other men and woman of the Dixie Mafia, had met in Biloxi a few weeks earlier. According to Mississippi Highway Patrol Intelligence files maintained by the Harrison County Sheriff's Department, an undercover agent watched them gather at the home of Christian's girlfriend, a nightclub worker and close friend of Mike Gillich. The meeting appeared to have been a planning session for upcoming Dixie Mafia crimes, including the Gypsy camp raid.

Of the four other men, William Mansker Clubb was the most interesting. He and Kirksey Nix were extremely close. Clubb was notorious in his own right, having been linked to (but never convicted of) several murders, including the killing of an FBI agent. He was under indictment in Oklahoma for perjury for testifying on behalf of Nix's old friend Bobby Joe Faubion in a gun-running case in Dogpatch, Oklahoma. Later, he would be accused of being the Dixie Mafia's premiere cocaine smuggler, in years to come achieving legendary status among his peers by crashing a small plane loaded with the drug, then escaping arrest by claiming to be a doctor responding to a medical emergency. His getaway was detected only because a news photographer inadvertently snapped him getting into a car, carrying a briefcase. He was at the controls years later in the crash of another plane just short of the runway in New Orleans, his body and the cocaine he was smuggling lost in the flames.

11. According to Jefferson Parish Chief Deputy Sheriff Gene Fields, who has extensively investigated Nix and other Dixie Mafia criminals, and retired Drug Enforcement Agent William Warner of Mobile, who was at the time a sheriff's detective. Warner interviewed Gwinn when he was picked up with Cook, five days before the murder. It was during this interview, according to Warner, that Gwinn promised to cooperate—and expressed fears that he might be killed for doing so.

12. Nix denies involvement in the Gypsy camp killing. In a March 1978 interview with the Louisiana State Penitentiary news magazine, *The Angolite,* Nix claimed the ballistics evidence in the case was trumped up by the police, and that bullet casings were planted at the dump to falsely match those at the scene of the murder. He admitted in the interview that he had been target-shooting at the dump outside Covington, but he said that proved nothing. He denied that any of the defendants was going to cooperate with authorities, and he denied any ininvolvement in Gwinn's murder. He said the case was dismissed not because of a key witness's murder, but because of the shoddy police investigation and manufactured evidence.

13. Within two months of his release, the Dallas police raided an apartment where Nix and three cohorts were living. Detectives found a few ounces of marijuana, along with three pistols, a sawed-off shotgun, the usual Nix kit of burglary tools, a police radio, and a telephone test set—this last item for tapping into phone lines. The police believed they short-circuited a burglary Nix had been plotting that involved a telephone alarm system of some kind, but because no major crime had been committed, charges were not pursued against Nix. Two months later, three million dollars in precious metals and gems were stolen by a sophisticated team of vault burglars, who spent a whole weekend in January breaking into a Dallas jewelry store protected by a sophisticated alarm system. The burglars

electronically circumvented this system and its connection
to telephone lines while drilling into the safe. The break-in
artists left no clues, but the Dallas police said at the time
they suspected Dixie Mafia burglars of returning to town to
finish what had been started in November. This was never
proven, and Nix was never arrested in the case.

CHAPTER 14

1. From the sworn testimony of Marian Corso, in *Louisiana vs. Nix, Mule and Fulford,* contained in transcripts filed
in the Louisiana Supreme Court, Case No. 56371.

2. Ibid. Also, from the testimony of Susan Corso in the
same case.

3. Nix denies any role in the ski-mask robberies, as well as
the Corso killing. Eugene Fields, chief deputy for the
Jefferson Parish Sheriff's Department and a sergeant for the
New Orleans Police Department at the time of the Corso
killing, had conducted the Mule-Nix surveillance, then took
a lead roll in investigating the Corso case. It was his
informant who first tipped police to the identities of the
killers.

According to Fields, shortly after the stakeout began, the
ski-mask robberies stopped. Investigators found this odd,
because until then, they had occurred once every two weeks.
The captain of investigations at New Orleans P.D. ordered
the surveillance ended a few weeks after it began, saying
Mule "wasn't worth the trouble." Only years later, long
after the captain had died in a car accident, would New
Orleans detectives learn he had been in the employ of New
Orlean's Mafia chieftain, Carlos Marcello, all along and had
tipped off Mule about the surveillance van outside his
apartment, according to Fields. The ski-mask robbers had
been warned off.

Investigators would also learn that robbery had not been
a motive in the break-in and murder at the Corso house,
after all. Instead, they learned Corso had refused to cooperate in an organized crime venture and had been targeted,
not for death, but for intimidation, perhaps a beating, when
the plan fell apart. That was why handcuffs were brought for
the whole family—they were to be held hostage and terro-

rized so that Frank Corso would willingly accept whatever terms the mob dictated. Marian Corso had spoken of this mob connection to the rogue police captain, who cautioned her to keep silent on the matter for her own safety. The captain never reported this to his department, again protecting his mob cronies, just as he had protected them earlier by canceling the surveillance of Mule and Nix.

4. From "Nix says paper seeks his ouster," Oklahoma *Journal,* October 30, 1968.

CHAPTER 16

1. Water Bill Sanford was a bookie to the Coast's wealthiest gamblers, a gentle con artist who knew every killer and crook in town, but who eschewed violence himself. He made his fortune in bootlegging, like some other now-respected families in Biloxi with old money. A shrewd businessman, he also was a Coast character—installing brilliant airplane landing lights on his Cadillac one year because, he said, he hated driving in the dark. He also killed, cleaned, roasted, and ate a two-hundred-dollar myna bird he had bought for his bar because it refused to talk as had been promised by the man who sold the bird to him. When his wife shot him in the head during an argument over her supposed involvement in witchcraft, Water Bill recovered, refused to press charges, and went home with her from the hospital, her bullet still lodged at the base of his brain.

Sanford died in the 1970s. The information on him is drawn from the author's interviews with Boyce Holleman, district attorney in Harrison County in the fifties and sixties, and a personal friend of Sanford's; and Mickey Ladner, of the Harrison County Sheriff's Department. Ladner and Holleman are in agreement on most points, though Holleman recalls Sanford being a small-time bookie, while Ladner pegged him as one of the Coast's biggest bookmakers. Mike Gillich confirmed his relationship with Sanford during his sworn testimony at his trial, without conceding any illegal activities.

2. From the author's interviews with Biloxi Detective Gerald Forbes and other law-enforcement sources.

3. The murder plot against the Gulfport chief unraveled

when an informant told federal investigators about the conspiracy. No convictions resulted. Hobbs was eventually arrested in a cocaine sting operation, convicted of a series of felonies, thrown out of office, and sentenced to prison. Larkin Smith, his archenemy, succeeded him as sheriff of Harrison County, the first man to hold that office in decades without scandal. Little Henry also went to prison, on unrelated charges.

4. Even when dozens of state investigators worked undercover on The Strip and elsewhere in town, documenting violations of the law on a nightly basis, nothing happened, records and press clippings show. City authorities, who had jurisdiction to prosecute misdemeanors within Biloxi's city limits, declined to act on most of the cases the Mississippi Highway Patrol put together. The county district attorney at the time, Boyce Holleman, tried to fill the void, using court injunctions to close down several of the worst offenders, with limited success.

But with a corrupt sheriff and police department as his only investigative tools, Holleman recalls that his main tactic was to forget the letter of the law and instead draw an arbitrary line: gambling, some prostitution, and B-drinking would be overlooked, but robbing customers, displaying perversion (Holleman was particularly riled by several acts on The Strip involving bestiality), and violent crimes would be prosecuted. When something particularly egregious came up, the D.A. called meetings with the club owners to discuss their "going too far." Gillich was particularly adept at walking this line of "now-boys-let's-be-reasonable" form of frontier justice. He yes-sirred Holleman, then did what he always had done.

5. Years later, James Granger, one of the thugs accused of the murders, returned to the Mississippi Gulf Coast after a long prison term and moved into a house owned by Kirksey Nix, according to LaRa Sharpe, John Ransom, and other associates of Nix's. After Granger supposedly absconded with several thousand dollars and a truckload of furniture that belonged to Nix, his body was found in Louisiana. He had been beaten to death with a baseball bat.

6. Then-MHP Investigator Joe Price, Harrison County's current sheriff, noted in a report at the time that Gillich knew about the murder in Texas of a Dixie Mafia burglar

and strip-club worker named George Fuqua as quickly as police on the Coast learned of it. The same day the bodies were found, Gillich knew the type of weapon used, the caliber of bullets, and the number of times Fuqua was shot.

"I just heard it through the grapevine," Gillich told Price. Every bit of Mr. Mike's information was accurate, demonstrating his intelligence-gathering network was as good as law enforcement's.

That same year, a February 1, 1972, report to then-District Attorney Albert Necaise from one of his investigators, Gene Evans, described at length the prostitution and other illegal activities in his clubs. "Mike Gillich . . . has been known to stop at nothing to make a dollar," the investigator concluded in his report. Necaise, like Holleman, moved to the criminal defense field, and later represented Gillich.

7. "Gillich always a step ahead," by Anita Lee, Biloxi *Sun Herald,* September 9, 1990. The newspaper performed a comprehensive review of court records for this story.

8. Gerald Blessey, now in private practice in Biloxi, declined to be interviewed by the author on this and other subjects. In a written response to a series of questions, Blessey responded to only two, saying he would have to conduct too much research to answer the author's other inquiries. The unanswered questions included queries about his administration's posture toward Gillich's operations, as well as the nature of Blessey's personal relationship, if any, to Gillich. In a subsequent letter, Blessey amended his explanation for declining to be interviewed by saying he was writing his own book and did not wish to share material with another author.

9. Cono Caranna, a city prosecutor in the Blessey administration, now district attorney in Harrison County, said he was never aware of any scheme to protect Gillich's operations. He suggested Gillich's longevity, compared to his rivals, owed more to his outside sources of income than any favoritism by the city. The income, he said, lay in the illegal enterprises he conducted with Kirksey Nix. Former District Attorney Boyce Holleman, who in private practice represented Gerald Blessey, said the Blessey administration did end up giving Gillich a de facto monopoly on vice, but only

because it tried to shunt strip clubs into a narrow zone of The Strip while cleaning up the rest of the city. It just happened that Gillich's establishments lay within this unofficially designated red-light district, Holleman said.

Others dispute Caranna and Holleman on this point and say Gillich was afforded special protection and virtual immunity from prosecution despite official knowledge and evidence of his law-breaking. The author interviewed five current members of the Biloxi Police Department and the Harrison County Sheriff's Department, and eight former members of those agencies, all of whom asserted personal knowledge of illegal activities by Gillich that were never prosecuted. The former chief of police under Blessey, Tommy Moffett, has testified that city police records pertaining to Gillich's criminal activities have been tampered with or destroyed to protect the strip-club owner, and that decisions were made at levels higher than the chief not to prosecute Gillich.

10. According to a federal grand jury indictment in U.S. District Court in Jackson, Mississippi, Criminal No. J89-0003(w), *U.S. vs. Roy N. A. Mattina.* Mattina was indicted for four counts of perjury for lying to the grand jury about receiving tips about police raids and passing them on to Gillich. He pleaded guilty to one count involving his receiving tips; the other counts, including the one referring to his passing on information to Gillich, were dismissed as part of the plea bargain. He was sentenced to six months of confinement in a halfway house.

11. Even when some enterprising policeman—always in the lower ranks and without permission from the department brass—managed to surprise Mr. Mike, the results invariably were decided in Gillich's favor.

• In 1972, when an investigator for then-District Attorney Albert Necaise witnessed prostitution operations at a Gillich club, the only consequence was a warning to Gillich to stop.

• In 1979, a sweep through The Strip by Biloxi police— with help from undercover officers borrowed from an outside department—netted sixteen arrests for prostitution and other crimes at eight joints. Three women were arrested for prostitution at the Golden Nugget and the Dream

Room; Gillich was pulled in for permitting indecent exposure there. As minor as those charges against Mr. Mike seemed, they theoretically could have ended his career on The Strip by preventing him from obtaining a work card from the city. Multiple prostitution convictions would have enabled the city to shut down the clubs as public nuisances. Strictly enforced, local ordinances coupled with convictions from this raid could have closed Gillich and his competitors down. Instead, most of the charges were dropped when city prosecutors decided that—contrary to common practice— two witnesses, rather than just one arresting officer, were needed to try the prostitution charges. It seemed almost as if the men hired to prosecute crimes were acting as defense attorneys, finding reasons not to go after the crooks on The Strip. The burden was impossible to meet in many cases, and the city decided to drop vice operations against the club for the rest of the O'Keefe administration. Gillich eventually pleaded his case down to allowing B-drinking, paid a four-hundred-dollar fine, then had some or all of it refunded by the city.

• In 1981, a group of patrol officers at Biloxi P.D. tried repeatedly to get detectives to investigate illegal gambling at Gillich's Horseshoe Lounge. None of the vice detectives would take the case, so the officers finally raided the place themselves, seizing bookie sheets, arresting Gillich's employees, then taking over the phones themselves, accepting telephone bets and building a case. Once again, though, city prosecutors decided to drop the case, telling the enterprising officers they had conducted an illegal search.

• In 1984 and again in 1986, undercover officers found prostitution, B-drinking, and other violations in all three of Gillich's clubs—the same type of evidence that was being used by the Blessey administration to shut down other rival joints. But once again, city prosecutors found insufficient evidence to take Gillich to court, allowing him to keep his monopoly on vice.

• Gillich's stranglehold on The Strip continued even after slot machines and crap tables were found in the Golden Nugget in 1986, and when he was found in 1988 to be operating without a work card from the city. In both cases, judges dismissed the charges.

12. When asked to explain his action to the Biloxi *Sun Herald* in an article dated September 9, 1990, Halat was quoted as saying, "A cursory reading of the [expungement] order will reveal that the petitioner and the city were both represented by counsel and that the order was issued in open court. A review of the file will also reveal that no objection was raised prior to the order and no appeal was taken on the actions of the court."

CHAPTER 17

1. From the author's interview with Biloxi Police Detective Gerald Forbes. Halat declined to be interviewed, so the account of the courthouse conversation is based entirely on Forbes's recollection. However, it is undisputed that Halat drove the Mercedes registered to Gillich for about two years.

2. From the sworn testimony of Pete Halat in *U.S. vs. Nix, et al.*, Criminal Case S91-40, U.S. District Court, Southern District of Mississippi.

3. From the sworn testimony of Kellye Dawn Newman Nix in *U.S. vs. Nix, et al.*, Criminal Case S91-40, U.S. District Court, Southern District of Mississippi. Kellye Nix gave similar testimony before a federal grand jury, and in statements to the FBI and the Harrison County Sheriff's Office.

4. From the November 20, 1990, report on a telephone interview with Kellye Nix by Harrison County Sheriff's Captain Randy Cook, contained in the Sherry Homicide File, Case No. 87-37181.

5. From the author's interview with Eugene Fields, chief deputy of the Jefferson Parish Sheriff's Department in Harvey, Louisiana.

6. From the sworn testimony of Peter Halat.

7. From the sworn testimony and police statements of Kellye Dawn Newman Nix.

CHAPTER 18

1. James Dickey's experience with Eddie Johnson took place over twelve days in September 1988. This account is

based upon the sworn testimony of James Dickey in U.S. vs. Nix, Gillich, Ransom and Sharpe; on police reports on the scam; on a written summary of events supplied by Dickey to police; on the author's interview with Dickey; and on the testimony and statements of other scam participants, including Roy Garland.

2. The penitentiary would seem an unlikely location for anything refined. There is nothing subtle or sophisticated about Angola's roots, just a legacy of brutality going back to 1880, when Louisiana prisoners were first moved from Baton Rouge dungeons to a plantation in the wild, near-impassable Tunica Hills. Since before the Civil War, the state had leased its prisons and all of its inmates to private entrepreneurs—turning its correctional facilities and the unfortunate souls imprisoned within into private property. Long after black slavery was abolished, prisoner slavery flourished, with inmates manufacturing rope and textiles, farming, and building levees for the lease-holder, a retired Confederate major named Samuel James who drove dozens of inmates to their deaths with inhuman conditions at his Angola plantation, earning a fortune in the process.

The notion of privatization of prisons, touted near the end of the twentieth century as new and revolutionary in an era of overcrowded and costly penitentiaries, is in fact an old, much-tried, and unworkable experiment. It finally ended in Louisiana in 1901 after a series of graphic newspaper accounts of brutality at Angola revealed that twenty-seven inmates had died of disease and overwork in the space of a year, all in the name of cost control and profit. Major James and his son, who inherited the lease and its inmate-money machine after his father's death, suffered no punishment. Their family had become one of the wealthiest in the state of Louisiana thanks to their prison lease.

In a gesture at reform, the legislature and governor created a three-man public Board of Control to take over corrections. But because no one in government knew anything about prisons—having leased their operation for more than fifty years—the men appointed to the board consisted of the major's son and two of his employees, the only living "experts" on corrections in Louisiana. They promptly bought Angola from themselves at a huge profit—

$200,000 for eight thousand acres. The fact that the state was able to buy ten thousand adjoining acres from other plantation owners twenty years later at half the price showed just how badly the James family had scammed the state of Louisiana, a fittingly corrupt beginning for an eternally corrupt prison.

3. From the author's interview with Captain D. K. Basco, Angola's chief investigator.

4. Guard D. K. Basco, later to become a captain and the prison's chief investigator, recalls Nix blithely scamming on prison telephones that year, with access to the phones far in excess of what prison regulations permitted. On a daily basis, Basco would receive orders from the warden's office to give Nix special access to the phones, supposedly to make legal calls to Pete Halat or other attorneys. With the warden or one of his deputies issuing the orders, Basco could not refuse. He would, however, stand by close enough to listen to Nix's end of these "legal calls." He would hear Nix using falsetto voices to woo suitors, making real-estate deals, arranging to have automobiles purchased, sold, or refurbished, and conducting all manner of business—anything but legal calls. Basco dutifully reported his observations to his superiors. Nothing was done. Nix began bragging to other inmates about having prison officials in his pocket.

5. From the statements and testimony of Robert Wright and Robbie Gant, and from the author's interviews with D. K. Basco, Captain Randy Cook, and others.

6. From scam materials seized from Kirksey Nix's cell in Angola in 1987.

7. Robbie Gant, a handyman and small-time crook introduced to Nix through Dixie Mafia connections, made some forty pickups for the scam. In a three-month period in 1986, Gant fetched about $24,000 for Nix at Western Union, all of it sent by lovelorn gay men throughout the U.S. and Canada, with a smattering of Australians and Japanese thrown in for good measure. In the course of a year, Gant picked up nearly $50,000 total.

Roy Garland, a convicted murderer recruited into the scam by Nix once he left Angola in 1988, did even better: Playing a bogus New Orleans police lieutenant and other characters, Garland picked up at least $200,000 in scam money in the space of year, he would later estimate. There seemed to be no end to the money Nix could generate with his various scripts, which included titles like, "The Second Step Plan," and Fabian's favorite, the "Quickie Method."

8. Prison authorities once managed to seize a pocket computer from Nix before he could erase the memory, but they were never able to break the access code Nix had used to protect his scam data. As for the larger personal computers his cronies maintained for him on the outside, investigators learned they had last been in the control of Kellye Dawn Newman Nix. Then they were taken to a preschool operated by Marlene Clubb, the widow of Nix's old Dixie Mafia partner, William Mansker Clubb.

9. From the testimony of inmate Arthur Mitchell.

CHAPTER 19

1. LaRa Sharpe, in an interview with the author, said Fabian deceived her mother, failing to mention he was a fugitive and almost getting her arrested. Fabian, however, said Granny willingly harbored him, knowing he was a wanted man.

2. According to Robert Wright, in his statements to police and the FBI, and his sworn testimony before a federal grand jury and in the trial of *U.S. vs. Nix, et al.* Wright's testimony came in exchange for a grant of immunity from prosecution, a factor cited by those he accused as providing motive for him to lie.

3. According to Robbie Gant, from a series of statements to the FBI and other law-enforcement agencies, and from his sworn testimony before a federal grand jury and in *U.S. vs. Nix,* et al. Like Wright and many other witnesses who ultimately testified against Nix, Gant received immunity from prosecution in exchange for cooperation. Those he accused of participating in the scam—principally Nix and Sharpe—and their lawyers attacked his credibility, saying he had a motive to lie about them in order to receive immunity from prosecution. Like Wright and others, Gant provided key evidence that investigators and prosecutors needed to pursue their case. LaRa has denied making the sort of scam calls Gant and others describe.

4. Ibid.

5. This incident was recounted by LaRa Sharpe in her sworn testimony in *U.S. vs. Nix, et al.*

6. From the testimony and statements to police of LaRa Sharpe.

CHAPTER 20

1. From the transcript of a recorded telephone conversation between Kirksey Nix and a confidential FBI informant on April 3, 1984, contained in FBI file No. 183B-815, with the date mistakenly stated as May 3, 1984.

2. From the August 3, 1984, report of FBI Special Agent William H. Deily Jr., in New Orleans, in FBI file No. 183B-815. The report, captioned "Administrative," reads in part:

"KIRKSEY NIX continues to telephone source from Angola State Penitentiary. NIX informed source that he continues to receive money from his lonely heart and homosexual scheme. He has asked source to pick up some money from a Western Union office and send it to PETER HALAT, Post Office Box 1346, Biloxi, Mississippi 39130."

The fact that the scam was known to authorities at least as early as 1984 would become a source of controversy in the case, since nothing was done for years while Nix continued to victimize hundreds, perhaps thousands, of innocent victims.

3. Kellye's run-in with the FBI, and Halat's role in her release, was described in the sworn testimony of Peter Halat and Kellye Nix, in *U.S. vs. Nix et al.*

4. From the police statements and sworn testimony of Kellye Dawn Newman Nix. Because of this comment, Kellye would later claim Halat knew all about the scams—something Halat would vehemently deny.

In an August 29, 1990, interview with FBI Special Agent Keith Bell and Harrison County Sheriff's Office Captain Randy Cook, Kellye used the word "fags." In subsequent testimony, Kellye paraphrased Halat by using the word "homosexuals" instead.

Although Halat has repeatedly denied having any knowledge of the scams, he was curiously equivocal when asked under oath about the statement Kellye attributed to him. In his sworn testimony in *U.S. vs. Nix et al.,* he said, "I do not recall having made that statement to Kellye Dawn Nix. And assuming that I would have made that statement, I would not have used the word 'homosexual,' which leads me to believe that I did not say that to Kellye Dawn Nix." None of the prosecutors or defense lawyers questioning Halat asked whether he might change his mind if the word "fag" was substituted for "homosexual."

The author did not have the opportunity to question Halat on this point, or any other. As previously stated, he refused repeated requests to be interviewed.

5. From the author's interviews with Angola's chief investigator, Captain D. K. Basco.

6. From the author's interview with D. K. Basco. LaRa eventually swore that the photo was hers, left over from a batch she had copied many months earlier for Nix. In this final version of events, LaRa explained that she had forgotten it was in her things and had not intended to smuggle the photograph into the prison. At the time, she later swore, she had disassociated herself from the scam and was just trying to help Nix with his case. She also blamed a boyfriend for hiding the pot in her car without telling her.

7. Ibid.

8. From "Envelope with nude photos was addressed to Halat," by Jerry Mitchell, Jackson *Clarion Ledger,* October 26, 1989, and "Nude photos addressed to Halat found at prison," by the Associated Press, Biloxi *Sun Herald,* October 26, 1989. Both stories quoted Halat through his spokesman at the time, Cliff Kirkland, who purported to provide the newspapers direct quotations from Halat.

9. From the testimony and statements to police of several of Nix's fellow inmates, including Bobby Joe Fabian.

10. From the sworn testimony and police statements of Charles Leger.

Chapter 21

1. The preceding account is based on the recollections of Lynne Sposito and Becky Field, in interviews with the author. Armistead declined to be interviewed.

2. This account of Harenski's comments to Lynne is drawn from the author's interviews with the women as well

as from police reports and a transcript of Harenski's interviews with the Biloxi police and the FBI.

3. From a tape recording of a conversation between Pete Halat and Lynne Sposito, made by Sposito without Halat's knowledge in January 1989.

4. From Lynne Sposito's September 1990 testimony before the federal grand jury in Jackson. Pete Halat refused requests to be interviewed and has never commented publicly on this particular recollection of Lynne's.

5. These comments were the subject of a press conference by Mayor Blessey, and an eight-page, February 26, 1988, letter to the FBI's then-director, William S. Sessions. The letter portrayed the FBI investigation as a groundless and politically motivated attack by racist conservatives intent on destroying a liberal, crusading mayor. It made clear that the prototypes of such racist conservatives were, in Blessey's opinion, Margaret Sherry and FBI Agent Royce Hignight.

"Mr. Hignight continues to engage in political terrorism to destroy the credibility and effectiveness of my administration in order to advance the political cause of his radical, right-wing allies in local politics," Blessey's letter said.

In decrying the Sherrys as inappropriate friends for an FBI agent, Blessey also claimed that Vince "went beyond the normal limits of defense counsel in associating with the business and social life of his underworld clients," and made suspicious appearances at a local house of prostitution where, Blessey reported, he had been spotted by an undercover policeman.

While he did not hesitate to use his police department's findings to further his attacks on the FBI agent and the Sherrys, Blessey bitterly criticized Hignight for doing the same thing: using his work for the Sherry murder investigation task force to further his own investigation of city officials. The mayor claimed Hignight promised to help investigate the murders, accepted assignments from the task force, then failed to carry them out, amounting to an "obstruction of justice" that hampered the murder investigation. Much later, Biloxi Director of Public Safety George Saxon stated that the assignment Agent Hignight supposedly accepted, then failed to carry out, was to go to Angola to talk to Kirksey Nix. In fact, other agents in the FBI were already fumbling an investigation of the Nix prison scams by then, making a trip by Hignight unnecessary. In any case, Biloxi Police Department detectives ultimately took the trip to the Tunica Hills themselves—after which they promptly and inexplicably dropped any thought of linking Nix and the scams to the Sherry murders. Saxon eventually admitted that decision could not be blamed on Hignight or the FBI—in other words, there had been no "obstruction of justice."

Blessey's complaint made a brief stir in the Mississippi press, but nothing more. The FBI shrugged off the letter and continued its investigations of Biloxi city government. A spokesman for the FBI explained that, contrary to Blessey's assertions, FBI agents never joined the Sherry task force because murder is a state crime, outside the jurisdiction of federal agencies. Judge Sessions never responded to the letter.

6. At Sheri's request, the author has agreed to withhold her full name. She is fearful about becoming a target, and about going public with her professed psychic abilities.

7. From the author's interviews with Lynne Sposito and "Sheri."

8. Ibid.

Chapter 22

1. From the author's interviews with LaRa Sharpe, her attorney Arthur Carlisle, and Lynne Sposito, who received a report from Armistead on his conversation with LaRa.

2. From the author's interviews with Michael J. Lofton, Biloxi Police Detective Gerald Forbes, and Harrison County Sheriff's Captain Randy Cook, as they recounted what Lofton said during his police interview. The author did not have access to the actual report or transcript of that interview.

3. The preceding quotations and paraphrases from LaRa's interview with the Biloxi police on March 8, 1989, are drawn from a transcript of the tape-recorded portion of the interview, captioned Case No. 87-30529. The tape covers about one hour and fifteen minutes of the interview, and therefore is not a complete representation of the three hours of discussion between LaRa and the police that day.

In an interview with the author, LaRa's attorney, Arthur Carlisle, confirmed that the transcript reflects the major points raised in the interview. LaRa, however, claimed in an interview that the police threatened her and told her she was a suspect in the murder during portions of the interview not tape-recorded. She said she left the meeting terrified and frightened for her life, although the conclusion of the tape—which coincides with LaRa's departure from the meeting—does not reflect this.

4. This description of Mike Gillich's visit is based upon Beau Ann Williams's sworn testimony before a federal grand jury in Jackson, Mississippi, on August 20, 1990, and on a report on an interview with her written by Harrison County Sheriff's Captain Randy Cook, dated July 2, 1990. In subsequent testimony and in an interview with the author, however, Williams seemed to back off her earlier account, saying Gillich was merely acting as Nix's friend, wanting to let him know that he was under investigation, and that he in no way intimated to her that he might be involved in criminal activity. Although her grand jury testimony cast doubt on Nix, Williams later told the author that she believes her cousin to be innocent of any involvement in the Sherry murders, and she criticized the grand jury process for forcing her to say negative things about Nix without allowing her to discuss any positives.

5. From the testimony of Robert V. Richardson, former security guard at the Ramada Inn in Biloxi, called as a witness in *U.S. v. Nix, et al.*

6. From the grand jury testimony of Beau Ann Williams.

7. From the author's interviews with Lynne Sposito and Bobby Joe Fabian.

CHAPTER 23

1. From the author's interviews with Lynne Sposito and Becky Field, as well as "Sheri," whose journals indicate she "received" names "that sounded like" John Rathman and Hicks in October 1988. Notes written by Becky Field that same month corroborate Sheri on the timing. This was long before Ransom's name had ever surfaced in the case, and long before Nix's name had been mentioned in any press

coverage related to the murders. There is no evidence that Sheri used any inside information or other trickery. Rex Armistead's initial reaction was, "What's her connection to the case?" None was found. She has never sought compensation or publicity of any kind. Thus there is no apparent motive for her to have contacted Lynne, other than a desire to help with the investigation. It should be noted that Sheri's psychic abilities, if they exist, have never been tested scientifically, and her contribution to the investigation remains little more than a curiosity, if a dramatic one. However, at least one investigator involved in the Sherry murder investigation has consulted with her repeatedly and confidentially.

2. A few months after this meeting, before he ever got a chance to see an end to the investigation's new direction, Mike Meaut slumped to the floor in midsentence while talking to a fellow officer outside the county courthouse's grand jury room. He died at age forty-two of heart failure.

3. The preceding account of Fabian's statement is drawn from a document entitled "Statement Under Oath of Bobby Joe Fabian," dated May 19, 1989, from the files of the Harrison County Sheriff's Department. Pete Halat has vigorously denied attending such a meeting at Angola, and points to prison visitor logs to support this. He has denied any role in the murder of the Sherrys, and he has denied knowingly aiding Nix's scams.

Chapter 24

1. The preceding account of Fabian's second interrogation is drawn from a document entitled "Statement Under Oath of Bobby Joe Fabian," dated June 21, 1989, from the files of the Harrison County Sheriff's Department, and all quotations represent verbatim extracts. Additional information was provided by Harrison County Sheriff's Captain Randy Cook, in interviews with the author.

2. With news breaking about the long-stalled investigation of his best friend's murder, Mayor Halat would have seemed a likely source for the media to seek out for comment. Oddly, though, the flood of stories detailing breaks in the Sherry case contained not a single quote from

the new mayor. His new police chief, however, complained bitterly in one story about being left in the dark about the investigation's new course.

3. Immediately after the broadcast of Fabian's interview, Halat said at his press conference, he had ordered his newly appointed chief of detectives, Kevin Ladnier, to call Angola and to ask if they had any record of him visiting in March 1987. The answer, Halat announced at the press conference, had been no.

Halat also informed the press corps that he had ordered his own Biloxi Police Department to resume investigating the Sherry murders, so that "the truth" could be brought out. Potential conflicts of interest notwithstanding, they had retrieved the department's files from the district attorney and were busily at work, Halat said. Records and interviews by the author suggest that this investigation was more concerned with absolving the mayor than with solving the murder, with Chief of Detectives Ladnier driving to Angola, then faxing pages from the visitor logs back to Biloxi for distribution to reporters.

CHAPTER 25

1. Although he initially told Cook that his encounter with Ransom occurred anywhere from one day to two weeks before the murders, Leger's recollection on this point has varied. He told his friend Betsy Walker in 1988—when his memory presumably was fresher—that he saw the gaunt man ten days to two weeks before the murders. Later, he testified that the range was one to two weeks, and that he was certain it occurred after Labor Day 1987. Labor Day fell on September 7 that year. The murders were discovered on September 16.

2. Attorney Betsy Walker, in sworn testimony, confirmed Leger's story, saying he first mentioned the dreams in 1988, and described a man who fit Ransom's description. Neither Leger nor Walker associated the recollection with the murders of Vince and Margaret at that time. Leger said he saw no need to report the matter to the authorities before seeing Ransom on the news broadcast.

3. The account of the Ransom encounter and ensuing

dreams is drawn from the transcript of a tape-recorded sworn statement of Charles Patrick Leger, taken August 9, 1989, by Sheriff's Captain Randy Cook and District Attorney's Investigator Hayward Hargrove, and from the federal grand jury testimony given by Leger on September 12, 1989, in Jackson, Mississippi.

4. From Leger's August 9, 1989, sworn statement and September 12, 1989, grand jury testimony.

5. Ibid. LaRa's truthfulness was a key issue. Her only obligations under her immunity agreement were that she cooperate with investigators, and that she tell the truth. Lying could provide grounds for prosecutors to revoke her immunity and to file charges against her.

6. Halat told police on the day the bodies were discovered that he personally tried the door, and that no one went inside the house with him—which might explain why the initial investigation bypassed Leger. The Sherry children later recalled Halat saying his elbow pushed the door open inadvertently. In any case, though Halat did tell the police Leger drove to the house with him that day, his taped statement to detectives did not mention many of the details Leger offered.

7. The account of the discovery of the bodies—and Leger's opinions on Halat—are drawn from Leger's statement to Cook and his grand jury testimony. Since then, Leger has been inconsistent in his opinions about Halat, at times expressing doubts, then later saying he believed in Pete's innocence.

A report on a November 13, 1990, interview of Leger by FBI Special Agent Keith Bell states that, because of Halat's declaration about Margaret being dead, "Leger believes Halat knew before arriving at the residence that Vince and Margaret Sherry had been murdered. . . . Leger stated that, looking back on the series of events surrounding Leger's contacts and observations of Halat since September 1987, it appears Halat has considerable more knowledge concerning the murders of Vince and Margaret Sherry than he has apparently yet shared with investigating authorities."

In subsequent testimony a year later, in *U.S. v. Nix, Gillich, Sharpe and Ransom,* however, Leger's account seemed to differ subtly, becoming more favorable to Halat.

In recounting the morning the bodies were found, for example, Leger omitted mentioning Halat's declaration about Margaret being dead, and prosecutors neglected to clarify the point. In a 1993 interview with the author, Leger said he did not believe Halat was "acting" on the day the bodies were found. He said he felt confident Halat had no involvement in the Sherry murders. He remained adamant, however, about seeing Ransom outside the law office.

CHAPTER 26

1. This account of Hallal's initial statement to the investigators drawn from an FBI report on an interview with Robert Michael Hallal dated October 7, 1989, File JN166-17725; the FBI interview of Hallal dated October 6, 1989, by Agent Keith Bell; a transcript of Hallal's sworn testimony before a federal grand jury in Jackson on October 18, 1989; and the author's interview with Captain Randy Cook.

2. From the Harrison County Sheriff's Office report dated November 1, 1989, by Captain Randy Cook, and the author's interview with Cook.

3. From the Harrison County Sheriff's Office report on an interview with Alice Powers dated May 5, 1990.

4. From police interviews and the testimony of Robert Wright. Both LaRa and her mother, Juanda Jones, eventually denied this gun allegation, though they admitted the mysterious meeting in Jackson with Ransom had taken place. LaRa claimed she made that long drive through the night with her two young girls in the car to meet with Ransom to pick up some jewelry.

5. From the author's interview with Randy Cook and his written report on conversations with Hallal's ex-wife, Pat.

6. Much later in the investigation, Hallal changed his story numerous times, providing details that could not be corroborated, badly damaging his credibility and providing a means for defense attorneys to attack his testimony. One of the greatest problems he created for himself lay in subsequent retellings, where he swore he phoned Gillich before visiting him. In his first interview with Cook and Bell, Hallal never mentioned calling Gillich and said that the first time they spoke was at the Golden Nugget, in

person. Later, though, he changed that story, insisting that he called Mr. Mike at Nix's direction. He even switched his story about the Jimmy James code name, saying Gillich told him to use it during this phone conversation, not Nix. Defense lawyers later pointed out that the phone bills from the Powers home in Leesville showed all sorts of long-distance calls by Hallal, none of them to Gillich, proving Hallal had lied. The defense lawyers tried to make this a pivotal point, but it remains unclear just what it proves. An examination of Hallal's grand jury testimony, in which he first mentioned the supposed phone call to Gillich, reveals that Hallal said only that he called Gillich from Leesville. He never actually said he used the Powers telephone to make that call. If he had used a pay phone, or if the call was a three-way—both techniques commonly used by the scam crews—there would be no record of a call to Gillich.

7. From the February 1, 1990, Harrison County Sheriff's Office report on an interview with William O'Neal Rhodes; the May 18, 1990, FBI report on an interview with Rhodes, File No. 166C-JN-17725; and from the sworn testimony of Rhodes in *U.S. vs. Nix, Gillich, Ransom and Sharpe,* Criminal Case No. S91-00040, in the U.S. District Court for the Southern District of Mississippi. Rhodes recalls the conversation took place in mid- to late March 1987, predating the Sherrys' comments about threats.

8. Indeed, the fact that law enforcement had known for years about the scam that ultimately led to the Sherrys' death, yet failed to shut it down, was intensely embarrassing, and the FBI and other agencies involved had scrupulously avoided mentioning it to the press. An argument could be made that shutting down the scam when it was first discovered in 1984 could have prevented the murders.

CHAPTER 27

1. The account of this conversation is based primarily on the recollections of Lynne Sposito. In an interview with the author, Cono Caranna recalled having such a general discussion with Sposito, but he could not recall the details. He did not dispute Sposito's account, and he made

similar observations about the Sherrys and the case to the author.

2. As district attorney for Harrison County, Caranna's job was to prosecute violations of Mississippi law. As in every state, the crime of murder falls strictly under state laws—except when it involves federal officials and a few other special circumstances, there is no federal crime of murder. Therefore, if Cook and Bell gathered sufficient evidence to prove who murdered Vincent and Margaret Sherry, only the D.A. could prosecute.

The investigation, however, was being directed by the U.S. Attorney, whose authority lay under federal law and who had a powerful grand jury system at his disposal that district attorneys in Mississippi lack. The only prerequisite for federal intervention was that the crime crossed state lines, which both the scam and the murder plots did, allowing federal conspiracy charges, which carried potentially severe penalties.

With ample evidence of multiple conspiracies but little to prove who physically entered the Sherrys' house and shot them, Cook's and Bell's first priority became putting together a workable federal case. But their hope, like Lynne's, was to find evidence for a state murder charge, the only venue in which the killers could face a capital murder charge and a possible death sentence.

3. From the author's interviews with Kent McDaniel and Lynne Sposito.

CHAPTER 28

1. From the sworn testimony of William Forehand before a federal grand jury in Jackson, Mississippi, May 20, 1990.

2. From the sworn testimony of Beau Ann Williams before a federal grand jury in Jackson, Mississippi, on August 20, 1990, and the original notes from Sheriff's Captain Randy Cook's interview with Williams that same month. In subsequent testimony and in an interview with the author, Williams revised her version of events, placing a far less damaging interpretation on Nix's and Gillich's words and actions, although the basic account remained the

same. She did, however, express the belief that the phone call from Nix had been on September 18, 1987, two days after the bodies were found—contrary to her grand jury testimony. In the author's interview, Williams harshly criticized the government's conduct in the case and said she believed her cousin to be innocent.

3. From the sworn testimony of Arthur Mitchell before a federal grand jury in Jackson, Mississippi, on November 15, 1990, and from his statements to investigators on November 16, 1990. Pete Halat has repeatedly denied receiving such large sums of money from Nix, and denies knowing anything about Nix's "standing offer" to pay $100,000 to anyone who helps arrange his release. Payments made by Nix to the trust fund maintained by Halat indicate a total of $71,286 sent during a three-and-one-half-year period between 1985 and 1988—far less than the quarter of a million dollars Mitchell spoke of. However, Mitchell also made it clear that the money he was speaking of was to be used for influence buying and possibly other illicit purposes—and, presumably, would have been paid "under the table" without being recorded in any official ledger.

Mitchell was unable to put an accurate time reference on when this conversation occurred—only that it came after a scheduled attorney-client meeting with Nix, perhaps in early 1987. The only such visitation by Halat on record at Angola occurred in December 1986. Another visit was scheduled for February 1987, but was canceled at the last minute.

CHAPTER 29

1. An added incentive came in the form of pressure from a long-lost half brother of Eric's, who wanted to reveal their shared parentage and reunite with Eric—which also would have tipped him off about being adopted.

CHAPTER 30

1. This account of the meeting with John Ransom is based on recollections of Harrison County Sheriff's Captain

Randy Cook, in an interview with the author. Ransom did not respond to requests for an interview made through his attorney, Rex Jones.

2. From police and FBI reports on John Ransom.

3. From a Harrison County Sheriff's Office report on Ransom's polygraph test, and the author's interviews with Randy Cook and Ransom's attorney in Mississippi, Rex Jones.

4. From the author's interview with Kent McDaniel.

5. The author verified this information through three independent sources who asked not to be named. Halat, as noted previously, declined to be interviewed. He was specifically asked to comment on the polygraph matter in a certified letter from the author. He never responded.

CHAPTER 31

1. From the author's interview with Assistant U.S. Attorney James Tucker and other prosecutors in his office involved with the case.

2. Ibid. Normally, evidence of one crime, in this case the prison scams, cannot be used to help prove a separate crime, in this case the Sherry murders. Defense lawyers undoubtedly would argue that the tie between the scam and the murders was too ambiguous. If that argument prevailed, then a judge might rule that the scam evidence, which was strong, would serve only to bias jurors called upon to decide the more iffy evidence in the murder case. Such a ruling would mean Tucker's indictment would have to be dismissed, and he would have to try to prove a murder case without discussing the Angola prison scams, an impossible task with the evidence in hand.

3. The account of the decision making leading up to the grand jury indictment is based upon the author's interviews with U.S. Attorney George Phillips, First Assistant Kent McDaniel, Assistant U.S. Attorneys James Tucker and Al Jernigan, and Harrison County Sheriff's Captain Randy Cook.

4. In interviews with the author, George Phillips and Kent McDaniel said they would have sought an indictment against Halat if they could have proven conclusively he had

gone to Angola in March 1987, as Bobby Joe Fabian and one Angola guard claimed, or if documentary evidence showed he personally profited from the scams. But the best evidence available suggested Halat had *not* gone to Angola to discuss murder in March, and that he had *not* profited visibly from scams.

CHAPTER 32

1. Nix's outrage was something of a pretense. A system-savvy jailhouse lawyer, he already knew the answer to his question: Prosecutors rarely polygraph their own witnesses, for the same reasons the tests cannot be admitted in court. Medical conditions, nervousness, a shading of truth rather than an outright lie, a host of mental states other than lying—all can influence the test, impairing its reliability. There also are some techniques for supposedly beating the test, as well as the fear that a true sociopath could lie with impunity, yet appear truthful—one explanation Randy Cook and Keith Bell offered for Nix's polygraph results. Finally, though law-enforcement officials are loath to admit it, there is an all-too-cynical bottom line dictating against the widespread use of polygraphs in criminal cases: Once a prosecutor decides he believes a witness and that his or her story is supported by independent evidence, there is no mileage in administering a lie detector test. Passing would only ratify a decision that had already been made. Failure— for whatever reason—could wreck a case.

The problem for the U.S. Attorney in this case was that the office already had used polygraphs to weigh the credibility of LaRa Sharpe, John Ransom, and Pete Halat. Once that door was opened, with potential legal immunity denied to Sharpe and Ransom based on the results, Nix's argument became more compelling, enabling him to label the government's position arbitrary and disingenuous.

CHAPTER 33

1. From the author's interviews with George Phillips, Kent McDaniel, and defense attorneys Rex Jones and Kelly Rayburn.

CHAPTER 35

1. The date of the phone call remained ambiguous throughout the trial. Williams's analysis on the witness stand of her phone bills remained unclear, even under questioning from both sides, leaving jurors uncertain just when the call had been made, and leaving prosecutors room to argue she had been right in her first version. The bills themselves show calls on both days, either of which could have been the one in which the Sherry murders were discussed.

2. From the author's interview of Lynne Sposito. Beau Ann Williams, in an interview with the author, maintained that she believed in Nix's innocence, and said the grand jury process had distorted her testimony to make it sound less favorable to Nix than she wanted.

CHAPTER 36

1. The defense attorneys eventually did successfully challenge one key recollection of Hallal's—that Mike Gillich had a telephone in his office at the Golden Nugget, which Hallal said Gillich used to arrange a drug deal in his presence. Several of Gillich's employees later swore there was no phone in the office, making the encounter sound like a fabrication by Hallal. The jury never heard it, but this most effective attack on Hallal was itself built on lies. Biloxi Police Detectives Gerald Forbes and Richard O'Bannon could have sworn that they used the phone in Gillich's office to call their department after busting some of Mr. Mike's girls on work-card violations. The phone apparently had only recently been removed. The prosecution could have damaged the defense and bolstered Hallal's credibility with this testimony, but it was never offered.

CHAPTER 37

1. From front-page articles in the Jackson *Clarion Ledger* and the Biloxi *Sun Herald* on October 23, 1991.

2. Ossie Brown did not testify at the trial, but he told the grand jury that he did not meet Halat that day. Phone

records show that Halat used his calling card to phone his office in Biloxi at 11:01 A.M. from Brown's office. He said he may have called his office to have his secretary cancel the appointment at Angola. Someone in the law office called the prison and canceled the visit with Nix at 1:23 P.M. Halat testified that he drove directly back to Biloxi, and should have been in his office by then. Prosecutors tried to imply that Halat could have gone on to Angola, but they had no evidence.

CHAPTER 38

1. In interviews with the author, defense attorneys Rex Jones, representing Ransom, and Kelly Rayburn, one of Nix's attorneys, said they believed the introduction of alternative murder suspects was a strategic error by the defense. Rayburn said he believed they might have had a better chance at winning acquittals if they had presented no defense at all.

2. Despite this suggestion made by the prosecution, investigators do not believe Swetman was present at the murders. Subsequently convicted with Nix and Gillich on a drug charge, he was paroled in 1994. Investigators have sought his cooperation in the Sherry case.

3. From the author's interview with Mike Green.

4. In his testimony, Green paraphrased Margaret Sherry's remarks. In a subsequent interview with the author, Green provided the more exact quotes reflected here—which, in substance, mirrored his original testimony.

CHAPTER 40

1. From the author's interviews with Kent McDaniel, George Phillips, and Al Jernigan, and the Biloxi *Sun Herald,* November 13, 1991.

2. From the Biloxi *Sun Herald,* November 12, 1991.

EPILOGUE

1. From the author's interview with Kirksey Nix.

2. From the author's interview with Rex Jones.

3. From the author's interview with Randy Cook.

4. From the author's interview with George Phillips.

5. Not long after leaving office, having issued a few bitter parting shots at press and prosecutors, Pete Halat landed on his feet. He returned to private practice.

Photo Credits

Read about the
SHOCKING and
BIZARRE
Crimes of our Times from Pocket Books

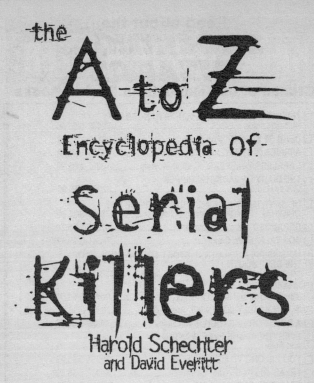

the A to Z

Encyclopedia of

Serial Killers

Harold Schechter
and David Everitt

"Harold Schechter combines the graphic style of a horror novelist with a keen eye for bizarre material....One of the few names that guarantee quality."

—John Marr, *The Bay Guardian* (San Francisco)

Coming mid-September 1996
from Pocket Books Trade

POCKET
B O O K S

The *New York Times* bestselling author of
FATAL VISION and *BLIND FAITH* takes us
to the outer limits of love and betrayal. . .

JOE McGINNISS

CRUEL DOUBT

"One of the best true crime stories ever written. . ."
— *The Philadelphia Inquirer*

Available in paperback from Pocket Books

POCKET
B O O K S

524-01